Developing Virtual Reality
Applications

Developing Virtual Reality Applications

Applications

Foundations of Effective Design

Alan B. Craig
William R. Sherman
Jeffrey D. Will

ELSEVIER

AMSTERDAM • BOSTON • HEIDELBERG • LONDON • NEW YORK • OXFORD
PARIS • SAN DIEGO • SAN FRANCISCO • SINGAPORE • SYDNEY • TOKYO
Morgan Kaufmann Publishers is an imprint of Elsevier

**MORGAN KAUFMANN
PUBLISHERS**

Morgan Kaufmann Publishers is an imprint of Elsevier.
30 Corporate Drive, Suite 400, Burlington, MA 01803, USA

This book is printed on acid-free paper.

Library of Congress Cataloging-in-Publication Data
Application submitted

British Library Cataloguing-in-Publication Data
A catalogue record for this book is available from the British Library.

ISBN: 978-0-12-374943-7

For information on all Morgan Kaufmann publications,
visit our Web site at www.mkp.com or www.elsevierdirect.com

Printed and bound by CPI Group (UK) Ltd, Croydon, CR0 4YY
Transferred to Digital Print 2012

Dedicated to Colleen and Cara, the future is yours

—Alan

Dedicated to Anthony, Thomas, Theresa, Danielle, Cindy, and Sheryl for their love and support throughout the years

—Bill

Dedicated to the Boy, the Girl, and the Mother thereof

—Jeff

Contents

Preface

HOW THIS BOOK CAME TO BE

This book, *Developing Virtual Reality Applications: Foundations of Effective Design*, has been many years in the making. Our interest in virtual reality came about as an outgrowth of our interest in, and our day-to-day work in scientific visualization. In the early 1990s the state-of-the-art in computer graphics used for scientific visualization was to take scientific data, clean it up, create geometry from it, place computer graphics lights, choose a camera perspective, and then render, *not in real time,* single images of computer graphics output. To create animations, one then created a sequence of images where either the camera perspective, or the underlying data evolves over time. The resulting images could be recorded to video tape or film, and played back as an animation.

There are several obvious drawbacks in that scenario. A fairly typical rendering time was about 20 minutes per frame. As technology improved, and rendering rates increased, frames still typically took about 20 minutes to render, because designers chose to render frames of greater complexity. Thus, scientific visualization animations were primarily used as an explanatory tool, rather than as an interactive, exploratory, real-time mechanism for exploring data. The use of computer graphics in other areas, such as Computer Aided Design, animated movies, architecture, and others followed a similar course of development.

The obvious thing that was missing was the *human in the loop*. The improvement in computer hardware and software allowed pseudo real-time computer graphics to be produced. This allowed new imagery to be generated as time evolved in the underlying data and/or the viewer changed their physical perspective to see the imagery from a different point of view.

Through our work with academic, government, and corporate partners, we began to see numerous areas where real-time imagery, in the form of virtual reality, could be applied with great benefit. A crystallizing application was when we were doing visibility studies to determine operator visibility from within the cab of a back-hoe loader, and were doing animations to show what the operator could see from the vantage point within the cab. However, those studies were not realistic in that in the real world, an operator could move his head in order to see around obstacles. This application (described in Chapter 3 of this book) provided the initial funding to develop our virtual reality lab.

As we developed the VR lab and started developing applications, we were invited to visit other VR labs and had a chance to experience and analyze the applications they had developed. Our home research lab at the University of Illinois was host to a plethora of visitors from academia, government, and industry. Visitors to the National Center for Supercomputing Applications at Illinois frequently requested a visit to the VR lab. As we met these visitors, we were constantly asked for information related to what applications had been developed in their area of interest. As such we became brokers between people looking for information, and those who were actively seeking information regarding VR applications. Additionally, because of the visitors to our lab and our visits to other labs, we were able to see many ideas and trends about what was working well, and what was not working well, and general observations across a vast array of VR applications. Visitors were constantly asking us to write this information down, and that if we did, that they wanted the very first copy. So, in essence, we wrote this book to satisfy the requests of many people who were seeking information of the very type that is included in this book.

When we met Mike Morgan of Morgan Kaufmann Publishing, he was looking for authors to write a book about scientific visualization. As we discussed that with him, we brought up the idea of a book that covers numerous VR applications in depth, in a way that could help VR developers learn from the mistakes of others, as well as to learn about ideas that worked particularly well. Simultaneously, the book would be useful to an audience of people who are interested in how VR can be applied in their area of interest. Morgan was enthused by that idea, and we wrote this book to fulfill that dream. Interestingly, we felt it important to have an introductory chapter to provide background to enable readers to understand the concepts and technologies we describe in the application chapters. That chapter grew to the point where it merited a book of its own, and it lead to the publication of *Understanding Virtual Reality: Interface, Application, and Design* by William R. Sherman and Alan B. Craig. Though the book you are reading has an introductory chapter that is sufficiently comprehensive to provide the background necessary to understand the application write-ups, the reader who is thirsting for a more in-depth treatment of VR is directed toward *Understanding Virtual Reality.*

WHO THIS BOOK IS FOR

This book was created as a resource for several different categories of readers. *Virtual Reality application developers* will find a wealth of ideas that are directly applicable to their own creations. By standing on the shoulders of giants, the developer can benefit from the trials, errors, and successes of other VR development projects. *Corporate research directors* who are interested in how VR might (or might not) benefit them in their own companies will find applications that are directly pertinent to their interests, as well as other applications that might not have crossed their minds, yet are likely to be of interest to them. For example, the manager who is interested in using VR for virtual prototyping may not have thought of the potential for using VR as part of an advertising campaign for their product. *University students* will find this book to be of considerable interest if their field is related to any sort of representation of information. We believe this book will be of interest to students of computer science, psychology, media studies, engineering, and many other disciplines. With the popularity of online virtual worlds, there are a number of people including teachers, students, and the general public who are interested in how online virtual worlds can be taken to the next level and implemented as full blown virtual reality applications. Likewise, this book can provide inspiration and insights for computer game developers.

WHAT THIS BOOK IS NOT

This book is not a book about computer graphics. There are a vast number of very good texts that cover the details of computer graphics. Likewise, this book is not meant to teach you how to write the computer code required for creating VR applications.

SPECIAL FEATURES OF THIS BOOK

This book contains a number of special features that will aid in accomplishing its task of providing inspiration and ideas for its various audiences. One feature to take note of is the "VR Discoveries" that are included with various applications. When one of those appears, designers are encouraged to take special note because they represent an "Aha!" by that VR application's designer.

Another key feature to this book is the cross reference system described in Chapter 10, and the online database reference on this book's companion website. The cross reference enables developers and interested parties to quickly find different applications in this book that have characteristics that are of interest, regardless of what field the application is in. For example, a reader might be interested to see all the applications that use audio in them. Or, they may be interested in those applications that have been deployed in public venues that use head-mounted displays. A printed book can only present information in a single organization. In this book, applications are grouped according to the area they are used in, such as business, education, or entertainment. Through the use of an online database, the reader can group applications by any characteristic such as the representation scheme, the displays used, or many other criteria.

HOW TO USE THIS BOOK

We anticipate that many of the readers of this book will skip straight to the chapter that is closest to their area of interest. We encourage that. However, if the reader stops at that point, they will miss some of the most valuable aspects of this book. After that, it would be prudent to read the book cover to cover to discover gems they might not have encountered in their chapter of choice. Of course, the cross references and the online database provide another path to find topics of interest. We believe it will be very beneficial to all readers to read Chapters 1 and 2 to gain an understanding of the field of VR, and also to learn the meanings we are using for a variety of terms. And of course we would be remiss to not encourage any reader who wishes to learn more about virtual reality and its applications to read *Understanding Virtual Reality*.

THE RELATIONSHIP OF THIS BOOK WITH *UNDERSTANDING VIRTUAL REALITY*

As mentioned above, *Understanding Virtual Reality* is a key resource for anyone who wants a very strong background in virtual reality. It covers VR systems, interaction schemes, and considerable depth in how information can be represented in Virtual Reality applications. The book you are currently reading is where the rubber meets the road, real world VR applications that are foundational to the field. Or the skeptic who wants to see the reality of the field, and understand what is concrete vs. hype will find this book of extreme value.

ABOUT THE APPLICATIONS IN THIS BOOK

This book provides a glimpse into dozens of virtual reality applications. The applications are from a wide variety of sources, and cover a broad expanse of application areas. The applications in this book are referred to as classic applications in that they are some of the earlier examples of virtual reality put into use. They are each foundational to the field in some way. It is important to note that each of the applications was chosen for a specific reason. We give full coverage of this criteria at the end of Chapter 2, but the litmus test for inclusion are:

- It must be possible to discuss the application in public.

- If at all possible, we strove to include applications that we were able to experience ourselves, and/or at least to have direct personal discussions with the application creators.

- The application illustrates a wide variety of technological implementations.

- To the extent possible, we include applications that were developed in different development environments, such as Academia, Government, and Private Sector laboratories.

- We include some applications that have ceased to exist, and some applications that have continued to be used, developed, commercialized, or otherwise exist today.

Acknowledgments

We wish to thank first and foremost our friends and family, who gave up seeing us as we produced this work. We also thank our home institutions, The National Center for Supercomputing Applications, the Desert Research Institute, and Valparaiso University for their support of our efforts. We would be remiss if we did not acknowledge the fantastic work of all the application developers whose work we describe in this volume and without whom this book would be impossible. Indeed, without them the genre of VR would not exist as we know it. Finally we would like to thank all of our colleagues in the field and our co-workers, from whom we have both learned so much and been so inspired.

There were many lynchpins at Elsevier on which the success of this book hinged, but we would like to single out Greg Chalson as our champion. In a sea of turmoil, he stepped forward, took control, and made the publication of this book happen. Thank you.

Our other heroes at Elsevier include Mike Morgan and Tim Cox, who started us off, Diane Cerra and Dave Eberly who saw us along, Chuck Glaser who propelled us forward, and Heather Scherer and Paul Gottehrer, the game-saving closers in the bottom of the ninth.

CHAPTER 1

Introduction to Virtual Reality

1.1 WHAT IS VIRTUAL REALITY?

When we speak of "virtual reality" (VR) we refer to a computer simulation that creates an image of a world that appears to our senses in much the same way we perceive the real world, or "physical" reality. In order to convince the brain that the synthetic world is authentic, the computer simulation monitors the movements of the participant and adjusts the sensory display or displays in a manner that gives the feeling of being immersed or being present in the simulation. Concisely, virtual reality is a means of letting participants physically engage in some simulated environment that is distinct from their physical reality.

Virtual reality is a medium, a means by which humans can share ideas and experiences. We use the word *experience* to convey an entire virtual reality participation session. The part of the experience that is "the world" witnessed by the participant and with which they interact is referred to as the *virtual world*. However, the term "virtual world" does not only refer specifically to virtual reality worlds. It can also be used to refer to the content of other media, such as novels, movies, and other communication conventions.

Here is a more formal definition for virtual reality from Sherman and Craig:

> *A medium composed of interactive computer simulations that sense the participant's position and actions, providing synthetic feedback to one or more senses, giving the feeling of being immersed or being present in the simulation.*

Note that the definition states that a virtual reality experience provides synthetic stimuli to one or more of the user's senses. A typical VR system will substitute at least the visual stimuli, with aural stimuli also frequently provided. A third, less common sense that is included is skin-sensation and force feedback, which is jointly referred to as the *haptic* (touch) sense. Less frequently used senses include *vestibular* (balance), *olfaction* (smell), and *gustation* (taste).

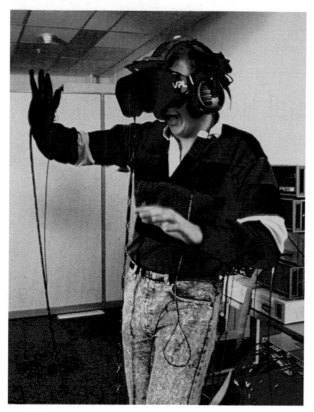

FIGURE 1-1

A virtual reality participant wearing a head-mounted display and a glove input device interacts with a virtual world.
Image courtesy NCSA

There are many specialty hardware devices involved in bringing the rendered sensory images to the user from the proper perspective. A familiar VR visual display device is the head-mounted display (HMD). An HMD is a device that the user wears on the head, containing a screen positioned in front of each eye. Another common technology used to display the visual part of a VR experience is to project the images onto a large screen or multiple screens that cover a sizable amount of the participant's view. Such displays date back to flight simulation projection domes and to the work of Myron Krueger (an early VR researcher) in the 1970s. This type of VR visual display is generically referred to as a large-screen stationary display.

As our formal definition suggests, an equally if not more important aspect of a virtual reality system is sensing the participant's position. Without information about the direction the user is looking, reaching, pointing, etc., it is impossible for the VR output displays to appropriately stimulate the senses. Monitoring the user's body movements is called *tracking*.

There are some related technological terms that are also often used in the discourse of virtual reality technology. However, these terms are not necessarily restricted to VR. One such term is "cyberspace." *Cyberspace* is the notion that people who are physically located in disparate physical locations can, through the use of some mediating technology, interact as if they were physically proximate. Thus, even technology such as the telephone can put two or more people in the same cyberspace.

Two other terms related to virtual reality and to one another are "telepresence" and "augmented reality" (AR). *Telepresence* is similar to VR, in that it is a means to virtually place a participant in another location in which they are not physically present. The difference from VR is that this location is actually a real place that for one reason or another is too difficult, dangerous or inconvenient for the person to visit in person. Like telepresence, augmented

FIGURE 1-2

Though often misperceptions surround the technology, virtual reality holds promise for a wide range of present and future applications.

FIGURE 1-3

Applications of virtual reality range from medicine to science to entertainment. Recent advances allow developers to port commercial computer programs to VR systems with relative ease.

Image courtesy of Jeffrey Jacobson

reality gives the user an altered view of the real world. However, the view they are given is of their current physical location, and using technology with many characteristics in common with virtual reality, additional (virtual) information is added to their normal sensory input. Frequently, it is the visual sense that is augmented, providing the user with abilities such as peering through walls, or into a patient's body.

1.2   THE BEGINNINGS OF VR

If one considers virtual reality to be the simulation of an environment that allows a person to experience some place and event other than where they actually are and what is actually happening around them, then flight simulators are an early example of this medium. Flight simulators based on interactive computer displays date back to the early 1970s. Earlier flight simulators made use of mechanically driven instrument displays driven by linkages to the pilot's flight controls such as the yoke, rudder pedals, etc. Many of the precomputer flight simulators were pedantic mechanical devices to give a future pilot the opportunity to become familiar with the flight controls and displays.

Later, by controlling the motion of a video camera over a scale model of some terrain, a sense of immersion was created. Although this did fulfill the criteria for virtual reality portrayed in the opening paragraph of this section, these early flight simulators were not general-purpose environments. A different simulator must be constructed for each type of aircraft, and additional terrain models created for new locations. General-purpose simulation was only possible after the advent of advanced computer graphics and display technologies.

In the following 11 examples of research efforts of different groups in VR development one can gain a sense of how VR technology came to be.

1.2.1   Morton Heilig's Sensorama

Early sensory display experiences included the Sensorama. The Sensorama was the brain-child of cinematographer and inventor Morton Heilig. Demonstrated in 1956, Sensorama was a scripted multimodal experience in which a participant was seated in front of a display screen equipped with a variety of sensory stimulators. These stimulator displays included sound, wind, smell, and vibration. The noninteractive scenario was driving a motorcycle through an environment with the appropriate stimulators triggered at the appropriate time. For example, riding near a bus exposed the rider to a whiff of exhaust.

The Sensorama system, however, was lacking a major component of the modern virtual reality system: response based on user's actions.

1.2.2   Ivan Sutherland's vision for computer-based virtual reality

In 1963, Harvard graduate student Ivan Sutherland demonstrated Sketchpad, a system to allow interactive, computer-generated visual imagery displayed on a cathode ray tube. In 1965, he described a vision for an immersive, computer-based, synthetic-world display system. His vision included the presentation of visual, aural, and haptic feedback in appropriate response to the user's actions. By 1968, Sutherland (as a professor at the University of Utah) had realized and publicly demonstrated a system that accomplished the visual component of his vision.

Sutherland's system included an HMD, mechanical head tracking using spooled retractable cables, and a computer program that rendered a simple stick representation of a cyclo-hexane molecule in three dimensions.

Sutherland later cofounded Evans and Sutherland Computer Corporation (E&S) and developed sophisticated real-time graphics rendering hardware for the flight simulator community.

1.2.3 Myron Krueger's Videoplace

Following Sutherland's demonstration, a variety of research and development efforts were born in university laboratories, government and military facilities, and, later, in the commercial sector.

In the academic community, University of Wisconsin researcher Myron Krueger was experimenting with a different perspective on virtual reality systems, which he referred to as *"Artificial Reality."* Whereas Sutherland's head-mounted display was especially suited for a first-person point of view in the virtual world, Krueger's artificial reality provided a second-person view of a virtual world in which participants could watch themselves within the world.

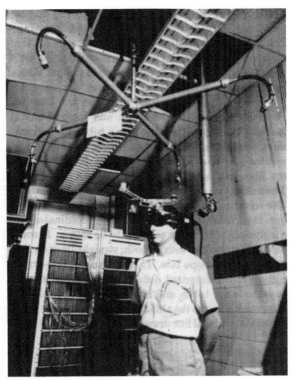

FIGURE 1-4

Ivan Sutherland demonstrates the first HMD virtual reality system.
Image courtesy Ivan Sutherland

Krueger's systems also differed from Sutherland's work in that he used video camera inputs to track the user's movements. Use of video camera technology resulted in two significant differences: The machine's perspective of the user was from the second-person point of view, and the user was not encumbered by any mechanical devices or other sensors attached to their body.

Other universities pursued various aspects of the virtual reality problem.

1.2.4 University of North Carolina at Chapel Hill

In the late 1960s, the University of North Carolina at Chapel Hill (UNC) computer science department founder and professor Fred Brooks espoused the need to have development work geared toward specific application problems. For example, a chemist would be interested in how two molecules dock together. Brooks' team also measured the benefits and pitfalls of their various innovations.

Due to the unavailability of capable hardware at the time, UNC also had to focus on hardware development, including high-performance graphics engines, head-mounted displays, and a variety of input and output devices, including devices to provide haptic feedback in

FIGURE 1-5

In Krueger's Artificial Reality, *a video camera is used to place an overlay of the participant's body on the virtual world.*
Image courtesy Myron Krueger

the form of responsive forces. Several commercial products have evolved from the innovative research at UNC.

1.2.5   Electronic Visualization Lab at the University of Illinois at Chicago

At the University of Illinois at Chicago, Tom DeFanti and Dan Sandin cofounded the Electronic Visualization Lab (EVL), where different types of graphical representations, input and output devices, and interaction techniques were explored. Most notable among their achievements were the development of the Sayer glove in 1977 (a glove outfitted to sense the bend of the wearer's fingers) and, in 1992, the announcement of the CAVE™ visual display system. The CAVE is a walk-in virtual reality theater typically configured as a 10-foot cube with three or more of its surfaces rear-projected with stereoscopic, head-tracked, computer graphics.

1.3   VR PARADIGMS

While we have already mentioned that VR systems provide synthetic stimuli to the senses, it is important to note that there are multiple ways by which this can be accomplished. Many

FIGURE 1-6
In the CAVE, participants stand surrounded by screens onto which the virtual world is displayed.
Image courtesy NCSA

suitable display technologies exist, but in general they can be categorized into three display paradigms. These three basic paradigms hold for not only visual displays, but also for display to other senses such as aural and touch (haptic) display systems. *Stationary* displays are fixed in place. Although the display doesn't move, the world is rendered in response to the user's bodily position. Examples of stationary visual displays include CAVE-type systems, single large screen systems, and desktop monitors. Loudspeakers are an example of stationary aural displays.

Head-based displays move in conjunction with the user's head. Consequently, no matter which way users turn their head, the displays move, remaining in a fixed position relative to the body's sensory inputs. Thus, visual screens remain in front of the users' eyes, and head-phones on their ears. Examples of head-based visual displays include the helmet-type display often seen in popular media, and BOOM™-type displays which are a display box into which a user peers that can be moved around on mechanical linkages. Headphones are an example of head-based aural displays.

Hand-based displays are a special case of the head-based paradigm. In this case, users hold the display in their hand. For visual hand-based displays, monitoring both the user's head position as well as the position of the display is required, because the direction of view is important. Most often visual hand-based displays are used to overlay computer graphics imagery registered with the real world. An example of a haptic hand-based display is the

FIGURE 1-7
The stationary CAVE visual display and loudspeaker aural display are often used together.
Photography by William Sherman

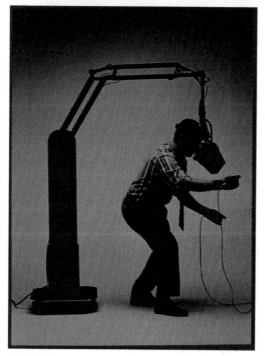

FIGURE 1-8
The BOOM head-based display mounts the screens on an arm that keeps the weight from being applied to the user's head.
Image courtesy Fakespace Systems, Inc

SensAble Technologies PHANToM™ arm. The PHANToM provides a dual role by mechanically tracking the user's hand as well as providing a force display to the hand.

1.4   COLLABORATION

One of the strengths of virtual reality is its capability to transcend the barriers of time and space. This transcendence leads to VR being a good vehicle for supporting collaboration. VR environments can foster collaboration in a number of different ways. Space can be shared, either physically or virtually. Dialog can be held synchronously, or in an asynchronous form.

Large-screen stationary systems such as the CAVE are the best type of VR system for collaborating in the same physical space. Many participants have a concurrent view of the virtual world, allowing them to point out items of interest to one another.

Most forms of VR systems provide a good way to collaborate in the same virtual space.

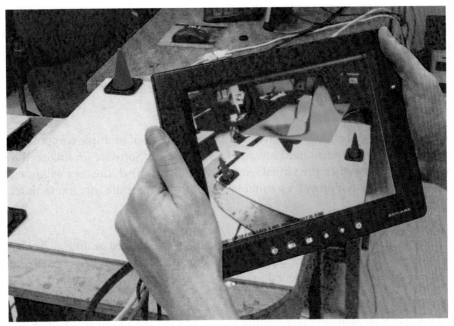

FIGURE 1-9

A hand-based display can provide an alternative view into the real or virtual world. In this example, researchers at the Colorado School of Mines use a hand-based display to superimpose virtual models on a stationary scene.

Image courtesy of Tyrone Vincent

A major benefit of virtual shared spaces is that they allow collaboration to take place via computer networks. Thus, not only can two workers share a space while remaining in their offices just down the hallway from one another, but they can also be an ocean away.

When working in a networked collaborative environment, each participant can be represented as a virtual entity. A virtual entity that represents a human in a collaborative environment is called an *avatar*. An avatar may be a somewhat realistic representation of the person, or an abstract representation. The mere presence of avatars can greatly improve the ability of the collaborators to communicate through nonverbal means. For example, pointing in a direction, waving an arm, or even just looking in a certain direction can convey valuable information from person to person.

Not every sense always needs to be transmitted in collaborative environments. For example, a telephone supports voice-only collaborations. VR, however, allows the option of participants sharing a three-dimensional world populated by 3-D objects that can be manipulated and worked with. Except for certain physical activities, most collaborative work relies only on the visual and aural senses, both of which are strengths of current VR technology.

Collaborators can inhabit the shared virtual world concurrently and engage in synchronous dialog and actions, or participate asynchronously by saving the state of the system after their component of the collaborative activity. Another possibility of asynchronous collaboration is to record all the actions of the participant(s), allowing other participants to replay that experience at a later time. In fact, the collaborators can leave annotations (such as messages or virtual pictures) for others who enter the space at a later time.

1.5   VIRTUAL REALITY SYSTEMS

The creation of a virtual reality system requires the integration of multiple components. These components include the system hardware, underlying support software for linking the display and input hardware together, the virtual world content with which the user will interact, and a user interface design that provides a suitable means for appropriate user interactions.

1.5.1   Hardware

Hardware used in virtual reality systems can be roughly categorized as display devices, input devices that a user consciously activates, and input devices that monitor the user, along with the computer that supports the modeling and rendering of the virtual world.

1.5.1.1   Computer/graphics engine

The main computing engine is responsible for calculating the physical behavior of the virtual world, and then rendering the state of the world into visual, aural, haptic, etc. representations. Because an effective VR experience requires real-time interactions, the computer system has some specific requirements.

The computational system can be implemented on a single large computer that meets all the requirements, or it can be implemented on multiple computers. In the latter case, the cadre

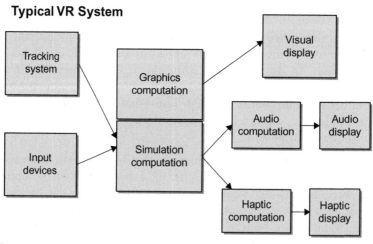

FIGURE 1-10

This diagram illustrates how the various components are integrated in a typical VR system.

of machines must be interconnected via a low-latency, high-speed communication network. Latency (the time delay between the time an event occurs and the time its results are apparent) is an important factor in any VR system. Any latency in the overall system reduces the effectiveness of the system. The use of multiple CPU components allows the system to achieve more computations both for the graphics and for the world simulation.

The primary needs that the computing system must meet include enough computational power to perform the virtual world's physics simulation calculations, sufficient graphical rendering performance from a "graphics engine" computational component, a means of rendering sounds, and perhaps rendering of other senses such as haptic (touch) information.

The specific computational needs vary based on the type of applications the system will be required to run. Representations of the real world generally require the ability to map pictures of the world onto surfaces to deliver a look of high detail (texture maps); however, an application to visualize a molecule could be done without the use of such features, requiring instead an increased geometric throughput. Some worlds, those that consist only of static objects, require no computation for world physics.

In addition to rapidly rendering the graphical representations, the graphics engine should have the capability to synchronize the display updates between multiple displays for rendering to both eyes (stereoscopic vision) in a head-based display, to multiple screens on a multi-screened projection display, or perhaps to multiple-projectors projecting overlapping left- and right-eye images to the same screen. Many high-end graphics engines and projectors have provisions to render and display stereoscopic images through a single mechanism. The absence of synchronization between displays leads to negative artifacts such as the world appearing discontinuous between two neighboring screens.

Modern computing systems include the ability to render sounds. If more advanced aural rendering operations are required, however, signals can be sent to an external audio processor. For example, the ability to make sound appear to come from a particular location relative to the user's head (spatialization) generally requires additional audio-rendering hardware.

The ability to perform multiple operations at the same time is also an overall requirement of VR systems. Thus, having an operating system capable of true multithreaded operation is a prerequisite of VR systems. The use of multiple computers is also a means of accomplishing this need.

Through the 1990s, many large VR projects relied on the use of larger (refrigerator-sized) computer workstations with multiple CPUs, and multiple instances of high-performance graphics-rendering hardware. However, with the advent of 3D graphics accelerators aimed at the consumer game market, it is now possible to utilize personal computers to implement VR systems with virtual worlds of significant complexity. This "low-cost VR" has made virtual reality systems available to a whole new class of users by decreasing the cost by an order of magnitude or more. A notable example of makers of such systems is Visbox incorporated, whose VisBox systems currently cost under $100,000.

1.5.1.2 Visual displays

The visual display portion of a virtual reality display generally has the most influence on the overall design on the virtual reality system. This influence is due to the visual system being the predominate means of communication for most people. It also tends to dominate how a VR system is defined, including which display paradigm is implemented.

Each type of visual display paradigm (stationary, head-based, and hand-based) has its own specific benefits and disadvantages, which are further influenced by advances in technology, and the amount of monetary resources available. In addition to these basic paradigms, all the visual displays can either display stereoscopic images, or monoscopic. In general, because virtual reality often attempts to mimic the sensation of physical reality, stereoscopic display is presumed.

Large-screen stationary displays such as the CAVE, wall displays, and table or desk displays use fixed-position screens to fill a relatively large portion of the field-of-view (FOV) for one or more viewers. Many of these displays (such as the CAVE and CAVE-like systems) wrap screens around the participant, surrounding the user as much as possible with the visual representation of the world. Even systems with a single display surface can fill significant portions of the user's view when the user stands near the large screen.

Thus, a primary benefit of the large-screen stationary display is FOV coverage. Other advantages include the reduced amount of hardware worn by users, which improves the ability to see colleagues physically standing next to them due to the reduced negative impact of latency. The ability of the user to continue to see the physical world while viewing the virtual world also improves the safety of the system.

Downsides of this style of visual display potentially include an incomplete view of the virtual world (field-of-regard), cost, and the difficulty of masking the real world if desired. The cost of these displays can vary greatly depending on the degree to which the user is surrounded and whether multiple projectors are used to increase the resolution of the imagery by tiling them together. An increased number of projectors also means more graphics-rendering hardware will be needed. Currently, with the use of projected images, the amount of space required is also one of the costs of using a large-screen display. The limited field-of-regard problem is solvable with an added cost. Six-sided (cube) CAVE-like facilities have been built that entirely surround the participant with screens (one being a door). The cost of such a facility needs to include creating a surface on which multiple people can stand, while being projected onto from below. This has been a significant challenge in the development of such systems.

Head-based displays (HBD) are perhaps the most commonly thought-of type of virtual reality display, having been popularized in movies and television. Early forms of head-based displays were often mounted onto fighter-pilot helmets, and thus were referred to as helmet-mounted displays (HMDs). Later the acronym HMD was also used for "head-mounted display." Either way, these devices were typically heavy headsets with attached screens positioned in front of the wearer's eyes. Two other types of HBDs that have also become available are a mechanical arm-mounted display that users pull up to their face, without any weight being placed on their body. The original of this class, the Binocular Omni-Orientation Monitor (BOOM), counterbalances the arm with the display. Later versions of HBDs use smaller screens, and weigh significantly less than the original HMDs. As these displays become closer to the sensation of wearing a basic pair of sunglasses, there is an increased tendency to label them "head-worn displays," with the superior connotations that phrase implies.

A major benefit of the head-based display is that users can turn their head to see any direction in the world. This is called 100% field-of-regard. Other benefits include being generally cheaper than large-screen displays, requiring less space, and being much more portable.

A significant disadvantage of HMDs is that any latency in the VR system is more noticeable to the user and thus more likely to cause nausea or a headache (thus limiting the interaction time). The more widely used head-mounted displays have the problem of the additional weight that users must carry on their head, along with cables to carry the video and tracking information. BOOM and BOOM-like display armatures often extend to the floor. Thus, the armature frequently causes blind-spots to which the user cannot move. Also, while BOOMs do not put the weight on the user's head, the display has a certain amount of inertia that can affect the experience. Head-worn displays therefore sound like an optimal solution, but they typically have screens with much lower resolution than what can be provided in BOOMs, HMDs, and stationary displays. Another disadvantage of head-based displays is that they are limited to a single user at a time, have a narrower field of view, and generally isolate that user from the people around the user, making it hard to discuss an ongoing experience.

Desktop VR displays (also known as *fishtank VR*) are similar to the large-screen displays in that they fall into the stationary display paradigm. The popular term "fishtank VR" is derived from the way one peers into a desktop VR display. A desktop VR display is basically a standard computer monitor, often augmented with the ability to display stereographically. By combining the monitor with the necessary tracking and other input devices and VR software, the scene appears to actually be inside the display—the way fish are inside an aquarium. Thus, if viewers moves their head left or right, they can see the fish from a different perspective, and similarly for the objects in the virtual world.

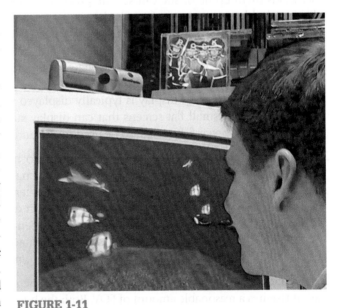

FIGURE 1-11

A computer monitor with a video camera can be a very simple VR display referred to as "fishtank VR" due to the similarity with looking into an aquarium.
Photography by William Sherman

The major advantage of the desktop VR display is that it can usually make use of an existing desktop computer with a few inexpensive additions. Thus, the cost of creating such a system is not excessive. Another significant benefit is that it can be used right at the user's desk. Frequently, the more difficult it is to use a VR system, the less often it will be used, and going to another room or building to make use of the system requires that the user expect significant improvements in the experience above what a monitor, keyboard, and mouse can provide. In fact, computer hardware has progressed to the point where, with the addition of a camera for user tracking, a VR system can nearly be completely implemented on a laptop computer, except not many laptops offer stereoscopic display.

There are some big disadvantages to the desktop display. These include very limited field-of-view and very limited field-of-regard. Users are only able to see what is immediately in front of them, and a little off to the side when they lean over, like looking through a window. Compared with the other types of visual VR displays, the cost is minimal, but there are costs to upgrade to a stereoscopic image, along with some input hardware and software to track the user's movement. The best tracking solution has been to use a video camera.

Hand-based VR displays are have not been widely used by VR systems. When used, they typically have a specific VR experience that makes use of them and generally have a specific need that must be fulfilled. The most intuitive type of hand-based display is a pair of binoculars that contain two small screens instead of the typical lenses. The binoculars continuously display a magnified (computer processed) view in the direction they are pointed, and when the user holds them up he or she can see the processed image. Another style of hand-based display is to hold a screen approximately the size of one's palm in the hand. The image on this screen shows the virtual world from the perspective of where the user's eyes are through the small window. This form of display works well as a "magic lens" display, giving the user an altered view of the "reality." The altered view might operate as if it were an "x-ray vision" device. The "reality" that is altered can be either physical reality or a virtual object itself. The palm-sized screen form of display is typically displayed monoscopically, in part because it is difficult to acquire small flat screens that can display stereo images. Modern cellular "smart phones" are now powerful enough to be used in VR, and more frequently in AR applications.

Although not widely used, handheld VR displays do have some advantages. In particular, they have an advantage when a VR experience has a natural interface for which the display is perfectly suited—as with the binocular, or "magic-lens" interfaces described. Because the user can choose when to look at a handheld display, it can be combined with either physical reality (as an augmented reality display), or in a screen-based virtual reality display such as a CAVE. Thus, a virtual reality world can be augmented—*augmented virtual reality*. Another nice feature of hand-based displays is that they tend to not be very encumbering.

Where hand-based displays do not work well is when there is no other VR display and the application requires a reasonable amount of FOV. Both the binocular and palm-sized devices provide very limited FOV. And while the field-of-regard is technically 100%, it requires the user to move the device through a large spherical motion to see in all directions. In general, handheld displays are less immersive, except when used to augment a larger view (real or virtual).

1.5.1.3 Aural displays

The inclusion of an aural display in a virtual reality system is generally a good way of enhancing any experience for a minimal additional cost. Unlike the visual display, it cannot be assumed that the aural image is presented stereophonically. In fact, the notion of "stereo" is more complicated with the aural sense.

Many virtual reality experiences can utilize a single (monophonic) channel of sound and still provide a deeply immersive experience. Experiences that provide just an ambient background sound, perhaps combined with some discrete sounds that mark an event in the world, seldom require more than monophonic. When this isn't the case, the question becomes whether traditional stereophonic sounds should be used versus a more complex method of sound spatialization.

The trouble with traditional (prerendered) stereophonic sound display is not that it only comes out of two speakers, but rather that it is preproduced (prerendered) to seem as though particular sounds come from particular locations. Because virtual reality is interactive, it is not generally possible to know a priori where the sound will be relative to the listener. Thus, sounds that must appear to emanate from a particular location need to be processed to create this effect. The processing is referred to as *spatialization*. Spatialized sound can be rendered to function in two-speaker (binaural) or multispeaker displays.

An interesting discovery regarding spatialized sound is that it can be effectively combined with prerendered stereo and monophonic sounds. For example, a VR experience might have a sound associated with a particular object or person in the world. That sound therefore should be spatialized to seem as if it follows the object or person. The scene might also have generic street sounds in the background presented as prerendered stereo. A monophonic, ambient orchestration to influence the mood can be added to the mix to create an overall highly immersive effect.

The two common sound display devices are loudspeakers and headphones. These two styles match well with the stationary and head-based visual display paradigms respectively. *Loudspeakers*, the aural display of the stationary paradigm, work well with CAVE-like displays, large wall displays, and desktop displays. *Headphones*, the aural head-based display paradigm, work well with head-mounted, BOOM, and other head-based displays. Of course, it is also possible and sometimes desirable to use headphones in a CAVE, particularly if the sound spatialization system works best with them. Likewise, there are good reasons to use stationary speakers with a head-based system.

Often, a single subwoofer is added to output loud, low-frequency sounds. Only one subwoofer is required because low frequency sounds are not easily localized by the human auditory system.

The cost of most aural displays generally pales in comparison with the cost of the rest of the VR system. Thus, neither form of aural display is more advantageous in that respect. The primary advantages of the two systems are that loudspeakers can be more easily heard by a group of participants, and headphones are generally easier to use when producing spatialized sounds. Also, headphones have a slight safety disadvantage in that if an excessive signal is presented, it will be very close to the listener's ears.

1.5.1.4 *Haptic displays*

Roughly speaking, haptic displays relate to the sense of touch. However, not all of the haptic sensations come via the skin. Some of what is called "haptic display" is related to the muscular and skeletal systems. Therefore, haptic displays are generally discussed in the two component terms: "tactile" (input through the skin) and "proprioceptive" (input through the muscular and skeletal systems). Sensing the coarseness of sandpaper or the temperature of water are tactile sensations. Sensing how much effort is required to lift a box, or knowing the current location of one's arm are proprioceptive sensations.

Different technologies are generally required for creating forces versus creating subtle skin-response sensations. Therefore, most devices designed for haptic display focus on either tactile or proprioceptive presentation.

Like visual and aural display types, haptic displays can also be divided based on the stationary versus body-based paradigms. However, when discussing haptic displays, these characteristics are typically referred to as "world-grounded" (stationary) versus "self-grounded" (body-based) displays.

World-grounded displays are those that have a base attached to the ceiling or that perhaps sit on the desktop or are affixed in some way to some object in the real world. Typically, the user holds the end of an arm with multiple linkages leading back to the base. Each of the linkages is capable of exerting an active or resistive force in a particular direction. Thus, when the user grabs an object and tries to move it, the ease with which it can be moved can be felt, allowing the user to sense the weight of the object and the friction or viscosity of the containing medium. Or, if the object is animate, such as a dog, then grabbing it (or its collar) can lead to an active force felt by the user.

Copyright 1994, University of North Carolina

FIGURE 1-12

This world-grounded haptic force-feedback device is attached to the ceiling, allowing a user to grab the controls and interact with the molecular world.
Image courtesy the University of North Carolina at Chapel Hill

Self-grounded displays are those that are somehow worn by the user. A common example is a glove fitted with some form of tactile display, such as small vibrators. Force display devices can also be self-grounded, such as a display that resists

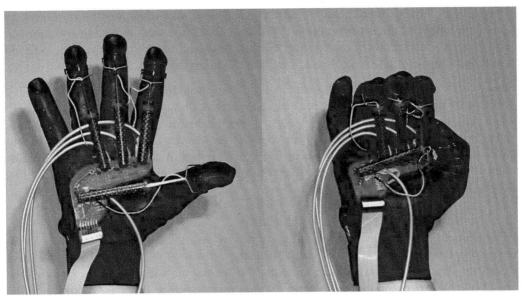

FIGURE 1-13

The Rutgers Dextrous Master II is a self-grounded display that can be used to prevent the fingers from closing all the way, simulating the effect of holding an object in the hand.

Image courtesy Rutgers University

the movement of the user's arm relative to their shoulder. The latter example works best however, either by ignoring the user's movement within the virtual world or by assuming that the shoulder is in a fixed location. In the latter case, the self-grounded arm display is effectively acting as a world-grounded display.

Another possible form of haptic feedback is that of the inactive prop device. In this case, the user gets tactile sensations from the skin touching a device and feeling its shape, texture, and sensing movement of buttons or other objects mounted on the prop. The prop device also provides some proprioceptic feedback by its weight and momentum. An example of an inactive prop is an instrumented (real) putter used as an interface to a virtual golf game.

1.5.1.5 Other sensory displays

Virtual reality systems make use of (in decreasing prevalence) visual, aural, and haptic displays. Use of other sensory displays has also been done. Of these the vestibular sense (the sense of balance) is the most common. In fact, it has been a very common form of display for flight simulation for decades. Olfactory display (smell) has been experimented with sparingly, and computer-controlled display of gustation (taste) is virtually nonexistent.

The most common form of vestibular display is the "motion platform." A motion platform is basically a large surface (the platform) mounted on top of hydraulic actuators that can raise, lower, and tilt the platform. The user (typically) sits on the platform, and in the case of flight simulators within a cockpit mounted to the platform. Sometimes the visual display is also mounted on the platform; other times it is projected onto a large dome that can be seen through the windows of the cockpit. By tilting the motion platform, the pilot can then sense when the aircraft begins to pitch, yaw, or roll, and by how much.

Another style of vestibular display is the bladder-equipped chair. By inflating and deflating different portions of the chair, the user can feel acceleration and deceleration. For example, when undergoing strong acceleration, pilots will feel themselves being pushed back in their chair. To recreate this, the bladder on the back of the display seat can be filled, and thus create a similar pressure sensation on the back of the pilot. A similar effect can be implemented for sensing the effective loss of gravity while riding in a roller coaster by deflating the seat of the chair.

1.5.1.6   *Input devices and user tracking*

Without input, a computer-generated display cannot be interactive, much less be considered a virtual reality system. In fact, virtual reality systems require not just a means for users to express their intentions, but also must track at least some subset of users' bodies. One can differentiate between these two types of input by referring to them as "cognitive input" (events specifically triggered by the user) and "user monitoring" (tracking the body movements of the user). Another way to think about this input dichotomy as an input that the user must specifically activate and an input that passively senses attributes, such as the position of the user.

The *position sensor* is the most important tracking device of any VR system. There are several types of position sensors, each with its own benefits and limitations. These sensors include electromagnetic, mechanical, optical, ultrasonic, inertial/gyroscopic, and neural/muscular devices. The most crucial factor of a position sensor is the type of limitations imposed on the system. Limitations generally arise from the technological means used to determine the relationship from some fixed origin and the sensor. For example, some trackers require an uninterrupted "line-of-sight" between a transmitter and a sensor. When the "line-of-sight" is interrupted (i.e., something comes between the transmitter and the sensor) the tracking system cannot function properly.

In position-sensing systems, there are three factors that play against one another (discounting cost): accuracy and precision of the reported sensor position, interfering media (e.g., metals, opaque objects), and encumbrance (wires, mechanical linkages). No available technology, at any cost, provides the optimal conditions in all three of these factors. Thus, the system designer must consider how the VR system will be used and make the optimal trade-offs. One of the driving factors is simply the ability of the system to produce an acceptable experience. Noise and low accuracy in the position sensor reports, as well as high latency decrease the "realism" or immersiveness of the experience, and often can lead to nausea in some participants.

Electromagnetic tracking systems are popular input devices for VR systems because they do not require line of sight to the tracked object. However, because they use an electrically generated and received magnetic field to determine the six degrees-of-freedom of the sensor device, metals interfere with the functionality of such a system. Ferrous metals are particularly problematic. Also, active electronic devices in close proximity to a sensor can be an issue. The magnetic properties of metals within the VR environment cause distortions in where the sensor is perceived to be with respect to the transmitter. If the interfering metals are stationary, then minor distortions can sometimes be corrected for in software.

Fortunately, the amount of metal within the environment can often be controlled. Cases where particular care must be taken to improve tracking accuracy are head-worn gear made of metal or with internal electronics, and wheelchairs. In the case of HMDs or stereo glasses with electronics, the best solution is to locate the sensor as far away from the electronics as possible. In the case of a wheelchair, a sensor mounted to the participant's head is less of a concern than a handheld device that will be located closer to the metallic components of the chair.

Standard electromagnetic tracking systems have wires that connect with both the transmitter and the sensor units. This is somewhat encumbering, with cables tethering the participant to the VR system. For a greater cost, some of these systems connect the sensors, not directly to the VR system, but rather to a radio pack worn by the participant. The participant thus has more freedom to physically move about the space without the concern of tripping over wires.

Mechanical tracking systems use transcoders mounted on physical linkages to report the movement of the linkages. The position of the end point can be calculated from the transcoder values. The use of transcoders provides extremely accurate and precise position readings. By improving position reports, the overall VR experience is improved by giving an increased physically immersive sensation, and perhaps also reducing the likelihood of nausea. The overriding

FIGURE 1-14

A low-level electromagnetic field is emitted by the large black box. The signal is sensed by a receiving antenna, which allows the system to determine the location and orientation of the receiver.
Photography by William Sherman

problem of mechanical tracking systems is that there is some physical attachment between the user and the real world. This attachment can often impede the user from moving in a natural way. However, there are some situations where the user's movement is already restricted, and therefore the mechanical system can be designed such that no additional restrictions are added, such as a pilot sitting in a cockpit.

Glove input devices generally fall within the realm of mechanical position sensor. However, it is the configuration of the hand that is measured rather than the overall location and orientation of the entire hand. To deduce the shape of the hand, sensors are placed throughout the glove to determine the amount of bend between various joints. Two common bend-sensing technologies used for hand-position sensing are optical fibers that transmit less light when bent and metals that alter their resistance when bent.

Ultrasonic tracking systems use a collection of transducers—transmitters (speakers) and receivers (microphones)—that pass signals from one point to another. By measuring the time taken for the signal to arrive, one can compute (using the speed of sound) the distance between the transducer pair. The key factors in accomplishing a proper measurement are that multiple transducer-pair measurements are required to determine the complete (X, Y, Z, roll, pitch, and yaw) position, and an uninterrupted line-of-sight must be maintained between transducer pairs. Thus, hardware systems that use ultrasound to measure sensor positions typically mount several transducers on the sensor device to provide some redundancy, allowing the sensor to go through different orientations and still maintain sufficient contact with the transmitters.

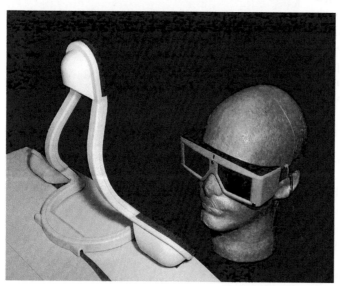

FIGURE 1-15

This basic ultrasonic tracking system uses three speakers and three microphones triangularly arranged to measure the distance between all the speaker-microphone pairs from which the location/orientation of the glasses can be determined.
Photography by William Sherman

Determining the orientation or location of a sensor requires that at least three transmitter-receiver transducer connections be made. In addition, there is a minimal distance that must exist between transducers in order to avoid ambiguous results. The number and spacing of the transducers can be cumbersome in some circumstances, such as adding significant weight to stereo-glasses, and requiring handheld devices to be large enough to accommodate the transducer distances.

Optical tracking systems can work along the same lines as ultrasonic systems, measuring distances by time and triangulation, or they may operate using computer vision by attempting to discern features of a video image to recognize where certain reference markers are located, and also how they are oriented. The markers used are generally designed to contrast with the rest of the scene. This contrast can be done by using illuminated objects such as light-emitting diodes, or by creating high-contrast signature shapes such as a white square surrounded by a black square.

Clearly, because the optical transducers work in the visual and near-visual spectrum, opaque objects will interfere with the operation of the sensors as there is a line-of-sight restriction with this form of tracking. However, optical tracking systems have some significant advantages over many other tracking systems. Specifically, a reasonable system can be constructed using commodity video equipment and freely available software. Another advantage is that video tracking can be done without the need for any wires emanating from the tracked sensor. One problem with video tracking is the reduced accuracy attainable using standard video resolutions.

Inertial and *gyroscopic* tracking systems are unlike many of the previously discussed methods in that they do not directly relate themselves to a fixed reference point. The downside is that they only report relative movements, not absolute positions. The benefit of this fact is that less hardware is required to implement these types of tracking. Thus, an inertial or gyroscopic tracker could be mounted in a small head-based display, and no other hardware would be required to give visually immersive feedback to the user. Another important benefit of this hardware is that there is very little lag between movement of the sensor and the reported movement.

The problem with such tracking systems is that because of the lack of a fixed reference, the reported values accumulate error. After a few minutes, when the user looks forward, the system may behave as if the user was looking ten or more degrees to the left or right. Frequently, inertial and gyroscopic tracking is combined with other tracking hardware so the benefits of each can complement one another. Because some VR systems, especially head-based systems, can cause nausea when there is significant lag between user movement and the visual image, the fast response of the inertial/gyroscopic system provides a low latency response to quick movements. Electromagnetic, ultrasonic, or other type of referenced tracking is then used to continually adjust for drift.

Neural and *muscular* tracking refer to the use of transducers placed on the skin of the participant to monitor muscular and other activity within the body, and make use of this information to provide inputs to the virtual reality system. For example, a sensor on the arm might be able to determine when the user clenches a fist. An example is a device called the Biomuse™. When the Biomuse is attached to the user's forearm, a virtual violin can respond to the user making bowing motions.

The tracking systems above are generally used to monitor the user's general body movements. This type of activity is referred to as that which is passively transmitted by the participant. Other VR input devices are designed to give the user more active and cognitive inputs. For example, pressing a button to jump forward in the virtual world is an active form of input.

Props and *platforms* are the physical places where such active input sensors are placed. The term "props" comes from the theater and film industry use of the word. Short for "prop-erty," a prop is any physical object that is not part of the scenery and can be manipulated by the actors. Thus in virtual reality systems a prop is an object that the participant can handle and use to interface with the virtual world. A prop may be embodied by a virtual object and might have physical controllers mounted on it.

Props themselves can be used for both passive and active user input. Handheld props are generally tracked in space, and thus a good indication of where one of the user's hands is located. Props also frequently have buttons, joysticks, and other input devices mounted on them, allowing the user to actively cause an action in the virtual world.

A platform is similarly used as a means of user input to the virtual world. It differs from the prop in that it is more like the scenery. Thus, a cockpit, or captain's wheel of a tall ship are both part of the "scene" where the participant is located and also provide a means of con-trolling the virtual world.

FIGURE 1-16

In this virtual reality system, a platform with a ship's wheel mounted on it provides the space where the participant takes a virtual voyage.

Image courtesy Randy Sprout

For gathering input about the real world for use in a virtual (or augmented) reality, there are many different types of data transducers. For example, MRI and medical ultrasonic scanners can produce data to recreate the internal organs of a patient. Real world objects and locations can be captured with laser scanning devices such as light detection and ranging (LIDAR). Larger scale locations and weather data can be collected by interpreting data transmitted by satellites.

Once the system has collected the input data it can further refine the data and otherwise filter it. Two common types of filters are for calibration/registration and gestures.

In order to provide a participant with a better sense of physical immersion, it behooves the system to respond in a manner consistent with the user's movement. In other words, if users move their head 4 inches, the system should not respond with an 8-inch movement. Many systems, and especially electromagnetic trackers, produce a consistent error that can be put in a table and used to compensate for the erroneous sensor reports. Other systems might be able to combine their data with fiducial (reference) markers that can be used to correct for slight errors in the data. Either method results in more accurate reports of sensor positions, at perhaps a slight increase in latency. Augmented reality systems are especially susceptible to poor calibration and registration to the real world because any errors are glaringly obvious against the real-world backdrop.

Another common form of filtering is to interpret patterns in the input from the user. For example, if the user extends both arms out the sides and repeatedly moves them up and down, the system may generate the "flap" input. Or if the system monitors finger movements and senses that the hand has closed into a fist, it may indicate to the virtual world that the user is attempting to grasp an object in the world. Sufficient tolerance must be built into a gesture recognition system to allow for variations from individual to individual.

Given the plethora of input possibilities, designers should consider the goals of the system and find the combination of input devices that best serve that goal.

1.5.2 Software

A variety of software components must be integrated to enable cogent VR experiences. Such software ranges from low-level libraries for simulating events, rendering display imagery, interfacing with I/O devices, and creating and altering object descriptions, to completely encapsulated "turnkey" systems that allow one to begin running an immersive experience with no programming effort.

1.5.2.1 *Laws of nature—simulation code*

Many VR experiences have some programmed laws of nature that govern the behaviors and interactions carried out by the objects in the world. The exception to this is the case where the only interaction possible is changing the user's viewpoint relative to the objects in the world. In this case, the user cannot manipulate the objects but only look at and work around them.

One option for "world simulation" is to merely allow several explicit cases of behavior to be executed under specific conditions. For example, in an architectural walk-through, the system

FIGURE 1-17

A simple, nonrealistic set of rules govern this fantasy space, providing both cartoon-like renderings as well as cartoon-like laws of nature.

Photography by William Sherman

may prevent users from walking through walls, and constrain users' vertical movement to be as if they were walking on the floor surfaces.

More advanced simulations can have global behaviors such as gravity, plus individual rules that apply only to specific objects. For example, a bee could be given a rule that allows it to fly in search of a flower, gather pollen, and then return to the hive. On the other hand, a flower could be plucked with a grasping gesture and when released, fall to the ground.

Other application simulations strive to more closely mimic the real world by adhering to mathematical descriptions of real physics. So, for a bee to fly, it would have to flap its wings sufficiently rapidly to generate the needed lift, and orient itself properly to send it in the desired direction.

Given that in a virtual reality experience there is no requirement that the world follow the laws of the real world, it is possible to give objects fantastic behaviors. Such behaviors might be to give the user "x-ray" vision abilities to see through objects or to see the interior structure of an object. Another possibility is to give the user the ability to move heavy objects such as walls and furniture in an architectural (or game-world) design application, and walk through walls.

The concept of world-physics also applies to how multiple users sharing the same world can interact and communicate with one another. Simple implementations of behaviors for collaboration might include representations of the other users (their "avatars"), and perhaps also an audio channel that allows everyone to communicate verbally.

1.5.2.2 Rendering libraries

Rendering libraries convert the form of the world from the internal computer database to what the user experiences. The rendering library must include the appropriate rendering algorithms for whatever sense is to be portrayed. Visual images produced from graphics rendering libraries are perhaps the most common of this class of software; however, such libraries have also been developed (and used in VR) for other senses, such as hearing and touch.

These libraries generally include features to render the basic elements of a "scene" along with features to enrich the display. For example, in a typical graphics library, along with the ability to render basic forms by specifying the vertices and colors of polygons, the programmer is also given options to add lighting elements, and overlay photographs onto polygons to make them appear more realistic. Also, such libraries can support higher level graphical functions like hierarchical object descriptions ("scenegraphs") and collision detection.

1.5.2.3 VR libraries

A complete virtual reality system is not comprised merely of rendering sensory outputs, but rather rendering appropriate outputs depending on the user's current position and actions. The paramount task of this VR library is to acquire the necessary information about the participant. This is done by interfacing with tracking and other input hardware. Information from the various sensors is integrated and provides the necessary parameters to the rendering systems. For example, the graphics (and also 3D audio) rendering process requires knowledge of the user's head position to give the proper visual/soundscape.

Another critical requirement of the library is to operate in "real time." It must perform all the input, simulation, and rendering functions at a rate that makes the world appear to be "real" by immediately responding to the participant's actions. Using multiple processing units on VR systems can help to achieve such "real time" responsiveness. Therefore, VR libraries typically include the ability to perform multiple tasks at once.

1.5.2.4 Ancillary software

The creation of a virtual reality experience also requires the use of various software in addition to the software required during the presentation of the experience. Examples of such tools include modeling software to aid in the construction of the form of the objects that inhabit the world; sound editing software to construct sound clips that will be heard in the experience, and image processing software to create appropriate texture maps.

Independent user interface libraries might also be linked with a VR experience to allow the operator to control parameters of the experience, for example a mouse-controlled widget panel. File formats such as VRML (a format for describing three-dimensional computer graphics objects and spaces) and other standard object formats also play an important role in the creation of virtual reality worlds.

1.6 REPRESENTATION

There are several stages to presenting information to the user. We have stated that virtual reality is indeed a medium for communication. As such, the choice of symbols one chooses to convey is important. Depending on the goal of the VR experience, one may choose to mimic the real world to a high degree of verisimilitude, or one can choose to disregard the structures and limitations extant in the real world and create surreal or fantastic worlds with never-seen-before objects, behaviors, and beings. One can choose to present aspects of real-world entities that are normally unseen, such as stresses within a structural beam, or present the world as perceived by someone who has undergone a traumatic brain injury.

Regardless of the application, a mapping must be made between concepts in the virtual world, and the stimuli that will be presented to the user's various sensory organs. When choosing representations for objects and concepts, tradeoffs must sometimes be made based on the limitations of the underlying systems and the requirements of the application. The choice of representations is clearly limited to the kinds of transducers available in the system. For example, most virtual reality systems provide a visual and aural display. Beyond these two modes of presentation, in some special cases there is extra hardware available for presenting certain tactile, force, smell, and vestibular feedback.

Within the modes of presentation, tradeoffs exist regarding fidelity versus cost and performance issues. For example a tradeoff in designing the visual aspects of an automobile lies between visual complexity/realism versus the real-time/interactive nature of the display. Limits on the real-time frame rate reduce the possible level of interactivity.

However, users who require highly complex extreme realism may be willing to accept the reduction in frame rate.

Often, specialized rendering tricks are used to increase the realism. This includes techniques such as texture mapping, level of detail (LOD) culling, and polygon decimation. Sometimes these tricks lead to a tradeoff between realism in the geometric form versus realism in the surface look. The technique of texture mapping photographic images onto a simple geometry is a common method of making a world look more realistic. However, the closer one approaches a texture-mapped object (especially when presented stereoscopically), the more apparent it becomes that the form is not a true representation of the object. The object looks like a cardboard cutout or stage background of a play rather than the actual entity.

As has been stated, users' avatars are their representation within the virtual world. There is a wide range in how one can create this personal representation. Perhaps the simplest is to restrict the avatar to a nonvisual, vocal presentation. In the realm of visual avatars, there are a variety of avatar options. The type of interpersonal communication required by the application affects the avatar representation requirements. If the capability of expressing nonverbal body language is required, then having a 3D model with articulated arms offers the ability to point, wave, and perform other gestures. If seeing the faces of other users is important to read their reactions to events, then an avatar comprised of a video representation becomes the preferred option. In a fantasy scenario, users may not want to accurately reflect their real-world counterpart at all.

1.7 USER INTERACTION

Virtual reality offers the opportunity for new modes of interaction not previously available with traditional computing systems. While offering new possibilities, a downside is that there is no established set of conventional idioms. Often interaction styles are borrowed from two-dimensional user interfaces. For example, pull-down menus can be imported into a three-dimensional virtual world.

Using borrowed idioms helps the user by providing a familiar means of interfacing with the computer. However, it may not take advantage of the potential richness of the 3D virtual environment. Even when using borrowed paradigms, questions still remain regarding where

FIGURE 1-18

The menu is an interface technique that has been adapted to the virtual reality medium from the realm of desktop computer interfaces.

Photography by William Sherman

to place them, which direction they should face, and other decisions that were obvious in the 2D worlds for which they were designed.

1.7.1   Interaction Techniques

If one starts with a blank slate, not considering previous 2D interface styles, then one can conceive of new interaction styles that can be broken down into four major categories.

The obvious mode of interaction in virtual reality is to mimic the actions required in physical reality. Thus, to move an object, a user can position their hand at the object's location, grasp it by closing their fingers, and then by moving their hand, change the position of the object. In the virtual world, this can be emulated by tracking the position of the hands and fingers. This is referred to as a *direct* form of interaction.

While *direct interaction* best mimics our methods of manipulating the real world, there are other ways in which we are accustomed to interacting with computers. These three other forms of interaction are referred to as *physical, virtual,* and *agent* interactions.

Physical interactions are those that are input to the virtual world through input devices that the user actually touches. In a conventional computer system, the most common physical inputs are through the mouse and keyboard. In a virtual reality system, devices such as a handheld wand, steering wheel, or glove input devices are examples of physical inputs.

FIGURE 1-19

Steering a vehicle is one way in which the participant can use a physical device to interface with the virtual world.
Photography by William Sherman

Virtual input interactions are ones in which the "devices" with which one interacts are a part of the virtual world itself. Thus, a virtual button is one that is rendered directly in the world and might be activated when the users hand comes in "virtual" contact with the button. Many virtual interactions rely on physical or direct interactions to activate the virtual device. So in the given example, a direct interaction is used to press the virtual button. An example in which a physical input is used to activate a virtual device is when a slider is rendered in the world (or just on the screen in a traditional desktop interface) to control a parameter such as volume. In both the VR experience and desktop metaphor, a physical button on the wand or mouse is pressed to manipulate the slider.

The fourth type of interaction is to express control parameters via an *agent*. In other words, by communicating with a computer entity (the agent), one lets their desires be known, and expects the system to comply. For example, to travel through a solar system world, one might say the name of a planet and be taken into orbit around the specified celestial object. In the real world, we might tell our chauffeur the name of the location to which we wish to travel, and expect to be taken there without any further input.

Having listed the four forms with which one can cognitively input information to the virtual reality system, it is appropriate to examine three broad categories of the types of interactions commonly performed in a virtual reality experience. These interaction categories are making selections, performing manipulations, and traveling.

FIGURE 1-20

Interacting with a graphical (virtual) controller is an example of a virtual input interaction, such as moving this table using a virtual slider.

Photography by William Sherman

1.7.2 Making selections

The primary selections one can make in a virtual world are selecting an object on which to act, or to select a direction in which to go.

There are a variety of ways of indicating a direction of interest. Many of these ways make use of the position of some part of the user's body, such as pointing with a finger, gazing with the eyes, or facing with the torso. One can also indicate direction with devices such as a joystick or steering wheel, or by referring to a coordinate system or some landmark-based reference system.

There are many natural ways in which a VR system designer might choose to allow the user to select an item in a virtual world. In some of the previous examples, the user makes contact with an item to activate it—making contact is one way to select an item. By making use of a selected direction, one can point to the object of interest. Through the use of voice recognition software, the user might just name the object, either from memory or from a menu listing possible selections. Or the VR system might provide a menu system that allows the user to point to the desired object or make contact with the object's name.

1.7.3 Manipulating the virtual world

Having selected an item, the user will often want to perform some manipulation on that item. In many cases, the process of selecting an item may be incorporated directly into the manipulation process. For example, moving a box might be performed by touching or pointing at the box, pressing a button, and then moving the hand that is making virtual contact with the box.

The manipulated element of the experience can be either an object of the virtual world or an attribute of the overall virtual reality system. For example, moving a car is manipulating an object of the world, whereas choosing a filename to store the current status of the world is an attribute of the virtual reality system.

There are two ways of acting on elements of the experience: in a way that mimics the action of forces on them, or by changing attributes of objects in the world or the system in supernatural ways. So, a car in the world can be changed from blue to red by applying virtual paint to the car (mimicking reality) or by selecting the new color from a menu (supernatural modification).

1.7.4 Navigation

Navigation describes how we move from place to place. In the real world, we navigate from place to place as we walk, drive, ski, fly, skate, and sail through the world. In a VR experience, there are several additional choices for how one might navigate through the environment.

For clarity, the term *navigation* can be divided into two subcomponents: *travel* and *wayfinding*. Travel is the act of controlling one's movement through the world, such as by physically walking or controlling an airplane yoke. Wayfinding is using information about the world to guide the direction and speed of travel.

FIGURE 1-21

The task of navigating through a world can be broken into the component tasks of wayfinding (figuring out where you are and where to go) and travel (moving through the world).

Photography by William Sherman

There are 10 common travel paradigms used in virtual reality experiences:

- *Physical locomotion* is the simplest method of travel in VR. It is merely the ability for participants to move their bodies to change the position of their point of view within the virtual world. Physical locomotion travel is generally available in VR experiences, often in combination with another form of travel.

- *Ride-along* describes the method of travel that gives participants little or no freedom. They are taken along a predetermined path through the virtual world, perhaps with occasional choice-points. Usually participants can change their point of view or "look around" while on that path.

- *Tow-rope* travel is an extension of the ride-along paradigm. In this case, the user is being pulled along a predetermined path, but with the ability to move off the centerline of the path for a small distance.

- *Fly-through* travel is a generic term for methods that give the user almost complete freedom of control, in any direction. A subset of the fly-through method is the *walk-through*. In a walk-through interface, participants' movements are constrained to follow the terrain such that they are a natural "standing" height above it.

- *Pilot-through* describes the form of travel in which users controls their movements by using controls that mimic some form of vehicle in which they are riding.

- *Move-the-world* is a form of travel that is often less natural than the previous forms. Here, users "grab" the world and can bring it nearer, or move or orient it in any way by repositioning their hand.

- *Scale-the-world* travel is done by reducing the scale of the world, making a small movement, and then scaling the world back to its original size. The difference between the points about which the two scaling operations are performed causes the user to reappear at a new location when returning to the original scale of the world.

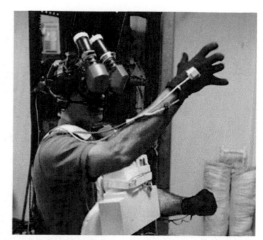

FIGURE 1-22

Astronaut Rick Mastracchio practices shuttle mission tasks in virtual reality.
Image courtesy of NASA

- *Put-me-here* travel is a basic method that simply takes the user to some specified position. This can be somewhat natural, like telling a cab driver your destination and arriving some time later, or this method can be totally unnatural such as selecting a destination from a menu and popping there instantaneously.

- *Orbital-viewing* is the least natural form of travel. In this method, the world (which often consists of just a model-sized collection of objects) seems to orbit about users depending on which direction they look. When users look left, the object orbits to their left, allowing them to see the right side. Looking up causes the object to orbit above them, showing the bottom side.

Some of the above methods of travel aid users in their movement through the virtual world by constraining where they can go. This constrained travel is one of many ways in which a virtual world can be designed to help users find their way around. Other wayfinding aids include the provision of maps, paths in the world to follow, obvious landmarks by which to site one, and instruments such as virtual compasses, among others.

CONCLUSION

This chapter covered the history, background, and terminology associated with VR technology and applications. The following chapter will address issues related to applying virtual reality to a problem or for some other purpose. The chapter will discuss basic issues related to the application of virtual reality, how the application examples in this book were chosen, trends in virtual reality applications, background on how the applications are related to each other, and commonalities and differences to watch for as you read the application descriptions. We present a taxonomy of virtual reality applications and explain the visualizations of the application database that is on the companion website of this book.

CHAPTER 2

Applying Virtual Reality

Image courtesy of the University of Illinois

While the technology that supports virtual reality is interesting in its own right, the real payoff of virtual reality comes when it aids in solving real-world problems, provides a creative outlet, or betters human existence in some way. The area in which virtual reality has been applied in order to bring about edifying personal experiences is wide and varied. These range from viewing architectural (re)creations to visualization of the human body. However, virtual reality has only begun to be applied to the myriad of possible uses.

33

2.1   VIRTUAL REALITY: THE MEDIUM

Virtual reality is a medium. Much like the media of music, painting, and dance, VR can be used for many purposes. A primary purpose for any medium is the communication of ideas. That is the primary focus of virtual reality in this book. The ideas can range from the purely abstract (what is it like to live inside an animated cartoon?) to the very practical (will this vehicle function appropriately after we build it?). The medium of virtual reality is much more fully explored in *Understanding Virtual Reality* [Sherman & Craig].

Although it is difficult to categorize works in any medium, it is sometimes useful to classify works for the purpose of study. This book focuses on virtual reality applications. It is helpful to classify applications to allow the reader to understand common elements, and to learn from other applications that are similar in some way to what they would like to create.

2.2   FORM AND GENRE

Form and *genre* are two terms often used to evaluate and discuss the content of media. Form is related to how the narrative is constructed and presented to the audience. An example of form from the movie *Citizen Kane* is the use of flashbacks to tell the story. Genre is a way to categorize style: Science fiction or mystery, opera or symphony, abstract or representational are all genres of particular media. Just as other media have their forms, in virtual reality there are different presentation and interaction styles that combine to make up the forms of VR. The elements of a created work are built around a basic structure that can take any number of forms (i.e., literary or interface styles). The form of an experience is manifested in the style of interface chosen for the experience; thus, in VR the form is for the most part the interface. In essence, the interface is the way things are presented, the shape of the narrative.

In VR we typically associate genre with the class of problem being addressed and form with the method of interaction and presentation. One form of interaction is the *walkthrough*. This form is a somewhat simple application interface that allows the participant to experience some model of a location through an undirected interactive narrative. Participants are allowed to move throughout the modeled virtual world. A common genre that makes use of this form is the architectural or site walkthrough, often based on a real-world location or plan, where the user can perhaps test accessibility of doors, sinks, and cabinets. However, not much else typically takes place in these spaces. One doesn't pass by the water cooler and see a conversation taking place, or hear a fire alarm, watch as people walk calmly to the nearest exit, and see them vacate the building (although one could).

In addition to the walkthrough, there are many other forms that are common VR interface forms, which we describe in the chapters that follow. Of course, the form of a VR experience is not limited to how users travel through the virtual world. Form also includes how they interact with the objects in the world. For example, to select and move an object, users might be required to make a fist near the object, move their hand to the desired location, and release their fist. An alternate form of this operation might be to point at the object with a wand, press a button, point to the new location, and release the button.

Along with these various classes of presentation/interaction styles (the forms), there is also a set of narrative styles and prototypical settings (the genres). Some virtual reality genres have begun to emerge, and, as with other aspects of VR, many are derived from other media. Examples of today's VR genres include games, scientific visualization, manufacturing procedure analysis and training, product prototyping, interactive story experience, and historical site recreations.

The choice of genre and form is orthogonal; that is, the selection of a particular genre does not (necessarily) put limitations on what form may be used. In practice, however, there may be certain combinations frequently used together; certain genres go hand in hand with specific forms. Similar forms can be used in different genres, however, as we see in the use of the newsreel and flashback in both the dramatic genre film *Citizen Kane* and the comedic genre film *Zelig*.

2.3   WHAT MAKES AN APPLICATION A GOOD CANDIDATE FOR VR

Potential new users of virtual reality should consider whether their objective will gain a sufficient advantage via this medium. Many people are attracted to virtual reality simply due to the newness of the technology. This is a perfectly valid reason to make use of virtual reality if one is tasked with investigating new technology, or if one is interested in attracting people to see your work (i.e., using VR as a means of advertising or marketing).

Apart from superficial benefits of using virtual reality, there are features of a task that can help determine whether VR can be advantageous.

Virtual reality provides a means of presenting information in a three-dimensional space, with three-dimensional input controls. Therefore, any problem that is inherently 3D can be made to work well in virtual reality. This proficiency includes any multidimensional data that can be mapped into some 3D form.

Much of what VR can do involves the creation of computer models of some real-world item or event. So, for real-world problems that rely on the use of models to achieve some goal, a virtual reality solution can often prove beneficial. Thus, model-based applications for which a computer construction can be created with fewer resources (time and/or money) than a physical mock-up would be likely to succeed as a virtual reality application. Likewise, VR is beneficial when computer models can be generated more accurately than the corresponding physical models. For example, a building can be modeled to a greater degree of detail and more lifelike scale in a computer than can be done with a hand-crafted model.

Another technological limitation that can eliminate otherwise potential applications is the degree to which the application requires input registration over a large space. Input registration refers to the ability of the hardware to maintain a stable relationship between the real world, and the sensed location of tracked objects. So, if an application requires that a user walk around a real factory, and have an augmented overlay added to their real-world view, that application must have good registration between the real world and the augmented data to work properly. There are techniques available for attaining good registration, but the current technology generally limits this to a smaller working volume.

2.4   PROMISING APPLICATION FIELDS

Through the examination of some of the application fields that have benefited from the use of virtual reality, one can get a better sense of how well VR can be applied in other fields. "Genres" of VR applications can roughly be categorized into four broad groupings: virtual prototyping, visualization, training, and entertainment. Other genres can be classified as a subgenre of these four, such as the architectural walkthrough style of application.

2.4.1   Virtual prototyping

A classic genre of virtual reality applications that strives to save money and reduce time in bringing a product to market is *virtual prototyping*. The product can range from something small such as an appliance to large complex machinery such as a wheel loader or submarine.

A virtual prototype might be used to evaluate a product from a variety of perspectives: ergonomics, constructability, and aesthetics.

The ergonomics, or usability, of the product can be examined by presenting a virtual representation of the device to its intended users and allowing them to try it out. By virtually using the product, users can discover the little annoyances that might tip a purchase to another brand, and they can discover the big problems that could make the planned item unusable.

Some product designs are also tested for how easy it will be to construct them, and for mechanical products how easy to maintain them. By putting the product through a virtual assembly, with workers experiencing it in a realistic manner they can uncover trouble that might require a redesign of the assembly process. Likewise, a maintenance worker can be asked to perform many probable repair and inspection tasks to verify their ability to be successfully completed.

Many products get their edge in the marketplace primarily through their aesthetic qualities. Therefore, the design team assigned to consider the look of the product can get a good sense of how the product might appear to the customer by using virtual reality. Because realistic rendering is even more important to this aspect of product analysis, the experience is generally tuned for maximum visual fidelity, sacrificing some interactivity if necessary.

Not only is it easier to change a computer file than a physical structure, it is also much easier to distribute a computer file. This feature of computer-based design makes collaboration across great distances much more feasible. In a world where companies operate on a global scale, with operations and customers spread across multiple continents, the ability to quickly pass information between sites is imperative.

2.4.2 Architectural walkthroughs

Visualizing and demonstrating not-yet-constructed buildings as envisioned by their designers is a widely acknowledged, appropriate use of virtual reality. But what is it about architecture that suggests this merit? In addition to having the quality of presenting three-dimensional constructions, virtual reality improves upon traditional methods of examining a planned structure by allowing the client to experience it "first hand." They don't need to imagine walking into the building by looking at the model. The goal of reviewing the design prior to beginning construction (using either traditional methods or VR) is to find undesirable features in time to make changes inexpensively. In this fashion, architectural walkthroughs can be thought of as a type of virtual prototyping application.

Models can also be presented using traditional computer animation renderings, which can be used to show lighting and visual aesthetics of the space. However, by being immersed, the participant can also evaluate the scale, accessibility, and usability of the space.

A standard architectural VR application has an obvious three-dimensional representation to make the virtual world look like the real world. There is also a natural choice for navigation scheme, which is a walkthrough that allows the user to move through the space in a manner similar to how they would do so in reality. The visitor to the virtual building is constrained to walking about on the floor surfaces, but with the ability to open doors, move up and down stairs, and take the elevator.

A similar application is to create nonexistent places for reasons other than design analysis. These places might be nonexistent in time rather than space. Historical places and situations can be created as a means of allowing people to learn about the past. Here, the architectural walkthrough genre acts mostly in the realm of visualization. This exploration of data is otherwise difficult to see with unaided human senses.

2.4.3 Visualization

Computer simulations and detailed sensor inputs both can provide an overabundance of data, making it hard for researchers to perform a useful analysis. This trend previously led to the use of computer animations and then to interactive tools to aid this process. By continuing this trend to the use of virtual reality, researchers can be provided a more natural way to navigate through the space into which the data has been mapped.

Although some simulated data is not three-dimensional in nature, much of it is, so it can be easily presented via 3D VR displays. For higher-dimensional data, techniques are being developed that provide users a glimpse of the features within.

In any case, virtual reality can provide a better interface to the data than is possible through the two-dimensional interfaces of the standard desktop mouse. This interface departure can be used with nonrealistic rendering techniques afforded via computer graphics. Nonrealistic rendering is common in scientific and medical visualization, and in VR the user can be given a natural interface to view the world through a variety of different "lenses."

2.4.4   Training

Training is also an application genre that is a rather obvious fit for VR. In fact, the oldest example of virtual reality, flight simulation, is of this genre. One basic reason for this natural fit is that mimicing the three-dimensional real world has a clear metaphor, that is, behaving in the virtual world should simulate behavior in the real world.

Virtual reality, however, allows one to do more than merely mimic reality. If reality imitation was the only goal, then it may be simpler to manufacture physical props with which a participant could practice some procedure. For example, much surgical training is performed on animals and cadavers. What virtual reality adds is the ability to practice uncommon, expensive, and dangerous tasks.

By practicing tasks in this computer-mediated system, other benefits are realized. Specifically, the simulation operator has more control over what scenarios can be presented to the trainee, and can change the scenario in response to performance. The other significant benefit is that their performance can be recorded and analyzed.

2.4.5   Entertainment

As a new medium, virtual reality has found a niche in the entertainment market. However, being new will draw people for a while, but to "keep them coming" requires an enhanced experience at an affordable price. A profitable, long-lived VR entertainment endeavor has yet to be demonstrated.

That said, the trend in computer gaming is toward more realism with techniques to render the world from the perspective of the player. This has led to an amazing improvement in the price/performance of computer graphics hardware. If this trend continues, it is likely that the cost of hardware for physically immersive displays will become low enough for many game enthusiasts to purchase them for the home.

The added feeling of immersiveness when comparing the desktop version of a game such as *Quake II* to an adaptation to the CAVE VR display indicates that the computer game community is likely to embrace virtual reality. *CAVEQuake II* is perhaps the most widely distributed of all CAVE applications.

2.4.6   Other application genres

Virtual reality has also been applied to other areas of use, such as medical, educational, and artistic uses. However, many of these uses can be categorized as subsets of the above genres.

Medical applications chiefly fall into the two categories of either visualization or training. Surgical suturing and minimally invasive surgery trainers are available commercially, and experimental work has been done on other procedures such as celius plexus block anesthesia administration. Visualization applications include analysis of CT and MRI scan data, sometimes with the ability to aid in planning for an upcoming surgery. Work has also been done at the University of North Carolina to allow a physician to visualize inside the patient's body while performing a procedure. Psychological treatment of phobias is a (clinician) controlled walkthrough of a visualization of some subset of the real world.

Educational applications can fall into the training, walkthrough, and visualization categories. The ScienceSpace application, a lesson in high school physics developed at the University of Houston and George Mason University, is an example of how physical processes can be visualized to allow students to come to a better grasp of the 3D nature of the subject matter than merely reading it from a book. Presently, virtual reality is being used at Valparaiso University to teach subjects such as electromagnetics and materials science. Architectural students supplement their education by creating virtual prototypes of their designs in the CAVE at the University of Illinois at Urbana-Champaign. A Japanese science museum has sought to make learning important lessons about their nation's ecology entertaining, as well as educational, by creating a virtual reality game that students participate in to learn about the ecological place of the dung beetle.

For art-oriented applications, the experience of the participant is the focus rather than the utility of what can be done in a virtual reality encounter. The goal of an artistic application may or may not be to entertain the participants, but it strives to give them a chance to view the world from another perspective and give rise to intellectual stimulation. Artistic applications also differ from many visualization, training, and virtual prototyping applications that strive to closely mimic the real world. Many artistic and entertainment applications choose to focus on the surreal or fantastic rendering and interactive possibilities offered by virtual reality.

New ideas for where to apply virtual reality are continuously arising. As virtual reality becomes more commonplace, the medium will be sought as a possible answer to many new tasks and many new artistic expressions.

2.5 DEMONSTRATED BENEFITS OF VIRTUAL REALITY

Much like any other technology, the adoption of virtual reality as a practical tool is dependent on showing that it adds some benefit unavailable through other tools. VR has promised to aid in lowering product development times, providing cost savings, scientific insight, improved learning, and engaging entertainment. In order to assess whether VR is fulfilling these hoped-for ideals, it is important to define criteria by which success is measured.

One measure is to see whether people are using the technology or not. If so, one can assume it offers something of value to the person beyond other tools they have available. If no one uses the technology, it could be because the technology is inadequate, or because it is not mature enough, still too expensive, or they haven't had an opportunity to try it.

Of course one reason to not use VR for a problem is that it is not the suitable tool for the problem. In general, VR is a tool for working with three-dimensional problems. Anytime one needs to recreate the real world (which is three-dimensional), VR is often a reasonable medium in which to work. Any task that requires the simulation of a real-world operation is a potential candidate for benefiting from VR. So, training in any number of areas is appropriate, including medical training and military training. VR is also useful for evaluating products and places, such as new machine prototypes, architecture, and cars. Some fields in which VR has been adopted and has been used in the normal course of working include medical training applications, virtual prototyping, aircraft manufacturing (e.g., Boeing has demonstrated wearable computers with heads-up displays), and entertainment.

However, the real power of virtual reality comes from what can be done in a simulated space that cannot be done in the real world. Although VR is generally useful for imaging objects that can be represented as a 3D physical entity, like a building or a human liver, this involves representing a real-world entity exactly as it normally appears, and may not make use of all the advantages provided by VR. In VR it is possible to change the surface of the objects to show additional information such as stresses, temperature, or other attributes that are not normally visible. Similar abstracted representations can be made in aural or other senses in addition to the visual.

Usefulness can be demonstrated by organizations that have already found VR to be mature enough to be useful in its present state. Uses have included automobile and machinery design, visualization of scientific and medical data, engineering analysis, artistic expression, training, and entertainment.

In 1992, General Motors began investigating the use of virtual reality for aesthetic evaluation of automobiles as well as analysis of an automobile's ability to withstand crashes. Automobile designers began making regular use of the CAVE, escalating to the point where, by 2000, GM installed their fourth CAVE VR environment. Most other automobile manufacturers also now make use of CAVEs and similar technology and have been shown in television advertisements to illustrate that the manufacturer uses high-technology tools.

In 1994 *CRUMBS*, an application to visualize a variety of three-dimensional scientific and medical datasets, was created at the National Center for Supercomputing Applications (NCSA). Though originally developed for a specific medical application, over the subsequent years it has been expanded and used by scientists and researchers in many different fields, including oil exploration, basic physics research, genetic research, veterinary medicine, and biomedical visualization. It has also been extended in its capabilities to allow it to be a useful application in support of education by allowing an instructor to create and share scenarios with students located at a remote facility.

Nalco Fuel Tech, a company that provides engineering consulting services for operators of large boilers and incinerators, developed a prototype tool for analyzing how to improve the burn process in a way that releases fewer pollutants into the atmosphere. By visualizing the output of supercomputer simulations in a VR environment, they found that the immersive interaction of VR could aid the analysis and reduce the amount of time necessary to reach optimal design solutions. Their initial experimental effort with the Argonne National Laboratory in 1995 was rewarding enough that Nalco began their own internal VR effort in 2000.

In addition to the proven benefits of flight simulation training, both the military and NASA have found VR to be suitable for training in other areas. For NASA, training for Space Shuttle Extra-Vehicular Activity (EVA, or "space walk") missions such as the repair of the Hubble Space Telescope in 1993 and 1996, and construction of the International Space Station have benefited from pre-flight exercises in a VR environment (beginning in 1998). One of the ways in which the military has used VR is training submarine officers in the seldom-performed task of bringing a submarine into port. A research project begun in 1994 at MIT has been successfully transitioned to a commercially supported tool for training this operation into the 21st century.

Another task that can benefit from VR training systems is surgery. Boston Dynamics, Inc. (BDI) has created a surgical task training simulator for the commonly performed task of suturing together two tubular structures (anastomosis). In addition to training for the task, an analysis mode was also created to evaluate the progress of medical students and determine when they were ready for the next phase of their training. BDI implemented the system in such a way as to make the training system match the real-world task as much as possible. The operator stood at a kiosk that mimicked standing over a patient, and held onto actual surgical instruments. The instruments were connected

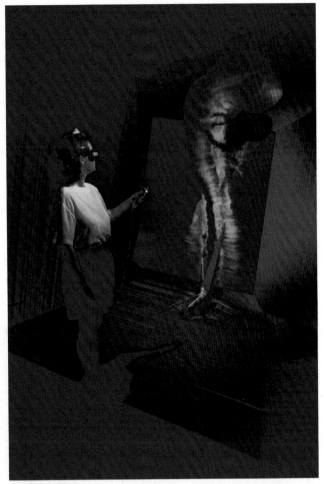

FIGURE 2-1
A user visualizes 3D data in the CAVE using the CRUMBS application.
Image courtesy NCSA

to a haptic feedback system that displayed forces calculated from a realistic dynamics simulation. As the operator looked down, a computer-rendered stereoscopic image hid the haptic display device, showing instead the virtual ends of the instruments interacting with the simulated tubular organs.

Photographer/artist Rita Addison turned to virtual reality as a means of expression after an automobile accident in 1992 impaired the visual centers in her brain, thus reducing her ability to use a camera. After losing her ability to express herself via the camera, in 1994 she turned to virtual reality as a means of artistic expression. In particular, working with a software developer, she produced a VR experience that gave people the ability to visually experience the world through the eyes of someone suffering the aftereffects of brain injury. Many visitors of her "Detour: Brain Deconstruction Ahead" VR experience respond emotionally, stating that they can better understand what life must be like now for Rita and other sufferers of brain injury. The experience is especially poignant for people who personally know others who have suffered a stroke or other form of brain trauma.

In 1997, Id software's *Quake II* game was adapted for use in a CAVE environment by Paul Rajlich. Although the game was developed for play on home PCs, the increased immersion offered by the VR version demonstrates an added dimension of play. "CAVEQuake II" has been downloaded and installed on more CAVE™ and CAVE-like systems worldwide than any other application.

CAVE facilities generally do not have open public access, so for many, the DisneyQuest venue offers a more likely place to have the opportunity to experience virtual reality. The DisneyQuest family arcade centers offer a variety of interactive experiences with which families can participate. Several of the experiences consist of either head-mounted display or CAVE-like VR systems. With many of their experiences based on characters from Disney films, the creators have the opportunity to experiment with how to transition these characters from the medium of film to interactive immersive experiences.

FIGURE 2-2
Vision becomes cloudy and warped in the "Detour: Brain Deconstruction Ahead" VR art experience.
Photography by William Sherman

2.6 MORE RECENT TRENDS IN VIRTUAL REALITY APPLICATION DEVELOPMENT

Virtual reality application developers have an advantage over the pioneering scientists, artists, engineers, and educators when it comes to creating their own virtual reality experiences. Not only do they have the benefit of the experience of the early application developers, they also have a plethora of new tools that help them to do their task more quickly, effectively, and at a lower cost.

This section looks at some of the trends in application development that developers are taking advantage of.

2.6.1 Converting extant applications to virtual reality without having access to the application code

A "Holy Grail" in virtual reality application development would be to "retrofit" existing computer applications to work as virtual reality experiences without having to do any extra work, without access to the application code, and without requiring a significant level of technical expertise.

Of course, even when the technical challenges of integrating user tracking, stereoscopic display, and multisurface display are achieved, the VR developer would still need to think about the issues discussed throughout this book related to interaction schemes, navigation paradigms, and other issues related to interacting with a computer simulation in a physically immersive virtual reality environment. Fortunately, several technologies have emerged that address the issue of tackling the problems of integrating tracking, stereo, and multisurface display.

One example is a product from Mechdyne Corporation called Conduit. The goal of Conduit is to allow users of existing computer graphics applications to automatically be able to run those applications on cluster-based systems, with integrated tracking and with stereo display. The idea is that one could use an application they currently run and without access to the source code or significant code development use that same application in a CAVE, head-mounted display, or other VR device to provide immersive head tracking for the experience.

The way that this is achieved is by hijacking the application's OpenGL calls and transforming them based on the display device and tracking information. While Mechdyne doesn't claim to support every application that exists, they provide a list of common applications that they have tested and made "VR-aware" in their own terms.

Another tool that provides a similar functionality to Mechdyne Conduit is a suite of products from TechViz that offers a similar functionality. Though these are commercial products, it is entirely reasonable to believe that open source products with similar capabilities will be created.

2.6.2 Developing virtual reality applications with game engines

The proliferation of computer games has brought along with it a variety of game development tools. Some of these are quite useful in developing virtual reality applications. As early

FIGURE 2-3

Recent games like Electronic Arts' Spore *allow the building of 3D models for creatures that even children can create.*
Image courtesy of Nickolaus Will

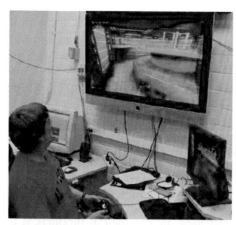

FIGURE 2-4

A nuclear engineering student at the University of Illinois tests a virtual model of a nuclear reactor that he created using the Unreal Editor with Unreal Tournament.
Image courtesy of UIUC

as 1997, Paul Rajlich modified the computer game *Quake* to run in a CAVE. Since then, many VR applications have been developed that use game technologies.

Unreal Tournament from Epic Games and Digital Extremes is a first person shooter game in which multiple players use various weapons to engage in various battles. The game, and the Unreal Editor, provide a low-cost way for application developers to create virtual worlds for virtual reality applications. The editor is straightforward to use, and provides support for creating walk-through spaces. The game also supports animation and other useful techniques.

Professor Rizwan Uddin at the University of Illinois uses these tools to create virtual recreations of nuclear power facilities. Graduate students, undergraduate students, and even high

FIGURE 2-5
The Virtual Pompeii application described in Chapter 6 is being modified to work with the CaveUT software platform.
Image courtesy of Jeffrey Jacobson

school students have used the Unreal Editor content creation tool to model the facilities they are interested in.

CaveUT is an adaptation of the *Unreal Tournament 2004* game engine that works with multiwall virtual reality display environments, including tracking of the users' point of view and also supports dome-style displays. The Virtual Pompeii application described earlier is being converted to work with the Unreal game engine and will be compatible with CaveUT.

2.6.3   Low-cost input devices

Another positive outcome of the popularity of video games is that the gaming industry has developed a variety of low-cost, durable game controllers. One that is particularly useful for virtual reality applications is the Nintendo Wii Remote (otherwise known as the Wiimote).

The Wiimote is a handheld device that an end-user can use to provide input to games that run on the Wii console. VR developers

FIGURE 2-6
CaveUT supports multiwall projection environments.

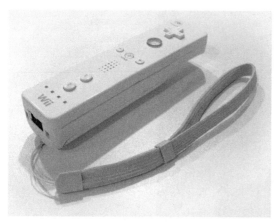

FIGURE 2-7

The Wii Remote has caused considerable change to the nature of input devices in commodity console game systems by providing the types of kinesthetic inputs VR developers have used for decades.

quickly recognized its potential as a VR input device and started creating applications that support the Wiimote.

The Wiimote provides sensing of acceleration on three axes, as well as an optical sensor that is used in conjunction with a stationary Sensor Bar to provide information on the direction the Wiimote is pointing. In addition to its utility as an input device, the Wiimote has a built in vibrator that the application developer can control. The low cost, combined with the functionality that the device provides, as well as the fact that the Wiimote operates without being encumbered by a wire makes the Wiimote an attractive option for many applications.

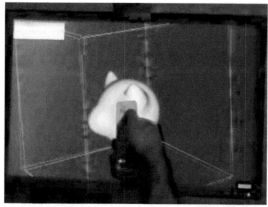

FIGURE 2-8

A Wiimote being used as an input device to a fishtank VR system.

2.6.4   Cluster-based compute engines and high-performance graphics acceleration

Many of the applications described in this book relied on high-cost graphics supercomputers. Application developers today have the advantage of the vastly improved price/performance ratio that has resulted from the mass marketing of computing and graphics technology.

Modern graphics cards, with very reasonable prices, provide an amazing level of performance compared to the technology of yesteryear that cost orders of magnitude more. The computer game industry has pushed the capabilities of the graphics cards even at price points that are attractive to the average mass-market consumer.

Likewise, the price of computers has decreased to such a level that the typical home computer now possesses more computational capability than the supercomputers of decades past.

Many virtual reality developers are taking advantage of the idea of clustering several low-cost computers together to gain computational capability. One scenario that is appearing more and more frequently is that multiwall projection environments, like CAVEs, are being driven by a computational cluster that has one computer and one high-performance graphics card per display surface. Other scenarios include using a multiprocessor computer with several graphics cards, using a handful of multiple processor computers, and others.

The trend toward using a computer per display wall is somewhat ironic in that the original CAVE environments were driven in that exact way, using a computer per wall, where the computers were interconnected with SCRAMNet (Shared Common Random Access Memory Network). As graphics supercomputers became available, the model was to use a graphics supercomputer with multiple graphics "pipes" or hardware accelerators.

Many virtual reality software libraries now provide support for using clusters of computers rather than a monolithic computation engine. Additionally, software solutions such as the Mechdyne Conduit provide a way to utilize extant software applications on clusters of computers with little or no modification.

2.6.5 Passive stereo displays

In the past, many projection-based VR environments used active stereo glasses, and for good reason. Active stereo works by time multiplexing the left eye view with the right eye view. The glasses shutter in synchrony with the display of each eye's view. A major advantage of active stereo glasses is that they work even when there is not an inherent "up" or "down" of the scene. That is, no matter which way a participant positions their head with respect to the display, the stereo still functions correctly. For example, the floor in a CAVE has no inherent up or down. Consequently, the shuttering glasses work nicely because they function no matter how they are oriented with respect to the display. A major disadvantage of active, time-multiplexed stereo is cost.

FIGURE 2-9

A small-scale computing cluster that drives the CUBE (six-sided CAVE-like device) at the Beckman Institute using the Syzygy virtual reality library.

FIGURE 2-10
A large scale computing cluster.

In an effort to reduce costs, many virtual reality environments now use passive stereo techniques. The most common passive stereo technique is using polarizing filters on the projection source, and corresponding filters in the participant's glasses. The most common polarization scheme is where the images intended for one eye are polarized horizontally, and the images intended for the other eye are polarized vertically. This works nicely as long as the display has an inherent up and down, and the participant does not tilt their head. If the participant tilts their head, the result is unsatisfactory.

One way to overcome the problems of linear polarizing filters is to use circularly polarized filters (polarized clockwise and counterclockwise). They have the advantage of not being affected by head tilt, but suffer from a worse rejection ratio.

Another passive stereo technique is to use anaglyphic stereo. The red and blue filters that were used in old-fashioned three-dimensional movies are an example of this technique. That technique, though, suffers from the problems inherent with filtering two colors. A more modern spin on the red/blue filters is implemented by a technique known as Infitec™ stereo separation. In this technique, filters are created that allow a wide range of colors to pass, but with a selected subset of each color wavelength being filtered. The filter for the other eye also allows the wide range of colors, but with a different subset of wavelengths being filtered. The end result is that users perceive the full color spectrum, but the left eye receives the image intended for it, and the right eye does as well. This technique does not suffer problems with head tilt.

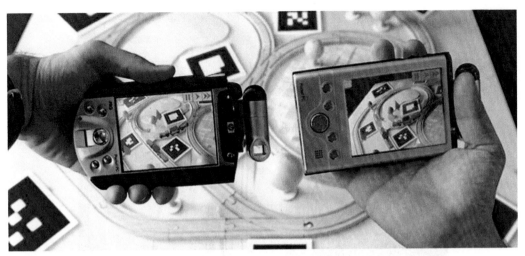

FIGURE 2-11
This example of handheld augmented reality from the Christian Doppler Laboratory at the Graz University of Technology allows the participants to use their handheld PDA devices to "see" a virtual train on the physical toy train track. Images courtesy of Vienna University of Technology

2.6.6 Augmented reality and handheld devices

Although augmented reality (AR) is not a new idea, new applications are being developed at a rapid pace. One area that is relatively new is using cellular telephones and/or other handheld displays as the interaction device. The Wellington Zoo Advertising Application is an example of hand held augmented reality that uses a cellular telephone as the viewing device. The telephone also has a camera built into it, so it serves as a fully functioning AR system.

2.6.7 Wireless interaction and optical tracking

One limiting factor in many of the foundational applications described in this book is that the participant is encumbered with devices and wires. Technology can solve that problem, and as technology progresses we expect to see many more examples of unencumbered virtual reality.

One area that has made tremendous strides in freeing the participant from wires is in the area of tracking. Optical tracking, which uses cameras to "watch" the tracked object or person, is becoming quite useful as a means of tracking without wires. In order to be most useful, optical tracking must utilize more than one camera in order to determine depth and to solve the problem of occlusion between objects (when something else comes between the tracked object and the camera, making it impossible for the camera to see the object).

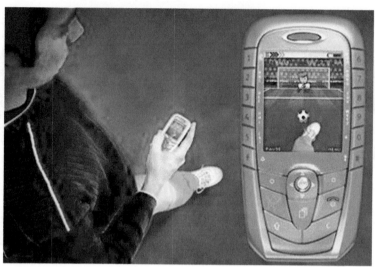

FIGURE 2-12

This person is using their cellular telephone to "see" an augmented reality soccer game. The AR application is allowing the user to interact with the virtual ball with their physical foot.

FIGURE 2-13

Current optical tracking systems determine the coordinates of the tracked entity. A camera "watches" one or more identifying marks in the scene. In order to aid the system, reflective markers are often used. The two styrofoam balls mounted on the glasses are covered with retroreflective tape so they appear as the brightest objects in the scene. The camera(s) can determine information about this person's location and orientation by where the markers appear in the camera's view.
Image courtesy of Valparaiso University Visualization Laboratory

Currently, many optical tracking systems use retroreflective tape or markers to make it easier for the camera to identify the tracked object. As research advances, optical tracking will be useful without requiring any markers.

Another advance is in the area of eye-tracking methods. By tracking the eyes, computational resources can be deployed where the participant is looking.

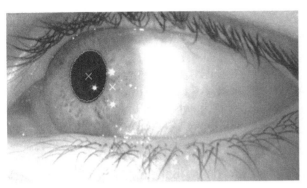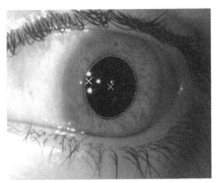

FIGURE 2-14

Eye tracking allows the application developer to utilize information about where the participant is looking, as opposed to just the direction their face is pointing.

FIGURE 2-15

Although still not common, some application developers are including treadmills into their applications for a more natural running/walking sensation. The image in the left shows a manifestation of an omnidirectional treadmill built in the form of a large hamster exercise ball. The image on the right is implemented as a treadmill of treadmills with additional technology.

Other devices can be made wireless through many different wireless technologies such as radio, ultrasound, or infrared communication.

2.6.8 More senses

Though it is still the case that most virtual reality applications rely primarily on visual displays, and to a lesser degree to aural displays, more sensory displays are becoming more common. Haptics is an area that is becoming more widely utilized.

FIGURE 2-16

Haptics is becoming more widely used in VR applications. In this example, surgical tools provide haptic feedback in similar ways to the BDI Surgical Simulator described in Chapter 5.

FIGURE 2-17

Multiperson augmented reality games can be played outdoors. Of course, people who are not in the game will not see the objects that are augmenting the view of the players.

2.6.9 Multiperson virtual and augmented reality

A major trend in computer gaming that has also followed in virtual reality and augmented reality is the inclusion of multiple participants. It is only natural to want to share your experience with other people, and it is often highly useful to collaborate with others in a virtual reality environment. By building VR applications with computer game engines, multiple people can participate in the virtual experience. While many of the multiperson virtual reality experiences were built without the use of game engines, for those that use the game engines, the multiperson characteristics come with little or no extra effort.

2.6.10 Tiled displays

One limitation of older virtual reality technology is that it suffers from poor resolution and is limited in brightness. Modern head-mounted displays are an improvement, as are modern projectors. There is a trend, though, to achieve higher brightness and more pixels by tiling multiple display systems together. This can be achieved by projecting multiple projectors onto a single display surface, or by abutting multiple displays together.

Of course, achieving a good alignment and registration, as well as color and brightness matching, is still a nontrivial engineering challenge.

Tiling together multiple flatscreen displays can be problematic if the bezels and frames are obtrusive for your application. Tiling projectors together to project on a single screen (typically, rear projected) brings with it the difficulty in aligning the displays. Image alignment can be carried out

FIGURE 2-18
This display was created by tiling together multiple flatscreen display monitors. The net effect is high resolution, and plenty of screen real estate.
Courtesy of Visbox, Inc.

mechanically (to line up the edges physically) or in software by allowing the images to overlap and using software to do edge blending.

Of course, the goal of tiling displays together is to achieve high pixel density with appropriate screen real estate. As display technology improves, there will be less incentive to tile multiple displays together.

2.6.11   Head-based projection

With head-based projection, the participant wears a small projector on their body or head. The net result is that there is a display wherever the participant looks. One example application would be to integrate head-based projection with augmented reality technology. A camera could "recognize" the person you are talking to, and project that person's name on their body to give you a reminder of their name.

2.6.12   Tele-immersion

Tele-immersion allows multiple people to interact together as though they are in the same place. Instead of using avatars to represent the participants, the system creates three-dimensional models of each participant in real time and reconstructs them at the other end of the system.

FIGURE 2-19

This picture shows a tiled display that is rear projected. The projectors are mechanically aligned.
Image courtesy of Visbox, Inc.

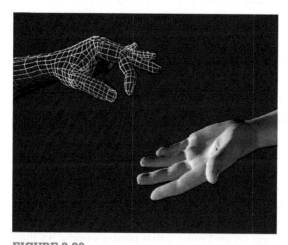

FIGURE 2-20

Tele-immersion allows users who are not located in the same place to interact as though they are. The system uses computer vision to interpret the scene, which is then integrated with the other locations and then reconstructed as a single environment.

2.7   A FRAMEWORK FOR VR APPLICATION DEVELOPMENT

This book presents several exemplary VR applications that are either inspirational or foundational in nature. The casual reader may be interested in a specific genre, or may have a specific application to develop for a narrow focus. Regardless, lessons learned in one area often can impact a topic in another area. To help in making sense of the following applications, we have developed a taxonomy and database to cross-reference applications, or to do searches for specific information that you may be interested in. This is described in detail in the final chapter. The database is available for access on the companion website.

FIGURE 2-21

A game player immerses himself into the game world.
Photography by William Sherman

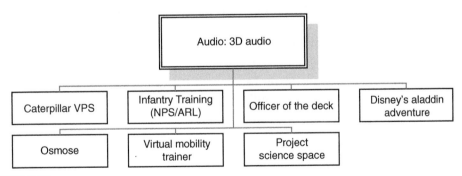

FIGURE 2-22

Results of searching for 3D audio show that a wide range of applications in different areas use the technology.

An example of how this can be useful is finding commonalities between applications in different fields. For example, you may be interested in 3D audio for entertainment VR applications. However, applications in business, military, science, and art all use 3D audio. By searching on such a topic in the database, you would find that the following applications all use 3D audio.

We have defined the fields for the database based on high-level categories. For each of the applications, their characteristics are identified. Again, we refer the reader to the final chapter for a full treatment of this topic. The main fields and their subcategories are:

- **Audio:** 3D audio, Non-speech, Sonification, World Referenced, Head Referenced

- **Direct Selection:** Pointer, Gaze, Crosshair, Torso, Device, Coordinate, Landmark

- **Display:** Front Projection, Rear Projection, Mono, Stereo, Reach-in, Computer Monitor

- **Genre:** Site Exploration, Game, Virtual Prototyping, Visualization, Training

- **Goals:** Analysis of 3D Data, Cost Savings, Profit, Improve Quality of Life, Artistic Expression, Informative Expression, Entertainment/Escapism, Simulation Experimentation, Safety, Marketing, Training, Education, Virtual World Creation, Modify Objects

- **Head-based:** HMD, Opaque, Video See-through, Optical See-through, BOOM, PUSH

- **Input:** Head-tracking, Prop-in-hand Tracking, Hand-tracking, Two Limbs Tracked, Two Hands Tracked, Feet Tracked, Objects/Props Tracked, 6DOF, 3DOF, Other DOF, Electromagnetic, Mechanical, Optical, Videometric, Ultrasonic, Inertial, Neural, Fingers, Eyes, Predictive Analysis

- **Item Selection:** Contact, Contact by Intermediary, Point, 3D Cursor, Aperture, Menu, MiniWorld, Name

- **Manipulation:** Direct User Control, Physical Control, Virtual Control, Agent Control, Machine Control, Ratcheting, Artificial Constraints, Natural Constraints, Distance AAAD, Local Action-Direct Action, Local Action–Remote Effect, Action through an intermediary, Laser Pointer Beam Scope, Expanding Pointer Beam, Adjustable Pointer Beam, Hysteresis, EGO Reference Frame, EXO Reference Frame, Feedback,

- **Navigation:** Path Following, Maps, Landmarks, Placenames, Bread Crumbs, Compass, Instruments, Exoxentric View, Coordinate Display and Grid, Constrained Travel

- **Objects:** Geography, Agents, Artifacts, UI Objects

- **Physical Input:** Correction Table, Buttons, Switches, Valuators, Wand, Joystick, 6DOF, Props

- **Physics:** Static World, Cartoon Physics, Newtonian, Aristotelian, Choreographed, Collision Detection, World Persistence, Dynamic World, Inference from Real World, Computational Model

- **Platform:** Ring, Kiosk, Ambulatory, Cockpit

- **Point-of-View:** First Person, Second Person, Third Person, Inside-out, Outside-in

- **Representation:** Realistic, Abstract, Cartoon, Mixture, Qualitative, Quantitative

- **Sharing:** One immersed with onlookers, Two or more immersed, Open Display, Multiperson Cockpit, Collaboration, Avatar Representations, Synchronous

Collaboration, Asynchronous Collaboration, Annotation, World Congruity Synchronous, World Congruity Asynchronous, Doctor/Patient

- **Speech Recognition:** Speaker Independent, Speaker Dependent, Push-to-talk, Name-to-talk, Look-to-talk
- **Stereo Display:** Time Interlaced, Passive, Linearly Polarized, Circularly Polarized, Anaglyphic, Spatially Multiplexed
- **Travel:** Physical Locomotion, Redirected Walking, Ride Along, Tow Rope, Fly-through, Walkthrough, Pilot-through, Move-the-World, Scale-the-World, Put-me-there, Put-me-there-WIM, Orbital Viewing, World-in-hand, Point-to-fly
- **Venue:** Home, Work, Museum, Arcade, Retail Store, Trade Show, Product Showroom, Classroom, School District, Outdoors, In-vehicle, Corporate Meeting Room, Physical Rehabilitation, Mental Therapist Office, Theme Park, Research Lab, Design Facility, Factory, Doctor's Office, Training Center

As you read through the applications in this book, take special mental note of how the developers chose to address such issues as input and navigation. Also keep in mind the constraints posed to the developers such as the application's display, venue, and goals. In developing your own applications, you may struggle with similar constraints. By looking at example applications and the lessons learned by other developers with similar constraints, you can optimize your users' experience.

We provide a complete system for exploring this taxonomy in the final chapter, but want to introduce the reader to this concept so that this framework can help you to interpret the information as it is presented.

ABOUT THE APPLICATIONS IN THIS BOOK

This book provides a glimpse into dozens of virtual reality applications. The applications are from a wide variety of sources, and cover a broad expanse of application areas. The applications in this book are referred to as *classic* applications in that they are some of the earlier examples of virtual reality put into use. It is important to note that each of the applications was chosen for a specific reason. While many modern-day applications utilize many of the same techniques as those covered in this book, we chose to go back to the beginning of the advent of virtual reality. It is in these early applications where one can discover not only good techniques and ideas, but more importantly the why of these ideas. Many aspects of these applications are seen in more modern applications, but it is often the case that the developers of the newer applications saw a technique in one of the more foundational applications and chose to implement it in their endeavor. Through personal experience, discussions with early developers, and review of extensive notes and documentation, our goal was to tease out the whys of the choices the developers made, and also to discover what was tried that didn't work as well as planned. In some cases, early technology was simply inadequate to implement an idea, but in other cases it turned out that there were other reasons at play that drove the application designers to choose a different path. It is important to understand how the applications in this book were chosen for inclusion.

Each application in this book was included because it illustrated some particular item or idea. Although the applications covered in this book were primarily developed and deployed in the United States, we are in no way implying that the bulk of the work in early virtual reality applications was done in the United States alone. Rather, due to the realities of logistics and travel, we were better able to offer an in-depth look at those applications that were chosen according to the criteria they laid out when this book was conceived. There were a number of heuristics that we used in order to choose which applications would be discussed in this volume. The heuristics were as follows:

- Heuristic 1: *It must be possible to discuss the application in public.* We are aware of many other virtual reality applications that illustrate the same points as many of the applications described in this book but, due to the confidentiality of the information, could not be published.

- Heuristic 2: *If at all possible, we strove to include applications that we were able to experience themselves, and/or at least to have direct personal discussions with the application creators.* This heuristic unfortunately led to most of the applications covered to be U.S.-centric.

- Heuristic 3: *The applications should illustrate a wide variety of technological implementations.* That is, our goal was to include some applications that used head-based displays, and some that used projection displays. Some applications were included because they utilized some novel device or technique. Some applications used haptics or sounds, or other sensory feedback in a unique way. This heuristic helped to ensure that the coverage was not limited to CAVE™ applications, or head-mounted display applications, or any single technology that was prevalent at the time.

- Heuristic 4: *To the extent possible, include applications that were developed in different development environments, such as academia, government, and private sector laboratories.* This heuristic was to ensure a heterogeneous coverage of developers. Academics often attend different conferences, read different journals, and so on, than do industry developers. We believed that it was important to report on the work from all of those groups

- Heuristic 5: *Include some applications that have ceased to exist, and some applications that have continued to be used, developed, commercialized, or otherwise exist today.* The important issue with this heuristic is the reason *why* some applications survive and some don't. In some cases an application has ceased to exist because it served its purpose, or a new solution to the problem it was addressing arose. In other cases, it is sometimes that the application was implemented in a way that caused the intended audience to not embrace the application. Likewise, some applications have survived because they genuinely aided in the solution of a difficult problem, there was commercial interest in the application, or the application developers saw the potential to fully realize the implementation.

The applications in this book have been organized into eight chapters. It is a difficult task to categorize the applications because any given application might be appropriate in more than one chapter. It is our hope that by presenting the highlights and problems with these applications that the reader can jump-start their own applications, get new ideas for techniques, and gain an overall appreciation for the breadth and depth of VR applications that came before.

> *If I have seen a little further it is by standing on the shoulders of giants.*
>
> **– Isaac Newton**

Throughout this book, we follow a standard template for describing each application.

Applications are divided into major applications and minor applications. For each major application, the following sections are included: Executive Summary, Introduction, Application Description, Representation of the Virtual World, Interaction with the Virtual World, Venue, VR System, Application Implementation, and Conclusion. Minor applications comprise a subset of these, including: Executive Summary, Application Description, VR System, and Conclusion.

CHAPTER 3

Business and Manufacturing

In the fast-paced world of business and manufacturing, competitive advantage can mean the difference between a successful endeavor and one that is surpassed by the competition. Being the first to introduce a product to the market may establish a company as a leader. A company's ability to harness the power of new technology can enable it to exploit its own competitive edge. Businesses also succeed by building and controlling market share. The novel medium of VR can often be exploited to generate interest in a company or product.

Early adoption and exploitation can give a competitive advantage. Three primary ways virtual reality has been used to increase competitiveness include product development, business education, and marketing. The underlying goal of exploiting VR in business and manufacturing has been, of course, to enhance profitability and/or productivity. Many have found that VR offers a means to improve productivity, increase safety, speed-up design cycles, raise product awareness, and other strategic advantages.

By using VR to increase productivity, an additional benefit can be gained through a variety of subtle marketing strategies. Companies using VR in new ways are enjoying considerable press coverage, which also enhances their public image.

The steps toward utilizing VR in business have been occurring since the advent of computer-based drafting and design systems. Companies that adopted such tools found they were able to make decisions and adapt to changing conditions quickly. Virtual reality is an extension to the evolution of the physical world into the digital realm. Often, physical models and prototypes will still be essential, but with VR it is possible to delay and minimize the creation of such models, thereby saving costs.

In its early inception, virtual reality was found mostly in research and development (R&D) departments. R&D departments are tasked with finding new technologies to help their company make more money. The pattern has been that after initial seed money is spent creating example VR applications, those researchers are required to seek out those within their company who are interested in using the applications. If there is not enough interest to justify further research on an application or technology, research typically ceases.

However, it may be renewed when other advances indicate an increase in its potential advantage.

3.1 AREAS OF APPLICATION

There are many ways in which VR has been applied in business. Some have been explored more than others. This chapter describes several applications of VR in the area of product development as well as examples of usage for training and marketing. Research has also begun on the use of VR for analyzing production flow, especially for factory floor machine layouts.

3.1.1 Product development

Perhaps the most widely explored usage of VR by the business world has been in product development. This includes the use of VR for *virtual prototyping,* which is the use of a computer to simulate a design of an object or system. While virtual prototyping does not require the use of VR, the two are often associated.[1] Examples of virtual prototyping that have successfully incorporated VR addressed in this chapter include efforts by Caterpillar Inc. and General Motors Corp. Another interesting example includes experimental studies performed by DaimlerChrysler on the perceptions of customers to possible car interior designs. VR has the potential to be used as a tool in which a product is designed. This is demonstrated in the collaborative work between Nalco Fuel Tech and Argonne National Laboratory, where optimal placement of fuel injectors within a boiler can be determined via an immersive, interactive tool (described in Section 3.4). Work has also been done by Lockheed/Martin to create a ship-designing tool that allows immersed participants to manipulate designs, with consequences such as pipe relocation performed automatically.

VR has also been tested as a means for improving productivity during the manufacturing process. In particular, The Boeing Company created an experimental augmented reality system that shows a human assembler of aircraft wire-bundles where to place each wire, a step at a time.

3.1.2 Business education

The use of VR as a training tool is spread across many fields. One notable example in the area of manufacturing is the training of assembly line procedures at Motorola University.

---

[1] An example of virtual prototyping that does not use VR is electronic circuit design, where a simulation of the circuit allows the results to be measured, and compared with expectations.

Motorola found that VR benefits the learning process in three ways: 1) the virtual assembly line is much cheaper to create and duplicate than a physical practice line; 2) the computer version is easier to transport to other training centers; plus 3), the workers being trained are more highly motivated to work with the virtual assembly line than previous training methodologies.

3.1.3   Marketing

VR is sometimes used as part of a marketing strategy to demonstrate that a particular company or product is high tech, forward looking, or just plain cool. In this case, getting people to remember and talk about the product is the goal. As a new, exciting, and often talked about technology, virtual reality has been used several times as part of advertising campaigns. Television advertisements include those by Honda, Starburst, and Bubble Yum.

Virtual Reality gives the opportunity to advertisers of providing advertising that people want to participate in. One way in which this has been done was through the development of a specific VR game that relates to the company or product. This game was then taken to several venues (stores, trade shows, etc.), where people literally stood in line to experience the advertisement. Since lines often attract attention to themselves, the effect often snowballs, bringing more people to see the message. In this chapter, we describe the usage of VR for marketing Cutty Sark scotch. The Fraunhofer Institute for Computer Graphics (IGD) has also done a project for a Swiss bank to help draw attention to a new bank card they were introducing.

The VR application (game) itself might be a good piece of advertising. However, because of the excitement, there are usually several people queued up to take their turn. This presents another opportunity to communicate with potential customers. While in line, people can be presented product information in more traditional ways as well as provide information back to the company by filling out marketing questionnaires. Most people do not object to providing this form of "payment" to try the experience. Examples of this include Virtuality for the Ford Galaxy (Chapter 9) and Matsushita for Kitchen and House products.

[Du Pont, P. (1995). "VR for thermal visualization: Analyzing air and temperature flow," VR world, May/June, 58–59.

hotwired.lycos.com/collections/virtual_communities/2.07_kitchen.html1.html]

Often, the use of VR in other areas of business and manufacturing has the secondary result of bringing attention to the company. This is generally intentional, and part of the company's marketing effort. It is likely that as VR becomes a less novel technology, this particular use of VR as marketing tool will wane.

3.2   OTHER AND FUTURE USAGE OF VR IN BUSINESS AND MANUFACTURING

As expertise in implementing VR applications grows, and the technology becomes more economical, it will be applied to many other areas and types of business.

Some research that is already underway includes the usage of VR as a tool for studying production flow, especially for factory floor machine layouts. Research has also been done on maintenance analysis of product designs, taking advantage of the LBE game *BattleTech* and using a simplified version of the experience as part of a team-building effort.

Another area in which VR has been used extensively includes collaborative work environments, allowing workers to more easily work with others who might be at a remote site. An example of this is the *Virtual Director* application described in Chapter 9.

Other potential areas for applying VR to business and manufacturing include the visualization of business information and farming data. Business visualization is currently a growing area of research among visualization experts, and has expanded into the medium of VR. Similar techniques will also be useful for people who need to access large archives of business data. A spatial organization of information can be helpful in being able to sort through such data. VR can provide a means of allowing a person to spatially experience a database. Spatial data in VR can be achieved by extending typical GIS representations into 3D, and also by developing completely new representations. Farming has become increasingly high tech. Many farms now use the global positioning systems (GPS), combined with soil analysis techniques, to apply specific fertilizers/pesticides for certain locations in the field. This and other information can be transferred to a VR visualization tool for analysis and/or telepresence applications for farmers.

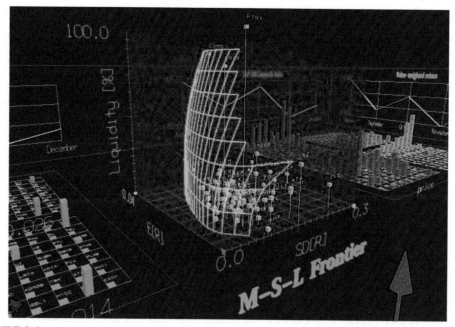

FIGURE 3-1

Virtual reality has allowed new visualizations of business information. These images from a portfolio analysis tool (above) and an oil pipeline monitor (the next page) show examples of such representations.

Photos courtesy of Visual Decisions, Inc.

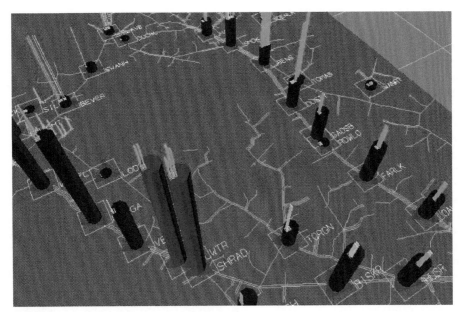

FIGURE 3-1
(Continued)

CASE STUDY 3.1: USING AUGMENTED REALITY FOR ADVERTISING

The Wellington Zoo

Executive Summary

Traditional print advertising suffers from several deficiencies that are difficult to overcome. Among them are that imagery is only visible as flat, two-dimensional pictures, and that they are required to be static. Until now. The Human Interface Technology Laboratory New Zealand (HIT Lab NZ) at the University of Canterbury in Christchurch, New Zealand, has successfully demonstrated that augmented reality techniques can allow advertisers to purchase a relatively small, two-dimensional, black-and-white advertisement in a newspaper, or magazine, and yet convey colorful, dynamic, three-dimensional virtual images. The way it works is that a customer sends a text message to obtain a small computer program that runs on their cellular telephone. The advertiser places a specially designed, black-and-white marker on the print ad. When the customer points the camera of their cellular telephone at the marker,

they can see and interact with the full-color, three-dimensional virtual world overlaid on the real print advertisement.

FIGURE 3-2

Potential zoo visitors are able to see a 3D rendering of a cheetah by pointing their cellular telephone at a newspaper ad. By moving the telephone around, they can see the animal from different perspectives.

The Wellington Zoo, in Wellington, New Zealand, is the first organization to exploit the advertising potential of the augmented reality (AR) medium. They wanted to create a dynamic print advertisement for their "Close Encounters" exhibit. Working with the Saatchi & Saatchi NZ advertising agency and the HyperFactory[2] mobile marketing provider, and powered by the AR technology developed at the HIT Lab NZ, they placed a print advertisement in one of New Zealand's largest newspapers, with a circulation of 750,000 people. Readers downloaded the software to their cellular telephone by text message, and then were able to interact with three-dimensional virtual views of zoo animals by pointing their telephone at the marker in the advertisement. They could see the virtual animals from all angles by moving their telephones around the image. The advertising was effective, with the zoo realizing a 32% growth in visitors and the campaign winning numerous international advertising awards.

Application Description
Representation of the Virtual World
One of the goals of this application was to allow potential zoo viewers to see some of the animals from the "Close Encounters" exhibit up close and from all perspectives. As part of this advertising campaign, the developers created

FIGURE 3-3
This person is reading a newspaper and pointing a cellular telephone camera at a marker in the paper. The cheetah is visible from different perspectives by moving the telephone in relation to the newspaper.

[2]http://www.thehyperfactory.com/

three 3D computer graphic modeled animals: a cheetah, a giraffe, and a bear.

The animals were modeled with an eye toward realism. That is, the cheetah model looked like a cheetah. Each animal was set on a grassy expanse to show it more or less in an appropriate environment.

VR DISCOVERY

Augmented reality advertising works. The zoo experienced a 32% increase in visitors. The techniques shown by this application can also be used on other print media, including books, posters, or even the side of a building.

DESIGN CONSTRAINT

Because the virtual world would be displayed on the tiny screen of a mobile phone, the developers primarily exhibited one animal at a time. The background was straightforward and showed the animals in the open, to allow a good view of them, and to avoid cluttering the display with background objects.

The application was only able to run on certain models of Nokia mobile phones (the N-series Nokia smart phones). So when the user sent a text message to the number shown in the print advertisement, back-end server software would first check to see if they had the one of the supported phones. If so, they were sent a 200 kB application that enabled them to view the AR animal models. If their phone was not supported, then they were sent a static image showing them what the application would have looked like running on their phone if they had a suitable phone model.

Although this application did not make use of audio to keep the download file size small, there is no technical reason why the telephone could not be used to play animal sounds, or an audio advertising message. In the normal mode of operation, the end user typically holds their phone

FIGURE 3-4

The Wellington Zoo print advertisement as it appeared in the paper. The black square is used by the AR application to track the camera phone position and overlay a virtual zoo animal on the paper page.

in front of them as they pan around the virtual world. Hence, to effectively utilize audio, the phone would need to be placed in speakerphone mode.

Interaction with the Virtual World

The typical way an end user would interact with this application is to point the camera of their phone toward the real printed marker (known as a fiducial marker) and view the virtual image on the telephone display. On the telephone display the virtual graphics are combined with live video from the real world, so the 3D model appears overlaid on the real print ad.

In order to see the virtual world from a different perspective, the participant has two primary options. The most obvious way to navigate about the virtual world is to physically move the cellular telephone around the marker. Thus, you can pan around the space just by moving the telephone (keeping the camera pointed at the marker). The other primary way to navigate about the space is to keep the phone in one position and move the newspaper, or other print media, around. This method might be more convenient if one were, say, sitting at a table reading the newspaper. One could point their phone at the marker on the paper, and then maneuver the paper around on the table to see the virtual world from different perspectives.

In this simple AR application the user did not need to use the keypad to interact with the virtual animal, and only one animal was shown. During the campaign three different print ads were presented in the newspaper and so users needed to download three applications to see all of the different animals. This particular application is not a collaborative experience, but mobile AR technology is conducive to collaborative applications.

Application Implementation

This application was created using the ARToolKit computer vision tracking library. ARToolKit[3] is an open-source library for building augmented reality applications that was initially created at the Human Interface Technology Laboratory at the University of Washington in the United States. Anders Henrysson[4] ported this software to the Symbian operating system for mobile phones, and the HIT Lab NZ used this port to create the mobile AR advertising

---

[3]http://artoolkit.sourceforge.net/.

[4]Henrysson, A., and Ollila, M. *UMAR—Ubiquitous Mobile Augmented Reality* In Proc. Third International Conference on Mobile and Ubiquitous Multimedia (MUM2004) pp 41–45. College Park, Maryland. October 27–29, 2004.

FIGURE 3-5

HIT Lab NZ director Mark Billinghurst uses a handheld display to view a "Magic Book" in collaboration with a colleague. Each person sees the virtual world (and the real world) from his or her own perspective.

FIGURE 3-6

Augmented reality can be experienced stereoscopically by using specialized see-through displays with an attached camera. This provides the most "authentic" AR experience.

application. The toolkit provides services such as the computer vision required for the optically based tracking, thus providing a real-time 6 Degree of Freedom marker tracking system. The toolkit enables the overlay of the 3D virtual objects on the fiducial markers. The 3D virtual objects were created by using the Maya modeling software and the initial complex models simplified down to a few hundred polygons in size. The final application delivered to the mobile phone used the OpenGL ES mobile graphics library to render the 3D virtual models.

The VR System

The Wellington Zoo advertising application was developed primarily for use on mobile telephones. However, augmented reality technology can be supported on other hardware platforms. The most basic hardware requirements for augmented reality are a camera, a computer, and a display. Thus, there are a number of other physical scenarios in which augmented reality can be done. One common example is the use of a laptop computer with a web camera. In this case the end user can point their web camera at a fiducial marker and see the 3D virtual world appearing on their screen. At the higher end of cost and complexity are specialized head-mounted or handheld displays that have

cameras integrated into them. By using a head-mounted display, a user can see the virtual world from exactly their correct perspective, and also see the images rendered stereoscopically.

Conclusion

The Wellington Zoo application has been a smashing success on many fronts. Although mobile phone-based augmented reality had previously been demonstrated on mobile phones, this was the first time the technology had been used in a real-world advertising campaign. The advertising campaign led to a 32% increase in visitors to the zoo's "Close Encounters" exhibit. The advertising has earned numerous awards and honors. More importantly, this application clearly indicates that augmented reality has turned the corner from being a laboratory novelty and has been used successfully in the commercial world. The HIT Lab NZ's accomplishment with AR technology has been recognized, and they have since been engaged to develop other advertisements and games on cellular telephones that exploit augmented reality.

FIGURE 3-7
This is an example of an augmented reality fiducial marker. The ARToolKit library provides tools to create, and to read such markers. Notice the black frame, and the nonsymmetry of the image.

FIGURE 3-9
The Institute for Computing in Humanities, Arts, and Social Science at the University of Illinois at Urbana-Champaign is exploring the use of "Magic Books" in education. Here is an artist's conception of a student reading a book about the Battle of Gettysburg. In the future, augmented reality will not require intrusive hardware.
Photo montage by Dave Bock

FIGURE 3-8
HIT Lab NZ's director, Dr. Mark Billinghurst, reads a "Magic Book" in which he not only sees the text and images of the book but also sees a three-dimensional model of a sailboat. If he wishes to see the other side of the ship, he can turn the book around. The ship can also be animated to see the sails flapping in the breeze.

Related Applications and Follow-on Work
The Wellington Zoo advertising application follows on a long history of augmented reality applications developed by HIT Lab NZ, and their sister center, the HITLab at the University of Washington in the United States.

Perhaps the most widely recognized VR applications prior to this advertising campaign were the "Magic Books" that use augmented reality to allow readers to see 3D, animated augmentations of traditional physical books, in place, and registered spatially with the physical book.

I-CHASS, the Institute for Computing in Humanities, Arts, and Social Science at the University of Illinois at Urbana-Champaign, is exploring the use of augmented reality (also using the ARToolKit) to enhance books with animated, three-dimensional scenes for educational purposes.

Other laboratories, such as the augmented environments laboratory at the Georgia Institute of Technology, the Graz University of Technology, and others, continue to develop core augmented reality technologies and applications. The ICT Center at the Commonwealth Scientific and Industrial Research Organisation (CSIRO) in Australia has integrated Augmented Reality with haptic feedback devices.

Another example of AR in advertising was at the 2008 Auto Show in Los Angeles, California. Nissan used a brochure that was enhanced with augmented reality that could be viewed with a web camera. Indeed, a search of the world-wide web shows that AR advertising is catching on very quickly. An especially interesting example is the Smart Grid Augmented Reality Web-based system by General Electric.

FIGURE 3-10

Sony's Eye of Judgment game for the PlayStation 3 uses a computer monitor, a camera, and trading cards with AR markers on them to provide a novel and exciting game experience.

On a different but related note, augmented reality has already been commercially used in the gaming market. Sony released its *Eye of Judgment* game for the PlayStation 3 in October of 2007. The game provides a number of "trading cards" that contain a graphical image, plus an AR marker. Players place their cards on the table, and a camera on a stand next to the playing area identifies the markers and the game responds appropriately. Since its release, *Eye of Judgment* has sold more than 250,000 copies, making it the most widely distributed commercial AR application.

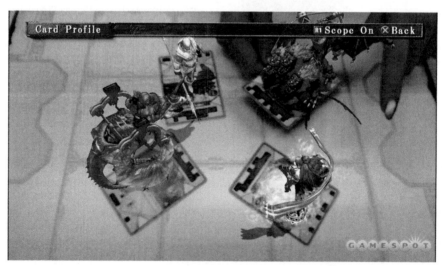

FIGURE 3-11

Sony's Eye of Judgment game allows players to move their cards near their opponents' cards to engage in battle.

CASE STUDY 3.2: CATERPILLAR VIRTUAL PROTOTYPING SYSTEM

Executive Summary

The Caterpillar Virtual *Prototyping System* (*VPS*) was created to allow design engineers to test new machine designs prior to building physical models. The preliminary usage of the system was for assessing operator visibility and allowing engineers to make corrective modifications very early in the design process. Later, the system was expanded to include the capability to evaluate a variety of different aspects including machine performance. Development of the system focused on enabling engineers located at geographically distant sites to collaborate on projects by sharing the same virtual world.

The initial VPS used head-mounted display technology to present the view of the virtual landscape. That technology was replaced by projection-based displays such as *CAVE*™, *ImmersaDesk*™, and Responsive *WorkBench*™. A prominent part of the system includes a physical platform with

an actual machine seat, steering wheel, pedals, and other control elements that are used to control the prototype systems in a near-normal operational setting. A dynamic model simulates the operation of the virtual machine. Additionally, a very simplified program gives the illusion of soil dynamics. The soil model was integrated to create typical scenarios for operating simulated earth-moving machines. The *VPS* has been involved in actual product design, including the Caterpillar® 914G Wheel Loader.

Introduction

Caterpillar, Inc. has been designing and manufacturing earth-moving machinery since the 1920s. Although machines have changed immensely over this period, one thing has remained constant. To be competitive one must constantly strive to stay one step ahead of the competition. Studying what the customer needs and providing it sooner helps to accomplish this goal.

FIGURE 3-12
Caterpillar, Inc. was an early adopter of the use of virtual reality systems for virtual prototyping. Shown here is Kem Ahlers navigating through a representation of the Caterpillar proving grounds.

To remain competitive requires Caterpillar to be leaders in the use and development of new technology as an aid in the design and manufacturing process. Caterpillar has been using computer simulation and modeling in the development of their vehicles since the 1960s. More recently, they began using scientific visualization and computer graphics to aid them in the design process.

Although batch simulation and visualization have proven useful, they do not support the level of interactivity required to include the "human in the loop" in the simulation—that is, to enable a human operator to "drive" the machine in real time with the simulation taking into account the human's actions. Designs that rate poorly based on static tests and simulations may actually be reasonable. For example, in a static test, an operator's view might be impeded by some obstruction. By integrating the operator's head position into the simulation, the operator may be able to adjust their seat and simply look around the obstruction.

The *Caterpillar VPS* went through several phases. Throughout the project's development, a physical machine cab where an operator sits and uses actual tractor controls was the primary means for interacting with a computer simulation of the machine. In the first phase, head-mounted display and single-screen projection systems were used as the display mechanism to evaluate the visibility of a virtual backhoe loader. In subsequent phases of the application, a *CAVE* projection-VR system has been used as the primary display device, and has been used to examine the design of many other machines, including a variety of front-end wheel loaders.

The *Caterpillar VPS* project encapsulates three overall goals:

- Shorten the time and cost in new product introduction
- Consider an order of magnitude more design alternatives
- Improve "early hour" discovery of problems

Achieving these goals has helped Caterpillar to be competitive in the global marketplace. Strengthening competitiveness is achieved by using simulation as a tool to understand how a product will behave for the customer. By developing virtual prototypes of a product, Caterpillar has uncovered such knowledge early in the design process, allowing changes to be made while changes are still easy and inexpensive to make. As a product's design moves from concept phase to design phase, changes to the design increase in cost by tenfold over what they would have cost in the concept phase. When proceeding from design to production, the cost of a change increases by an order of magnitude. Once the product is in the customer's hands, the cost of fixing a problem is even greater. Thus, it is extremely advantageous to find any problems as early as possible in the process to remedy them inexpensively.

In addition to finding "fatal" errors in a design that must be corrected, virtual prototyping enables designers to make more iterations. Each iteration can improve the product in many small ways, ultimately resulting in a better product at a lower cost. Also, it is easier to compare different design alternatives. Virtual prototyping enables up to 10 times as many design alternatives to be tried than by conventional methods.

Prior to using the VR virtual prototyping system, designs were modeled using physical prototypes. These prototypes were very expensive and took considerable time to build. Physical prototypes are still the norm for most machine development. The VPS has allowed Caterpillar to create fewer physical prototypes.

Caterpillar has used computer simulation of products for many years, as well as desktop computer-aided design (CAD). In the early 1990s, Caterpillar Inc. enlisted the aid of the NCSA Visualization Group to collaborate with them to explore the possibilities of using computer graphics and animation to aid them in prototyping vehicles. The earliest efforts in this joint research explored what could be learned about operator visibility problems in a particular machine. The goal was to learn of problems *before* building physical model of the vehicle. NCSA animator Mark Bajuk developed frame-animation techniques to aid in assessing operator visibility in new tractor designs that existed only within their computer CAD and simulation models. Caterpillar already had the CAD databases for their designs, as well as real-time simulations of the vehicle dynamics. The next step was to incorporate real-time computer graphics, user tracking, and operator interaction.

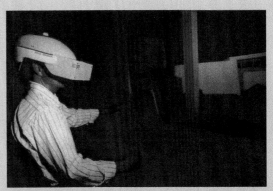

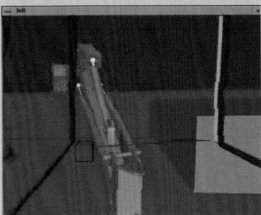

FIGURE 3-13

The image on top is an example of an early visualization to assess operator visibility. This image is a frame from an animated movie created by NCSA. The image on the bottom shows the view from an early example of the VPS with the operator controlling the system interaction.

Application Description

The virtual prototyping system is meant to serve many purposes. Some of the uses Caterpillar envisions for the use of the virtual reality system include:

- Ergonomic studies
- Machine performance in the work cycle
- Serviceability audits
- Manufacturing and assembly
- Marketing
- Training

FIGURE 3-14

The original Caterpillar VPS made use of a head-mounted display (above). The image below shows a view of the original, simple virtual world.

Since the original project was to assess operator ergonomics through the complete work-cycle of a virtual backhoe, a physical platform that emulated the controls of an actual backhoe was built to allow the operator to control the virtual backhoe. To view the world, the operator was placed in a head-mounted display.

In this system, the user was able to see (from the first-person point of view using the HMD) and control the arm and bucket of a backhoe loader. The tractor was stationary (as in real life). There were simple cubes in the virtual scene that a skilled operator was able to lift with and drop from the bucket. The operator in the head-mounted display was unable to see their own hands, so an assistant was required to help them find the control levers when first "suiting up." In this installation visibility analysis with an operator free to move their head was possible. They were also able to get out of the cab, and walk around the tractor and see the tractor from the appropriate points of view, although to help rendering performance only the most important parts of the tractor were modeled.

Building on the success of the original backhoe system, the *Caterpillar VPS* was extended to simulate a wheel loader, and a control platform was built to match. The front end loader was much more complex, adding driving controls such as steering wheel, gear shift lever, accelerator, clutch, and brake to the levers required for controlling the bucket and lift arms. These functions not only were added to the physical control mechanism (the platform) but also to the world dynamics simulation. The visual scene of the virtual world was also raised in complexity by changing the

small generic yard previously used for practice into a more complex area with a variety of visual elements including buildings, piles of rocks, and other entities. The loader and a dump truck were also rendered more realistically.

Representation of the Virtual World

The virtual world in the later editions of *Caterpillar VPS* consisted of models and simulations of a variety of real locations where new tractors are tested under a variety of conditions: a mining pit, a factory, a sanitary landfill, and a highway construction site.

Virtual world physics are calculated by a very simplified computational model of the dynamics and kinematics of the machine being prototyped—including the powertrain, hydraulics, wheels and tires, steering system, and suspension. While models for engines are available, the models used in *VPS* are simple mapping functions from gear selection, throttle and breaking to a speed. There is also a very

FIGURE 3-15

As part of the Caterpillar VPS, a simple model of the Caterpillar proving grounds in Peoria, Illinois, was used to enhance the operator's experience.

Image courtesy of Caterpillar, Inc.

simplified soil model that portrays frictional soils such as gravel, sand, or coal. Complex, highly realistic soil models are difficult to compute in real time, so a simple, volume conserving model was implemented. The soil model allows the machine operator to test scooping and digging operations, on the delivery of soil to a truck, bin, or pile.

The *Caterpillar VPS* is an interesting application in that one of the goals is highly realistic representation. In this sense it is similar to a traditional flight simulator, with the notable difference that since it is a design tool, it is essential to be able to make changes to parts of the virtual world very readily. Caterpillar engineers are able to put a new design in the *CAVE*, rapidly utilizing the tools they have built for converting CAD data into a format suitable for the *VPS*. Since the goal is a realistic simulation, many decisions such as how the user will navigate in the system are very simple. The user should navigate in the same way they do in the real world; for example, operation involved pressing the gas pedal and rotating the steering wheel.

For a prototyping system it is also important for realism to extend to accurately representing the scale of the object as life size. This is important for doing studies that involve how the user will interact with the product. Accurately registering the size of the virtual object to the size of the object in the real world also allows testing of maintenance procedures (such as checking to see if a mechanic can reach an object or fit a tool into position to make an adjustment). By enabling designers to manipulate a ruler in the virtual space they can take measurements, but if the world is not to scale, then they may not trust those measurements.

Internally, the objects in this application are represented in a polygonal manner. These objects initially come from CAD engineering files. However, because these CAD files are very detailed and complex, the models must be simplified before being imported into the *VPS* to reduce the number of polygons required by each object.

The system designers believe that realism in interaction is of higher importance than attempting to achieve "photorealism" in images. This is in contrast with the approach taken by the General Motors VR design team, who consider photorealism to be more important than real-time performance for their application (see next section). Each group made the decision based on the goals for their application. In the case of GM, the goal is to allow users to see what the product would look like visually, whereas Caterpillar is more interested in those aspects that require the "human in the loop," such as how the machine performs and how well the operator can see from any position, or state of the machine.

The original computer graphics visibility animations were done outside of real time, in a batch mode. This yielded very high-quality imagery. For the VR system, real-time performance was required. Thus, the graphics were computed at much lower resolution, and with much lower scene detail.

The operator is able to see "out the window" views in any direction covered by the field-of-regard of the display device. The operator can also see a realistic representation of the interior of the cab, including a control panel overlaid with instrument status indicators. Some parts of the control panel are fixed texture maps, others are rendered in each frame to reflect the state of the simulation.

In the *Caterpillar VPS*, the machine is represented as visually accurate as possible within the constraint of real-time rendering. Representations of additional information such as stresses or other invisible aspects of the machine were not added to the visual rendering of the virtual world. The goals were more along the lines of seeing whether or not the bucket was visible throughout a work cycle, and with the operator's head in various locations.

The designers feel that audio cues help to augment the sense of manipulating the machinery. This sense of presence is important to help operators be less conscious of the artificial environment, and to behave more naturally as they perform the task. If the system seems "odd," operators may focus on that aspect of the virtual world instead of the task under study.

As with the visual representation, realism with the audio representation is the main goal. Both the old and new versions of *VPS* have made extensive use of sampled waveforms of recordings made from actual operating machines under real work conditions. Realistic examples of sample sounds include the engine, back-up indicator alarm, and pieces of the machine banging and clanking as they go through the paces of a typical work cycle.

FIGURE 3-16

Left: An operator seated on the platform can see appropriate "out the window" views from the virtual machine. Right: Bob Fenwick raises the bucket of a simulated loader in the CAVE. The instrument panel is visible and emulates its real-world counterpart.

FIGURE 3-17

The Caterpillar VPS attempts to render the environment as realistically as possible while maintaining a frame rate suitable for real-time interaction.

The physical platform the operator sits on and manipulates to control the machine is a prominent and key component of the *Caterpillar VPS*. The platform is equipped with an actual tractor seat, steering wheel, gas and brake pedals, gear shifter, and control levers. Each of these components provides haptic feedback to the operator that closely resembles that of an actual machine. The main difference is that rather than controlling hydraulics, these mechanisms provide electrical signals to provide feedback to the computational simulation.[5] None of the controllers provide force feedback other than that innately provided by the spring loading of the control.

_____

[5] In fact, "fly-by-wire" controls are pervasive in present-day systems. Control levers produce electrical signals that are interpreted and converted to inputs to the hydraulic system.

The platform has evolved throughout the project. Though it began simply, it has increased in complexity over three or four generations to accommodate the additional capabilities supported by the system, and required for more sophisticated prototyping. The most recent platform allows the system maintainers to swap different control systems with fairly short lead time.

Caterpillar has also done experiments with motion platforms, including a Frasca flight simulator, and a full-motion, limited visual, decommissioned B52 flight simulator at the University of Iowa Driving Simulator (part of the Center for Computer-Aided Design). They have done studies to determine the need for motion cues before integrating them with the *VPS*. In preliminary tests, they found that the ability to display "jerk" to the machine operator greatly enhances their ability to judge how the machine interacts with the simulated environment.

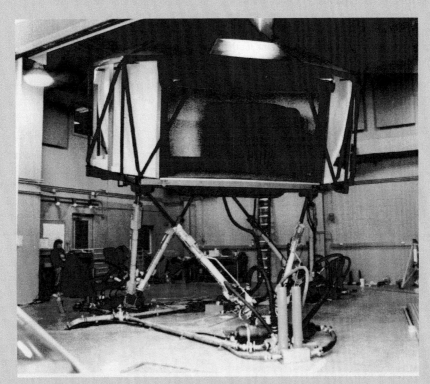

FIGURE 3-18
Caterpillar has experimented with a full motion flight simulator at the University of Iowa.

In the physical machines, the engine and hydraulic system produce many smells. These smells can actually be useful as a means of diagnosing trouble brewing with the machinery. However, no research has been done by the Caterpillar application designers along the lines of integrating such sensory display into the system.

Interaction with the Virtual World

The genre of this application is virtual prototyping. Specifically, virtual prototyping using a VR display system—not all prototyping done on computers in a virtual world requires the use of a VR display (an electronic circuit simulator, for example). The form is a participant vehicle pilot-through with control inputs from a platform mimicking the actual controls.

The narrative of this application is using the virtual machine in a typical work cycle. While the machine is put through its paces, machine-operator performance can be analyzed. Some sample questions the developers are interested in assessing are: How many passes does it take for operator to load a dump truck? How effective is the machine for the task at hand?

The travel interface for the *Caterpillar VPS* is simple. Control is a basic pilot-through interface that allows the operator to drive the machine as they would drive the real-world counterpart. However, it is not always appropriate for the user to interact in this way. There are many situations in which a user will need to be able to move around independent of the machine, perhaps while redesigning a particular part of the machine, or during collaborative sessions, while they watch other participants drive the equipment. For these reasons, it is also possible to move to a view outside of and untethered from the cab of the machine.

When traveling through the virtual world untethered from the machine cab, the *CAVE* wand prop is used. A pressure joystick mounted on the *CAVE* wand provides the user with two degrees of input. Pushing left or right rotates the world about them, and pushing forward or backward (toward themselves) translates them through the world in the direction they point the wand.

The system also has a menu system to control various options within the *VPS*. For example, operators can activate or deactivate sound rendering, or they may choose to jump to another environment, such as a mining pit or highway road construction site.

The menu takes the form of an object that floats within the virtual world. The user can summon the menu by pressing a button on the wand. While viewing the menu, a marker indicates the currently selected item. This marker can be moved to the next item by making a quick downward gesture with the wand. To activate a submenu, a quick rightward gesture is performed. Once the marker is on the desired selection, another button on the wand is pressed, after which, the menu system is deactivated and the representation disappears. If no selection is made, then the menu representation remains in place in the virtual world.

Any of the menu options can also be invoked by using a keyboard equivalent shortcut. In general, the keyboard is outside of the *CAVE* environment, so keyboard commands are usually invoked by an assistant who is helping to run the *VPS*.

There are no computer-controlled agents in the *Virtual Prototyping System*. However, there are situations where such an agent would be useful. In particular, situations where a work cycle involves operations that must be performed in conjunction with operators controlling other equipment. For example, a dump truck agent may drive the truck away when it is full, with another truck driving into place.

A more current focus in the development of the *Caterpillar VPS* is support of distance collaborative capabilities. Caterpillar has design facilities located throughout the world, and requiring designers to congregate at a single location can be expensive in time and money. At the same time, not bringing designers together can allow less than ideal designs to propagate through the design process. By providing a shared virtual world in which geographically distant collaborators can see, speak, and work with one another while remaining at their home facility, *Caterpillar VPS* can provide a means of reducing the costs of travel, while enabling joint projects to gain the advantage of collaborative development.

Collaboration is seen as such an important aspect of working on a design project that the effort to incorporate multi-site collaboration capability within the virtual environment is considered a project unto itself—the *Distributed Virtual Reality* (*DVR*) project.

FIGURE 3-19

A menuing system allows the operator to change various aspects of the virtual world. The menu is summoned by pressing a button on the CAVE wand.

As human communication is both a verbal and visual operation, each site sharing the "conversation" is equipped with a video camera and microphone. The audio of each site is mixed with the overall audio of the virtual environment, and the video images are integrated into the avatar that represents the position of each site within the space. For sites without a video input, the avatar consists of a box-like shape colored based on the site it represents plus a matching-colored pointer that shows the position of their wand. When video is available, the avatar's front side has the live images texture mapped onto it.

A multicasting approach was chosen for information sharing between sites involved in a collaborative gathering. Multicasting was chosen over a client/server model because of the reduced overhead of not needing to maintain a server application that duplicates most of the information already stored in the individual clients, and because

information between sites would all need to pass through a single server, which would result in increased latency. Other benefits of multicasting are that any site can begin interacting in the virtual environment first, and any other sites can join and leave the collaborative session at will.

The use of multicasting does raise some problematic issues that must be addressed, however. A major problem is that multicasting is not a fully supported feature over many networks. To enable a multicasting route between multiple sites requires special requests be made to the network administrators of all the intervening network "hops" to activate multicasting in their network routers. The other concern with multicasting is that it uses a data transfer protocol designed to keep network latency down by discarding old packets. Thus, when an application is too busy to read all the data, it will miss some information. In many cases, this is exactly what is desired. For example, only the

FIGURE 3-20

In the Caterpillar DVR project, participants at various geographically separated sites are able to share the virtual world in real time. Caterpillar engineer Bob Fenwick takes his turn in a CAVE that is a shared resource of the NCSA VR research facility. Avatars consisting of a box displaying a video of each person appear in the location and orientation the person is in the virtual world.

most recent information about the position of other participants is important. However, it is more difficult to handle situations where information regarding other collaborators joining or exiting the session is lost.

The data for the user and pointer locations, video images, and audio are transmitted from each site to the others over a multicast-enabled route over the Internet. The application also passes simulation information between sites. This allows the remote participant to see what actions the other participant has taken. The audio and video signals are captured using microphones and cameras connected to a computer, transmitted using standard network collaboration tools, and displayed by mixing the received audio with the simulator-generated audio, and integrating the video signal into the scene by converting it into a texture map that is rendered onto the avatar.

The goal of the world simulation is to reflect realistic performance of the machine and objects with which it interacts, in a real-time environment. The *VPS* uses a simplified transfer function from control inputs to speed, a simplified vehicle dynamics model, a simplified soil model, and a simple method for determining elevation for terrain following. Although Caterpillar has proprietary software that can simulate these systems very accurately in non-real-time simulations, they had to simplify the simulations to allow the required real-time performance in the *VPS*. Caterpillar used a proprietary dynamics simulator to simulate the various vehicle forces, including steering, hydraulic implement control, braking, and so on.

Venue

Design and testing of the *Caterpillar VPS* was performed in the research labs of the National Center for Supercomputing

Applications (NCSA) at the University of Illinois at Urbana-Champaign. Caterpillar later built a *CAVE* at their design facilities. Design engineers traveled to the VR facilities at NCSA in Urbana to spend 1 to 2 hours per session in the *VPS*. The engineers worked at their own pace subject to the availability of the *VPS*. The NCSA facilities are shared among several other researchers working with virtual reality, so the design team and users were required to schedule time to run the *VPS* in the NCSA *CAVE*. This scheduling constraint was lifted with the development of the on-site *CAVE* at Caterpillar.

VR System

The early implementation of the *Caterpillar VPS* used a Virtual Research Flight Helmet 2 HMD (aka "VR2") and Polhemus Fastrak tracking system available in the NCSA VR facilities. A custom-built platform that emulated a backhoe machine was integrated into the NCSA environment. A large single-screen display was also available in the VR lab, and the developers also made use of it in the early application development and testing.

The most severe limitation of the original system was the low resolution of the HMD. It was evident early on that the resolution of the VR2 was insufficient for Caterpillar's needs. During the course of early development, a *CAVE* system was installed at NCSA in collaboration with the University of Illinois at Chicago Electronic Visualization Lab. The NCSA *CAVE* was the second *CAVE* in existence, and Caterpillar quickly put the new display to the test.

The machine platform could be easily wheeled into the *CAVE*. The operator sat on the platform in the *CAVE*, and wore tracked Crystal Eyes shutter glasses. Since the original configuration of the NCSA *CAVE* included only a front wall, left wall, and floor, there was not an "appropriate" view for the operator's right window. The NCSA *CAVE* could be configured to use the front and both side walls instead of the floor, but most of the other users of the NCSA cave found the two walls plus floor configuration more useful, so this was seldom done. In late 1995, with the upgrade to a new Silicon Graphics rendering engine (Onyx with dual Infinite Reality engines), the NCSA *CAVE* could more easily render to four separate walls, allowing for the addition of the right screen.

The latter system ran on a 12-processor SGI Onyx with two Infinite Reality Engines. The original NCSA VR lab was equipped with Silicon Graphics' first multipipe rendering system, the dual-display SkyWriter™. The tracking system for the *CAVE* is a Flock of Birds electromagnetic system from Ascension Inc. The platform was originally connected to the VR system via an IBM PC equipped with an analog-to-digital input board connected to the Silicon Graphics via a serial connection. Later, an analog-to-digital board was directly installed into one of the lab's SGI Onyx's using a standard VME bus device.

In the original *VPS*, a Symbolic Sound Kyma system was used to play triggered audio samples. The current version uses the NCSA VSS audio system to play triggered audio samples directly from a Silicon Graphics workstation. Prior to sound hardware becoming available on the powerful Onyx series of machines, an SGI Indy workstation served as the audio serving device.

Application Implementation

The *Caterpillar VPS* and *DVR* projects are ongoing research-and-development efforts. The projects began as a collaboration between Caterpillar and the NCSA Visualization group in 1990. The *VPS* was developed by Caterpillar, NCSA, and the Electronic Visualization Lab at the University of Illinois at Chicago. Work on *DVR* formally began in September of 1995, with functional experiments running in July and August of 1997.

The project represents many "mythical person-years" of development. Project personnel have included project leads Rich Ingram, then Kem Ahlers, and Bob Fenwick, and project developers Dee Chapman (NCSA), Mike Novak (NCSA), Valerie Lehner (NCSA), Brian Keenan (NCSA), Lance Arsenault (NCSA), Volodymyr Kindratenko (NCSA), Erik Zentmyer (NCSA), Joe Lohmar (NCSA), Mike McNeill (NCSA), and Milana Huang (EVL).

In the first version of the system, very simple scenes were rendered using a research graphics toolkit from the University of Iowa. The only parts of the virtual world rendered were the cab frame and digging arm of the backhoe loader. The interior of the cab was not visible, including the control levers.

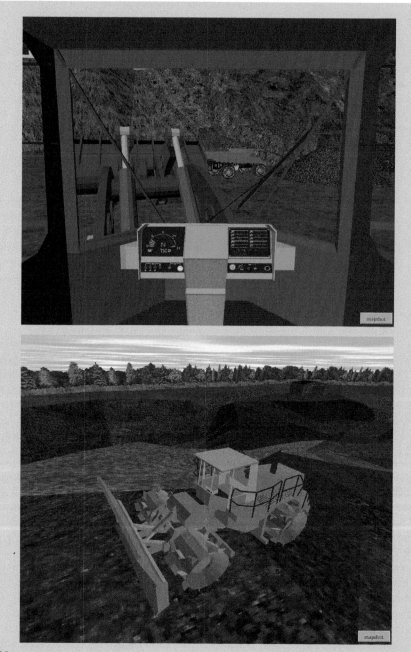

FIGURE 3-21

In order to provide a more useful experience, Caterpillar modeled several testing locations. The image above depicts mining pit, and the image below depicts a strip mine.

The Front End Loader was developed using the University of Iowa toolkit, but later, the project developers decided to move to a more robust toolkit with built-in capabilities for virtual reality. They chose Sense8's *World Tool Kit* (*WTK*). The graphics are computed with a combination of *WTK* and portions of the *CAVE* Library. Once the switch was made to the *CAVE* environment, the HMD specific work was abandoned—although the *WTK* and *CAVE* libraries both allow for the possibility of rendering to HMDs.

Conclusion

In addition to the direct benefits to Caterpillar from the use of the *VPS*, they also enjoyed a great deal of publicity about the project. The public is very interested in the use of high technology in development of products they know and understand. The Caterpillar project has aided in allowing the public to get an early glimpse of how virtual reality can be put to very practical uses. In 1993 Caterpillar Inc. was awarded NCSA's Grand Challenge Award for their work on the *Virtual Prototyping System*.

The fact that actual design engineers used the system is an encouraging indicator of the utility of the *VPS*. The Caterpillar® 914G Wheel Loader is one example of a released product which used the *VPS* in its design. One of the benefits attributed to the *VPS* is enhanced rear-view operator visibility. This influenced a major design change in the product line. Engineers used the *VPS* in the development of other products and to make major design changes to existing products that had not been released yet.

It is not clear to what degree user's become "immersed" in the virtual environment presented by the *VPS*. However, designers frequently made trips to the NCSA *CAVE* specifically to try new design or control interface ideas because of the realism that they simply could not achieve with a desktop computer interface. On the other hand, in instances where the test operator needs to have a good feel for how the unit drives over rough terrain, a motion-base display is almost essential to provide an appropriately immersive experience.

Over the course of the years during which the *Caterpillar VPS* has evolved, the developers have learned many lessons about implementing a large, collaborative virtual reality system for a design environment. The first major lesson was the necessity (and difficulty) of converting the CAD files used in product design to a format more suitable for real-time VR rendering.

Many of the other lessons learned involve the integration of collaborative capabilities into a virtual environment. The developers found that low-latency audio was essential, but more easily producible than video. Telephone-quality (8 Khz) audio and 8 Hz video were sufficient and producible within the virtual world. The use of standard multicasting protocols and tools proved practical and suitable as the means of adding a collaboration interface. However, challenges still existed regarding the difficulties in acquiring a high-bandwidth, low-latency, multicasting route between sites (especially trans-continental sites).

Caterpillar is also interested in obtaining customer opinion on potential future product designs and design alternatives in products that have not yet been released. They may ask customers for opinions on joystick versus steering wheel methods of steering control, for example. Connecting these interfaces to a virtual representation allows them to place the new concept on any of Caterpillar's virtual machines operating in a variety of settings. Input controls of modern machinery are a "drive-by-wire" control system. This means that it is now easier to replace or change how the input controls affect the machinery. Putting new devices through human factors studies before they are integrated in physical machinery is an appropriate use of VR.

Finally, Caterpillar continues to see potential in using VR in training operators to drive machines with which they are not familiar in a safe environment. Often, the operators must use the machines in rugged or hazardous conditions. Caterpillar is making every effort to teach operators how to operate machines safely in such environments.

Bob Fenwick of Caterpillar summarizes the *VPS* effort:

> Even though Caterpillar has used virtual reality
> in product design for a number of years, we
> still consider this to be an infant technology.
> Its ultimate potential will not be realized until
> it becomes an integrated everyday tool that
> product design engineers use in the new product
> development cycle. Advances in hardware, software
> and communications brings us a step closer to that
> realization every day.

CASE STUDY 3.3: GENERAL MOTORS CORPORATION

Executive Summary

General Motors developed an in-house Virtual Reality Facility as an extension of their *VisualEyes*™ project. The *VisualEyes* project enables them to do virtual prototyping of new vehicle designs prior to creating physical prototypes. An important aspect of the design process was to be able to see models at life-size. To enable this, General Motors utilized *CAVE*™ and other stationary projection devices. The *CAVE* system allowed designers to view vehicle interiors from the interior perspective. They also used large, single-wall displays with no user tracking to display crash test data, which was best seen from outside the car.

A primary goal of the GM VR project was to display the models with a very high degree of realism. Thus, they chose to render highly detailed images at the expense of high frame rate and interactivity. Audio was not a critical element of this application, and the developers planned to enable collaboration between design teams located at geographically disparate facilities.

Introduction

General Motors (GM) has a history of early adoption of computing technology. They are credited with the development of the light pen, and are among the first users of computer-based solid modeling. Thus it is no surprise that they are among the first businesses to investigate the use of virtual reality toward improving products.

GM virtual reality efforts fall within the scope of their *VisualEyes*™ project. The primary purpose was to allow design engineers to see a visually realistic, life-size model of their design in an immersive environment. The *VisualEyes* package refers to a software program developed by GM to aid in virtual prototyping ranging from the desktop to large-screen and immersive displays.

The old adage "faster, better, cheaper" describes some of the primary goals of this application of VR. Any technology that offers the possibility of more rapidly bringing a better product to market attracted the GM researchers. Virtual reality, via a *CAVE* display, was their chosen venue.

One of the more explicit goals of the *VisualEyes* project was to reduce (or eliminate) the time and money spent on producing physical prototypes of a future product. Physical prototypes are very costly, and in iterative design processes, many are built. If the number of physical prototypes constructed can be reduced, especially in the early design stages, a considerable cost savings can be realized. It is also the case that physical prototypes take time to construct, so reducing the number that need to be constructed results in a faster path to a final design. These concerns are very similar to those experienced by Caterpillar Inc. and Boeing Corp.

Interestingly, the goal at GM focused on visual realism in a virtual prototype, even if it came at the expense of response time and interactivity. In order to use the virtual prototype in design evaluation, they required a high-quality rendering to allow evaluation of overall impact of design, visual quality inspection, human factors, and packaging studies. While they were also interested in using interactive tools for the added ability to view a model under different lighting conditions and from different perspectives, they directed most computational resources toward creating a realistic rendering.

Without the virtual reality system, design engineers make use of a variety of real-world physical models. In the earlier stages of the design process, they used clay models, usually scaled down in size, but occasionally life-size clay models were created. Although much more costly and time consuming, life-size models were created because people are much more adept at understanding and reacting to "models" that are full scale.

Designers have also become accustomed to viewing computer graphics renderings of their designs on their desktop workstations. The *VisualEyes* software renders to a variety of visual displays ranging from desktop viewing to a *CAVE* projection-based VR system. Hence, the virtual reality aspect of the project was part of an exploration into an alternative method of viewing virtual worlds previously viewed on conventional desktop monitors.

Finally, in traditional design practice, full-size prototype physical models are still constructed. The cost of these models can be prohibitively expensive, so they are utilized only when absolutely necessary. However, they do provide a very accurate representation of the visual aspects of the

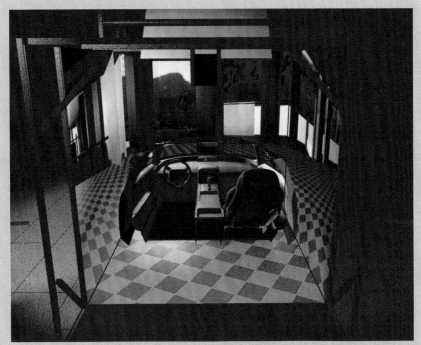

FIGURE 3-22
General Motors chose the CAVE to examine the aesthetics of an automobile interior.

final product. The accuracy of the representation allows designers to uncover most problems in the design.

The paradox is that by the time the stage of design is reached, it is difficult and costly to make drastic changes. *Virtual prototyping* allows an intuitive way of exploring new designs. In GM's case, they were more interested in finding problems rather than validating the design. Virtual prototyping allows this to happen much earlier in the design life cycle, yet still provides a representation that visually emulates the final product.

Application Description

GM's initial focus on using VR was to render a surface model of the interior of a vehicle for evaluation of the aesthetics and ergonomics of a design. *VisualEyes* already provided an acceptable means for lifelike viewing the exterior of a virtual car, a large-screen wall projection. Such a display matches how one naturally views a car: from the

outside; standing next to it; looking at one side at a time. Viewing the interior of a car, however, is not typically done in this manner. To get a good feel for the interior of a car, one needs to be inside. This means that the user is able to turn their head to see what the interior looks like from any perspective.

Virtual reality capabilities were integrated into the *VisualEyes* package to enable the proper viewing and design analysis of automobile interiors. By positioning the viewer in different locations in the car, they can evaluate the interior from the perspective of the driver, or any of the passenger seats. Having a physically immersive display also allows users to do things such as poke their head under the hood to see the interior of the engine compartment.

One of the key points of the system is that it provides a life-size view of the car. This allows the engineer or designer to exploit their past experiences of sitting in many actual cars. One designer exclaimed on seeing a computer screen display, then a life-size immersive display: "That is a model, but *this* is a car!"

Representation of the Virtual World

The virtual world for design analysis is a simple one, a highly detailed visual model of a car. This is sometimes enhanced with a showroom or outdoor scene in which the car is placed, but the car is the important element. As a visual design tool, aural elements in the scene are not very important, with the exception of feedback from the control interface. The virtual world display is often augmented by the use of physical props such as a seat and steering wheel.

In many VR applications, the choice of visual representation is not obvious. Considerable thought goes into how things should be represented, such as which symbols or graphical elements can be mapped to particular components of the virtual world. In this application, however, the choice of representations is simple. The virtual world

should be represented as realistically as possible, a lifelike representation of the automobile.

In many virtual reality and computer graphics applications, datasets are simplified in order to increase rendering speed. In this application, with the explicit goal of attaining as much realism as possible, data simplification is avoided unless absolutely essential. Models are represented within the computer as polygonal objects, as well as texture maps. Standard culling techniques based on distance are not useful in environments such as a car interior, where everything is nearby. This problem also occurs for other types of information-visualization needs, such as many scientific visualization representations.

Frequently, the objects in the virtual world can be distinguished between the object of interest and background objects. One technique they use to help maintain more reasonable frame rates is to direct more computational resources toward the focal object, presenting it in full

FIGURE 3-23

A designer views the interior of a car through the window in a CAVE display. Note that the virtual car is life-size.

detail, while spending less on the background objects. The background objects may be rendered with less polygonal detail, as points, or in wireframe. Another option is to simply not display the nonessential objects. Their highest concern is to maintain the aesthetic integrity of the object of importance.

DESIGN CHOICE

In this application, realistic rendering was done at the expense of frame rate, rather than model simplification. Compared with standard VR practices, this decision was carried to the extreme, delivering frame rates that would generally be considered quite bad or unusable for out-the-window visual simulation—often approximately 5 frames per second (FPS), but sometimes as low as 1 FPS. For visualization of a static scene, low frame rates are preferable to cartoonish simplifications of higher rates.

To achieve a very realistic-looking display, details are very important. For the interior of a car, the most critical element is the dashboard display.

In some instances, texture maps can be exploited to aid in presenting a lifelike appearance. A variety of different texture map techniques are used in this application. Some of the textures are photographs of actual components of a car. Others are hand drawn. In special cases stereographic texture maps are used. In general, for VR, stereo texture maps are not useful because they must be viewed from a particular point of view. In this application, however, the developers had the luxury of knowing the most important and most common point of view (the driver's seat) and can create the stereo textures appropriately.

Although the system did model the mirrors in the interior of the car, the participant in the simulation does not see their own reflection. A mirror view could be accomplished by using a video camera and texture mapping the video image onto the mirror surface, but this does not contribute significantly toward the goal of design analysis.

This particular application focused on the visual aspects of design. There was no audio representation, though feedback at the control interface could have been integrated.

Haptically, the application involved a participant sitting in an actual car bucket seat, giving the strong sense they were sitting in a car. Ideally, the best choice of seat to use was found to be one from the car being designed. However, depending on what stage of the design process the car was in, a physical copy of the seat itself may not yet exist.

Allowing the user to hold and manipulate an actual steering wheel, or a steering wheel prop, also raises the sense of realism. Since vehicle dynamics were not part of this evaluation, the steering wheel did not provide any input to the system. However, its usage was enough to improve the perception of the design.

VisualEyes was used to simulate a stationary car; there was no need for vestibular display as might be needed for an off-road driving simulator. Likewise, the senses of taste and smell are not important to the task (though using "new car smell" aerosols may add to the mood.)

Interaction with the Virtual World

This application is of the genre *virtual prototyping*. In virtual prototyping, an ephemeral model is put before the designer for evaluation. The main method of interaction (the form) is simple—physical locomotion. There are also menu interactions given via a wand that can be used to select the make and model, or modify the color of the body or interior. The focus is to let the designer naturally move about the space within the vehicle to make their evaluation.

The "narrative" is typical of design and visualization applications—look at some pre-created data from different perspectives, and with some user-selectable options.

The best way to determine the quality of a vehicle design is to interact with the representation in a manner as similar as possible as one would with the final product. This means climbing in, sitting down, reaching for the radio controls, etc. Thus physical movement (locomotion) is the travel method best suited for this application. The application developers also implemented other travel options, including fly-through methods. One option that is sometimes used to interact with the design prototype is the *grab-the-world* method of travel.

Most of the interaction that takes place in immersive use of the *VisualEyes* system took the form of physical body movement to judge the appearance and human factors issues of a design. For some design analysis situations some additional interactions were available, such as being able to choose the style of the interior dash, or to choose the interior and/or exterior color scheme. For these interactions, a simple menu-based interface was provided using the buttons on a handheld wand.

The *VisualEyes* software system as described here does not have built-in support for remote collaboration. The system was developed in the GM research and development center in Warren, Michigan. During the initial development states, designers went to the R&D center to try *VisualEyes* on their designs. Later it was exported to the Warren Design Center.

The *CAVE* itself is ideal for multiple people at the same physical locale to work together on a design. One reason for choosing to use a *CAVE* and large-screen displays is the ability for many people to view the environment simultaneously. This means that there is opportunity for people to share ideas while experiencing these images, all in an immersive environment

The virtual world in this application was a static model. Car designs are examined as they remain motionless in the virtual world with the occasional exception of simulating the car placed on a rotating base in a virtual car showroom.

There is no collision detection done within *VisualEyes*. This allows the participant to do things such as stand up in the car, and enter and exit through the side panel. There is also no notion of gravity in the system, but there typically aren't

FIGURE 3-24
A life-size rendering allows a more intuitive visual interpretation of simulated crash data.

individual parts to pick up and move, so this is not a major consequence.

Another use for *VisualEyes* is visualizing computational simulations generated for crash analysis. Crash analysis rendering is typically displayed on the nonimmersive (untracked), large-screen display as this data is more suitable for observing the car from the exterior. The crash physics themselves are pre-computed, and not part of the rendering package.

Venue

The venue for this application was a research lab at GM. Another possibility was to use the system in dealership showrooms, allowing customers to experience a virtual replica of a car they are considering with various options, color choices, etc.

At the GM R&D center, the normal scenario was for small working groups of 5–6 people to visit for sessions of about 30 minutes to 1 hour. These working groups were often subsets of a larger group who meet around a table, then proceed into the *CAVE* to discuss some aspect of the design. The car designers typically used the shuttering glasses less than 30 minutes at a time.

In addition to actual design meetings, many demonstrations of the system were held. This is a price that system designer Randy Smith says is required for promoting a new technology.

VR System

VisualEyes was first used to display models in stereo on large monitors using head tracking and hand (wand) tracking with Logitech ultrasonic tracking systems. Later, *VisualEyes* was used on larger projection screens to view larger models of full-sized cars that were sometimes head-tracked, sometimes not.

When displaying cars and parts on a small screen with head tracking, the developers found that designers were not particularly interested in looking at the cars, but reacted significantly when shown a (smallish) part at life-size. Thus, they strove to push their displays to be large enough to display a car at actual scale. Providing the user a life-size view of the exterior of a car worked well, even when head tracking was disabled. For this purpose and for viewing visualizations of crash simulations, untracked rendering was satisfactory.

FIGURE 3-25
Rear projection of a vehicle allows designers to inspect the image without casting shadows on the screen.

To examine the interior of a car requires the ability to see all around. Thus, *VisualEyes* was extended to work in a *CAVE* environment, a visual display that surrounds the user. Installed in 1994, GM's was the first *CAVE* at an industry facility. From its creation, their *CAVE* offered a full three-wall display plus the floor display. Lack of a rear projection wall was not a major hindrance.

DESIGN CHOICE

From the outset of this project the application designers had planned to use projection VR rather than an HMD-based system. There are a variety of reasons for this choice. One of the major reasons is that typical usage would involve a team of people discussing a design. Projection VR allows team members to easily see and converse with one another. Another reason is that the developers felt that HMDs were too heavy and clumsy, and many of their clientele, including executives who are interested in viewing designs under development, would not wear them. They also felt that the HMDs available (when the decision was made) were not adequate with respect to resolution and field-of-view. GM was quite satisfied with the choice of projection VR, and even if given adequate resolution and field-of-view, it is unlikely they would shift to an HMD system.

Interestingly, they chose to build a *CAVE* measuring 8 feet on each side as opposed to the more common 10 feet per side cube. This was done to more closely map to the size of a car interior, minimizing the disparity between focal distance of the model and the physiological measurements calculated by the human optical system. Thus the screens (where the eyes will focus) are approximately the same distance from the participant as the interior wall of the car. Secondary benefits are that by reducing the size of the screens, the apparent resolution (pixel density) of the display is increased, less floor space is required, and the display is brighter.

In comparing the *CAVE* environment to the large, single-screen display used for the crash simulations, the application developers said that they believe the advantage of the *CAVE* was that it allows the inside-out view that gives the participants a chance to climb inside a crashing car, or to poke their head into the engine compartment. The advantage of the large single-wall projection was that it is more suitable for external viewing of a vehicle, and allowed even larger groups to watch the simulation.

The application designers' primary concerns with the projection-based system were insufficient resolution, brightness, and color uniformity across screens. They wanted improvements in each of these areas. An upgrade to SGI Infinite Reality Engines provided an increase in pixels per screen from 1024×768 to 1280×1024 (66% increase), while continuing to provide a 96 Hz refresh rate (48 Hz per eye when in stereoscopic display mode). This has resulted in a noticeable improvement in visual quality, but they felt like they were an order of magnitude away from where they would like to be. For example, lines on dashboard gauges were in reality 1 mm wide. On the old system, they were only able to resolve 2–3 mm, which was not quite good enough for presenting a realistic display.

Like most *CAVE* displays, the GM *CAVE* used the Ascension Flock of Birds extended-range electromagnetic tracking system to track head position and the position of one handheld device. Because electromagnetic tracking systems are susceptible to errors caused by metal in the environment, tracking performance is improved by calibrating the rendering system to correct for the inherent errors. At GM, they used a mechanical position measuring system from FARO (the FAROarm™ to measure the difference between the values reported by electromagnetic system and the (more accurate) values from the

FAROarm. These comparisons were the basis from which the tracking system is calibrated. The FAROarm itself can serve as a tracking device, and such an option is available in *VisualEyes*. This is very useful when recording the virtual environment with a video camera. The camera was attached to the FAROarm, so the perspective is rendered from the camera's point of view.

The computing and graphics system utilized an SGI rack Onyx with Infinite Reality graphics engines. The Onyx system included multiple processors enabling it to render and compute interactions in parallel. This was the typical system for a *CAVE* environment at the time.

Application Implementation

This project was developed around the already existing *VisualEyes* software environment. Rather than rewriting their existing software to work with the *CAVE* library, the application developers integrated the basic functionality of the *CAVE* libraries directly into their existing software, providing the ability to display head-tracked, stereoscopic images in a multiwall display. By integrating the multiwall display techniques directly into their existing system, the application developers felt they were able to reduce time of software programming and maintain the use of the advanced rendering techniques they developed for their visualization system.

GM began exploring VR in 1992 as part of a continually evolving company-wide internal project. By 1992, they felt that the supporting technology for VR had finally reached the threshold to make VR a usable medium for their purposes. The GM VR project was a boot-strapped effort that grew as necessary. They evolved the system to fulfill the need for an inside out view of full-size models, stereoscopic depth cues, and tracking to make the perspective accurate.

The *VisualEyes* project was developed in-house, within the GM Research and Development Center by a team consisting of Randall C. Smith, project creator and team leader; Tom Celusnak and Larry Peruski, also early members of the core software team; and Don McMillan, who was responsible for some of the more recent developments.

By corporate standards, the development and usage of the system proceeded rapidly, though the designers wanted to move even faster. Gaining buy-in from the users and company required time, demonstrations, and energy.

The typical mode of interaction with users and potential users was to tell them to BYOD, or "Bring your own data." Usually the design data came available in a CAD format that could be readily transferred over the company network, and imported into the system. Using the participants' own data allowed them to better understand the capabilities of the new system. In fact, they saw many repeat visitors who came to see their designs in the *CAVE* environment.

Conclusion

An interesting anecdote is that people reported that virtual cars viewed in the *CAVE* seemed wider than expected. A possible explanation of this phenomenon is that it is a result from the fact that the *CAVE* was slightly wider than a typical car, and eyes focus at the distance of the *CAVE* wall. The brain uses this information to help determine the size of the interior, resulting in the wider perception. The focal distance depth cue may be overridden by stereopsis[6] when directly looking at the walls of the car, but when the head is facing the front of the car stereopsis is not a factor because each side-wall can be seen by only one eye.

When examining the car from the driver's seat, the viewer sat about 2 feet from the left wall (driver-side in the United States). This put the passenger-side wall about 6 feet away from the viewer, which caused the single right eye to sense the distance of objects displayed on that screen as being 6 feet away, which is larger than most cars.

Although *VisualEyes* probably has not directly saved any lives,[7] it is likely that it saved GM time and money. GM has not

---

[6]Lack of stereopsis in peripheral visual is not the result of projector or head-based VR displays, but rather is an inherent trait of the human visual system.

[7]It is, however, used in crash simulation analysis to make safer cars.

published any data to verify whether any time or money has actually been saved, but the longevity of the system implies that was indicative of payback in the near future. Although the system was used on real problems within GM (indicating that the system is useful to designers), users do report that there are additional capabilities they would like to have.

The developers state that the system probably allowed the designers to reduce the number of early physical models resulting in some monetary savings. However, they did not reach the point where construction of all physical models could be eliminated. This is particularly true for the end of the design cycle, where physical parts are at least required for use in manufacturing analysis and crash testing. Government agencies are not yet to the point of trusting computer simulations enough to alleviate the need for physical crash testing. But any reduction in the number of stages requiring a physical model results in significant savings of both time and money, which can add up to considerable savings.

Although participants in this experience probably don't feel like they are actually in a real car, the application designers did relate some anecdotes that indicate participants' sense of immersion, and the transparency of the user interface.

One anecdote involves an executive who was examining a design for a specially designed ride vehicle for display at a future technology venue at Disney's EPCOT center. The executive looked carefully at the vehicle, squatted down, sat in the seat, etc. He remarked that the carlike ride vehicle required too large a step to get in, and worried about how people's heads would block others' views. The interesting aspect about this story is that the executive was not remarking on, or testing, the technology. He was doing his job, and the VR system supported that task.

Other anecdotes include the excitement participants display in the system, and the fact that many would hesitate to step on the console and tended to reach to set their notebook down on the dash, etc.

One of the more significant things that this group has learned is the importance of detail over frame rate in their application. In other words, sometimes using sufficient detail makes the system much more useful even if it costs a rapid display update.

Having begun on the path of projection VR, the application designers did not regret that decision. The application designers felt that projection gave them the ability to see and more easily work with collaborators. Also, there was no need for suiting up, and the resolution and field-of-view were better when using projection technology. They also learned that VR was not a suitable technology as a tool for fine modeling due to tracker error and low resolution.

In turn, GM learned that people who are not designers by trade typically have difficulty visualizing from a drawing or a sketch. It turns out in practice that what they had built primarily as a design tool actually turned out to be primarily a communication tool.

In the future, the application developers envisioned using the system for worldwide collaborative efforts to reduce travel time and expense. Design discussions can be held between collaborators working on different continents to work together more frequently and cohesively. Designers have specific concerns related to their location. Many of these different concerns might not be raised as early in the design process if meetings are held only at times when they could meet in person. In general, fostering early communication during design helps the team to find out about the little things that will be major issues down the road. It also helps keep continuity during the design process. VR is becoming part of GM's virtual prototyping effort. Application developer Randy Smith likes to quote an old Chinese proverb to describe the usefulness of VR: "If I hear—I will forget if I see—I may remember if I do—I will understand."

CASE STUDY 3.4: NALCO FUEL TECH

Executive Summary

The BoilerMaker application was a joint development project between Nalco Fuel Tech (NFT) and Argonne National Laboratory (ANL). This collaboration created a virtual reality application in which one can interactively do visualization, analysis, and design of significantly reduced-emission boilers and incinerators. The raison d'être of this application was to provide a way to find the optimal locations for fuel injectors in an industrial boiler. By accomplishing this, NFT augmented the pollution control systems of industries to help them meet the requirements of the 1995 Clean Air Act. The *BoilerMaker* application was designed to aid and assist designers for placement of fuel injectors in their boilers. This application allowed designers to view simulation data and interact with the changes that varying injector placements resulted in, especially temperature gradients and effects of design changes.

Application Description

Placing boiler fuel injectors in locations that result in optimal (cleaner) burn is a difficult, iterative task. The optimal location is influenced by flue-gas temperatures, velocity fields, and slag buildup. The application authors created a computational model of the interaction of these elements that allowed them to predict the effectiveness of an injector at a specific location. The VR application gave them a tool to interactively place injectors and get quick feedback of spray coverage and burn efficiency. By interactively moving the injector nozzles and particulate matter in the virtual boiler, the designer could quickly iterate over several placements to arrive at ideal locations.

The heart of this application is the computational model that simulates the fuel-burning phenomena of a boiler. A separate software package (*TrackPack*) computes the

FIGURE 3-26
Participants begin their experience with the Nalco Fuel Tech BoilerMaker application by making menu selections via a CAVE wand while standing outside a virtual boiler.

dynamics of particulate matter. Simulated particles can be massless, massed, or evaporating, and calculated on a variety of meshes for both steady-state and time-dependent flows in noncoupled two-phase flows. Although the model is computationally intensive, it does respond adequately for real-time interaction—20 frames-per-second (FPS) for moving an injector, while the computation of a handful of injected particles proceeds at about 2 FPS. By distributing this application over multiple machines, each computer can do the part for which it is best suited (parallel computation/graphics rendering), resulting in a useful tool. The display and interaction with the simulation is carried out in a *CAVE* equipped with a wand and electromagnetic tracking system.

The utilization of networking hardware to allow running an application in distributed mode has both advantages and disadvantages. The primary advantage is that each component can run on a system especially suited for a particular computation. The main disadvantage is the added complexity of building a distributed system, as well as the need for high-speed networking to connect the components. When the *BoilerMaker* VR experience begins, the user is located above the ground (a grid of green lines) facing the external structure of a boiler. Interaction with the environment is accomplished via wand-based travel controls, and a menu interface developed by ANL. Basic operation includes three modes of interaction:

- Display features mode
- Visualization mode
- Injector placement mode

The display features mode allows the user to increase frame rate by toggling the display of graphically intensive geometric features. For instance, the user can toggle the display of the internal water and steam pipes representation. These cylindrical graphical objects are made of many-thousand polygons, and put a strain on the rendering system. This noticeably reduces the visual frame rate of the application. By removing this visual feature, the frame rate jumps to a very comfortable level—about 40 FPS even when flying vectors are in use—making interaction much more effective.

The visualization mode allows a user to display a variety of common visualization idioms including a streamline from a point, an isosurface, and static or flying vectors.

FIGURE 3-27

The BoilerMaker application presents a menu of three modes of operation: the small sphere in the upper right is a three-dimensional compass to aid the participant in determining their orientation in the virtual world.

Streamlines are released using the wand location to position the release point, and a button press to activate. An arrow loops over the path of each streamline showing the speed of flow along the path. Isosurfaces can be used to visualize a scalar data field such as the region for which temperatures are within the range for highly efficient particle burn. The overall flow of gases can be viewed with a collection of vectors (represented as darts). These darts can be visualized either as a static collection covering the entire boiler, or as a smaller collection that traverse the flow of the boiler beginning at the fire.

Any of the visualization idioms can be colored based on different scalar fields within the simulation, primarily temperature and optimal burn. Coloring for optimal burn is also a temperature-based mapping, but highlights the region where the temperature is ideal. Specifically, bright colors are mapped to the optimal region, light purple to regions that are too cold, and dark purple to regions that are too hot.

FIGURE 3-28

Colored stream lines indicate the effectiveness of the fuel injector placement. Here we see that light purple regions show areas that are too cold for effective burning, whereas dark purple indicates regions that are too hot. The very bright areas indicate optimal burn temperature.

The injector placement mode allows the user to interactively position up to 25 injectors by pointing at a location on the boiler wall, selecting an existing injector or creating a new one if none are nearby. By pointing at exterior walls, the wand is then used to drag the selected injector to the desired location. As an injector is moved, computations are performed to aid in visualizing the effective burn of the current position. Characteristic sprays are made from the injector, showing calculated burn of entering particles. The participant uses the visualization to place injectors at locations appearing to have effective burn efficiency.

The *BoilerMaker* user interface also provides for computational steering. Computational steering is the term used to describe controlling a running computational simulation

from within a virtual environment. In addition to the menu interface, widgets such as 3D scrollbars allow the user to modify the numerical model parameters and visualization parameters. The initial particle size, speed, and distribution from the injector source can be adjusted using the scrollbars when studying particulate matter.

Audio is used to enhance the feedback to the user. The user can hear the transition between being outside the boiler and being inside the boiler by a marked difference in the volume of the ambient fire burning rumble. A trumpet fanfare marks the event of a new dataset being received from the computation application. Also, each release of flying vectors into the flow field is marked by a swoosh sound. However, no audio feedback is provided for user interface features such as the menu or controls relating to the travel interface (which would be useful).

The method of travel in this application is fly-through, with no constraints on orientation. This is unlike many applications that allow three-dimensional flight through space but constrain the view to have a specific up vector (i.e., if standing, the ground is always in the direction of the feet). In *BoilerMaker*, the user can rotate to any orientation with respect to the world. Such freedom can lead to disorientation. To compensate for this, they introduced a "3D compass." The compass is displayed at a fixed position relative to the user. Drawn as a sphere, it uses colors to disambiguate directions. The most dramatic distinction is between up and down. The top hemisphere is white, the bottom black, giving the appearance of an airplane pilot's attitude indicator with the equator acting as the artificial horizon. The four vertical meridians are colored red, green, blue, and yellow to help the user determine their orientation.

The developers' initial goal for travel was to design something that emulates a flight simulator. Because the user can hover, the resultant method is perhaps more akin to a simplified helicopter interface.

Travel control is divided into two components: rotational and longitudinal motion. Rotation is controlled by rotating the wand about the wrist. The Y-component of the joystick on the wand is used to move longitudinally through the world (along the line the user is facing). The participant can lock travel by pressing right on the joystick. Pressing left reactivates travel control. Locking travel means that both rotational and longitudinal movements are deactivated, freezing the user at the current position.

This travel technique is a little complicated but can be mastered in a single session, and is quite effective, with only a couple of small difficulties. One problem is that there is no way to directly move laterally other than physical locomotion. The other annoyance is that because the travel-lock control is part of the same device as the speed control, there is a tendency to activate the freeze mode when turning right. This is exacerbated since there is no aural feedback to indicate when this happens.

Once in operation, a typical design process using *BoilerMaker* begins with the application experts constructing the 3D and computational model of the boiler (or incinerator). This step can be done in about one half day. They then used the *BoilerMaker* virtual reality application to explore the gas flow and efficient burn regions of that particular unit. Once they had an understanding of the burn process of the unit, the engineers begin to design the injection system. This step generally took several iterations, and without VR is the most time-consuming phase. Then, if necessary, the *BoilerMaker* application can be used again (with remote collaboration) if the on-site engineers encountered an injector that cannot be placed as planned.

An avatar consisting of simple body, head, and hand representations allows a user to determine where another participant is looking and pointing. While this can be effective for collaboratively exploring the data of a system under design, it can be even more effective for working on last-minute changes that are found to be necessary during the implementation of the design. In particular, if the engineers on-site at the installation of the actual boiler discovered that placement of an injector was not possible as planned, they could use a more portable system to collaborate with the (off-site) design experts to determine a feasible alternate location. The experts at the home office would have the advantage of more powerful computers and better VR display systems. Thus, they could more quickly evaluate other possible injector placements and show the result to the engineer on site at the boiler/incinerator.

VR System

This application was developed for use in a typical *CAVE* installation, using the *EVL CAVE* library. However, the *CAVE*

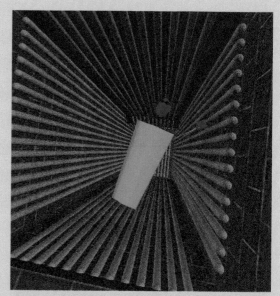

FIGURE 3-29

The BoilerMaker application supports synchronous collaboration between multiple sites. Here we see the avatar of one participant exploring the pipes in the Argonne's CAVEComm library, used to enable distributed computation of simulation and graphics, also allows collaboration between multiple sites.

library allows for use in all other styles of VR visual displays, so it can be used at remote sites with different available hardware. Collaboration between sites, and between the visualization simulation and the renderer were both handled by the *CAVEComm* library developed at Argonne.

The *BoilerMaker* design and implementation team consisted of the principal investigators from Argonne, Lori Freitag and Paul Plassmann, and Nalco Fuel Tech William Michels, plus a team of programmers who contributed significantly to the design and implementation of the software. The programming team included Darin Diachin, Daniel Heath, Jim Herzog, and Bob Ryan, all working at the Argonne National Laboratory.

Conclusion

Initially, the *BoilerMaker* application was tested as a proof-of-concept, using public domain computation algorithms. The *Boilermaker* application demonstrates how virtual reality can be used as an interactive design tool. By allowing

FIGURE 3-30

A splash screen in the BoilerMaker application gives credit to its many developers.

a designer to instantly see the results of the placement of injectors, the VR experience can aid in saving time, money, and potentially lives. *Boilermaker* also is an example of an early use of a virtual reality environment for computational steering and collaboration. The end result of this application development effort was worthwhile. The prototype system demonstrates that the time required to analyze injector configurations for pollution control systems can be significantly reduced. The ramification of this is that better, environmentally safer boilers can be designed at lower cost.

CASE STUDY 3.5: CUTTY SARK

Executive Summary

Who could resist the lure of donning a head-mounted display, grabbing an actual ship's wheel, feeling the rocking of the ocean beneath their feet, and heading out on a high-sea adventure? Of course, such a virtual reality experience has a grand appeal, and Cutty Sark chose to create such a scenario for people throughout the United States.

Their motivations, however, were more than the altruistic idea of providing compelling entertainment. Cutty Sark chose to develop the first virtual reality application with content specifically tailored to their product for the purpose of advertising. They spent a large fraction of their advertising budget to create a touring VR platform with an actual ship's wheel, and other accoutrements such as a handheld gun and moving deck. Computer graphics were driven by an SGI graphics engine. The plan was to allow participants to experience smuggling Cutty Sark scotch whiskey across the sea while battling pirates, weather, and other hazards. Their goal was to create an indelible brand imprint in the minds of the tens of thousands of people who got to try the system throughout the United States. The results included increased brand recognition and increased sales.

Introduction

The *Cutty Sark Virtual Voyage* was a virtual reality experience used as part of a product promotion campaign. Designed to help promote Hiram Walker's new slogan for Cutty Sark—"The Real McCoy"—the *Virtual Voyage* puts the spectator aboard the ship of smuggler William McCoy during the days of prohibition.

Of course, as is part of any product marketing scheme, the ultimate goal is to increase sales. With generally limited means of advertising available (print media, store advertising/promotions, and billboards), a novel medium was selected to help boost awareness of the scotch—virtual reality. After taking the promotion on the road for more than 18 months, sales that had been sliding for over a decade turned around, and brand awareness was up.

The slogan "The Real McCoy" raises the comparison of Hiram Walker's scotch vs. all other brands. Legend has it that "The Real McCoy" refers to the scotch smuggled by William McCoy during Prohibition, when lesser-quality homebrewed "whiskey" was the norm. Telling such a story in print advertising is difficult. Although it is an interesting tale, it is unlikely that many readers will expend the effort to read it. Thus Hiram Walker sought to do something different; so when Scaros & Casselman proposed a virtual reality experience, Hiram Walker was interested. Scaros & Casselman then put together a team experienced in producing VR experiences, including Horizon Entertainment and GreyStone Technology Inc.

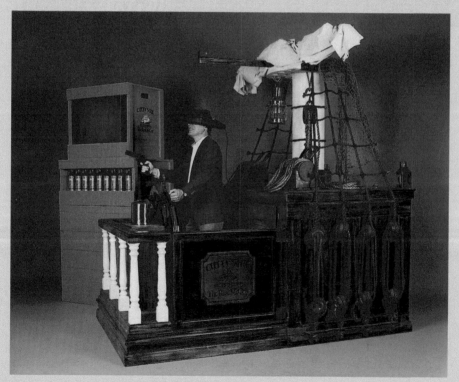

FIGURE 3-31
Virtual reality was used as part of an advertising campaign to increase brand awareness of Cutty Sark scotch.

Application Description

The VR promotion was packaged as a pair of touring VR platforms, each equipped to run a game experience based on the legend of Captain McCoy. The storyline of the game is of the participant taking the role of a captain trying to get "his" shipment of 1000 cases of Cutty Sark scotch delivered safely. Facing numerous hazards along the journey, the experience scores participants based on how many cases they successfully transport to the destination.

The experience presents McCoy's journey from the Bahamas to Long Island via a series of vignettes. The journey begins in a "sheltered harbor," where novice ship pilots can get their bearings and experiment a little with the controls. They are then given 3 minutes to face many hazards—"fierce sea storms," "marauding raider boats," "attacking planes," and "treacherous narrows"—before arriving at the "safe cove" with a "torch-lit welcoming party."

Representation of the Virtual World

Presented as realistically as practical, the world of *Virtual Voyage* is a cartoon-like polygonal world on a foundation of fairly realistic physics. Objects in the world include the ship itself, its cargo, the ocean and shore, and the computer-controlled agents that serve to impede players during their journey.

During the experience, the participant is positioned at the helm of the ship, enabling them to view the world from the vantage point of the captain. In particular, they see the fore of the ship and can look out over the ocean as they navigate the world. They are also able to see an avatar of their hand (equipped with an avatar of a pistol). However, the focal visual element of this experience is the cargo of Cutty Sark scotch cases on the deck. Players keep a watchful eye on the precious cargo before them, as the loss of each case reduces their score.

In keeping with the attempt for reasonable realism, the rendered visuals are the type comfortably produced by a typical high-end graphics engine—a large number of texture-mapped polygons. This type of rendering approaches, but is not quite "photorealistic." It tends to result in the cartoonish countenance mentioned above. Fog was used in some circumstances to allow polygon culling in scenes with high polygon counts.

Somewhat realistic audio cues (marker sounds) are heard when events occur during the adventure, helping to make the world seem more alive. Sounds were played from basic sound sample files and processed into spatialized sounds through a Beachtron™ system. By having the sounds of the boat and airplane follow the objects through the world, participants get a greater impression of being in the world of the experience.

DESIGN CHOICE

No active feedback to the other senses was provided in this experience.

Because the platform units had to be set-up and dismantled many times during their travel, the designers felt that the added technology required for other senses would increase the cost, as well as the susceptibility to failure. At the same time, it would not heighten player (mental) immersion significantly.

However, the platform structure was constructed with springs underneath the helm where the participant would stand. This was done so as participants shifted their weight in correspondence with the rocking boat, they would feel the deck moving beneath them. The developers were uncertain of the effectiveness of this method as a means of increasing realism and immersion, so provision was made to lock down the platform in the event it proved ineffective or caused motion discomfort. David Polinchock of the CyberEvent Group reports that the springs were not locked down for most people, and that he feels that the added realism of standing on an unstable platform helps immerse the player.

There are some other interesting haptic possibilities that might have increased the realism, had the technology been available. One additional sensation could have been to use the ship's wheel give feedback indicating the difficulty of turning the rudder against the sea. Other interesting haptic possibilities include providing wind and water spray, helping to put the player in the middle of the raging storm—though of course this would require extra precautions to keep the water from coming in contact with any of the electronics.

The rolling, choppy seas could result in active vestibular feedback. A simple olfactory display might also have been an interesting addition to this application. An ambient sea-smell would require no connection to the computational system, yet would reinforce the setting in the player's mind. Also, whiffs of gunpowder smell could be generated relatively easily each time players fire their weapons.

Interaction with the Virtual World

Although the use of the *Cutty Sark Virtual Voyage* experience was for product promotion, it falls within the genre of the *mission game*. In this case, it is a game that happens to be designed with an eye for promoting a certain product. The overall form of interaction is that of *pilot-through travel*, with agent communication done through the business end of the pistol.

As mentioned, the narrative of this experience is reenacting the voyage of Captain William McCoy as you smuggle scotch from Bermuda into the U.S. The "plot" of the story runs along the lines of a 1920s smuggler who must maneuver the ship while thwarting numerous hazards in an (your) effort to get the scotch through. As the ship's captain, you are responsible for safely transporting as many cases as you can. The score indicates how successful you were in the mission.

To keep throughput high, the game was limited to a 3-minute session for each player. The game's narrative is divided into five story elements, each of which lasted for a prescribed amount of time. An introductory sequence welcomed the participant and began the story of Captain McCoy while allowing the player to get a feel for controlling the ship. They were then presented with three sequences in which they face hazards along the journey typical of those that the real McCoy may have had to endure. After bearing through the hazards, and likely losing some but not all of the cargo, the experience is brought to a close by sailing into a safe cove where they are welcomed by a party of revelers at the Gatsbys'. Sequences are segued with a fade to a still image of the product, displayed along with the player's current score.

During the main body of the game, three of four possible hazards are presented. The possible hazards are:

- "Fierce sea storms"
- "Marauding raider boats"
- "Attacking planes"
- "Treacherous narrows"

During the "fierce sea storms," high winds and rough seas force the captain to pilot the ship to keep it from listing. As the ship rocks and rolls, the cargo slides across the bow, and if the motion is severe enough, cases will fall overboard. Lightning is also a concern during the storm, as it may strike and destroy cases of cargo. The player could reduce the chance of lightning strikes by orienting the ship such that the sail remained over the cargo—this is a faux maneuver, added to give the player an opportunity for protecting the cargo in this game experience.

Likewise during the "treacherous narrows," the primary task is maneuvering to avoid grounding the ship, causing it to list and dump cargo. The narrows were also obscured by fog. The fog served two purposes. It made navigation through the narrows more treacherous, and it also allowed the models of the rocky seas to be more complex because polygons hidden by the fog can be culled.

The "attacking planes" and "marauding raider boats" hazards fly and sail around the player's ship, harassing and shooting at it. The player loses cargo when it is shot by the attacking entities (or accidentally by the player). The biplanes and cigarette boats can be thwarted by hitting them with a certain number of shots. After a couple of good hits, the enemy boat will burst into flame, or the plane will crash into the sea, creating a large water plume and sinking after a few moments of bobbing in the sea.

A fifth hazard is ever present. This hazard is Jocko the stowaway, who attempts to make off with his own supply of scotch.

Finally, after surviving the hazards, the user sails to the Long Island shore for the clandestine meeting at which the "Real McCoy" is delivered to the awaiting party.

The participant pilots the ship while standing on a physical platform that looks like the helm of a real sailing ship. A ship's wheel mounted on the platform is a physical prop that provides the means by which the player can control the virtual rudder on the ship. The sails automatically properly align themselves to jibe with the wind. The effects of the wind and ocean on the sails and hull of the ship determine the speed and tack of the ship.

In addition to the vehicle platform, the participant is able to control one other object—a pistol. In either hand, the user

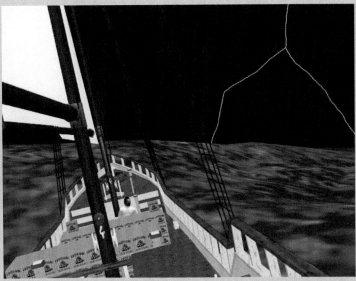

FIGURE 3-32
Participants in the Cutty Sark Virtual Voyage game must steer their ship through "fierce sea storms" while attempting to deliver their cargo.
Photo courtesy of GreyStone Technology Inc.

FIGURE 3-33
While traversing the "treacherous narrows" the participant must avoid running the ship aground.
Photo courtesy GreyStone Technology, Inc.

FIGURE 3-34
The participant must protect the cargo by shooting at attacking planes (left) and marauding raider boats (right).

FIGURE 3-35
The experience culminates in the delivery of the cargo in the stealth of night.

can hold a tracked pistol grip fitted with a trigger under the index finger. Firing the pistol is the only mechanism the user has for nontravel interaction. However, since all of the agents the participant can interact with intend to harm them, it comes in handy. The weapon provides unlimited ammunition and does not require reloading. It is aimed by the participant physically positioning their hand, and fired by squeezing the trigger.

A significant portion of the interaction within the *Virtual Voyage* is in response to the computer-controlled agents that strive to reduce the amount of the cargo. The boat and airplane hazards are both agents that navigate around and take shots at your ship when possible. Interacting with these agents involves steering the ship to avoid their fire, and firing your own weapon to keep them at bay.

The more interesting agent is Jocko the stowaway. Jocko stows away in the hold, coming out of hiding to steal cases of cargo during any of the hazard phases of the journey. Jocko is programmed to pay attention to when the participant is involved with activities that take their attention away from monitoring the cargo—such as fighting the marauders, or just gazing out over the horizon. When the Captain (being played by the participant) is not paying attention, Jocko will make for the cargo and begin to steal it. The user may notice Jocko absconding with a case out of the corner of their eye, or when they turn their head rapidly toward the cargo. Once spotted, the participant can shoot at Jocko with the gun. Jocko cannot be killed, but if a bullet comes too close, he will return to his hiding spot.

The *Virtual Voyage* attraction travels with only one platform going to any particular venue, so was designed strictly as a one-person experience. However, the touring attraction does include a monitor to encourage kibitzing by people waiting to play and other onlookers. Thus the experience becomes a communal activity in the conversations that arise comparing scores and interesting scenarios.

As a game, there are no rigorous requirements to emulate real-world physics such as might be required by a ship-training application. However, to make the experience as engaging (and thus memorable) as they could, the designers strove for realism wherever possible. The physics of the

FIGURE 3-36
Jocko the stowaway lurks on the ship trying to steal the participant's precious cargo.

world simulation were accurate enough that the Captain could sail the ship using typical sailing techniques. With only a one-person crew, the sails were automatically trimmed to match the tack of the ship and the wind and sea conditions. The interface between the hull of the ship and the ocean waves and wind were also fairly realistic, producing an accurate feel of buoyancy and stability. The boat would heel drastically when inappropriate sailing technique was employed.

As the player sails through difficult conditions, the ship's cargo would slide across the bow from side to side in accordance with the rocking of the boat. When the boat was sufficiently listing, some cargo would fall off, reducing the player's score.

Collision detection, which is often very computationally expensive, is not needed to any great extent. Most of the user interactions are with physical objects that limit their motions, allowing the physical world to handle collisions appropriately. The one type of object that did require collision monitoring were bullets and determining what object was struck.

Venue

Venues included stops at restaurants, nightclubs, trade shows, food festivals, and other high-traffic (adult) locations, beginning with the National Restaurant Association

FIGURE 3-37
The Cutty Sark application uses a kiosk platform to enable participants to feel the ship's wheel and provide a general ambiance for the experience.

Trade Show and Expo in Chicago on May 14, 1994. Over the 18-month tour, the two units were booked at over 600 events covering every major U.S. market—most of them multiple times. The majority of cancelled shows were caused by logistical rather than system problems.

The touring nature of this advertisement was the major drawback for the advertising agency. Although a company specializing in such events was hired to manage the tour, bookings were typically done through liquor sales distributors. Since these distributors handle many different brands, not all of them were enthusiastic about making bookings for this single product.

Each unit handled only one player at a time. In addition to the 3-minute game time, 1 or 2 minutes were required to suit and unsuit each person. Over the course of the 18 months, approximately 55,000 people tried the system first-hand. Each player had to provide two proofs of purchase and be 21 years of age or older.

VR System

The system for the *Virtual Voyage* was designed within the constraints imposed by the cost, the tour, and the audience. In this case, there are multiple venues, and the system had to be easily transportable between sites. The primary concerns were portability and durability. The platform structure was designed to include all the hardware into a single unit. The structure included the helm at which the participant would stand, plus concealed locations to hold the computer system, etc.

SYSTEM CHOICE

A head-mounted display was selected as the visual display paradigm for this application. Specifically, they chose a relatively high-resolution HMD (640 × 480 pixels), the n-Vision Datavisor 9c.

The n-Vision Datavisor is a stereo-capable display, but the development team chose to display a monoscopic image for better rendering speed. The amount of money budgeted for the rendering system allowed only one SGI RE2 engine, and using it in stereoscopic mode would have reduced the resolution to a value below the level required by the stated system specifications. A nearby monitor was positioned to allow onlookers to follow the action.

A typical electromagnetic tracking system was selected, the Polhemus Fastrak™. Tracking was done using full six DOF positional tracking. The tracking transmitter was hidden in the ship platform to keep it from standing out obtrusively.

Two "prop" input devices were used in this experience. The most prominent prop was the platform, which was rigged to look like the helm of a tall ship, including the ship's wheel, used to give steering input to the simulation. The other was a basic handheld pistol-grip equipped with a trigger switch and a tracking receiver used to aim and shoot at enemies in the game.

Graphics and computation were done on a Silicon Graphics desk-side Onyx with the RE2 graphics option. Sound file playback was done by the Onyx, with spatialization performed by a CRE Beachtron™ system.

A technician traveled with each unit to set up, run, power down, and do some repair work on the system. The HMD was the most fragile component of each unit, so a second HMD was kept on hand. If an HMD broke, the technician had the tools and knowledge to do some limited repair work on site. For more serious problems, the HMD was shipped back for repair.

The cost of system and software development was about $1 million. Cost of the touring systems was $1 million to $1.5 million each. After adding in the cost of the tour (including promotion), the overall cost was less than $10 million. This amount was a significant portion of the Cutty Sark advertising budget, much more than would typically be spent on a single campaign.

Application Implementation

From the time the idea was conceived to the time the system began appearing at venues, the development of the *Virtual Voyage* was fairly rapid. The general notion of using virtual reality in an ad campaign for Cutty Sark came from the Scaros & Casselman advertising agency after seeing a Bubble Yum campaign that used a touring VR show in early 1993.

The Bubble Yum display did not use a virtual world created specifically about the product; it was just a device to attract crowds.

In the summer of 1993, Scaros & Casselman contacted Horizon Entertainment, which was responsible for the Bubble Yum exhibit. Horizon Entertainment suggested the possibility of creating a customized game for the Hiram Walker product that would be simple to play. Scaros & Casselman would require players to be 21 or older and provide two proofs of purchase to play. After some proof-of-concept development, Scaros & Casselman brought the idea to Hiram Walker and won the advertising account.

Once the account had been won, development on the full application began in February of 1994. Horizon Entertainment served as the project's executive producer, bringing in other experts to help with development, including Silicon Graphics Inc., Spinnaker Design Inc., and GreyStone Technology Inc. Horizon was also responsible for the tour technical support, though the tour management was handled by the CyberEvent Group. Silicon Graphics provided the graphics/computer systems. Spinnaker, a theatrical set design company, produced the physical platform, and GreyStone provided the software and system design, development, integration, and implementation.

GreyStone Technology Inc. was specifically subcontracted to provide the VR operating system (their proprietary VR library built on SGI's IRIS Performer), the application code (including the audio features) and the interfacing to the tracker and other input devices. This work also included designing the individual game scenarios and putting the overall experience together.

Using their proprietary VR library, GreyStone added the components necessary to model an ocean world, with a selection of interesting locations, a two-masted barque (the ship), and the physics to provide a fairly realistic sailing experience. The sailing physics were such that without the constraints of the game narrative, one could freely sail around the world in a realistic fashion, sailing from one point of interest to another.

The ship itself was modeled by GreyStone after the brig *Pilgrim* in Dana Point harbor, based on detailed measurements and photographs of the actual sailing ship. The collected data and images were used to construct a realistic-looking virtual ship, and photographic textures were applied to the virtual model. Jocko was modeled by scanning the face of a GreyStone employee and putting it on the agent's avatar.

The original concept for the experience was simply to allow the participant to sail from one point to another in a race situation. However, the GreyStone developers pointed out that this scenario would result in the better players having a shorter, less rewarding experience. As a way of increasing interest in the product, the player should be made responsible for the safety of the product. The advertising agency liked this idea, so they pursued the experience with the more complex narrative.

During development and play-testing, players experienced each hazard sequence for 60 seconds. This provided enough time to become familiar with each new environment and learn enough skills to survive. However, as a marketing device, the number of people given the opportunity to try the experience was very important. Thus, the entire experience was limited to 3 minutes, from the time the player signaled they were ready to set sail to the display of the final score. This length meant the time spent with each hazard had to be reduced by about half, and the game was never play-balanced for the shorter times.

The shorter play sequences also meant that many of the details present in the application were not apparent to the participants. For example, the raider boat contained two men, one steering and one on the bow holding a tommy gun and balancing himself against the waves. As the boat approached, the man lowered the gun and aimed it at the player's ship. The sense of self-protection is lessened when the player is too rushed to notice such details.

Conclusion

The goal of the application was to raise product awareness, so as with any campaign, the effectiveness of the advertising was measured both in awareness levels and sales.

In follow-up surveys, 80–90% of the players were found to remember the brand name associated with the experience four months later. Overall brand awareness levels were at an all-time high, and sales that had been declining for over a decade had turned around.

It is difficult to directly measure the relationship between who participated in the experience and who makes future purchases. Gregg Zegras, account executive for the Cutty Sark campaign at Scaros & Casselman, suggests that other industries have better opportunities to make such measurements. For example, if the NHL, or specific hockey teams, sponsored a VR experience, they could compare the list of VR participants with new purchasers of season tickets.

Although it consumed a large percentage of their advertising budget, the turnaround in sales and awareness were very effective for Hiram Walker. They saw their sales increase for the first time in 15 years. In addition, the campaign itself was the winner of the Advertising Age Media and Marketing award in the "Consumer Kiosk" category.

However, the difficulty of booking a touring exhibit and moving the units from venue to venue made continuing this line of advertising impractical. Zegras feels that using VR to draw in customers can be effective in the right situations. In particular, it would be more beneficial if enough display units are constructed to allow them to remain at venues for much greater lengths of time. Again, a hockey experience located at a fixed venue in towns with professional hockey teams may be able to hit the right market, without the need for the logistical difficulties of a touring event.

Although the participants probably don't think they are actually breaking any laws by their action of smuggling "the virtual McCoy," and wouldn't have considered the dangers encountered in the experience to be life-threatening, they certainly found the experience to be memorable, as shown by the follow-up surveys. The experience was successful at accomplishing the goal of creating an application that would get people to live an experience associated with the product, and therefore remember the message (advertisement) longer.

It is vital to understand, however, that what is of the utmost importance is the story itself, not the medium. Virtual reality may be part of why people come to expose themselves to the experience, but it is the story that draws them in and stays in their memory. Content is key. However, the participatory nature of the experience may have been compromised by the constraint of increasing throughput. Participants would be yanked from one scenario to the next without much opportunity to settle into each scene.

This was the first time a virtual reality advertising experience was created that included the product as part of the virtual world. The result was a resounding success both as a means of advertising and in introducing the medium of VR to several thousand people. In general, Gregg Zegras believes that while the cost of using virtual reality experiences as advertising is much higher per person than traditional advertising, achieving the same impressions using direct mail would have cost a lot more. The advertisement doesn't reach 10 million people, but the thousands of people it does reach are left with an indelible impression. In this case, Zegras feels that overall the VR Cutty Sark experience "helped the brand's recognition more so than anything else they'd done in the last 3 to 4 years prior."

CHAPTER 4

Science Applications

Achieving breakthrough science requires brilliant people, dedication, and the proper laboratories and tools. The computer has become an essential, sophisticated laboratory tool that provides capabilities that were not possible before. One thing the computer does is enable the scientist to manage huge volumes of data. Scientists acquire data through observations, often using instruments such as radio telescopes, electron microscopes, etc., as well as by synthesizing data by computational modeling of natural phenomena that result in highly refined simulations.

A major problem that confronts the scientist is how to make sense of the billions of numbers provided by these data sources. Hence, the field of scientific visualization was born in which scientific data is represented as visual images for the purpose of data analysis and presentation. Virtual reality is also a powerful tool in enabling scientists to explore the world via related techniques such as telepresence. Telepresence allows a scientist to be virtually present in places that are not normally possible because they are too dangerous, too far away, too small, too large, or otherwise not conducive to human visitation.

Many of the phenomena that scientists study are three-dimensional (or more) in nature. Thus, it is a natural outgrowth of the field of scientific visualization to take advantage of the three-dimensional nature of virtual reality display and interaction techniques.

4.1 AREAS OF APPLICATION

Scientists have applied virtual reality to scientific visualization in a number of fields. Computational fluid dynamics allows the scientist to simulate flow under various conditions. The ability to visualize flow allows the scientist to better understand the fluid's interaction with objects in the environment (such as the flow of air over a wing, or blood through an artery). Because most flow is three dimensional, the three-dimensional virtual interface is often advantageous.

The buildings we live in are three dimensional in nature. Understanding their structural properties allows engineers to design and build safer buildings that are able to stand under heavy wind conditions, earthquakes, etc. Finite element models of structures, beams, automobile fenders, etc., can be visualized in virtual reality and allow the scientists to understand their behavior under varying conditions. Chemists, biochemists, and others are interested in how atoms and molecules interact. The ability to visualize those interactions is a powerful tool in understanding basic reactions, drug design, properties of materials, and much more.

The ideas discussed above are but the tip of the iceberg in current and future uses for scientific visualization in virtual reality environments.

4.1.1   Exploration

Many areas of science require the scientist to leave their laboratory and go into the field for observation, data collection, experimentation, and other duties. To do so sometimes involves considerable expense, danger, time, and inconvenience. Consider space exploration. NASA has spent billions of dollars, as well as the cost of lost lives, to allow scientists to gather data from space. However, the benefits from such exploration have been immense. Virtual reality and related technologies such as telepresence are allowing scientists to explore remote areas from the safety and comfort of their own laboratories. These technologies are also allowing scientists to explore areas that have never been explored before, such as the bottom of the ocean, within nuclear waste dumps, and other areas that are hostile to human life.

This chapter illustrates the use of telepresence as an aid in exploring under the ocean, as well as the surface of Mars.

4.1.2   Physical system simulation and interaction

In many cases it is advantageous to be able to visualize and manipulate objects in a simulated or real system. For example, in the *GRIP* application described later in this chapter scientists are able to reach out and physically manipulate representations of molecules, and observe visually their interactions. In addition, the scientist is able to feel the forces between molecules via a haptic interface. Another example of physical simulation and interaction is the Air Force solar system modeler, which allows scientists and engineers to observe locations of planets and other celestial objects, as well as satellites and other man-made objects from various perspectives, and at various times in the past and in the future.

There are many overlaps between applications in this chapter and applications discussed in other chapters of this book. For example, the scientific visualization application *Crumbs* has found many applications in the medical field due to the reliance of physicians on image data from three-dimensional objects. In the field of virtual prototyping, additional information can be overlaid on the models to visualize concerns such as stress, strain, temperature hot spots, etc. In much the same way that scientific visualization tools educate the scientist in matters of what data indicates, these same tools can be used for educating students about scientific phenomena. Finally, these same tools may find use in the fields of anthropology, archeology, and any study of natural phenomena, such as Sandia's RAPTOR study, detailed in Chapter 7.

Another path for visualization in virtual reality is to enable current visualization tools to exploit the new capabilities of virtual reality. This allows scientists who are already familiar with visualizing their data using common software packages to take advantage of the immersive VR environment. This process includes packages such as *AVS, COVISE,* and *SciRun* adapted to *CAVE* environments.

Finally, as computational power increases, existing bottlenecks in simulation and visualization will be relieved. For example, Professor Eric Loth extended the notion of computational fluid dynamics visualization in *CAVE* environments to also support multiphasic conditions. Virtual reality has already demonstrated its utility in the scientific process, and new developments will allow scientists to use VR to aid them in understanding and explaining more areas of difficult scientific problems.

Scientists are often among the early adopters of applying new technology in their work. Virtual reality is no exception. Many early examples of applied VR come from the labs of NASA, where researchers began exploring it as a means for space exploration and visualization in the 1980s. Whereas NASA had to develop the technology as well as the applications, more recently many more scientists have been able to experiment with VR by using established VR hardware and software.

The primary goal of science is to explore natural phenomena around us, and derive explanations of what is found. We often refer to the originations of new explanations as *insight*. The use of various media (sketches, written word, x-ray photography, and now virtual reality) has played an important role in the process of gaining insight.

4.1.3 Areas of application in science

Scientists have used virtual reality to interface with their work in three primary ways: the visualization of observed and simulated data, exploration of places that are difficult to travel to, and direct interaction with simulations of physical systems.

- Scientific visualization
- Scientific exploration
- Physical system simulation and interaction

The applications presented here cover these application areas in whole or in part, and give insight into the possibility of virtual reality for scientific applications.

CASE STUDY 4.1: VIRTUAL WINDTUNNEL

Executive Summary

One of the earliest scientific uses of virtual reality was the application from NASA Ames known as the *Virtual Windtunnel* The *Virtual Windtunnel* portrays many interesting ideas that persist to this day, which is remarkable since the application designers had virtually no predecessors to emulate. The *Virtual Windtunnel* is used in a head-mounted display with a data glove, a *BOOM* display, and in projection-based displays.

The *Virtual Windtunnel* allows scientists and others to experiment with computed flow fields in a virtual environment that allows an actual wind tunnel to be emulated, as well as allowing additional capabilities not found in typical wind tunnels. The *Virtual Windtunnel* emulates many common tools used in an actual wind tunnel, such as allowing the scientist to release "smoke" in the flow field. In an actual wind tunnel the act of introducing smoke affects the flow field. In the simulated environment, however, the scientist can choose to have their tools affect the flow field or not. The *Virtual Windtunnel* application provided an example to others of the capabilities of virtual reality for scientific discovery and explanation. Although the application was built in the laboratory, many versions of the application have been demonstrated in numerous venues allowing others, including the general public, to learn more about computational fluid dynamics, fluid flows, and virtual reality.

Introduction

A critical problem for scientists and engineers is to understand the unsteady flow of fluids. In particular, it is of great importance to analyze the effects generated as a solid object passes through some fluid medium, or vice versa. One means of understanding these flows is through computational modeling. However, computational models of complex systems generate too much data to be analyzed as individual numbers. Instead, scientific visualization is often used to aid in the analysis process.

The task of visualizing the output of computational simulations in three dimensions is itself a nontrivial problem. The *Virtual Windtunnel* from the NASA Ames Research Center is a system that addresses the problem of visualizing the results of such complex three dimensional simulations using virtual reality. The *Virtual Windtunnel* allows a researcher to interactively explore flow fields in a three-dimensional virtual world using common visualization techniques.

Steve Bryson and Creon Levit began work on The *Virtual Windtunnel* application in 1989. The concept of the visualization tool came out of the NASA Ames Virtual Interface Environment Workstation (View) Lab (Michael McGreevey and Scott Fisher) working with physicist Creon Levit as a project to establish the potential benefits of the medium of virtual reality. The project has continued to evolve, and in 1998 was released on the Internet for others to use.

Application Description

The *Virtual Windtunnel* application was a pioneering virtual reality application in the field of fluid dynamics. Prior to the existence of the *Virtual Windtunnel*, experiments such as studying the airflow over a wing were carried out in actual wind tunnels. In an actual wind tunnel, techniques such as releasing smoke into the wind tunnel allowed scientists to see the flow of air over the wing. The *Virtual Windtunnel* allowed scientists to see flows over a virtual wing using scientific visualization techniques such as particles and streamlines. The *Virtual Windtunnel* was primarily experienced using a *BOOM* device.

The *Virtual Windtunnel* was also made into a desktop application for those scenarios that did not require VR hardware, and for times when VR equipment was not available.

Representation of the Virtual World

In the immersive display systems the virtual world consists of any objects involved in the computational experiment (such as an airplane wing, or the body of the space shuttle) as well as the flow field and its representations. There are a variety of tools that allow the user to visualize the flow with some graphical metaphor to a real-world equivalent representation. For example, as in the real world, "smoke" can be released into the virtual world to view the flow from an arbitrary location. Unlike the real world, the presence of measuring tools does not affect the flow. The ability to measure without interference is very useful in exploring sensitive areas such as boundary layers and chaotic regions.

The visualization tools are derived from common idioms used in many computational fluid dynamics (CFD) visualization applications. Idioms include vector data fields represented by streaklines, particle paths, streamlines, and material tracing. Scalar data can also be visualized with techniques such as global or local isosurfacing, pseudo-color mapping, and probing the data to view the underlying numeric values [Sherman et al. 1997].

The location of the gloved hand or handheld pointer is represented in the scene as a 3D crosshair marker. This avatar allows the user to get a better sense of the position of their hand relative to the other objects in the world. Only visual information is displayed to the participant. Users of the tool have not expressed a significant interest in other sensory modalities such as sound or haptic feedback. Therefore, no effort has been made to integrate other sensory rendering/display into the package.

Interaction with the Virtual World

Each tool has a set of "grab points" that allow the user to do different things. Depending on which "point" is grabbed, the user can "grab-and-move" in order to move the source of the visualization to a new location, or resize or otherwise adjust the tool. The display is continually updated to reflect the flow in the new region. There are a variety of visualization techniques, and display options that the user can control.

Travel is performed by a method common to all the interface devices that this application has been used in the "world-in-hand" paradigm. In both the *BOOM* and the *Responsive WorkBench (RWB)*, the user can grab the world to move and orient it in any direction, allowing them to view the world as they desire. Both display types also allow for some form of physical locomotion to adjust the user's perspective on the world, but with some limitations imposed by the nature of the displays.

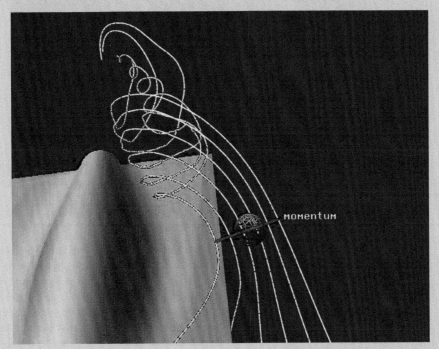

FIGURE 4-1

This example visualization shows streaklines over an airfoil. The control bar allows the user to change the location by grabbing the ball, or to affect the number of streaks by stretching or contracting the bar.

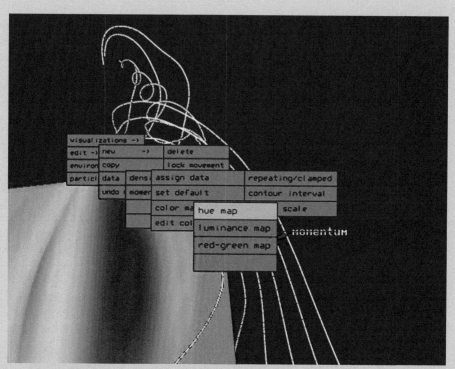

FIGURE 4-2

The Virtual Windtunnel *provides hierarchical, pop-up menus to allow users to select from various options.*

The *BOOM* display allows users to physically walk through the data, and turn their head in any direction, but has limited reach. The mechanical linkages of the *BOOM* also limit the user from walking to certain locations. When using the *RWB* display the user cannot walk around to all sides of the table or through the table, and consequently the virtual world. Thus, physical locomotion must be supplemented by other travel techniques. The "world-in-hand" interface paradigm accommodates both types of displays and allows the user to view the world from any relative position. To activate world-in-hand travel in the *RWB*, the user points to open space, presses the pointer button to "grab" the world, and moves the pointer to cause the same relative movement of the virtual world. Both the *BOOM* and *RWB* version provide controls for the users to change the relative scale between themselves and the world, as well as move and manipulate the visualization tools.

In addition to physical locomotion and world-in-hand travel, some demonstration versions of the *Virtual Windtunnel* also provided the point-to-fly travel paradigm, which may be more familiar to participants at the particular demonstration venue. In particular, the *BOOM*/glove system allowed the user to travel by putting their gloved hand into the pointing posture and guiding the direction of travel by pointing to their desired destination.

A user can also control the visualization parameters. This interaction is done from within the virtual world via hierarchical pop-up menus. Menus are invoked by making a "pointing" posture at empty space with the gloved hand. They then select an item by pointing their index finger to their choice and releasing the hand-posture. The menus are hierarchical to better organize the set of choices.

Venue

Although the *Virtual Windtunnel* was originally designed in a laboratory setting, the application has been demonstrated in many venues using a variety of technologies. Many people

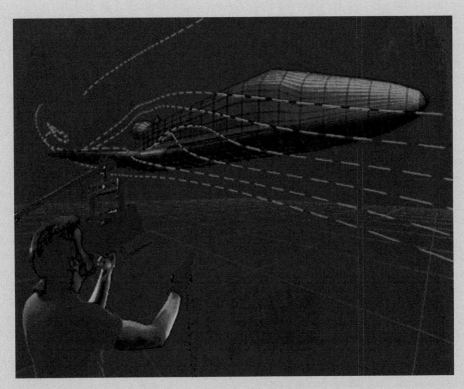

FIGURE 4-3

A view of Virtual Windtunnel *creator Steve Bryson using a* BOOM *to view streamlines over the wing of a space shuttle. The upper portion of the photo shows the image Bryson is currently viewing. Bryson uses a DataGlove to enter commands via hand gestures.*

gained their first exposure to virtual reality by witnessing the *Virtual Windtunnel* at conferences and other public settings. The application has been experienced by numerous people, from rocket scientists to first-graders. In addition to its originating lab at NASA-Ames, *Virtual Windtunnel* has been ported to different display technologies in other laboratories such as the *Responsive WorkBench*. Additionally, researchers at Brown University have created a separate user interface.

VR System

The initial version of the *Virtual Windtunnel* used a *BOOM* display device, a stereoscopic, head-tracked viewing device. A glove was worn to allow the user to interact with the system by issuing commands via hand postures. Parameters of the visualization tools were entered via a traditional keyboard and mouse. Use of the *BOOM*-style VR display was

convenient because it still allowed the user access to the computer keyboard.

With little time involved in "suiting up," transitioning between the VR display and the keyboard is quick and easy. The user can remove their head from the *BOOM*, use the traditional workstation for manipulating selected parameters, tand hen bring the *BOOM* back to their face.

Later, the *Virtual Windtunnel* was equipped to handle a variety of input and output devices such as the RWB tabletop projection system.[1]

----

[1]or the *Immersive WorkBench,* as the version marketed by Fakespace Inc. is called.

In the *WorkBench* version, a handheld pointer device with a single button replaces the glove input. This changes the interface somewhat in that there are less direct control inputs available to the user because they can only push a single button. With the *BOOM*/glove system the user can generate multiple hand postures and still use the buttons mounted on the handle of the *BOOM* display, allowing the operator more flexibility.

The *Virtual Windtunnel* also gives the option of using a desktop monitor and mouse interface for situations when it is impractical, or unnecessary, to utilize the VR displays. Because the application was designed to be interactive, many people have found benefits in using the *Virtual Windtunnel* even as a desktop application.

Application Implementation

Though commonly used to examine precomputed datasets stored locally on the graphics workstation, the application developers extended the capabilities of the application by providing an interface that enables the simulation computations to be calculated on a remote supercomputer, and delivered to The *Virtual Windtunnel* via a high-speed network. The first step was to introduce an asynchronous process to produce the visualization representations, apart from the rendering of the visualization. This separation allowed the user to continue interacting with the virtual world in a smooth, continuous manner.

Access to greater computational resources enabled the exploration of time-varying simulations. However, expanding from the visualization of static steady-state flow simulations to time-varying simulations led to a significantly more complicated data management issue. There are a variety of time-management issues that arise in applications that allow the user to control simulation time. Recent implementations of the *Virtual Windtunnel* address many of these issues in interesting ways [Bryson and Johan].

A particularly interesting feature of The *Virtual Windtunnel* is the use of a "computational budget" to maintain high frame rates of both the graphical rendering and the computation of subsequent time steps. Bryson and Johan assert: "Many researchers have indicated that when interactively exploring a data set they would rather have a fast, less accurate answer than a slow accurate answer."

Thus, for example, if a large number of particles are used to show the flow in some region, the computation of the particle locations cannot be done quickly enough with a more complex algorithm (e.g., fourth-order Runge-Kutta). In these cases, computation switches to a less accurate but faster algorithm (e.g., second-order Runge-Kutta) until there are enough resources to reinstate the more accurate algorithm.

Related Applications and Follow-on Work

We use the term "Virtual Windtunnel" in this chapter to refer to the specific virtual reality application. However, many programs and systems bear the same moniker. One system by Denford Ltd of West Yorkshire England provides CFD simulation and visualization for vehicles and is aimed at a wide audience of general users. Though the creators advertise the product with the term "virtual reality," the application does not involve any tracking, stereo, or kinesthetic input and therefore does not fit the genre of virtual reality as we define it in this work. Other "virtual windtunnels" include freely available simple Java programs, interfaces through Web pages, and specific applications of Flovent software (made by The Mechanical Analysis Division of Mentor Graphics Corporation, formerly Flomerics).

The obvious application that (Bryson and Johan's) *Virtual Windtunnel* addresses is the need to visualize computational fluid dynamics data, and the adoption of the "Virtual Windtunnel" name by several related applications testifies to this fact. Perhaps a most illustrative example of a fully VR implementation to merge the CFD and visualization worlds is *VE-Suite*. Originally developed at Iowa State University by the Virtual Engineering Research Group under the direction of Professor Mark Bryden., *VE-Suite* is now available in open-source format under the GNU Lesser General Public License.

VE-Suite focuses on allowing the user to simultaneously generate engineering simulations and visualize the resulting data. The integration of these two often-disconnected actions allows fast design iterations and real-time decision making. Bryden states,

> *"VE-Suite is a tool to develop complete virtual environments that include graphics, physics, and*

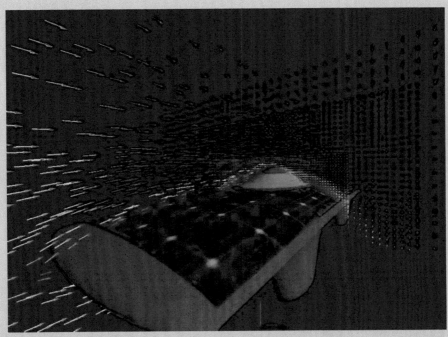

FIGURE 4-4

VE-Suite *provides a multifaceted interface for visualization of computational fluid dynamics data as well as several other engineering applications.*

easily understood user interactions. It can be used across many display hardware configurations, from desktop to the largest multiwall stereo displays. VE-Suite is currently used in a number of companies, national labs, and universities. VE-Suite has been used on applications ranging from finance, engineering, biology, processing plants, and materials science. In 2006 VE-Suite won a R&D 100 award for being one of the top 100 R&D developments of the year."

Conclusion

The *Virtual Windtunnel* is an example of a virtual reality application that is based on a complex simulation of natural phenomena. Many of the "virtual" techniques implemented in the application have their origins in real-world measurement techniques. In the virtual world, however, there are fewer constraints on the number and location of tools since the "virtual" tools don't interfere with the experiment.

Most of the equipment used during the project was also shared with other efforts, especially the large Silicon Graphics workstation computers. The budget for this project varied, but was approximately one million dollars spent over the course of the first 7 years.

The *Virtual Windtunnel* was a successful VR application on many levels. First, it was an early demonstration of a scholarly use of the medium of virtual reality. Second, it provided some users within NASA a tool that helped them gain new insights about their data. Finally, it led to interaction techniques that were found to be useful even on a nonimmersive desktop system.

FIGURE 4-5

Mark Bryden and Steve Gent use VE-Suite *to analyze the airflow through the fan blade of an engine.*

Prior to release to the general public, there were few users at NASA and elsewhere that worked with various versions of the application. Feedback from these users was generally positive. Many users reported that they like the ability to directly manipulate the visualization tools to view their data, and some reported that they found new features in datasets with which they already had considerable experience viewing via other technologies. The release of the code to the public was done in order to gain a wider audience of application.

In addition to cofounding programmers Bryson and Levit, other significant contributions have been made by Sandy Johan, Brian Green, David Whitney, Leslie Schlecht, David Kenwright, David Kao, and Tom Meyer.

Steve Bryson summarizes the benefits he sees in virtual reality as demonstrated by the *Virtual Windtunnel* project:

> *The virtual windtunnel presents abstract phenomena with a strong 3D presence and allows you to explore that phenomena in a completely intuitive manner. We've found that from first grade students to seasoned CFD researchers, people reach a quicker understanding and have a stronger memory of the abstract phenomena through intuitive exploration combined with a strong 3D presentation. I think this is the power of virtual reality: by hiding the computer interface, total intuitive and natural focus on the virtual world provides a quicker and more compelling grasp of what's happening in that world.*

CASE STUDY 4.2: ARMY CORPS OF ENGINEERS

BayWalk

The Army Corps of Engineers Waterways Experimentation Station (CEWES), in Vicksburg, Mississippi, completed an extensive study using VR to visualize the Chesapeake Bay. CEWES collaborated with the National Center for Supercomputing Applications (NCSA) to produce another VR application for visualizing the bay. This project served several purposes. One of the primary purposes was as a technology transfer project. CEWES had acquired an *ImmersaDesk* and was interested in doing a collaborative project with NCSA to gain experience in applying it to scientific applications. Of several possible projects, NCSA was especially attracted to the Chesapeake Bay project due to the importance of the bay, as well as the fact that the simulation of the bay was computationally complex and highly multivariate.

Application Description

The *BayWalk* application was created primarily as a scientific visualization and collaboration tool for exploring the results of a complex computational science simulation. In the computational model, the three-dimensional bay was divided into 4000 volumetric cells or "bricks." The simulation calculates flow information and the presence of certain substances throughout the bay over time. There are many variables at each cell in the simulation. However, for the initial study only three were visualized—*chlorophyll, salinity,* and *dissolved oxygen*. More recently, two more variables were added—*nitrogen* and *phosphorus*. (The latter two are of particular interest because they are contained in fertilizer, one of the sources of ecological concern.) The computational model has been calibrated to match observed data by modifying coefficients and other computational parameters so that the simulation results based on known initial conditions match the actual results observed in nature.

Representation in *BayWalk*

As with most virtual reality experiences, *BayWalk* is represented primarily visually. To begin with, the participant sees a planar representation of the bay with text markings and symbols to give landmark locations, including city and river names. On command from menus controlled by the wand, the participant can turn on and off a variety of visual representations, including the computational grid, glyphs,

cutting planes, and volumetric idioms. These representations are very useful for the scientist, and given some explanation, can also aid the nonexpert viewer in understanding how the computational model works.

One of the visualization tools available is a display consisting of "glyphs" that indicate the scalar values of some subset of the data within each cell. In the original version, the three variables were mapped to a three-vector axes where the length of each axis indicated the amount of that chemical. Chlorophyll was mapped to the green vector, salinity to magenta, and dissolved oxygen to white. These glyphs enable the researcher to see relationships between the variables as the simulation proceeds over time.

One modification was to add two new variables (amount of nitrogen and phosphorus-limiting potential) to the glyph display. The glyph was modified to show all five variables on a five-pronged display. The nitrogen-limiting potential is represented as blue and phosphorus red.

Over the change of seasons one can observe that in the spring runoff, high levels of nutrients are carried into the bay generating an algae bloom (indicated by an increase in chlorophyll). Later in the season the algae dies and falls to the bottom of the bay. It decomposes there, consuming oxygen in the process. This is evident from the shortening white vectors in the depths of the bay. The researchers indicated that this tool has proven effective, and even nonscientists have been able to understand the dynamics of these environmental interactions. By including the phosphorus and nitrogen-limiting potentials, the viewer can see that over the course of a year there is a seasonal switch from phosphorus to nitrogen. During the spring algae bloom, the system is phosphorus-limited, whereas during the period of summer maximum productivity, the system is nitrogen-limited. Another visualization tool available in the system is an "orthogonal" slicing plane—orthogonal with respect to how the data are stored. The slicing plane is a two-dimensional surface that cuts through the data. It displays a color mapping based on the value of the chosen variable at each point the plane intersects. The data grid is irregularly shaped, but it is roughly aligned to and regularly spaced across the Cartesian axes. The plane can be

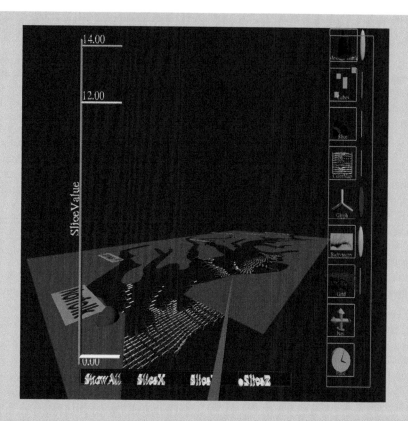

FIGURE 4-6

Abstract glyphs are used to show the concentrations of oxygen, chlorophyll, and salinity. The length of each axis of the glyph represents the amount of each substance. The color indicates the substance.

translated along any of the Cartesian axes, and a submenu provides a selection of data values that can be represented (Salinity, chlorophyll concentrations, etc.).

A simple crude isosurface can be generated by selecting a tool that colors all the bricks that fall within a user-selected range of data values.

Travel and other Interaction in *BayWalk*

The handheld wand is used by the participant to travel through the virtual space, travel through time, and select menu items. Travel is by pointer-directed fly-through, allowing the user to easily control movement throughout the entire data space. All other interactions are performed through a menu system.

The menu system is context sensitive and displays a list of choices based on the current interaction mode. The main menu (for toggling visual representations and setting the current mode) can be activated either by holding the wand above it (useful on the *ImmersaDesk* display), or when the wand is pointing at it (more useful for Wall or *CAVE*-projected displays). Once the main menu is activated, the pressure joystick on the wand is used to slide choices up and down the menu, and to stop on the desired selection. Certain selections may invoke other controls, such as submenus, or a slider.

The interface limits the user to control only one thing at a time. More importantly, this co-use of moving the wand and its joystick both for travel and for menu interactions

FIGURE 4-7
A slicing plane is texture mapped with colors that represent the chosen variable.

can cause interference and confusion. As the user travels through the space, they can very easily activate the menu system as they move the wand to specify direction. This accidental activation of the menu causes them not only to stop moving, but also to change the menu selection, since the pressure they are applying to the joystick now affects the menu.

A slider interface appears on the screen when specific menu selections are made. The slider is used for moving a cutting plane throughout the data, or to manipulate time. The dataset used in the original version covers a period of one year allowing the user to analyze the annual stages of the ecosystem. The slider, located at the left side of the main viewing surface (e.g., front wall of the *CAVE*) is used to select the time value for which simulated data to use. Animation of the data over time can only be done by manually sliding the time control. Thus, there is no way to put time in motion, and simultaneously manipulate other features or navigate through the data as time advances.

Collaboration in *BayWalk*

Because of interest in the bay by geographically diverse researchers, this VR experience was created as a collaborative tool that can be used by multiple participants in

FIGURE 4-8

In the BayWalk application, the main menu is vertically oriented, whereas submenus related to the chosen menu appear horizontally.

separate geographic locations. It was designed to allow any number of participants, but was tested with only two.

Each user is represented in the environment by a fish-shaped avatar. The position and orientation of each user's wand is represented by a pointer emanating from the fish. Combined with an audio communication channel, collaborators can have discussions and observe where other participants are looking and pointing.

In a collaborative session, a multicast connection is usually established. The multicast session appears on an *ImmersaDesk* and allows the participants to see and hear each other as well as the surrounding environment at the remote location. The multicast connection has proven especially valuable when demonstrating the system to observers who are unfamiliar with the system. Even if appearing in a separate window on the screen, seeing the remote collaborator and their lab makes it more obvious that collaboration is taking place, and that the fish is a representation of what the remote users are doing in the virtual space. The video feedback also aids the collaborators in understanding what is happening at the other end.

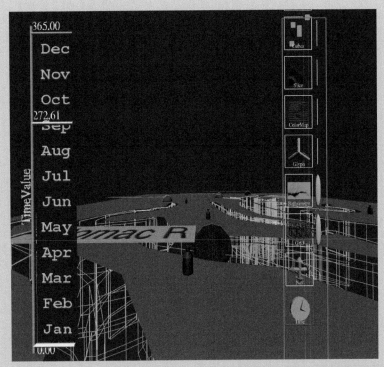

FIGURE 4-9

The passage of time in the BayWalk application is depicted by a vertical timeline. The timeline can also be used to set the view to a particular time.

For example, the local user can see when other people enter the collaborator's lab and call them away from the system. If the other participant takes off their glasses and lays them upside down on a table, without the video/audio connection, it would look as though that person's fish went "belly up" with no explanation.

In addition to collaborating in a live two-way communication session, some experiments have been done to allow researchers to collaborate by leaving annotations in the *BayWalk* world. Messages can be deposited in the virtual world in the form of voice annotations. The voice messages are left using the metaphor of a "message in a bottle," that is, wherever an annotation is left a bottle icon is placed in the world. By pointing at the bottle and pressing a button, other researchers can access the information. The same researcher may even access the annotation in a future interactive session.

The message in the bottle paradigm enables a certain amount of asynchronous collaboration to take place. In the initial instantiation, the annotations do not persist across sessions. To reduce bandwidth requirements for collaborative data exploration, each site has a copy of the computational data on their local computer. Thus, the only data transmitted between sites is user positions with the positions of their wands, and if utilized, the multicast communication and voice messages.

VR System

This application was written using the *SGI Performer* (2.0) library and C++. The *CAVE* library handles the multiple-screen display, tracking, wand events, sharing user information between sites, and other virtual reality aspects of the interaction. The initial version, demonstrated publicly at the Supercomputing '96 conference held in Pittsburgh, took about 6 months to complete.

Initially, it took approximately 8 hours on a Cray Y-MP supercomputer to run a simulation encompassing 1 year. This is not fast enough for the researchers who had a goal of doing a 50-year simulation. Thus, the VR application was run as a post process to the supercomputer simulation. The simulation results were computed and stored, and could then be explored using a variety of tools at whatever time scale the researchers desire. Later, the code was optimized to calculate a 20-year simulation in less than a real day, a 50-fold speedup. The researchers later moved the program to a Cray T3E. Running on 64 processors, this platform could simulate 20 years in less than a day on a 10,000-cell grid.

Originally designed for the *ImmersaDesk,* the application also runs in the *CAVE* environment. Because the application was specifically designed for the *ImmersaDesk,* which has an angled viewing surface, some user interface elements required minor adjustment to display correctly on the other devices. The *CAVE* library also supported display in head-mounted displays.

The application authors originally planned to enhance the ability to interactively probe a region of interest in the bay in high detail. This capability would more fully exploit the capabilities of a VR system by offering an "inside out" view of the data in addition to the "outside in" view that is how the current system is typically used. Without the ability to probe the dataset in detail at a given place, it is less relevant to know where your collaborator is positioned in the virtual environment. When allowed to probe into the data, it then becomes interesting to see what region the collaborator is exploring.

A possible enhancement to the synchronous collaboration interface that was considered was to duplicate control information between sites, so one user could manipulate how all sites see the visualization. Such a capability would allow a scientist who is trying to demonstrate a feature or an interesting aspect of the data to those at another site to show them directly by controlling their movement and

tools, rather than have to explain exactly how to set all the controls and requiring them to make those adjustments. Changing to a persistent storage of annotations between collaborative sessions would also enhance the usefulness as a collaborative tool.

Other than the multicast session and the voice messages, there is no audio used in this application. There are no immediate plans for using audio to provide sonification, but some feedback for menu interaction, etc., is desirable. Voice input is also a desired feature. With voice input, much of the problems caused by interference of the menu with the travel interface can be reduced.

Related Applications and Follow-on Work

One of the first applications of virtual reality to the visualization of oceanographic data was a collaborative effort between Old Dominion University and NCSA entitled *A Walk Through Chesapeake Bay* [Wheles et al.]. This *CAVE* application, first shown at the VROOM venue of the SIGGRAPH '94 computer graphics conference in Orlando, Florida, consisted of a three-dimensional graphical representation of a Chesapeake Bay bathymetry dataset textured and colored according to depth. Integrated into the virtual world were transparent isosurfaces derived from monthly composites of Chesapeake Bay surface salinity observations.

The bay research at Old Dominion focuses on seasonal effects on the marine life of the bay caused by pollutants and nutrients carried into the bay via the river systems and its interface with the Atlantic Ocean. The initial version of this application cycled over a full year. The user could activate the movement of time and simultaneously walk about the bay to explore the data. The passage of time was indicated by a clock icon that displayed one revolution per year, with each season identified by an icon on the clock. The user can observe the annual changes in salinity found in the bay due to increased freshwater runoff in the spring and heightened evaporation in the summer and fall. By peering just under the translucent sea surface, the user could view the main shipping channels and the abrupt topographic variations in the bathymetry.

An ambient soundtrack aided in achieving a sense of participant immersion. When the participant was above water,

FIGURE 4-10
The Chesapeake Bay application provides a number of visual representations, including colored isosurfaces and vector arrows.

sea gulls and other beach sounds could be heard. Under water, bubbling and other underwater sounds helped the participant realize they were under the surface of the bay. A splash sound was made each time the participant crossed the boundary entering the water. When leaving the water, the participant heard the squawk of a gull indicating their return to the atmosphere.

In the initial prototype version of this experience, the virtual world consisted only of the bathymetry, salinity isosurfaces, and a few landmarks to indicate the geographic location of the bay. This allowed the researcher to examine and explain to others only some of the seasonal changes of the estuary system. Although the early prototype VR application was groundbreaking from both the standpoint of applying virtual reality to oceanographic information

as well as for viewing the annual salinity cycle in the Chesapeake Bay, it was obvious that more functionality was necessary. The next logical step was the development of a visualization framework to more easily integrate the results from *any* coupled physical-biological model into the virtual environment.

The application developers routinely use *CAVE5D* on their *ImmersaDesk* located in the Virtual Environments Laboratory at the Center for Coastal Physical Oceanography (CCPO) at Old Dominion University, where the freely available software is maintained and enhanced. It has been used to create virtual environments useful for the examination of the effects of flow on fish distributions in Beaufort Inlet, North Carolina [Wheless et al.], as well as the tidal circulation in Ponce Inlet, Florida.

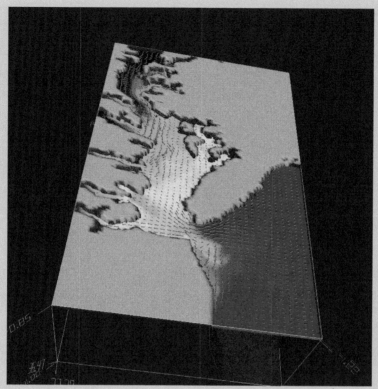

FIGURE 4-11

Color, vectors, and depth provide details regarding the Chesapeake Bay in a virtual reality experience utilizing an ImmersaDesk.

Conclusion

In summary, this application works well as a demonstration of applied computational science. It is a good example which people are likely to understand because the content is familiar to them and can be used to tell an interesting and educational story. The public seemed to enjoy the notion of going for a virtual "walk under the bay." From a science perspective, this application demonstrates great promise. The scientists involved have stated that this tool appears to be useful and beneficial to their research.

For the ODU *CAVE5D* project, the visualization files for *CBVE* provide the basis for the virtual environment and normally consist of a few hundred frames of multivariate data. These files routinely were as large as 450 Mbytes. Complete functionality in the networked interactive mode would

require that these visualization files be rendered at a sufficient frame rate (usually greater than 20/sec). If all graphics information is sent across the network, a sustained network throughput of much greater than 155 Mbits/sec would be required, which was too aggressive at the time. The commonality between the CEWES application and *CBVE* indicates that collaborative work between the sites would have enhanced both applications.

In addition to research on the Chesapeake Bay, other research institutions have used VR to visualize oceanographic simulations. Many of these institutions would be able to use some of the packages developed by ODU and CEWES in conjunction with NCSA. For example, Mississippi State University has done some interesting visualizations of water flow through the Sea of Japan using a FakeSpace

PUSH display, and in the NCSA *CAVE* [Gaither et al.]. They have now built their own *CAVE*-like system, which enables collaboration with other *CAVE* sites. By sharing work and combining efforts teams of researchers throughout the world will be able to create better tools for the specific purposes such as the oceanographic research.

Wheless says:

At present, the use of VR allows environmental scientists, educators, students and managers to collaboratively view, analyze and interact with very large data sets in a way that is understandable and intuitive. By adding persistence to the shared virtual environment, so that the virtual space remains operating and changing independently of the users involved, we will enable worldwide participation and will allow raw data to become usable information and then cognitively useful knowledge.

CASE STUDY 4.3: NASA TELEPRESENCE

VEVI toolkit

The mere mention of the name "NASA" conjures images of high-tech equipment, adventure, and exploring new frontiers. And while NASA's primary mission is the exploration of space, they put many new technologies to the test right here on Earth. Two technologies that NASA has used for exploring unfriendly terrestrial terrain are virtual reality and telepresence.

Historically, NASA has been at the forefront in developing applied virtual reality systems. Earlier in this chapter we looked at the *Virtual Windtunnel,* which is one of NASA's uses of VR for the visualization of fluid flow around a solid body. The NASA Intelligent Mechanisms Group (IMG) is using telepresence and immersive displays to learn how to improve their ability to more efficiently control remote devices (e.g., robots).

The application described in this section uses telepresence to allow scientists to view the depths of the ocean from a first-person point of view while remaining in safety on land or on a ship. The device they use can be operated either by using a typical computer system, or by using a tracked head-based display system that remotely controls the positioning of the device and cameras on the device in a natural way, by moving their head in a manner similar to what they would do if they were actually under the ocean. A specific focus of the IMG is to investigate technologies for the exploration of

planetary surfaces and space vehicle control. When testing these technologies, the preliminary stages of development are done right here on Earth, but often in hostile locations, including under the sea, in the desert, and in and around active volcanoes. Part of the research involved the creation of a software tool to control a variety of vehicles in a variety of situations. This tool is the *Virtual Environment Vehicle Interface (VEVI).* This section focuses on the use of telepresence and other VR techniques employed in a particular mission of exploring the undersea world—one of the first where these elements were brought together at NASA.

Application Description

The first vehicle controlled by the *VEVI* system was the "Telepresence Remotely Operated Vehicle" (TROV). The TROV was designed as an undersea vehicle, where the buoyancy of the water acts as an analog to space vehicle travel. By putting the vehicle in a situation where real science is done, the system is put through a more realistic set of exercises. The TROV allowed scientists to explore, collect data, and chart the undersea world from the relative comfort and safety of the surface. The specific mission was to explore the undersea waters of the Ross Sea Ice near the McMurdo Science Station (McMurdo Sound) in Antarctica, including a benthic (ocean floor) ecological study of the region.

Much like a mission to another planet, the McMurdo Sound mission was a full-fledged scientific research project. The

FIGURE 4-12

An actual robot (top) explores the depths of the ocean. The operators are remotely located and control the robot via telepresense. A virtual re-creation of the ocean floor and the robot are seen below.

expedition leader, Dr. Carol Stoker, looked forward to discovering and cataloging the ecology of a previously unexplored undersea region. Other scientists involved with the mission include James Barry from the Monterey Bay Aquarium Research Institute (MBARI), James McClintock of the University of Alabama, and a team from the Antarctic Science Project S022. Barry was interested in learning how the dominant life-forms on the shelf vary as the depth increases, while McClintock planned to use the TROV to collect animal specimens to study their use of chemical defenses.

The TROV itself is an unmanned device for underwater exploration, remotely controlled by an operator at a significant distance. It has thruster motors to propel and steer the vehicle. Power, communication, and other electrical connections are supplied via a 340-meter tether from a console at the surface. An interface between the user and the remote location is provided via video cameras and a grasping arm mounted on the TROV. A satellite uplink connection allows the TROV to be controlled from NASA Ames Research Lab in California. Alternatively, a system at the dive site can be used.

Two control interfaces were used to interact with the TROV in this mission. The basic interface, which could be used at either site, consisted of a stereoscopic-capable computer display screen for output, and a keyboard, mouse, and joystick-equipped control box for input. The operator could view stereoscopic images and control the vehicle via the control box. No audio feedback was provided, apart from an intercom loop between the operator at Ames and the operator on the ice. This enabled the collaborators to coordinate activities, but did not provide any direct feedback from the interface with the TROV.

When controlled from NASA in California, another interface option was available—NASA's *Virtual Environment Vehicle Interface*. Using *VEVI*, the operator could view a stereoscopic computer monitor identical to the monitor used at the dive site, or use a head-tracked, stereoscopic, head-mounted VR interface.

The *VEVI* software system provides a user interface appropriate for different methods of teleoperative control. The primary methods available are supervisory control (infrequent task-level commands planned using *VEVI* and

FIGURE 4-13

A user in California controlling the vehicle in the Antarctic Ocean. The immersive interface is provided by a VR2 HMD, Logitech Ultrasound tracker, and Spaceball.

then sent to the vehicle to perform) and traded (or direct) control (commands and results are passed instantaneously between vehicle and operator) [Sheridan 1992].

The rendering system was independent of *VEVI*, and could be chosen by the mission programming team. For TROV, rendering was done using Sense8's *WorldToolKit (WTK)*. The goal was for the rendering to work adequately on a mid-range SGI (in 1994, they used an Indigo2 Extreme).

To test missions involving remote space operations, time delays can be artificially added to the communications to simulate the lag of space communication when doing terrestrial experiments. For example, whereas Moon communications take only 2.5 seconds for round-trip communications, communication between the Earth and Mars can take 4 to 40 minutes. More significant delays in communication force the usage of supervisory control methods. This feature has been utilized in the Nomad vehicle experiments conducted in the barren terrain of the Chilean Atacama Desert [Piguet et al.].

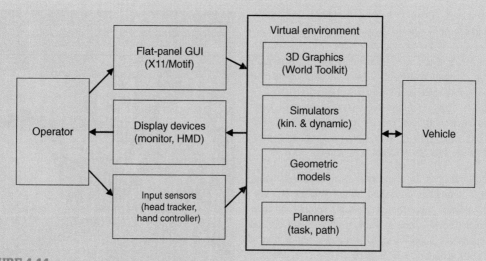

FIGURE 4-14

The system contains two layers of abstraction between the user and the vehicle. [Fong et al.]

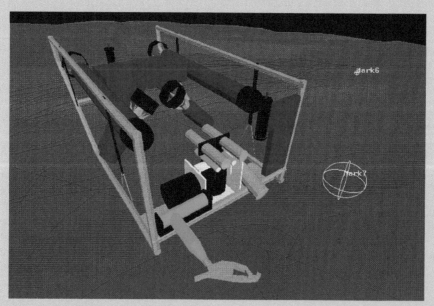

FIGURE 4-15

The Sense8 WorldToolKit *was chosen to provide the graphical rendering for the* VEVI *system.*

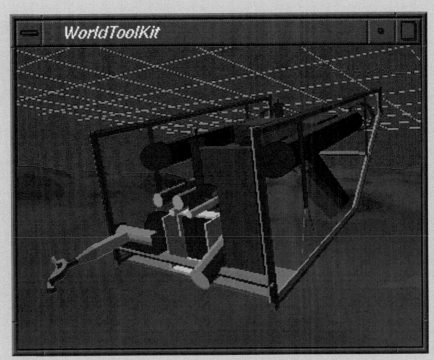

FIGURE 4-15
Continued

FIGURE 4-16
VEVI *was used in controlling Ranger, an orbital robot used to repair satellites.*

FIGURE 4-17
The Nomad planetary surface rover performed a 40 day mission to explore the Chilean Atacama Desert.

The *VEVI* system provides two methods for representing remote locations. In the TROV McMurdo Sound mission, one method was to directly view the world via the live video cameras onboard the TROV. The other method was to use a computer-generated representation of the underwater terrain. The computer-generated representation was constructed using information gathered by a set of sensors carried on the TROV. A virtual-world model representing the real world was created by traversing the terrain with the TROV to gather the appropriate data.

The virtual-world display also included a representation of the position and state of the TROV, plus information such as the vehicle's track and science markers. Science markers are icons placed in the 3D world representing the location at which certain measurements were taken. The researcher can see the markers, to see where data was collected, and in later versions of the software, hyperlink to the raw or processed data. The data collected could be from any number of input sensors, resulting in a mixture of data types, such as images, salinity values, temperature, or light measurement.

The two presentation methods give the operator a choice between viewing the remote locale via first- or second-person points of view. The first-person POV view is obtained from a pair of video cameras mounted on the vehicle. This technique includes separating the cameras by the distance common to human interocular spacing, and rapid tilt-and-pan movements to be able to follow quick human head rotations. Rapid response between human input and the visual feedback is an important factor in a telepresence application. The visual lag of a poorly responsive camera will cause perceptual difficulties for the operator. The stereoscopic camera-pair helps provide depth cues to the viewer, although since the cameras do not translate relative to the craft there is no depth cue from head-motion parallax.

In addition to the use of the stereoscopic camera-pair to produce a first-person view from the TROV, several other

FIGURE 4-18
The development team works on the Nomad planetary surface rover in the field.

cameras and sensors help to relay the current situation to the user. A monoscopic camera helps the user see what is immediately in front of the craft, and another monoscopic camera is mounted to the bottom of the craft to observe what is directly beneath. The forward-looking camera is equipped with a power zoom lens, used to obtain close-up views. The vehicle also carries sensors for ambient light, direct light, dissolved oxygen, and temperature.

VR DISCOVERY

A significant difference between virtual reality and telepresence/AR applications is the increased demand for sensor devices. In order to allow interaction with a world, the interface must be able to accurately represent the world. When the world in question is the real world, the representation (and hence the ability to interact) relies on accurate sensing of the world plus the registration of the virtual-world representation to the real world.

When we directly view the real world around us with our eyes, we see it from a first-person point of view. The computer generated version of the real world can also be presented from a first-person perspective. However, the computer version is also able to be presented as a second-person view of the world. Using this capability allows the operators to see "themselves" (i.e., the vehicle they are piloting) from an external point of view, giving them the ability to see the relationship between them and the environment.

Another important feature of telepresence is the ability to manipulate the world. Accordingly, the TROV was

(continued)

VR DISCOVERY (Continued)

equipped with a manipulator arm for gathering samples and executing other necessary activities in the ocean floor expedition. The TROV manipulator arm was furnished with a simple gripper claw to provide a mechanism by which the operator can affect the real world from within the virtual world.

The vehicle's position is tracked in much the same manner as ultrasonic and visual tracking systems are used to track the human body. Specifically the *SHARPS*™ (by the Marquest Group) navigation system tracks the TROV by transmitting and receiving acoustic ranging signals. Transponders are mounted on the front and the rear of the vehicle. The transponders are referenced against three known position units. The fixed units are arranged in the water in the formation of an equilateral triangle. The transponders are positioned at a depth of 100 meters

(hung in the water by cables). Onshore, a 386-PC uses the tracking data to compute the vehicle's relative position from the dive hole from the tracking data. The PC also records the vehicle's movements, and keeps track of the sections of the sea covered by the vehicle's movements.

During the course of the McMurdo Sound benthic ecology project, the system was in nearly continuous use for over 2 months. The complete system was implemented with a variety of hardware, including Sun SPARCstations, Silicon Graphics systems and an assortment of special-purpose processing and communications boards. To aid in integrating this variety of platforms, the developers used NASA's *ARCA (Ames Robotic Computational Architecture)* standardized communications package for interprocess communication and synchronization of the heterogeneous, distributed system [Fong 1993].

VR System

The nonimmersive stereoscopic monitor display was implemented using CrystalEyes LCD shutter glasses. The VR display was implemented using a Virtual Research VR2 HMD. The HMD was tracked by a Logitech ultrasound position tracker. Both the immersive and nonimmersive systems used a Spaceball™ for input. The operators at the dive hole using the nonimmersive system also had a pair of joysticks on a lap-belt controller that they could use. In the immersive system, a head-tracking system provided user point-of-view input.

Vehicle movement was controlled using joysticks. Unlike some other telepresence applications, the manipulator arm was not controlled by a glove interface, but instead it was controlled using the joystick. The arm had limited possible configurations; thus it was sometimes necessary to manipulate the vehicle to achieve certain positions.

The terrain model is created by piloting the TROV along the sea floor while the system records data from the tracking system and onboard measuring devices. This data is then used to build the model. Once the terrain maps exist in the *VEVI* software, the vehicle can be driven purely within the virtual world, to an accuracy of .25 meters.

As with many explorative missions, multiple scientists were involved; each with their own goals to accomplish. One goal was to produce a video record of benthic (ocean floor) organisms gathered during passes of the TROV through several areas ranging from 60 to 1000 feet in depth. Another goal was to gather life-form samples from the region, and bring them back to the surface for further study. In addition to the marine scientists, the NASA engineers were interested in studying how VR and other displays could help the operator's ability to perform teleoperations.

To collect the samples, a separate basket constructed from PVC pipe and netting was created. A hinged door on the top of the basket opened by pushing on it. The scientist could explore by driving the TROV, finding samples, controlling the manipulator arm and claw with a joystick to procure a sample, bring it to the basket, and push it through the door. When the basket was full, they could grasp it in the claw and carry it to the surface with the TROV.

The developers feel that telepresence techniques provide significant advantages for studying the undersea world. Stereoscopic display was considered important in this application for several reasons. Stereoscopic imagery helped provide a sense of depth that helped in using the manipulator arm. Also, the use of stereoscopic images provided a means to calculate the size of objects and the distance between objects. The navigation and tracking system also allowed the scientists to record measurements such as the distance traveled and the distance between objects.

This application shows an interesting integration of both telepresence and virtual reality techniques for use in the visualization of a remote environment, as well as controlling a vehicle within that environment. These techniques show great promise for exploring, analyzing, and manipulating in hostile, inaccessible, or extreme environments. Such techniques could feasibly be implemented in applications that require the control of vehicles in distant, dangerous, or extreme environments.

While the McMurdo Sound Project was focused on an undersea environment, NASA has also done similar exploration on extraterrestrial environments. One of the key hurdles to overcome in such applications is the lag between the remote vehicle and the control operator. Even with sufficient bandwidth, the absolute distance creates a time delay that can lead to problems with conventional telepresence techniques.

The IMG researchers have made some interesting discoveries over the course of their research with this and other telepresence projects using the *VEVI* system. One thing they found was that once the move was made from the original text-based control systems to even the 2D interfaces, no one went back to the old method. The text method of reading enormous amounts of numbers and offering "indecipherable" command options was too "daunting."

They also learned which interface features were key to aiding the understanding of the vehicle's situation and how it could be controlled. Many of these features were added to the *VEVI* 2D interface for the descent of the *Dante* land vehicle into the rim of the Mt. Spurr volcano. In particular, they added visual reference aids such as grids, axes, landmarks, and orientation indicators to the display. The *VEVI* authors also found that improved registration between the real and virtual worlds greatly enhanced their ability to control the device. Many of these lessons are described in Fong's paper on the Dante project [Fong et al. 1995]. Fong also found that "traded and shared supervisory control can improve system performance through synergistic human-machine interaction," and that user situational awareness and information processing can be enhanced via a virtual reality interface.

Butler Hine, Group Leader of the Intelligent Mechanisms Group during the TROV and *Dante II* missions, felt that the *Dante II* mission was where using VR as part of the operator interface resulted in a significant improvement in usability. In many ways, TROV was "basically a telepresence device retrofitted to use a VR interface. It lacked the on-board control system and sensors required to really do a good job in the VR interface." Hine also stated that "*Dante II*, on the other hand, was very sensor rich and had a high-level control system. The vehicle was complex enough that the gain in situation awareness from using a VR interface was substantial."

One feature that had not been used in many NASA telepresence missions was the use of audio feedback, either as part of the control interface or to hear sounds from the remote location. In one mission to Mt. Kilauea, an active volcano in Hawaii, an audio pickup was placed on the rover, providing sounds as well as sights back to the operators. Hine points out that "it is amazing how good the human ear is at determining the health of a system by sound alone," indicating the value of being able to hear as well as see the telelocation.

Related Applications and Follow-on Work

VEVI was used in the *Pathfinder* mission to Mars, but as a visualization tool rather than a control tool. Terrain data received from *Pathfinder* was displayed and validated using *VEVI*. Control operations for *Pathfinder* were planned out a day ahead of time and sent as a mission for *Sojourner* (the Mars rover component of the mission). The planned operations were created using a separate, custom, tool also developed by the NASA IMG. The daily preplanned operating method did not require many of the features of *VEVI*, such as real-time telemetry display, or real-time control of the vehicle.

Conclusion

In addition to Butler Hine, the architects and implementers of the *VEVI* system include Laurent Piguet, Terry Fong, Erik Nygren, and Phil Hontalas. This team collaborated with many other people when integrating *VEVI* for the hardware of a specific mission. Some of the robotic vehicles were made by the Carnegie Mellon Robotics Institute, including the *Dante II* and *Nomad* vehicles.

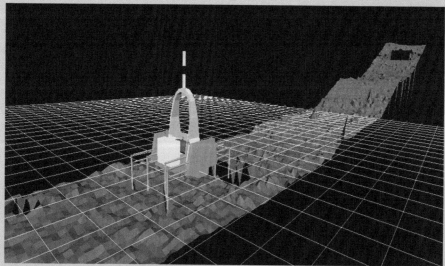

FIGURE 4-19
The actual system and its virtual representation.

FIGURE 4-20

Operators utilize both conventional video and virtual representation for remote control of the system.

FIGURE 4-21

In addition to real-time control, applications for virtual reality include visualization of remote environments and reconstruction of explored spaces through collected data.

Many of the IMG researchers responsible for the *VEVI* system have gone on to found a company to extend and support *VEVI*, as well as produce new technologies for telepresence applications. The name of their company is Fourth Planet Inc. Butler Hine, now president and CEO of Fourth Planet, seeing a great need for putting this type of technology to use, states:

I think that virtual reality and telepresence can have an enormous impact on how we explore and work in remote hazardous locations. These techniques will ultimately give us the ability to send our best minds and talent to places which would otherwise involve prohibitively extreme physical risk.

CASE STUDY 4.4: GRIP

Molecular Visualization

The University of North Carolina at Chapel Hill has used virtual reality to investigate interactions between molecules, such as drug-protein interaction using virtual reality. A significant feature of their system is the use of a six-degree-of-freedom force-feedback device called the Argonne Remote Manipulator (ARM). The ARM allows the scientist to "feel" the forces between two molecules as they are placed in different locations and orientations while using the ARM also as an input device.

One could consider this set of applications to be as much about haptic feedback as it is about molecular visualization, the fact that a significant investment in investigating the use of haptic devices makes this virtual reality application stand out from the pack of other molecular visualization application. It is very interesting to use the ARM to place the molecules in different orientations and "feel" when the molecules are attracting or repelling each other.

Application Description

Most of the applications described in this book rely on the visual sense to convey a virtual world to the human participating in the world. Many of these also use sounds to enhance or augment the information conveyed visually. However, very few use the sense of touch, or in this case more specifically kinesthesia, to transmit information about the world to the participant. (See Chapter 5 for an application that uses force feedback for surgical training.) The *GROPE* series of projects are significant in that not only

are they one of the few uses of haptic display for scientific visualization, but that this research has been ongoing at the University of North Carolina at Chapel Hill (UNC) since 1967 [Brooks et al.].

Inspired by Ivan Sutherland's description of *The Ultimate Display*, the UNC Department of Computer Science set out not only to implement such a device, including haptics, which was also part of Sutherland's vision, but also to put this ultimate display to work in aiding with real-world tasks. Founding department head and Computer Science pioneer Fred Brooks spearheaded the effort to create the new technology in such a way that it would be demonstrably useful.

Significantly, this project has been as much about analyzing the benefits of haptic technology as much as it has been about producing a single application that was useful to a particular set of scientists. The UNC research team has conducted a series of experiments on the usefulness of the concepts of the *GROPE* project while technology has allowed the application to advance.

From the outset of the project, the research team led by Brooks strove to implement an application for interactive exploration of molecular docking. Until *GROPE III* the research focused on taking steps that would take them in the direction of the originally conceived molecular docking application. The initial experiments focused on much simpler tasks.

Their research project has expanded into other application areas. The overall research for molecular "visualization"

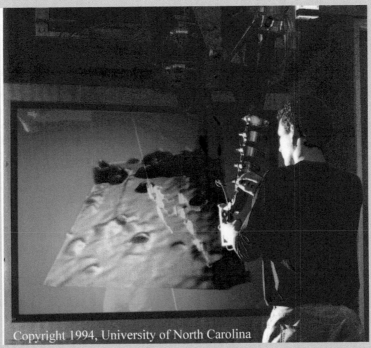

Copyright 1994, University of North Carolina

FIGURE 4-22
The ARM provides six-degree-of-freedom force feedback of interactions in the virtual world.

at UNC is now referred to as *GRIP (GRaphical Interaction with Proteins)*, with the *GROPE* project and others falling within. Of the *GRIP* projects, *GROPE* and *nanoManipulator* use haptics as a means of perception and interaction.

The generalized result of their data indicates that haptic display increases performance of a molecular docking task by about twofold in the *GROPE* task, and the *nanoManipulator* project has anecdotally demonstrated tasks that can only be performed with the haptic interface.

The *GROPE* project had evolved through many generations to become a software application usable by a number of chemists at multiple facilities. The resultant application (*GROPE III*) still provides for the same basic operation—finding the best docking configuration between a drug and a protein—while offering a variety of representational idioms to aid in this task.

Although "scientific visualizations" often map a variety of data to the visual sense (and to a lesser degree the aural sense) typically only simulated forces are mapped to our kinesthetic sense. This phenomenon is probably mostly due to the limited number of haptic displays that are in use. Thus, the primary owners of such systems are groups that see a direct need for perceiving forces. In the case of the *GROPE* project, the forces displayed to the user are the natural attraction and repulsion forces between molecules.

The molecular docking task was chosen because it involves real-world forces and torques that need to be analyzed by chemists working on drug design. While mapping a force phenomenon to the force display, the *GROPE* system must map the force "across scale." That is, it represents a force that is very common, but not otherwise perceptible at human scale. Bringing the drug interaction phenomenon to the level with which a human researcher can interact on their terms allows them to get a better "feel" for the chemical process by exploring it directly.

A variety of representational choices are provided to the user of the *GROPE III* system. The representation of each molecule can be selected separately from a choice of none (i.e., invisible), ball and stick, stick only, as well as a Connolly dot surface to represent the active site.

The forces between the drug and protein can be represented in one of two fundamental ways. The force can be represented visually, using an arrow that points in the direction of the force, with the length of the arrow proportionate to the magnitude of the force. The force can also be rendered haptically, producing directional forces on the user's hand or finger on all types of haptic display, and rotational forces on those capable of full 6DOF force rendering.

Two graphical-only representations in the *GROPE III* application include energy "thermometers" that show the total energy and the internal energy or the drug molecule, and a vector representation that shows forces and torques as arrows, with the force arrow emanating from the point, and the torque arrow shown as a tangent to a sphere surrounding the point. When subjects were only given the visual representation of the force and torque, they used the non-optimal strategy of attempting to first minimize the force and then the torque, versus doing both at the same time as a single operation. Those subjects interacting with the force display generally minimized both at the same time.

VR System

Development of the *GROPE* system stepped though some specific advances in force and computational technology over the years. These steps can be categorized as four distinct stages:

- 2DOF force system (called *GROPE I*, 1971)

- 3DOF force system with a simple task (*GROPE II*, 1976)

- 6DOF force system with a simple task (*GROPE IIIA*, 1989)

- 6DOF force system with a 6D molecular docking task (*GROPE IIIB*, 1990)

Because force feedback is not a commonly sought form of sensory display, a major problem with experimenting with force rendering systems was simply acquiring the hardware. This was particularly true in 1967. The main source of haptic display devices at that period were produced for tele-operation devices. UNC managed to acquire an orphaned Argonne Remote Manipulator (ARM) teleoperator unit.

As better force displays and computational systems became available, the task stepped closer to the original goal of the project. The initial 2DOF application (*GROPE I*) used potentiometers and servos to sense and move a small knob within a 2-inch by 2-inch square. The application was an experiment to measure how well people could judge a continuous 2D force displayed on this device. The *GROPE II* application used the ARM device as one means of interacting with a simple block world. Subjects were asked to make comparisons of particular cues in the virtual world using force, perspective, stereoscopic, and other representational cues about the world.

As the results of the *GROPE II* project were published, Brooks and the research team decided that computers would have to improve by 100-fold before full 6DOF forces could be calculated in real time. By 1986, this threshold had been reached, and the *GROPE* project was reborn as *GROPE III*.

The *GROPE III* system also used the ARM haptic device, but with more powerful computational and rendering computers. Computers were now powerful enough to calculate a 6DOF force in a simple world at about 80 Hz (which was determined to be the rate above which people could not sense any difference on the ARM system). The world was rendered on an Evans and Sutherland PS-330 color vector display, and computed on a dedicated Sun4/280 UNIX workstation.

Brooks' research team hoped to answer several questions about the potential usefulness of haptic displays in a scientific visualization task. The primary questions were:

- Do haptic displays demonstrably aid perception?

- How big is the effect?

- What models are best suited to force display?

- How good does the display need to be?

- Where is the perception threshold above which there is little/no gain?

In *GROPE I* the major finding was that people could learn from the system, but that if they weren't interested in the task, there was no gain in knowledge.

In the *GROPE II* research experiment, the team found that while each individual relies on different cues to discern the three dimensional nature of shapes, there are cues that are stronger than others. Specifically, they found that force feedback (touch) provides a better perceptual cue regarding the shape of objects in the world than either stereoscopic images or motion parallax. They found that force cue was somewhat weaker than the cue provided by shadows. Another finding was that when the user interface mediates 3D movement with 2D widgets, then people tend to limit their work to 2-DOF at a time. They separate the orientation portion of maneuvering from location, making the task less holistic.

In *GROPE III*, where the experimental task approached the original concept of using force as an interface to a molecular docking task, they found that adding haptic augmentation to the interface improved the results by a factor of two. Chemists who have used *GROPE III* have demonstrated that they are able to find good docking positions with it. More importantly, these chemists report that they acquired a better understanding of the details of the drug receptor site by experiencing the forces at work on the docking molecules. Thus in general, the UNC developers have shown haptic interfaces to have a potential benefit in a variety of computer applications.

Related Applications and Follow-on Work

Another project in the *GRIP* domain that uses haptic display is the *nanoManipulator*. The *nanoManipulator* project was begun in 1991 to use force feedback devices as an interface to scanned-probe microscopes (SPM). SPMs operate by scanning the surface of a material at the atomic level. The probe of these microscopes can also be used to modify the surface. By using force displays as an interface to these devices, users can both feel and affect the object under purview.

As with the *GROPE* applications, different force feedback devices can be used to interact with the *nanoManipulator*. However, they typically use a SensAble Technologies PHANToM device (a 3DOF point force display). Unlike *GROPE*, the *nanoManipulator* can use head tracking to visually immerse the user as well as haptically immerse them. They have used both workbench-style visual displays with and without head-tracking, and HMD visual displays.

Because the *nanoManipulator* generally uses live, real-time data, it is as much a telepresence application as it is virtual reality. In effect, what it is doing is allowing the user to jump from the world around them to the atomic world near the tip of the microscope, at one-millionth the scale. The real-world information can then be augmented with colors, forces, or other information to enhance the user's perception of the world.

With the *nanoManipulator* application, the UNC researchers found that the haptic VR interface enabled insights that were not made by scientists who had worked with the same data using traditional methods. Of course, this does not imply that the previous visualization methods should be abandoned.

One group they had collaborated with discovered a feature of their own data ("graphite sheets coming out of the surface") that they had not noticed using their traditional methodology—pseudo-color imaging [Taylor et al., 1997]. The spectral highlights caused by viewing the surface from a particular angle caused the feature to become apparent while flying over the surface. On the other hand, there is often a substantial amount of noise in the SPM data that can become prominent in 3D renderings and thus obscure features that are readily evident in the traditional 2D pseudo-color view. Both the 2D and 3D views are made available to the user to allow information to be gathered using the most appropriate view for a particular task.

The graphite sheet anecdote speaks favorably for using head tracking for visual displays, but such use could not make use of the haptic interface provided by the *nanoManipulator*. The primary benefits afforded by the *nanoManipulator* from the haptic interface device are in the improved user interface it provides with the scientific instruments. Without the *nanoManipulator* acting as mediator between the user and the instrument, the user has limited options for interacting with the surface. Two new features that emerge from the computer mediation of the device are extending how the tip can be used to interact with the surface, allowing the user to feel the material during times when the visual scan is unavailable.

Normally, the user of an SPM has only the brute force method of using the microscope tip to interact with the material. This brute force interaction is like probing and manipulating a block of ice with an ice pick. The *nanoManipulator* adds the ability to interact with the surface in a variety of ways that are more appropriate for certain tasks. These "virtual" methods of tip control include a "broom" tip and a "sewing" tip. The broom tip allows nanotubes to be "swept" accross the surface by rapidly moving the tip back and forth between the two ends of the "broom." Specifying the two end points of the broom is a far easier task for the user than trying to move the tip back and forth on their own. Another example of a "virtual tip" is the "sewing" tip. This tip is used when the user wishes to create a "trench" in the surface of the material, but doesn't want the tip to plow through the material and cause a "snow plow" ridge to form. To prevent material from building up, the tip presses into the surface, then rises up, moves a little, and then presses down again in rapid succession, much like a sewing machine needle.

The other major benefit that arises from computer mediation between the user and the "remote" environment is that the haptic display can continue to allow the user to perceive the material even when the visual display cannot be updated. Because of how scanning-probe microscopes work, they can either use the probe to scan the surface of the material or to interact with the surface. Thus, when interacting, the standard (non-computer-mediated) interface is to operate "blind." The visual display can provide an image from the most recent scan, but it won't show any changes that the user is making to the material. Also, because doing a scan on the surface leaves the microscope tip in an indeterminate location, the user cannot request a scan in the middle of a manipulation and expect to continue where they left off.

Operations that might otherwise be impossible to perform, such as sliding a particle across a surface to fill a gap in a wire, can now be done. The user cannot see when the particle is slipping from the front of the tip, but they can feel it and readjust their movement accordingly. Another example is that the depression between two carbon filaments can be sensed allowing the user to "tease" them apart [Taylor et al.].

In addition to allowing users to perceive the microscopic world during times when visual representation is not possible, haptic feedback can also provide perceptual cues that are masked by the visual representation. For example, adenovirus particles appear roundish in the visual display, but the discrete edges can be felt with the haptic interface.

Conclusion

Although many people assume that virtual reality is about visual imagery, and sometimes sounds, this application shows a cogent use of haptic representation of information. By integrating the participants' bodies in a way that allows them to feel the intermolecular forces of the subject of study, they are able to gain another channel of information to assist them in gaining insight into the inner workings of the virtual world they are experiencing. As a tool for science, the *nanoManipulator* allows data to be stored and retrieved. This is done because scientific research must be reviewable in order to be helpful. As Fred Brooks states as a general principle of scientific research: "If it isn't in the lab notebook, it didn't happen." In other words, "an experiment is performed once, but may be analyzed many times." In the case of the *nanoManipulator*, the "notebook" can store the entire history of a user's interaction with a material—both the scan data and the user modifications or touching of the surface. Researchers have already had occurrences where they saw things during the replay that hadn't been noticed during the experiment.

In general, the *nanoManipulator* demonstrates that by mediating the interface between user and instrument, the VR interface increases the usefulness of the instrument itself. In turn, the virtual reality application becomes a valuable tool for scientific exploration. At the same time however, it is important to keep in mind the lesson the *nanoManipulator* team has learned that the addition of new representations and interfaces does not mean that the previous methods are not valuable and should be discarded. Often there are features that are still best detected with the old method, and by switching back and forth between representations, the scientist can make a better overall mental model of what is being presented to them.

A number of people have worked on the *GRIP* research projects. Professor Fred Brooks is the overall project lead, and he conceived the drug-docking application. The *nanoManipulator* project was conceived by Warren Robinett and Stan Williams, and included Professor Russell Taylor, Richard Superfine, and Sean Washbur. The University of North Carolina research was funded by the National Institute of Health/National Center for Research Resources (NIH/RCRR) and by the National Science Foundation (NSF) in support of these efforts.

The *GRIP* projects are interesting both because there is anecdotal evidence that they have benefited some scientists and, more importantly, because there is experimental evidence that the haptic interfaces can improve performance with the virtual or teleworlds.

Other sites have begun to use the *GROPE III* software for their own molecular docking research. In particular, the Wright-Patterson Air Force Base, working with the National Center for Supercomputing Applications (NCSA) and Russell Taylor at UNC, has evolved the software to use more visual representations of the molecular systems, use the PHANToM device, and run in the *CAVE* environment.

CHAPTER 5

Medical Applications

The medical community actively seeks new technologies to enable them to provide better medical care. Tools such as the stethoscope, x-ray machine, microscope, and many more have enabled doctors to provide better patient care, medical research, and enhance and prolong life. While some tools have been specifically developed for medical uses, others that were not developed specifically for medicine are applied with positive results. Virtual reality applications for medical use are being developed and tested for a wide variety of tasks. While most applications are still in the development and testing phase, others have already been deployed for production use.

It is interesting to note that a significant amount of funding for research in medical applications of virtual reality has been provided by the U.S. Navy. The Navy sees promise that virtual reality can be a useful tool in support of their work in the medical care of our troops while they defend our country. In addition to the enhancement of more conventional medical care, they are also interested in applying virtual reality techniques to a more specific area of interest called "telemedicine." Telemedicine is a combination of telepresence, augmented reality, and virtual reality focused on allowing physicians to diagnose and treat patients at a distance. Telemedicine offers the promise of bringing high-quality doctors into a war zone that may be thousands of miles away.

Although many compelling demonstration applications have been created, relatively few have made it from the laboratory into daily production use. There are a number of reasons that account for this. Among them are the rigorous testing and government approval that new technologies are required to go through prior to adoption. Also, the medical community is largely very conservative, so they are often slow to migrate from the tried and true to the new and different. Many physicians are skeptical by nature, and have little time to devote to learning new techniques unless they are convinced the effort will pay off.

In order to have a high likelihood of adoption, a medical application of virtual reality must provide a benefit that outweighs the costs associated with adoption. One is that the system must be easy to learn and relate to techniques and procedures that the physician is accustomed to, while providing new capabilities. Later in this chapter, we cover the University of Virginia's *Neurosurgical Visualization* application which specifically addresses this concern.

Applications must provide accurate results, sufficient resolution, and any sensory output appropriate to the task. Because touch is a critical element in many medical procedures, haptic feedback is often important. Likewise, the use of olfaction in virtual reality is likely to occur in medical applications in the future.

5.1 AREAS OF APPLICATION

Virtual reality is being used in a variety of ways in the medical field ranging from drug design, to empathy training (see *Detour* in Chapter 8) to Phobia treatment (see *Fear of Flying* later in this chapter) There are four primary areas of medicine that are covered here. In each of these areas, there is a broad division of whether applications are primarily focused on supporting medical research or focused on clinical use. These application areas include:

- Training
- Scientific visualization
- Preoperative planning
- During-operation assistance

New application areas continue to emerge. Virtual reality is being applied in dentistry, otolaryngology (ear, nose, and throat), balance dysfunction, training for patient interviews, endoscopy, and other fields. The medical community is sufficiently interested in virtual reality that there is a conference specifically dedicated to VR in medicine. The "Medicine Meets Virtual Reality" (MMVR) conference provides a venue for interested participants to exchange ideas, view the latest products, and publish important findings. The MMVR conference has been active for over 15 years.

CASE STUDY 5.1: BDI *SURGICAL SIMULATOR*

Executive Summary

When medical students learn the complicated process of surgery, they use all of their senses. In contrast, many virtual reality applications rely primarily on visual and auditory information. Surgery, however, relies very heavily on the sense of touch. A surgeon reacts not only to what they see, but also what they *feel.*

In this focus, Boston Dynamics Inc. tackles the issue of the sense of touch in their turnkey surgical simulator system. Their system uses actual surgical instruments in tandem with a visual display housed in a kiosk that emulates the actual surgical environment. The instruments are actively manipulated by the VR system to provide realistic haptic feedback to the student. The system also evaluates the

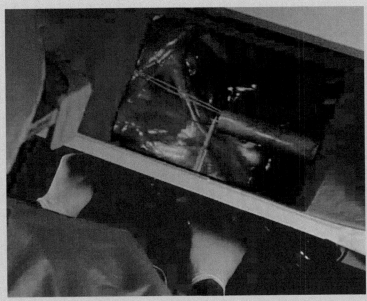

FIGURE 5-1
A surgical student wears shuttering stereo glasses to look into a virtual body cavity while practicing the surgical procedure of anastomosis.
Image courtesy Boston Dynamics, ©1997–1998

student and provides a report of their progress in learning new skills.

Introduction

The BDI *Surgical Simulator* is a medical training tool that uses force feedback to give life-like responses to a specific surgical procedure. Boston Dynamics Inc. (BDI) has been involved in creating realistic (physically based) motion dynamics simulations and haptics applications. The company slogan—"Focusing on the Science and Art of How Things Move" reflects their emphasis in applying real-time motion simulation to tasks that can be significantly enhanced by such technology. BDI has also used this technology to develop applications related to aircraft maintenance training and design and human factors analysis. Here, we will focus on their surgical simulator for training open surgery and anastomosis tasks.

The *Surgical Simulator* product is an integrated set of hardware and software utilizing VR techniques to provide an experience which represents reality within a set of commonly used surgical procedures. Of particular interest is the usage of haptic feedback as a primary form of display. In fact, the haptic feedback is based on user-position data, whereas the visual display is not, thus making the haptic display a significant factor by which the participant is physically immersed.

The specific goal of the *Surgical Simulator* is to re-create the experience of doing "end-to-end anastomosis"—the task of suturing tube-like organs together. This task was chosen partially because anastomosis is found in many surgical procedures involving various organ systems, such as blood vessels, esophagus, colon, and bile ducts. BDI designed the simulator to accommodate these various organs by providing an adjustable set of parameters, such as tube diameter, tissue stiffness, surface texture, surface friction, needle piercing forces, and so forth. Models of the different tissues and tube organs are created to both look and feel like the real thing.

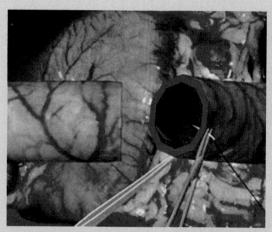

FIGURE 5-2
Body organs are rendered as realistically as possible within the constraints of real-time interaction. In this image a student uses a needle holder and forceps to practice end-to-end anastomosis.
Image courtesy Boston Dynamics, ©1997–1998

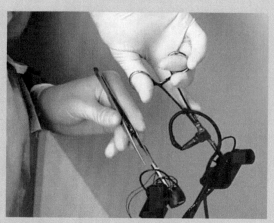

FIGURE 5-3
Actual medical instruments such as forceps and needle holders are attached to force-feedback devices. The end result is that the student can feel their interactions with virtual organs. They can sense the elasticity and stiffness of tissue and can sense when a needle penetrates an organ.
Image courtesy Boston Dynamics, ©1997–1998

Application Description

In the BDI *Surgical Simulator*, participants hold actual medical instruments to practice surgical tasks in a virtual world. This allows the medical student to practice without the use of hospital space, human patients, animals, or constant supervision by a surgeon.

In the simulator, medical students practice the various aspects of end-to-end anastomosis by using forceps, a needle, and a needle driver to touch, grasp, and suture two compliant tubular organs. Actual medical instruments are used as the interface to the virtual world. A student grasps the real instrument, and in the computer graphic view can see a realistic avatar representation.

The surgical instruments are connected to force-feedback devices to provide haptic feedback to the student. Haptic feedback is an important aspect of performing surgical procedures. Simulators like this can allow students to encounter unexpected conditions and rare medical disorders, which they might not have the opportunity to encounter in standard training methodology. The simulator allows the student to practice and be prepared for either routine or unusual procedures. To use the surgical trainer, the student grasps the forceps in one hand, and the needle driver in the other. Using the actual forceps, the student grasps a virtual tube in one hand, and punctures it with the virtual needle held by the needle driver in the other hand. The student then sutures the tubes together by puncturing the other tube with the threaded needle and then pulls the suture tight. The actual knot tying is performed automatically by the simulator, as there are other effective ways to teach this skill.

In conjunction with the *Surgical Simulator*, BDI has also developed a simpler system created to measure task performance on specific actions such as time to completion, needle placement accuracy, tissue surface damage, tangential tearing force, and others.

Representation of the Virtual World

The content of the virtual world is the small work volume of normal open cavity surgery, including the organs involved in the procedure and the instruments with which the user operates.

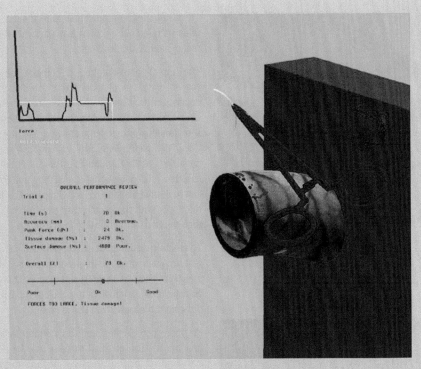

FIGURE 5-4

A simpler skills assessment simulator allows students to practice subtasks of anastamosis (e.g., pushing the needle through at well spaced intervals without damaging too much tissue), plus provides feedback on how well they did.

Image courtesy Boston Dynamics, ©1997–1998

The world is visually and haptically represented as realistically as feasible for the task. The graphics and haptics are driven by a fairly realistic dynamic model in real time. However, constraints on software development limited how many features could be incorporated as part of the initial product. For example, blood and other fluids that normally obstruct a surgical procedure are not rendered, resulting in a much cleaner opening than a surgeon would normally encounter.

While students are performing the task and feeling the results via the instruments, they are also able to see what they are doing on a visual display arranged to mimic looking into the patient's open cavity. In the visual display, they can see the deformation of the tubes and organs. In real life, there can be obscuring factors such as blood and

other tissues, as well as a constricted maneuvering space. Some of these factors are being developed for integration with training scenarios.

The world is visually rendered with a realistic visual representation of the tissue surfaces using texture maps. Two open-ended tubular structures can be seen at either end of the operating area, with a view into the body cavity below. Also included in the computer-generated scene are avatars of the medical instruments. The instrument avatars move in correspondence with the movements of real instrument props that the student manipulates.

Ordinarily, the student will see their own hand holding one end of the instrument, and the other end of the instrument represented via computer. If they put their hand far

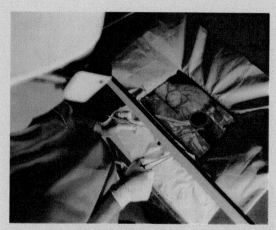

FIGURE 5-5
Avatars of the forceps and needle holder are evident as the student practices suturing.
Image courtesy Boston Dynamics, ©1997–1998

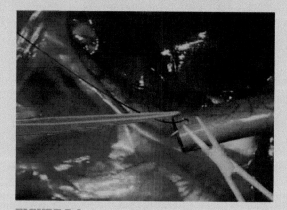

FIGURE 5-6
Haptic feedback devices are hidden from view by a mirror in which the surgical student sees the virtual body cavity and organs.
Image courtesy Boston Dynamics, ©1997–1998

enough into the scene, then the entire instrument could be viewed, but as though floating in space. When the application designers added hand avatars in the scene, experienced surgeons found the avatars to be distracting, so they were removed from the final product.

There is no audio representation in the surgical simulator other than the natural sounds made by the physical instruments held by the student.

The haptic representation is perhaps the most notable aspect of this application. Force-feedback systems are connected to the two medical instruments—a needle holder and a forceps. The trainee uses both instruments simultaneously to manipulate and feel the environment. Using the instruments, the student can grab the tissue, drive the needle through the tissue, and bring the thread together to generate a knot. As they pull the tissue, they can feel its resistance to stretching, and as they puncture the tissue with the needle, they can feel the resilience, and then the pop as the needle glides through.

To create realistic feedback on the medical instruments, a real-time dynamics model was incorporated using physical models of tissue stretching and tearing. This model can be adjusted with parameters to simulate tubular structures of different thicknesses and tissue type.

For more complicated surgical training tasks, one might imagine the use of smell to be a clue for detecting substances that might otherwise be undetectable, such as necrotic tissue. Much like audio often provides a great enhancement for mental immersion in a space or task, in a surgical environment, smell may be just as powerful, if not more so. There is no need for vestibular feedback, as the task itself is performed with the surgeon standing over the patient, and not moving into very many orientations.

Interaction with the Virtual World
The BDI *Surgical Simulator* can clearly be classified as an experiential *training* application. The form that the interaction takes is that of mimicking the real-world task where the surgeon stands next to the patient lying on a table and manipulates surgical implements.

The procedure followed by the students using the *Surgical Simulator* is a subset of actual surgical procedures. As much as is feasible, the students are made to feel they are working under normal operating conditions.

There is no travel necessary in the simulator beyond the physical locomotion of the hands. It is entirely through the use of the hands manipulating the prop instruments that the user interacts with the world.

There is no true interaction with other users or with autonomous agents in the virtual world. The only other being that is represented is assumed to be anesthetized.

The simulator is an attempt to represent the real world and is based on a real-time dynamics model to produce responses that reflect real-world laws of nature. This includes some collision detection necessary for determining when the instruments make contact with the organs as well as when the organs make contact with one another.

The deformable tube simulator is optimized for real-time performance. The simulation supports tube bending and stretching, as well as local surface deformation such as dimpling and puckering. The simulation allows parameters of the tubes such as length, diameter, thickness, mass, surface friction, compliance, and resistance to puncture to be varied to allow the system to represent different anatomical elements. The system parameters were adjusted by tweaking them until the results felt "correct" to experienced surgeons. This technique led to a more realistic "feel" than trying to take measurements from actual tissue.

Physical characteristics that are not supported include tissue folding, contact against puckered or dimpled regions of tube, or layers of tissue.

In order to approach the desired rate of 1000 Hz for interactions with rigid objects (soft tissue and other compliant objects are less demanding), the number of possible contacts between different objects was limited. One contact, for example, that was not computed was the instruments contacting each other.

Venue

The surgical simulator is based on a kiosk-style stand that closely resembles the station at which a surgeon would perform an operation. The typical location of this kiosk would be a medical school or hospital.

After a session with the full simulator, or the skills assessment package, a "Surgical Report Card" is delivered to the student.

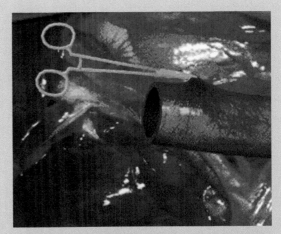

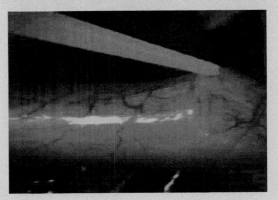

FIGURE 5-7

Physical characteristics of tissue, such as elasticity are modeled and rendered both visually and haptically. Here the student can feel the tissue stretch under their grasp.
Image courtesy Boston Dynamics, ©1997–1998

VR System

To view the graphical scene, the student stands at the kiosk looking downward toward a mirror that reflects the visual display from above. The reason for the mirror is to mask the mechanics of the haptic devices from view. The student then holds onto the instruments beneath the mirror. Cotton sheets disguise the monitor, in much the same manner that they hide the rest of the patient from view during an operation. As available during actual operations,

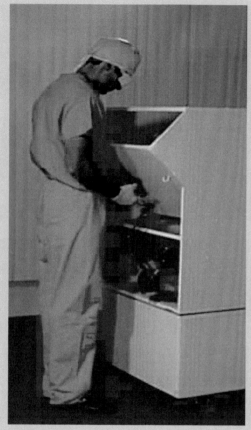

FIGURE 5-8
The BDI Surgical Simulator is a turnkey system that is housed in a kiosk. The kiosk provides hand rests and resembles an actual surgical station.
Image courtesy Boston Dynamics, ©1997–1998

a hand rest is provided on the kiosk to allow the surgeon to stabilize their hands.

The medical tools provide a prop-style interface to the virtual world. The tool "props" are instrumented to sense the amount of closure or clamping pressure is being applied by the user. To sense the position and provide force feedback to the user via the props, they are attached to haptic I/O devices.

Specifically, two SensAble Technologies' PHANToMs™ are used, one for each instrument.

The student wears untracked shuttering glasses to allow them to see the stereoscopic visual representation. Although the head is not tracked, the developers felt the benefits (motion parallax) would not outweigh the costs (latency and instability in viewing). The application does qualify as a VR application, because the hands are tracked (via the instruments), and the virtual world responds directly to those actions.

The hardware components consist of an SGI Maximum Impact Indigo II workstation to compute the graphics. A PC runs the simulation and controls the haptic feedback devices. A PHANToM device for each hand provides the haptic feedback.

The graphical software for the system is written using the *OpenGL* library. The scene consists of about 1200 polygons and is rendered and displayed at about 20 Hz. Other software consists of modules to perform the deformable tube simulation, fast contact detection, contact force calculation, the kinematics for the force feedback devices, and the force-feedback device drivers.

Application Implementation

Surgical Simulator required over 3 years to develop, representing over 12 man-years of effort. Funding for developing this product was provided by Dr. Rick Satava of DARPA, and Dr. Tom Krummel of the Pennsylvania State Hershey Medical Center. The application was created as an integration of a dynamic simulation of human tissue properties, stereoscopic display, and haptic feedback. An interesting aspect of this application is that actual surgical tools were used rather than more generic props.

Conclusion

Although the BDI *Surgical Simulator* does not fully replicate all the details involved in an actual surgical procedure, the system designers feel that it is a significant step toward that goal. The system has been tested with a variety of medical students, residents, and surgical instructors, including a few well-known surgeons. The response has been quite positive. Many of those who have tried the

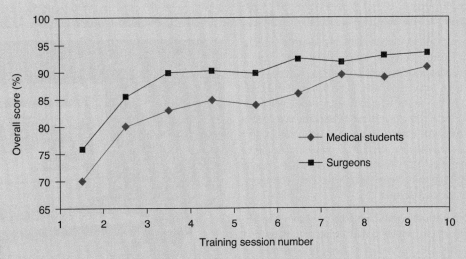

FIGURE 5-9

This graph shows that while experienced surgeons have a higher overall skill level than student surgeons, both groups improved their skills by using the VR Surgical Simulator.

Image courtesy Boston Dynamics, ©1997–1998

simulator are of the opinion that it would be a valuable tool in surgical training.

The results of these users (12 students and 9 surgeons) have been compiled into an informal study (overall results shown in Figure 5.9). Two observations from the overall results are that there is a marked difference between the skills of the surgeons and those of the students, and each group showed improvement over the eight trials.

The use of virtual reality in surgical training enables surgeons to be better prepared, and more skilled, as they prepare for real-world procedures. The *Surgical Simulator* may also prove useful to veteran surgeons by enabling them to practice for a rare or unusual cases prior to an actual procedure.

In closing, Marc Raibert, president of BDI, says: "Surgical simulators revolutionize how surgery is taught and how surgical skills are measured. The BDI Anastomosis Simulator is a significant step in that direction."

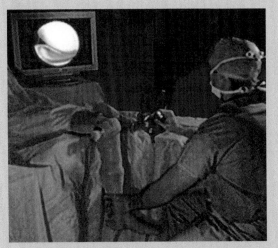

FIGURE 5-10

BDI has developed another simulator that is used for training students to do knee arthroscopy procedures.

Image courtesy Boston Dynamics, ©1997–1998

CASE STUDY 5.2: CELIAC PLEXUS BLOCK SIMULATOR

A celiac plexus block is a medical procedure for injecting a drug in a particular region within the torso of a patient. This procedure is carried out by inserting a needle into the back of a patient who is lying on their abdomen, and injecting a drug in the appropriate location. Finding the precise location of the needle inside the body is a difficult skill to learn. The physician uses a combination of their knowledge of anatomy with periodic x-ray views displayed on a fluoroscope. The physician uses their sense of touch when directing the needle through the skin, soft tissue, and other anatomic objects.

A problem that can occur during the procedure is injecting the drug in the wrong location, which can have catastrophic effects (if injected in a major blood vessel, for example) or, more likely, cause the procedure to be ineffective. Another potential problem is damaging good nerves as a result of repeated repositioning of the needle.

Researchers at the Center for Human Simulation at the University of Colorado Health Sciences Center have developed a simulator for training physicians in this procedure. The primary benefit of this VR application is the accelerated learning possible with the simulated procedure.

Application Description

The medical procedure supported by this VR application is normally done by having the patient lie on their stomach. The physician chooses a location on the back as the needle entry point best suited for delivering the drug to the target area. The patient is typically given a local anesthetic at the point of entry of the needle, but is normally awake during the procedure. As the physician inserts the needle, they can feel the different tissues as it moves through the body. When they feel that the needle tip is at the appropriate location, or need help determining its location, they can request a fluoroscopic update.

Because the actual procedure relies so heavily on the haptic feedback provided by the needle encountering the various parts of the body, the simulator provides an excellent platform in which to utilize haptic-feedback devices.

The simulator closely replicates the environment the physician would encounter in their actual practice. The elements

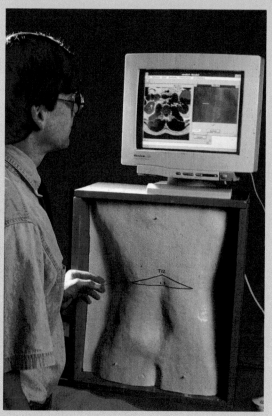

FIGURE 5-11

A user grasps the end of an actual needle (controlled by a force-feedback device inside the back) to practice the celiac plexus block procedure and can view the results on the nearby simulated fluoroscope display.
Photograph courtesy of Karl Reinig

that are readily visible to the physician include a life-size physical model of a human back, an actual needle identical to ones used in the procedure, and a computer monitor that mimics the display of the fluoroscope.

The *Celiac Plexus Block Simulator* attempts to mimic as much of the actual procedure as necessary to convey a realistic sensation of performing the operation on a human patient. During the simulation session, the physician can use the integrated "virtual fluoroscope" to display x-ray views of the patient, including the location of the needle on the computer monitor. Although the monitor is smaller than an actual fluoroscope, it is closer to the physician, with the net result being a realistic simulation. The system is capable of delivering continuously updated views on the display. However, in the real-life scenario the physician is only able to get updated views periodically, so this constraint is maintained in the simulator. During the actual procedure, each time the physician requests an updated view, everyone but the patient must leave the room while the image is being taken. This can be replicated with the simulator.

In this simulator, the PHANToM™ from SensAble Technologies provides the force feedback. The PHANToM itself was hidden from view, housed within the shell of the virtual patient's back. This simulator is a good example of how technology can be hidden from the user, thereby decreasing the likelihood of the illusion being broken by its physical presence. When the doctor inserts the needle into the virtual patient, the PHANToM provides forces on the needle that cause the physician to feel the needle penetrate the skin, soft tissue, be obstructed if it encounters bone, etc. Additionally, the physician can feel the pulsing of blood flow when the needle is positioned near or in a major blood vessel.

The prototype system uses the data from the Visible Human Dataset.[1]

Additional patients could be modeled from MRI and CT data. However, it would be a tedious process since every volume element of the data (voxel) needs to be segmented and classified in order for the system to determine the appropriate force feedback to provide. If each voxel in the area the needle is penetrating is not classified, the trainee cannot make (and recognize)

all the mistakes that should be allowed in a useful simulator.

While the interactively controlled needle provides fairly realistic haptic feedback based on user input, the back—which is modeled out of fiberglass—is inflexible, and thus not quite as haptically realistic. The inflexible back is also counter to the notion of a dynamic body in which the physician is positioning the needle. Internally, the application does simulate some dynamic tissue movements within the body. For example, the aorta changes in correspondence to a beating heart. They plan to implement more internal movements in future versions, such as the movement of the diaphragm to replicate the breathing of the virtual patient.

In addition to the haptic and visual sensory displays, the *Celiac Plexus Block Simulator* also provides aural feedback cues. In particular, if the user attempts to push the needle into a bone with forces that would cause pain in a patient, the system triggers the playback of a digital recording of the sound of a cry of pain. The expert advisors to the application developers provided input as to how hard a push into the bone would need to be to cause significant pain in a patient.

The fiberglass shell, representing the patient's back, was created by using the visible human dataset to drive a Dremel™ grinding tool attached to the PHANToM. They then cut the back from an alpha cradle block (the same expanding foam used to restrict the motions of patients in CT or MRI scanners). The block was then used to create a plaster mold from which the fiberglass model was made. The current model is positioned upright as though the patient were seated. The PHANToM can be reoriented to lay the model down as though the patient were on their abdomen, more closely replicating the typical real-life scenario.

The model of the back was created from the Visible Human Dataset, also created at the University of Colorado's Center for Human Simulation (UC-CHS). The same dataset was used to model the internal organs of the simulated patient. Some modifications were made to the dataset to correct artifacts that were introduced as a result of the procedure used to acquire the dataset.

---

[1]The Visible Human Project produced large, high-resolution datasets of a male and a female body using multiple imaging techniques [Spitzer et al. 1996].

The project took about four months to develop with the creators working approximately half time on it. Karl Reinig (a post-doctoral fellow at the UC-CHS) came up with the idea after encountering a haptic feedback device. Reinig was responsible for the basic design and haptic algorithms. Kenneth Niedjadlik, MD, Christopher Loeffler, MD, and Jose Angle, MD, were the anesthesiologists who lent their expertise to the program by teaching the developers about celiac plexus blocks, and conveying how the needle insertion should feel. Helen Pelster segmented and classified the visible human data to make it work for this project. Chuck Rush developed the PHANToM-NT driver, the application GUI, and helped Reinig develop the overall hardware and software system. Jim Heath helped Reinig develop the method for creating the fiberglass shell. Extensive use was made of data from the Visible Human Project led by Victor Spitzer, PhD, and David Whitlock, MD.

VR System

The primary hardware used by the *Celiac Plexus Block Simulator* is the PHANToM™ haptic device. The PHANToM—mounted inside the physical shell of a molded or carved back—is connected to the end of an actual needle that would be used in this type of operation. The PHANToM provides resistance to the motion of the needle. The simulation (including the PHANToM driver and fluoroscope graphics) was run on an IBM-compatible, Pentium Pro™–based personal computer. Sounds, such as the "yelp" of pain, were generated by loading WAVE sound sample files into memory and playing the sample when a specific event occurs.

A footswitch provides an emergency stop control for the PHANToM in the event of a software error, or other anomaly that may cause the PHANToM to go out of control. The consequences of a runaway condition in a haptic display can be more severe than in other displays.

The Center for Human Simulation also involved in several other VR applications. The *Dental Probe Simulator* uses the PHANToM in conjunction with a three-dimensional graphical display to allow a student to practice and be tested on their ability to diagnose tooth decay. They use the PHANToM to simulate a dental explorer tool. Rather than using an actual dental explorer, they use the generic PHANToM probe extension. The tool can be constrained to only allow the movements that would be allowed in the real world in the patient's mouth cavity.

The data is created from CT scans, and caries are artificially added to the tooth model. The participants feel the soft area, the movement of the jaw when pressure is applied, and the resistance to the removal of the explorer tool.

Another project is a *Scalpel Simulator* that allows the student to practice cutting through different types of materials, including fat (easy), tendons (a little harder), bone (very difficult), etc. This application uses the PHANToM for the force feedback, and an SGI for the 3D, texture-mapped graphical display.

Later, the UC-CHS VR team developed what they call the *Haptic Workbench* to create medical-related VR applications requiring force feedback. Mirrors are used to colocate a 3D visual image with the haptic devices. The haptic devices can be used to mimic a variety of operating tools such as a scalpel, a palpator, a needle, or a scope, all of which can be used to allow the user to interact with any part of the anatomy rendered on the screen.

One demonstration application they developed with the *Haptic Workbench* used two haptic devices to practice a distal targeting of a femoral nail procedure. In this procedure, a drill is hammered into a hole in a titanium shaft planted in the femur. If the drill is not lined up properly, then no amount of hammering will advance the drill into the hole. The two PHANToMs allow the user to line up the drill bit with the virtual patient's leg. The *Haptic Workbench* display provides both a 3D view and a fluoroscope display of the leg and tools. The benefits of simulating such a procedure extend not only to the patient, but also to the doctors because they are not exposed to harmful x-rays while practicing the operation.

Conclusion

Many of the doctors who have had the opportunity to try it have found it to be quite accurate. While the lab has not continued to work on the *Celiac Plexus Block Simulator*, they have remained active in pursuing other possible uses of virtual reality for simulation and training of medical procedures.

FIGURE 5-12

A physician practices a femoral nail procedure on the Haptic Workbench.

Photograph courtesy Karl Reinig

The *Celiac Plexus Block Simulator* is a pioneering example of multimodal representation in a medical VR application. The sense of touch conveys a great deal of information to a physician when performing this procedure. The *Celiac Plexus Block Simulator* used several forms of haptic feedback to provide a meaningful experience to the physician practicing with the VR application. Real world medical instruments were used as props to allow the physician to feel the actual mechanics of those medical tools.

A PHANToM device provided force feedback based on the type of tissue that was being penetrated. The shell of the body of the patient also provided haptic feedback, though not with a great deal of haptic verisimilitude to a patient's actual back. Sound was also used to emulate sounds that a patient might make during the procedure. In fact, the haptic components of this application were the elements that set this application apart from other similar applications at the time. The visual feedback was very similar to that conveyed during an actual procedure. An interesting aspect of this application was that while the hands of the physician were tracked via the instruments, there was no tracking of the head in this application. Hence, this application provides immersion via haptics rather than from the visual display. In summary, the combination of visual, haptic, and auditory feedback combined enabled a new type of simulator to be created that allowed physicians to practice a procedure they currently couldn't practice without an actual patient.

CASE STUDY 5.3: AUTISM THERAPY

Government regulations guarantee that all children in the United States receive an education. This includes children with special disabilities and handicaps. Unfortunately, current educational practices do not always meet the requirements of all children with special needs. Computer engineer Dorothy Strickland led a joint project between the North Carolina State University Computer Science Department and staff therapists from the Division for Treatment and Education of Autistic and other Communications handicapped CHildren (TEACCH) at the University of North Carolina at Chapel Hill School of Medicine. The project was an exploration of whether virtual reality would be a suitable technology for enhancing the education of one such group of children.

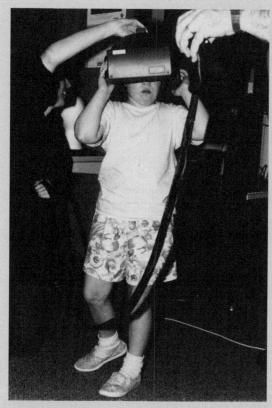

FIGURE 5-13

One problem with using virtual reality to teach children with autism is the fact that head-mounted displays are designed for adults. Here, you can see that not only is the HMD too large for the child but also heavy, as is evident from his using his hands to support the helmet.

Image courtesy Dorothy Strickland

For her project, Strickland chose to work with children with autism. Autism is a disability that causes children to be disconnected from their surroundings. They often display symptoms that include abnormal response to input stimuli, lack of human engagement, and inability to generalize between environments. People with autism often exhibit rigid, limited patterns of action and compulsive or ritualistic behaviors.

Application Description

It often takes longer to teach tasks to children with autism, and this can lead to real-world training involving dangerous environments resulting in considerable exposure to risk. Strickland hypothesized that VR would provide a safe learning environment for children with autism, and that a number of the special requirements for learning tools for these children can be met by virtual reality. This would be particularly beneficial for tasks that can be dangerous to learn in the real world, such as knowing what to do, and more importantly, what *not* to do, at street intersections.

When making an experience in any medium, it is always important to know (preferably early in the design/development process) who your audience is and what needs exist to specifically address this audience. The traits of autistic behavior constrain how and what information can be presented to people suffering from autism.

Strickland compiled a list of features that should be included in an environment for teaching children with autism [Strickland 1996]. Each of these features matches abilities of virtual reality, strengthening the possibility of the usefulness of VR for this task. Her list of features include:

- Controllable input stimuli
- Modification for generalization
- Safe-learning environment
- A primarily visual world
- Individualized treatment
- Learning with minimal human interaction
- Vestibular stimulation

The reasons for these features become more apparent when one considers the primary attributes of autistic behavior. Some common behaviors that make interacting with autistic people challenging include difficulty in focusing (easily distracted), difficulty in attending to more than one sense at a time, they often don't like things placed on their head, and (children especially) tend to get agitated when they are in unfamiliar surroundings. One thing they do seem to enjoy is "vestibular mismatch." This is when the sense of balance doesn't fit what the sense of sight is reporting. In the past, causing vestibular mismatch in students has even been used as a reward mechanism.

Of course, there are degrees to which individual people with autism can cope with the rest of the world. Their level of functioning is broadly classified as being low-, mid- or high-functioning. Low-functioning people with autism are not able to perform verbal communication. High-functioning people with autism are able to perform complex tasks well enough to hold a job. Mid-level function people with autism can do rudimentary verbal communication, but are not able to cope in most situations.

Strickland's initial work has been with mid-level functioning children with autism. This group needs more educational help than the high-functioning group. The level of communication with mid-level individuals with autism is limited to a few words. In this case, they cannot speak or understand normal sentences, but they can understand a few simple verbal instructions. Even this limited vocabulary of a few words and ability to follow simple directions makes it more straightforward to work with mid-level than low-functioning children with autism.

For months prior to designing the application, Strickland visited a classroom to study the children's behaviors and get ideas for how to best design the experiment and how to create an environment amenable to the children. One measure that was used was to have the toys that were familiar to the children at the lab environment. Since many autistic children tend to get agitated when in unfamiliar surroundings, or when not allowed to follow their normal routine, providing familiar toys to the lab environment and maintaining a consistent schedule helped to alleviate some agitation.

In order to build a VR environment based on her list of important features, Strickland created a simple scene with a street, a sidewalk, and texture-mapped buildings. She chose not to include any people or animals, or any objects in the sky. An important consideration when dealing with children with autism is to avoid unwanted distractions, so the only nonstationary object in the scene was a single car that passed by periodically.

The only output of the system was visual. Instructors gave verbal instructions to the subjects, but the computer simulation generated no sounds. Because children with autism often get agitated when required to attend to more than one sense at a time, the decision was made to focus on only the visual elements of the task. The application authors created a low-contrast environment using gray as the predominant color. The cars were made bright red and blue, the two colors recognized by the selected subjects in pre-VR cognitive testing. These colors also provide high contrast against a gray background.

Each trial would begin with the subject located in one of a selection of different places to allow the child to experience different scenery at the street crossing position.

Since the children were minimally verbal, it was difficult to give the children instructions, and likewise difficult for them respond to the instructors. To overcome this difficulty, the parents aided by physically helping the children carry out the instructions the first time. When successful, they rewarded the children and repeated the process in order to help the child associate the words with the task.

Strickland altered the scene between sessions to accommodate each subject's response patterns. Features that she could control from trial to trial include the speed of the car and the particular intersection at which they stood. A small virtual downtown was modeled, and the child could be placed at a variety of locations such as the middle of the street, in front of a gas station, across from stores, or at the corner of a two-way intersection. Strickland edited the world file by hand between trials to setup each particular scenario.

The First Experiment

Strickland developed an experiment to test whether a child with autism would understand the virtual world presented in an HMD, could learn a task in VR, and whether such learning would generalize to the real world. Two subjects diagnosed as being autistic were chosen for this study, a 7-year-old girl and a 9-year-old boy. Both were classified as mid-level functioning. Each child was exposed to the VR environment 40 times over a 6-week period.

The first task was for the child to learn to recognize an object. In this application, the object of primary importance was a car on the street. Once they were able to accomplish the recognition task, the child was instructed to find the object in the scene, walk to it, and stop. In addition to the car, there was also a stop sign located in the scene that the child had to find and walk to.

FIGURE 5-14

A simple virtual world was modeled that had some simple buildings and vehicles.
Image courtesy Dorothy Strickland

Because children with autism are often not skilled at knowing the most important things to attend to, it was important to provide an environment that promoted attention to the appropriate task. Also, there were no human representations in the virtual world. To avoid the distraction of room noises, and the sounds of the hardware, they placed padded inserts in the headphones of the head-mounted display. The occlusive nature of the HMD helped prevent visual distractions. The students could not see the other people while they were in the helmet. This feature of HMDs is one of the major advantages over a projection VR environment for this type of application.

No exposure was over 5 minutes. A trait common among children with autism is an aversion to having things on their heads, so there was concern over whether or not the children would even accept wearing the head-mounted display. Preconditioning was used to increase the likelihood that the children would wear the HMD. The boy practiced with a football helmet and the girl a riding helmet prior to trying the HMD. Also, the children's siblings were present as an aid in getting the children to accept the HMD. The subjects were more accepting of the HMD when they saw their siblings using and enjoying it. The girl subject immediately accepted the helmet. The boy, on

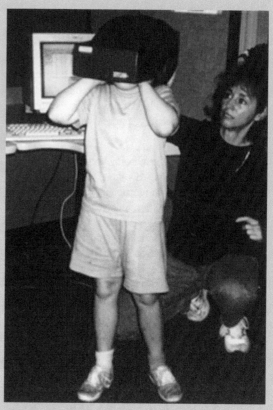

FIGURE 5-15

Children were able to see the virtual world on a computer monitor before they experienced the application using the HMD.
Image courtesy Dorothy Strickland

the other hand, didn't take the helmet until the second session. Interestingly, once he donned the helmet, he became calmer.

Since the virtual world was also displayed on a monitor in the test area, the children were able to see the car and virtual world on the monitor when they were not in the HMD. Interestingly, even though the children could not see the flat monitor once they had donned the HMD, both insisted that the monitor display be present before accepting the HMD.

Once they accepted the helmet, the children were able to learn to do the tasks. They would turn their bodies physically as appropriate to track the movement of the cars.

However, each child seemed to have a different acceptance of the idea of being immersed in the illusion. For example, when asked to point to the stop sign the boy would point to the front of the HMD (i.e., the location of the physical image of the sign), whereas the girl would walk to the stop sign and point to a position in the virtual world, although she too sometimes pointed to the front of the HMD. The boy was familiar with conventional PCs, so this may have contributed to his overlapping the immersive and real worlds. For this reason, they were instructed to walk to the object rather than point at it.

There was evidence of generalization in that the children responded similarly to three different street scenes, but Strickland knew that further study was necessary to determine if the children were generalizing across environments. Overall, the fact that the children seemed to accept and respond to the virtual worlds shows that VR might be a tool that can aid in the treatment of autism.

VR System
The virtual world was created using the Division dVS development environment and the *dVISE* authoring and simulation program software provided with the system. Development of the experiment was done over the course of a month of evenings by Strickland, on her own time. Use of the hardware was donated by Division Inc. Strickland was allowed to use equipment at Division's sales office in North Carolina during off-hours.

The VR system used in this application was centered on a ProVision 100™ integrated VR system provided by Division Inc. The system included an integrated Pixel-Plane hardware board for rendering the imagery, and an HMD. The HMD was a Division dVisor that provides 345 by 259 pixels of resolution with approximately 105 degrees horizontal FOV. The images were displayed stereoscopically, and adjusted for each child's interocular distance. The HMD weighed about 8 pounds, which was heavy for the children. Near the end of the sessions, the children were supporting the weight with their hands. A Polhemus FasTrak™ magnetic position tracker tracked the HMD in full 6-DOF.

In addition to the isolation benefit derived from wearing an HMD, the head-based type of visual display device is also less expensive and far more portable than projection VR displays. For all these reasons, HMDs were considered by Strickland to be the best choice for this particular application.

The Follow-up Study
A 6-month follow-up study was funded by an SBIR (Small Business Initiative Research) Phase I grant from the National Institute for Health (NIH). This grant was given to test whether students with autism who learn in the virtual environment will transfer that information to the real world, whether the training can be done on low-cost machines, and whether such a system is commercially viable.

The specifics of the experimental test were to analyze how well children with autism accept the technology, how well they learn concepts in the technology, and whether what is learned will carry over to the physical world.

In this study the specific task was "object identification." Strickland used subjects who were already participating in a cooking class, and who had mastered the ability to use a standard computer mouse. The task was to learn the names of different utensils used in cooking, such as a spatula. Objects used in the experiment were ones that had not yet been learned. The student identified objects by "picking out" the object in the HMD using a standard 2D desktop mouse.

Strickland reports that the results were impressive. Three objects were presented during 5-minute sessions. All of the subjects were able to learn the objects and identify them quickly in just two or three sessions. Once the students accomplished the object identification in the HMD they were tested in the real world with the real, physical objects. If they were not able to identify the real object, then they were retrained in the HMD. One to two weeks later, the students were retested with the real-world objects, and the statistical measure of their ability to identify them was better than chance.

To reduce costs both in development time and hardware expense, the object models were extremely simplified. By representing objects as simple 2D-texture images mapped onto a 2D polygon, the laborious task of object modeling and the computationally expensive task of rendering objects both become feasible in a small scale project.

This study was done without any user tracking, so no hardware beyond the computer and HMD was necessary. In fact, without tracking, the HMD was only beneficial because of its occlusive nature and the reduced distraction it provided the user. Strickland states that a flat screen with a hood to block distractions may have worked almost as well. However, once the children were used to the HMD, they liked it enough that it became a reward for the learning endeavor. The specific HMDs used in this study were Virtuality arcade-VR displays rented from n-Vision for the 3-month duration of the trials.

A Related Project

A related project was *Project S.O.L.V.E. (Studies on Learning in Virtual Environments)*, a joint effort between the Education and Outreach group at the National Center for Supercomputing Applications and the Transition Research Institute at the University of Illinois at Urbana-Champaign. The goal of *Project S.O.L.V.E.* was to research how VR can be applied in training and education. One specific skill they also chose to investigate using VR is children crossing streets. As part of this study, they chose to compare children with various disabilities to those without. The disabilities included autism and brain injury, among others.

The NCSA street-crossing simulation was created for the *CAVE* environment. The *CAVE* was chosen for a variety of reasons. Foremost was that the application was developed at NCSA, where a *CAVE* was readily available. However, use of the *CAVE* also provided an interesting contrast to other efforts at educational tasks. The *CAVE* can be more of a group experience, and at the very least does not isolate the subject from the instructor. The NCSA *CAVE* trades off loss of field of regard for wider field of view.

This application provides multiple street-crossing scenarios, including crossings protected by traffic signals, crossings protected by stop signs, and unprotected crossings. The *S.O.L.V.E.* simulation is designed to be a more realistic representation of the practice environment. Thus it is more complex than Strickland's worlds with multiple cars, buses, and a very rich environment with buildings, trees, and other details such as fire hydrants and street-lamps. One of the corners is a model of an actual intersection in Urbana, Illinois, near the school of the children involved in the study, which would thus be familiar to some of them.

FIGURE 5-16

A student stands in the CAVE *ready to cross the street after the truck passes. An instructor watches from within the* CAVE.

In this version of the street-intersection training task, the students were asked to go ahead and cross the virtual street at the appropriate time based on traffic and the type of traffic signs. To move the distance necessary to cross a street requires some travel paradigm other than physical locomotion as the *CAVE* is smaller than a street intersection.

Since the audience was young children a simple method of virtual travel was necessary. The experimental task only requires that the subject move forward to cross a street, so travel is controlled by pressing a button to move forward, and releasing the button to stop. This method of travel allows the student to approach the street, stop, look both ways, and when safe to do so, continue across the street. To familiarize subjects with the VR environment and practice the travel control, they were given a training session in a special pretask application. This task involved standing in a colorful field with a flower and tree ahead of the subject. They were instructed to approach the flower and stop. Stopping at the appropriate time rewards the child with sounds of applause and cheering.

FIGURE 5-17

Since many of the students in the study were from the same school, a corner near the school in Urbana, Illinois, was modeled for the study. Many students recognized the corner.

Preliminary Results

The project collected experimental data on 81 schoolchildren to see whether they could follow directions and safely complete the task and generalize between virtual environments. Half of the subjects had various disabilities. The data was analyzed at the Transition Research Institute. Analysis showed positive effects from training in the *CAVE*.

Another interesting preliminary finding indicates differences in difficulty based on the type of intersection. Based on the number of "virtual" accidents, the four-way stop intersection was found to be the most complicated intersection for children to maneuver, versus two-way stop and stop-light controlled intersections.

In addition to the findings regarding children and street crossing tasks, the researchers also learned an important lesson about VR application design. In an attempt to prevent the subject from walking laterally off the sidewalk, they implemented a scheme to move the world with the subject's head. The inadvertent result of this was to eliminate the motion parallax depth cue. The resultant loss of motion parallax makes it harder for viewers to get an accurate sense of scale of the virtual world, plus makes it seem as though the world "swims around" whenever the viewer moves their head. As it turned out, subjects don't really do much physical movement anyway, so it wasn't really necessary to do anything to keep them from walking sideways off the sidewalk.

Another design issue involved the 3D glasses. The NCSA *CAVE* uses the Crystal Eyes shuttering glasses, which were too large for most of the children involved in the study. To accommodate the smaller size of the children's heads, the researchers attached the glasses to a hat that the children were able to wear more comfortably. After one of the parents mentioned that they had a hygiene concern regarding the sharing of the hat, they went back to using the ill-fitting glasses.

Conclusion

These projects laid groundwork for future work in using virtual reality to teach children potentially dangerous tasks in the safety of a virtual world. The *S.O.L.V.E* project expanded toward training of potentially dangerous scenarios to a wider base of children, and relied on the expectation that what is expensive VR today will be affordable in the not too distant future. Strickland, on the other hand, looked at getting

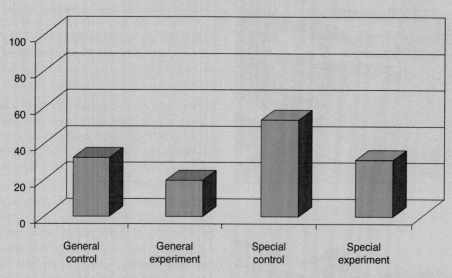

Percentage of individuals hit by vehicles

FIGURE 5-18

Researchers from the Transition Institute at the University of Illinois studied the participants in the experiment. This chart shows the percentage of children hit by virtual vehicles in each experimental group.

FIGURE 5-19

This picture drawn by a fifth-grade special education student after his experience crossing the street in the CAVE shows one way in which the visit can be augmented through post-visit activities.

low-cost systems into use as soon as possible, and expanding the potential user base to help train low-functioning (nonverbal) children with autism, by using EEG monitoring to determine the response of the subject.

The expense of the *CAVE* makes such applications impractical for daily use by a majority of students. However, the use of special field trips to interact with applications specially designed for the students' skill levels can be a beneficial learning tool. Such experiences can be augmented by preparatory instruction about what they will do/see at the *CAVE*, and post-visit discussions about the experience. The education continues after the time spent at the VR facility ends. Discussions and other activities continued back in the classroom build on the experience in the *CAVE*.

CyberEdge Journal awarded Strickland its product application award for 1995, stating it to be an example of "finding a new way to use a powerful technology to help the least empowered."

CASE STUDY 5.4: ULTRASOUND DIAGNOSIS USING AUGMENTED REALITY

Executive Summary

Visualizing complex three-dimensional structures using tools capable of only two dimensional representations can be a difficult task for many people. Yet many professions require this very feat, and eventually the practitioners learn how to create 3D mental models given the 2D display as presented by 2D tools. Of these professions, perhaps the medical field offers the greatest challenge to coping with this task because new technologies and new uses for existing technologies are frequently introduced. Medical procedures often have the requirement of visualizing structures internal to the body, with only limited access to seeing the 3D structure directly.

Aiding doctors in overcoming this challenge is one way that researchers at the University of North Carolina at Chapel Hill (UNC) Computer Science department are using their programming skills. Fred Brooks, professor and founding department head of Computer Science at UNC, believes that computer scientists should do their work with an eye toward what is required to solve real-world needs. The CS department was interested in researching augmented reality (AR)—a technology related to virtual reality that combines the senses of the real world with computer-enhanced imagery. Building on a history of collaboration with members of the medical profession, they chose to work with doctors to create a system with the goal to "develop and operate a system that allows a physician to see directly inside a patient." Doctors use a variety of imaging technologies to help them visualize the internals of the human body, including x-ray, CAT scans, MRI scans, and ultrasound scans. The UNC team chose to work with ultrasound scanning technology for three reasons: it is fast, noninvasive, and does not use harmful radiation. An AR ultrasound system could be useful to doctors to "see in" patients during procedures such as obstetrics exams, cardiology exams, and diagnostic procedures such as needle-guided biopsies.

Ultrasound is widely used for procedures such as breast biopsies, removing tissue lesions, and localizing lesions prior to biopsy and cyst aspiration. Using ultrasound scans in these operations is "difficult to learn and perform." It requires good hand-eye coordination as well as 3D visualization

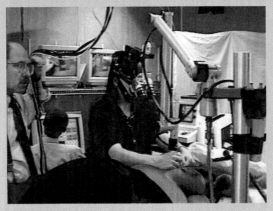

FIGURE 5-20

Prof. Henry Fuchs watches as Dr. Etta Pisano performs a simple visualization procedure using an augmented reality visualization system.
Image courtesy University of North Carolina

skills. Prior to using an augmented reality display, physicians performing such operations had at their disposal only a "non-registered two-dimensional ultrasound image (and perhaps prescan 2D medical imagery such as x-ray images) to assist her in the inherently three-dimensional task of guiding a needle to a biopsy target." [State, Livingston, et al.]

Challenges of Augmented Reality

Although augmented reality was not an entirely new technology (Sutherland's original head-mounted display allowed the viewer to simultaneously see the real world and virtual imagery), AR application development and research had a very limited scope. Besides the development in the military of head-up displays, few VR developers have shown much interest in the technology until more recently.

Part of the challenge for this project was to find out what was possible with then-current technology, and then set out to try to solve the problems that prevented the system from being useful as a medical tool. The project was begun by Professor Henry Fuchs in 1992. As the first medical procedure to explore with AR, he chose obstetric fetal exams as a good starting point. For reasons discussed below, the research team later changed their focus to other medical operations. A major focus was on the use of AR for "ultrasound-guided needle biopsy of the breast" operations.

Although virtual reality benefits from rendering the virtual world in as many senses as practical, augmented reality benefits from the circumstance that the user is already immersed in the real—physical—world. The physical world itself provides feedback for all the senses, including vision, so an AR system need only focus on particular senses to help convey additional information about the real world. For this reason, augmented reality systems often focus on representing, rendering, and displaying only visual information. Such is the case with the UNC *Ultrasound Visualization* project.

One thing they knew from the outset was that the artificial world would need to be rendered and displayed such that viewers "believe that the synthetic objects exist in the [real] environment." [Jacobs et al.] To realize this goal would require advances in registration, latency, resolution, and information representation. Problems on all fronts were encountered, and to a great extent reduced during the course of this (ongoing) project.

Registration

Registering the real and virtual worlds, such that objects coincident in both worlds appear to be in exactly the same place at all times, is one of the most critical problems for augmented reality. Registration affects the mental immersiveness/believability of the illusion, and in this case, usefulness. If the artificial objects are not properly registered, it is very difficult for the viewer to determine where those objects are supposed to be positioned with respect to the real world. Solving or reducing registration errors is crucial.

Both spatial registration and temporal registration are important to merging the two realities. Spatial registration is fairly obvious, but if objects are not aligned temporally, then when the user turns their head, they will see the real-world change, followed by the virtual-world change a few instances later. This delay makes it apparent which objects are real, and which are not. The delay between the real-world view and the virtual world objects is referred to as *relative latency.* In his research at UNC, Rich Holloway

found that about 1 ms of latency in tracking results in up to 1 mm of registration error at arm's length, ignoring positional error and assuming a peak angular velocity of 100 degrees/sec for the user's head. [Holloway 1995].

Latency

Latency is a common problem for both virtual reality and augmented reality, but usually more so for the latter. Latency can enter a system in many different ways. From work done by Wloka [Wloka 1995], Mine [Mine 1993], and Taylor [Taylor et al. 1995], the UNC research team compiled a list of six ways in which latency is introduced to an AR or VR system:

- "Off-host delay"—the delay between the actual event, and the *sensing* of that event by the computational system.

- "Computational delay"—the delay caused by doing computations on the incoming signal to produce a world-state.

- "Rendering delay"—the time required to render the world imagery.

- "Display delay"—the time between creating the rendered image, and the display of that image. (In visual rendering and display, this is generally the time spent waiting for the next screen refresh to occur, and presenting the new image at the beginning of the next display scan).

- "Synchronization delay"—the time waiting for some other crucial data path to catch up.

- "Frame-rate-induced delay"—the amount of time since the current image was first presented. For example, in the visual system the image is already latent when first placed on the screen, but as time passes waiting for the next "frame," the current image continues to age and become increasingly delayed from the incoming data.

Using the above terms, the relative latency is a combination of "off-host delay," "computational delay," "synchronization delay," and in some cases "rendering delay." Rendering delay is particularly problematic when the optical see-through style of HMD is used because the "rendering" of the synthetic imagery cannot be fast enough to match the real world (which does not exhibit a rendering delay). The other forms of delay will of course negatively affect the overall latency of the images presented, but do not affect the relative latency because all the data go through these steps together.

Resolution

The degree to which one can precisely sense the environment plays a large role in how we relate to it. The greater the amount of detail we perceive adds to both the realism of the image and its usefulness. If a visual image is so blurry that we would be considered legally blind, then we will have less ability to perform functions than if we had simulated 20/20 vision.

The need for greater resolution is even more crucial when the functions being performed have real-world consequences. This is obviously true for the medical procedures where fine hand-eye control is necessary to perform the operation.

Visual resolution can only be as good as the display device supports. When using the video see-through style of AR display, even perception of the real-world visual scene is limited by the HMD. In the case of needle biopsy operations, the 22-gauge needle that is typically used is less than the width of a single pixel in the VR-4 HMD used for many of the early UNC experiments (about 0.7 pixels thick). A 3 mm breast lesion would be about 3×3 pixels in size on the VR-4 display.

The solution to this was fairly obvious—use higher-resolution displays and cameras. At the time (1996), the UNC team did not concern itself with trying to solve the problem of video resolution themselves, because it would be reduced by natural advances in video technology. For their analysis, they have instead chosen to use thicker needles. Of course, this limited their testing to training dummies, since they cannot use the thicker needles on real subjects. They have subsequently upgraded to a higher-resolution HMD, allowing more realistic testing.

Interface with the Augmented World

AR systems are constrained by how the user can interface with the world. One constraint for most AR systems is that the user must occupy the same physical location as what

is being represented in their display. While limiting the options for how the user interfaces with the "virtual" world, it also makes the task much simpler. For instance, the only method of travel that makes any sense is *physical locomotion*. If the user doesn't move in the real world, then they shouldn't move in the augmented world. Also, many of the world-manipulation operations are done exactly as they would be done in the absence of an AR system. For example, to move the position of the ultrasound-augmented sensory input representation the user simply moves the physical ultrasound probe as they would under normal circumstances.

An example of a scenario that is not subject to these constraints is when AR is combined with telepresence. Because telepresence provides a remote position for the human participant, their interactions with the real world are mediated. Thus other VR interaction paradigms are possible. Also, the constraint requiring the participant to occupy the same physical location is replaced by requiring the participant's surrogate senses (robot) to occupy that space. So a point-to-fly method of travel could be implemented provided the sensory-surrogate can perform the maneuver in whatever real-world space it might be (e.g., underground, in space, or on land).

One freedom is that there is less need to attempt to represent a "photorealistic" picture of the augmenting information. In general, when particpants are using an AR system, they want to see something not directly viewable, and therefore not directly able to be represented. Thus, the challenge is to find ways to represent what is behind the walls, or beneath the skin, in an intuitive manner, despite the fact that seeing directly through solid objects is not something with which the users will have had a lot of experience (although doctors will of course have experience in seeing 2D representations of 3D structures, but this information is gathered "off-line" and is not viewed in registration with the solid object). The UNC research team discovered many features of good and bad representations as the project progressed.

Representation of the Augmented World

A significant factor in whether an AR system will be considered useful to a doctor is how well the information presented to them is represented in a way that makes it easier

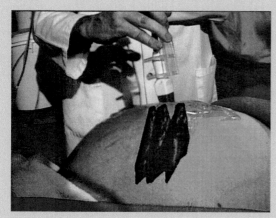

FIGURE 5-21

Visualizing ultrasound images without adding proper cues that indicate placement causes the images to be ambiguously floating in space.

Image courtesy University of North Carolina

for them to grasp the nature of the situation. In basic terms, doctors are interfacing with three-dimensional objects using two-dimensional sensing devices. By moving these 2D sensing devices around, they can scan the entire 3D structure, but it can still be difficult to perceive the overall nature of the object. A goal of this project has been to find effective representations for these objects within the constraints of the scanning technology.

Floating Slices

At the beginning of the project (when using a fetus examination as the prototype task), the first style of representation was to simply place 2D ultrasound slices of the developing child over the image of the woman. This technique was not very good at all. It was nearly impossible for the doctor to determine the position within the body where the slices were located.

The Pit (hole)

A direct result of trying to solve the problem of the "floating slices" representation, the use of a *pit* to represent a hole in the object (i.e., the patient) was found to be a much better representation. The pit gives location context to the scanned data, and allows the data to be rendered with the proper occlusion cues.

The pit appears as the inner-surface walls, floor, and rim of a hole in the object. Other forms of data are then rendered to appear within the pit, such as 2D ultrasound slices. Representation of material that is inside the body but not within the pit is occluded by the pit walls. Later representational experiments removed the inner-pit surfaces, leaving just a hole through which the doctor can explore the inner cavity of the patient. The plain hole allows the viewer to look obliquely through the hole, which is useful if there is some benefit from not "removing" too much of the skin surface, yet still wanting to be able to see underneath a larger area of the skin.

For best results, rendering a pit or hole requires that the edge of the pit/hole match the surface into which one is peering. Without this edge matching, the problem of the floating slices begins to resurface as it becomes difficult to determine how the pit/hole matches to the body, and therefore how the objects within the pit/hole are positioned. In order to properly render these edges, the system must know the shape of the surface, thus requiring more sensing technology.

The first representations placed inside the hole were the same floating slices as in the earlier versions. However, any type of representation can be placed within the hole, including isosurface and volumetric rendering techniques. Two other representations implemented by the research team thus far are a sphere to represent the target tissue (a cyst or tumor), and a representation of the biopsy needle (which must be registered with the actual needle).

Radar Slices

Ultrasound data is "accurate" only for the exact moment of each scan, because tissue within the body (especially a developing child) does not remain motionless. Thus, continuing to display all previously scanned data can misrepresent the hidden tissue. To address this, a "3D radar" idiom was created in which older scan slices are faded out over time, eventually disappearing altogether. This is very reminiscent to how radar displays represented information about echoes from the environment—as the probe scans in a certain direction, a bright blip is produced on the screen. When the probe moves away, the blip begins to fade.

The rate at which old slices are eliminated can be selected by the user. Choosing the fade rate is influenced by the

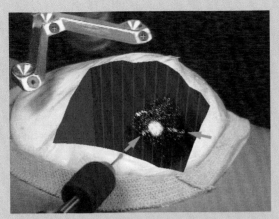

FIGURE 5-22

Two methods of the "pit" representation. On the left, the pit extends several inches, with a floor on the bottom. On the right, the walls of the pit are only about an inch deep, showing the rest of the body cavity beneath.
Image courtesy University of North Carolina

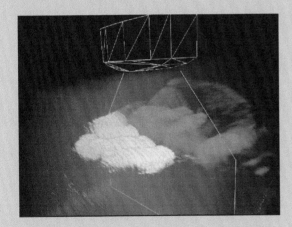

FIGURE 5-23

As the ultrasound scanner moves, old scan images begin to fade away, indicating the degrading confidence in the data.
Image courtesy University of North Carolina

amount of clutter versus the need for lots of data, and by how much the underlying tissue can be expected to move. For example, a developing child is likely to move a lot more than a lesion within the breast.

Depth Cues

Depth cues are always important in rendering a believable visual scene. In augmented reality, they become even more important as a means by which the synthetic imagery is represented to appear as though it occupies the same space as the real world. Four visual depth cues that are particularly important for enabling this effect are head motion parallax, stereoscopic imaging, proper occlusion, and lighting and shadow effects.

Head Motion Parallax

Head motion parallax is treated no differently than with typical VR display systems, and is vitally important to creating a world that responds appropriately to user movement. An added concern for AR display systems is that the synthetic and real worlds should respond the same to any user movement of the head. This concern is another manifestation of the registration problem.

Stereoscopic Imaging

Physicians typically work in small nearby working volumes. This situation is very conducive for using the depth cues provided by stereoscopic visuals. The stereoscopic depth cue is needed to help the physicians work, and was thought to be required for acceptable performance.

Occlusion

Nearer objects occluding objects that are farther away is the strongest of all depth cues. Therefore, appropriate merging of synthetic objects into the real world must avoid improper object occlusion at all costs, or else the virtual imagery will not seem to be of the same world. In some cases, this may simply be accomplished by preventing synthetic objects from moving to locations where they are likely to be occluded incorrectly. However, especially when working in close quarters, these circumstances cannot always be avoided. Therefore, other techniques must be employed to produce a proper image.

There are two situations that need to be addressed: real objects in front of virtual objects should result in the virtual object being (perhaps partially) occluded by the real object, and similarly, virtual objects need to be able to hide real objects in the scene. These may seem to be the same issue, but the latter requires the use of the video see-through method of AR display, whereas the former can be accomplished with any AR display.

In either case, proper occlusion-rendering requires knowing the positions of the real and virtual objects that might be involved so the rendering system can determine where to render the synthetic objects. This means that any real-world objects that might occlude virtual objects need to be tracked or kept out of the way.

In addition to tracking the real-world objects, the system must know the shape of those objects. Objects for which the shape cannot be known *a priori* must be scanned just prior to the procedure. In particular, the shape of the body region that will be involved must be determined. Knowing this shape is particularly important for aligning the edge of the virtual hole with the surface of the body. If the edge of the pit doesn't match the body shape, then the parallax from head motion will result in the pit moving slightly separately from the body and thus not appear to be attached to it. To get the shape of the body, it is prescanned by a mechanical tracker just prior to the procedure. Once scanned, it is assumed that the patient does not move until the procedure is completed. This assumption is of course an approximation of what will happen, but according to developer Mark Livingston, it is a surprisingly "acceptable approximation that does not cause significant

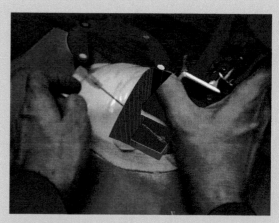

FIGURE 5-24

Images of the probe, pit, and patient are properly overlain, providing correct occlusion cues, but the doctor's finger is not occluded properly.
Image courtesy University of North Carolina

error compared to other problems." He continues: "Until we have accurate head tracking, it doesn't pay to worry about accurate surface tracking."

To properly render virtual and real objects together in the same scene, the developers take advantage of the z-buffer technique[2] common to most computer graphics rendering hardware. This is done by rendering the depth information of the real-world objects, but not their physical appearance. This "trick" then allows the virtual scene to be rendered normally, and any information from virtual objects that would be rendered behind other objects, including the z-rendered real objects, will not appear in the image. This technique works for both the optical and video methods of see-through HMD displays.

Proper occlusion rendering allows the scene to include virtual objects that visually behave as expected. For example, a virtual object can penetrate the skin but will only be seen if it happens to be within the pit. Some real-world objects

---

[2] *The z-buffer rendering technique is described in* Computer Graphics: Principles and Practice *[Foley, VanDam, Feiner, and Hughes],* Computer Graphics *[Hearn and Baker], among others.*

FIGURE 5-25
Lighting techniques are used to create more photorealistic representations of virtual objects. Here, a computer-generated teapot has a realistic reflection map to enhance the appearance of the object. Fiducial markers in the world allow the objects in the world as well as the viewing camera to be accurately tracked.
Image courtesy University of North Carolina

are too difficult to track effectively (such as the doctor's hands) and thus will not properly occlude the synthetic objects. The best solution in this case is to reduce the need for the hands to come between their eyes and the virtual objects. Of course, this cannot always be accomplished.

Lighting and Shadows
Lighting effects (including shadows) are also useful in helping a viewer determine the relative location of objects. Of course, when dealing with the representation of non-real, in fact, ethereal images, lack of shadows and interaction with lights is less important than when photorealistic imagery is the goal. The UNC research efforts toward producing a medical visualization system have thus been able to avoid addressing lighting effects. A separate effort at UNC has done research on photorealistic rendering of augmented reality scenes [State, Hirota, et al.].

Technology Enhancement for Useful AR Systems
Just as important as the efforts to produce a usable VR tool are, producing an augmented reality tool requires not just

the development of the interface and the representation, but also requires the pursuit of advances in the technology. That is, there were certain problems not related to the specific task of medical visualization that needed to be solved to bring their system to fruition.

One goal of the UNC project was to uncover what shortcomings and needs existed in technology that precluded the creation of a usable augmented reality application. These shortcomings were not so great as to cause the developers to give up in their pursuit to develop AR applications. Rather, it required parallel development efforts to solve, reduce, or avoid problems that were showstoppers in the original implementation.

One such effort was to develop a video that would demonstrate some high standards to which they could aspire. This attempted "gold standard" would be produced using as many of the same technologies as the struggling AR system as possible. The video was produced by recording all the incoming data along with time-code information such that it could be rendered and edited together in non-real-time. By freeing themselves from the constraints of insufficient computational power and delays in the data gathering and display systems (resulting in the total elimination of all types of latency), they were able to present a view of the possibilities of an AR application in the absence of technological bottlenecks. The result of this effort was not quite as good as they hoped for, and they deemed the video to be a "brass standard" that still represented something to strive for.

To make the "live" system function at a more acceptable level, the UNC research team created a system that was more usable by confronting three main issues: addressing a simpler problem, reducing relative latency, and enhancing tracker performance.

A Simpler Problem
After their initial work with visualizing a child developing within the womb, one of the main problems that made the AR system less than optimal was the fact that the baby frequently moved during the exam, making it difficult if not impossible to use the system in a meaningful way. Since other medical procedures that rely on ultrasound information examine tissue that doesn't move around quite so much, it was decided to address those procedures first.

 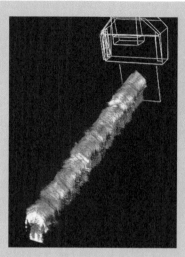 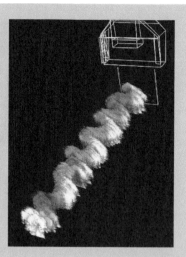

FIGURE 5-26

Without paying attention to relative delays between inputs, the path followed by the scanner can cause the data to be similarly skewed. The image on the right shows the more accurate representation obtained when information is properly aligned.
Image courtesy University of North Carolina

The research could return to the fetus examination later, once some of the other problems had been resolved technologies improved.

Relative Latency

Relative latency between incoming data streams leads to two problems: faulty temporal registration and incorrect recreation of scanned objects. When the ultrasound data is not properly aligned in terms of time, objects that are physically straight can end up being stored internally and represented in a shape highly affected by the scanning. For instance, if a zigzag or curving pattern followed during the scan is used, a straight object will look zigzagged or curved.

The two primary ways of addressing and reducing relative latency are to use time stamping and predictive filtering to temporally align data input streams, and also to delay inputs of lower latency to match those of higher latency. By using the video see-through method of AR visual display, the system can delay the real-world imagery to match it with the computer-rendered world. This temporal matching of images comes at the expense of delayed response of the real world to user movements. Thus, it is

imperative that the overall delay not be very long, or the user can experience nausea and/or other problems.

Time-stamping the ultrasound data at the moment when the scan was made and recording the location of the probe across time allows the resultant data to be positioned at the spot where the probe was located when the scan was made rather than where the probe is at the time it is displayed. This means that the user will see a delay between the probe's movement and the appearance of scan information, but the representation of the world will be more accurate.

Tracking Performance

Good tracking is important for a virtual reality system to give the user the opportunity to suspend disbelief and mentally immerse themselves into the virtual world. For an augmented reality system, it is vital. The error in registration between real and synthetic worlds caused by bad tracking spoils the illusion that the two worlds coexist.

As described in *Understanding Virtual Reality* [Sherman and Craig], different tracking technologies offer different abilities and constraints.

Magnetic tracking systems are nice because they are not very encumbering, allowing the tracked object (e.g., head, ultrasound probe) to be freely moved about the space. However, these systems suffer from being not very precise or accurate in high-metal, high-RF environments. It is not possible to eliminate all the sources of distortion from the environment, because the list includes the ceiling, lights, floor, and the ultrasound scanner itself. Thus, if magnetic tracking is used, other ways must be integrated to reduce tracking error.

Mechanical tracking systems are nice because they are very accurate and precise, and have very low latency in reporting the current position. However, the mechanical linkages that connect the probe to the fixed reference point can encumber the user. Because of the benefits of mechanical tracking, if feasible, it would be ideal for as many of the objects as possible to be tracked mechanically. In some cases, this does not even add an extra burden to the system, because of linkages already in place. For example, the ultrasound probe is already linked to the ultrasound processing box, and adding the mechanical tracking to this only slightly reduces how the probe can be maneuvered. In general, though, mechanical tracking, while okay for many props and medical devices, is not good for tracking the head.

Optical tracking systems can also provide good precision, without the added movement constraints of the mechanical systems. However, it depends on a clear line of sight being maintained between the unit being tracked and the sensors. In a hospital setting, it is not unreasonable to expect that there will be little visual interference between the head of the doctor and the ceiling, so this is an acceptable alternative.

Videometric tracking is a feasible choice for tracking in any AR system using a video see-through HMD, as is the case for the UNC project. Videometric tracking is done by processing the incoming video stream, locating multiple landmarks, and using the location of these landmarks in the video field to calculate the position of the camera. The benefit of using a videometric system is that given enough landmarks, it can be very accurate, and when used in a system that already has a camera input, it doesn't add any encumbrances to the system. The major problem

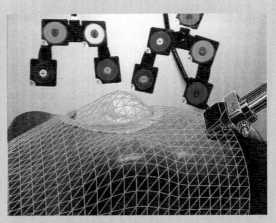

FIGURE 5-27

This image shows a wireframe representation of the body as it is scanned by a mechanical arm. A collection of colored fiducial landmarks are used to help register the real and virtual visual images.
Image courtesy University of North Carolina

with this type of tracking is that it can be computationally expensive.

The UNC developers describe two techniques that they use to reduce the computational expense of tracking: using a known approximation for the tracked position to begin the process, and using easily identifiable fiducial landmarks for the vision system to make use of. The UNC system uses color-coded fiducial landmarks to enable quick identification of any particular landmark. They use two concentric circles, each colored by one of four bright colors, which allows them to have up to 12 unique landmarks.

A hybrid tracking system was ultimately chosen as the method of tracking the user's head. Implementing this system required the development of algorithms to integrate information from three separate tracking systems into a single data stream. The implementation details are described in a paper by Andrei State and colleagues [State, Hirota, et al.]. We will briefly summarize the technique and results.

The hybrid tracking system was chosen only for tracking the user's head. Because the simpler (and better) mechanical tracking method was feasible for the ultrasound probe, that is how the probe was tracked. The hybrid head-tracking algorithm began by using the raw data from a magnetic tracking system, then using a static correction table (generated ahead of time using the mechanical system as the reference) to determine the amount of correction needed for many points in the working volume. This technique results in a decent approximation of the head's position, which can be fine tuned using the video information from the cameras.

In their research on tracking, the UNC team found that in a high-metal environment location errors of the magnetic tracking system could be up to 10 cm (i.e., huge), with orientation errors averaging 3.5 degrees (maximum of 6.6 degrees). The static correction table alone reduced maximum location errors by 80% (down to 2 cm), but only reduced the average orientation error by 40% (down to 2.1 degrees). The further enhancement from the videometric system reduced the errors to virtually nil.

The computational need of the videometric tracking approach can be reduced by basing the first-guess of the sensor position from the statically calibrated magnetic tracking information. Using a reasonable first-guess allows the image searching routines to know where to look for the fiducial landmarks. The location of the fiducial landmarks is preset by touching the mechanical tracker to each of them prior to beginning the operation.

It is sometimes difficult to keep many fiducial landmarks in view of the cameras. The operator cannot be concerned with this detail, so they must be strategically placed where they are likely to be within view of the camera. Three landmarks are all that are needed for "perfect" tracking. With two landmarks in view, then the camera's orientation can be completely determined. If only one landmark is in view, then two of the three camera orientation angles can be calculated. When no landmarks are visible, the system continues to use the latest known correction values.

Of course, better initial tracking reduces the necessity for more fiducials. After switching to an optical tracking system for tracking the doctor's head, the accuracy prior to correction from the videometric tracking was found to be good enough that a single fiducial reference point in view was sufficient to produce tracking results as good as the hybrid magnetic/videometric system with multiple fiducials.

Proper Rendering of Multiple Slices

The use of translucent slices results in loss of the ability to use the normal z-buffer method of fast rendering. Without the z-buffer, objects must be rendered in order from furthest to closest to the viewer. A technique for enabling objects to be quickly sorted is the binary space partitioning tree (BSP tree) algorithm. However, the BSP tree algorithm assumes objects are not added and deleted at a rapid pace as is the case of the fading radar slices. The application development team developed a method to use dual BSP trees to overcome this limitation as described in [Garrett et al.].

The AR System

As mentioned earlier, the UNC research team chose early on to use a video see-through HMD for the AR display device. In 1996, the HMD was a composite of a Virtual Research model VR-4 HMD with two Panasonic GP-KS102 cameras mounted on top, and a 3-pound counterweight added to the back. The VR-4 displays about 250 by 230 pixels per eye with a stereo image overlap of about 80% (in the range of the 50 mm working volume). Each of the cameras was equipped with a Cosmicar F1.8 12.5 mm lens. This camera configuration provides a 28-degree horizontal FOV. The primary concern in coming up with this configuration was to keep the optical distortion minimal. The cameras are mounted 64 mm apart to match the typical inter-pupillary distance of most people, and are oriented to have a fixed convergence of 4 degrees. Later, they upgraded the HMD to a Kaiser Electro-Optics ProView30 system with the same camera system attached.

Magnetic tracking was done with the Ascension Flock of Birds™ tracker. This system can operate at a sample rate of 103 Hz. Mechanical tracking for the ultrasound and ancillary operations were done with a Metrecom IND-01™ from FARO Technologies, Inc. The FARO tracker had a maximum sample rate of 27 Hz. The ultrasound scanner was a PIE Medical Scanner 200.

Later, the Ascension head tracker was replaced with the FlashPoint™ 5000 optical tracking system by Image Guided Technologies designed specifically for the medical market. The FlashPoint system was also used to replace tracking many of the instruments used in the procedures.

The mechanically linked (and still more accurate) FAROarm is still used for calibration, but most other tracking is handled by the FlashPoint 5000.

In 1996, the graphics and computational unit was a Silicon Graphics Onyx™ equipped with RE2™ graphics engines and a Sirius Video™ unit for real-time video integration. This has subsequently been upgraded to an Onyx with Infinite Reality™ graphics. In the prototype development for a fetal examination (done in 1992), a Pixel-Planes-5[3] graphics system was used. The video unit can access two simultaneous video input channels into the frame buffer, main memory, or texture memory with some constraints, and different time delays involved for each path. The camera images are combined by a QD Technology QD-1110 and sent to the Silicon Graphics frame buffer. The ultrasound video is captured directly into main memory by the Sirius Video hardware and resampled by the CPU to produce 256×256 monochrome (8-bit) pixel images. The resampled images are then transferred to the Reality Engine (RE2) texture memory.

It would be too difficult to buffer the incoming camera video signals, and it would be highly undesirable to add any delay to the user's view of the real world, so this input stream was used as the timing-anchor reference. Fortunately, the camera video inputs were found to have the lowest latency of all the devices, making it easier to make this the baseline for measuring input latency. The Faro mechanical tracker and Ascension magnetic tracker were both found to lag behind the camera by 30 ms, and the ultrasound scanner lagged the camera by 250 ms (as measured at 10 Hz). The considerable lag in the ultrasound video was due to the path the data took to get from video to the computational memory, as well as the processing required converting it to the appropriate format.

The Silicon Graphics RE2 is capable of displaying to multiple devices. In the UNC AR system, three outputs are used. Two outputs are set to 640×480-pixel VGA format (approximately the same resolution as NTSC television), and fed to the two HMD screens, and to separate monitors for others to watch. A third high-resolution image

---

[3]The Pixel-Planes series of graphics hardware were developed as part of a research program at UNC.

(1280×1024) is fed to a computer monitor and used to display the user interface.

The resultant system is capable of sustaining a frame rate of 10 Hz both for the HMD display and the ultrasound image capture. At slower frame rates it can render up to 16 million ultrasound pixels—255 two-dimmensional slices each with 256×256 pixels. To achieve 10 Hz, only up to about 20 slices were rendered at a time.

SYSTEM CHOICE

Display Paradigm

Perhaps the most significant choice made in designing the system for ultrasound diagnosis using AR was choosing the video see-through rather than the optical see-through method for merging the real and synthetic worlds. The benefits of using the video method are that it supports "proper occlusion relationships between real and virtual objects (provided that depth of real objects is known or can be determined)," there is better "ability to balance the brightness of real and synthetic imagery," it allows the latencies between real and virtual imagery to be matched, and it makes it easier to integrate videometric tracking into the system [State, Livingston, et al.].

The four major disadvantages of the video method are the lowered resolution of the real world because of the cameras and displays, the spatial offset between the location of the camera and the user's eyes, the added weight of the cameras, and the limited depth of field of the small ("lipstick") cameras. However, all of these disadvantages can (and likely will) be solved by improved technology. Even without the effort of the UNC team, cameras will become lighter and capable of higher resolutions. The use of some simple optics can adjust the incoming images to match those of the human observer, eliminating the spatial offset. In fact, the UNC research team has already developed an HMD to eliminate the eye offset [Fuchs et al.].

Credits

A great number of people have worked on this and other research efforts at UNC to support this project. Henry Fuchs, professor of computer science at UNC, conceived the project in 1992 and has nurtured it from the beginning. Mike Bajura was the principal designer of the system featured in the 1992 paper [Bajura, et al.]. Andrei State has been the technical leader on the project since 1993. Mary Whitton is the project manager. UNC professor Stephen Pizer helped with the research.

Several graduate research assistants have been involved with the project, including Ryutarou Ohbuchi, Michael Bajura, David Chen, Hong Chen, Christopher Tector, Andrew Brandt, William Garrett, Gentaro Hirota, Mark Livingston, Paul Rademacher, Jessica Crawford, Jeremy Ackerman, and Michael North.

The UNC computer scientists also worked with several physicians in their effort to produce a tool designed for use by doctors, including Vern Katz MD, Nancy Chescheir MD, Ricardo Hahn MD, Mark Deutchman MD, Matt Mauro MD, David Casalino MD, Etta D. Pisano MD, Anthony A. Meyer MD, Matt Mauro MD, and Melanie Mintzer MD.

Conclusion

Overall, the UNC project for ultrasound diagnosis using AR proved to be quite successful. It was successful at both demonstrating the real possibility of this technology to be useful in the medical operating arena, and successful at unearthing and reducing the technological barriers of implementation.

In general, project leader Henry Fuchs finds that implementing an AR system for visualization has greater "demands than either virtual environments or scientific visualization individually." This is due in part because, as Fuchs states, "Virtual environment and scientific visualization systems lack the error-emphasizing cues that a combined system provides" [State et al.].

There are a host of specific advances of technology that could significantly enhance the ability to produce a higher-quality AR system.

- Data-sensing hardware could include the capability of time-stamping the data stream to enable better predictive and corrective calculations.

- UNIX could be enhanced to behave in a real-time manner.[4]

- Standard ultrasound scanners scan at a thickness of 1 cm to 2 cm. While this is beneficial in many procedures, it does not work well with the AR system. The UNC team is striving to acquire a special thin-slice ultrasound scanner like the type used in cardiology exams.

- The weight of the HMD/camera unit must be decreased.

- The resolution of the cameras and HMD displays need to be significantly increased.

- The light sensitivity of the cameras needs to be increased.

- A method of scanning the patient's body (and the doctor's) to more faithfully produce the proper occlusion cues between the real and virtual objects must be developed.

Because the system could not be used by the primary doctor during a medical procedure, they equipped another doctor with the system. The second doctor would then observe the procedure "over-the-shoulder" to evaluate the system. The doctors report that the primary problems are insufficient resolution, overweight HMD, and difficulty in keeping enough fiducial landmarks in view to keep the trackers operating at maximum performance. They also reported some problems with the synchronization of input sources [State, Livingston, et al.].

---

[4]Silicon Graphics does offer a real-time variant of their IRIX flavor of the UNIX operating system.

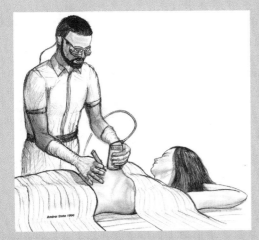 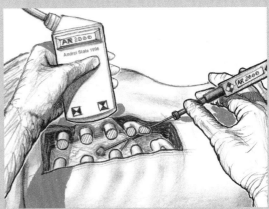

FIGURE 5-28

An artist's/developer's conception of the UNC AR system once the technology becomes less obtrusive.
Image courtesy University of North Carolina/artwork by Andrei State

FIGURE 5-29

Doctor Anthony Meyer, M.D, tests a new laparoscopic version of the UNC AR system on a patient phantom.
Image courtesy University of North Carolina

Once these problems are reduced, the UNC team "envisions the introduction of a system such as [theirs] into the operating room."

The next step will be to take advantage of the fact that the scanned data exists in the computer and use that data to automatically detect features such as lesions, cysts, etc. Pointers to the location of these features can be added to the augmented view.

In closing, the system developers report that "the system is sufficiently robust and accurate for the physician to report that the procedure on the breast model was easy" [State, Livingston, et al.].

Dr. Fuchs has even been re-encouraged in the possibility of fetus ultrasound imaging after seeing the results of another researcher comparing the face of his yet-to-be-born child with the baby's face after birth [Sakas and Walter].

CASE STUDY 5.5: VIRTUAL REALITY EXPOSURE THERAPY

Executive Summary

The treatment of psychological disorders might not be the first thought that comes to mind when looking for ways to apply a new technology like virtual reality. However, researchers have found success in treating patients with overwhelming fears using a technique called *exposure therapy* in virtual reality environments. Early successes have spawned a number of commercial entities that supply software, and turnkey virtual reality hardware systems that can be used in therapists' offices resulting in better treatment of phobias, and lower costs.

This section looks at applications related to fear of flying, fear of heights, fear of spiders, and treatment of post traumatic stress syndrome.

Introduction

Phobias, or persistent illogical fears of some particular thing, can range from minor nuisances to devastating disorders. Phobias can result in suffering and embarrassment to those who have them, and can have financial ramifications that reverberate throughout the economy. For example, it is estimated that 10–25% of the general population fear flying [Roberts, R.J.]. In 1982, the estimated cost of fear of flying to the U.S. travel industry was 1.6 billion dollars.

Because of the prevalence of the fear of flying, as well as the costly consequences of that fear and the high cost of traditional therapy, Professor Larry Hodges and his colleagues at the Graphics, Visualization, and Usability Lab (GVU) at Georgia Institute of Technology (Georgia Tech) began a collaboration with clinical psychologist Barbara Rothbaum from Emory University School of Medicine to develop programs that integrate virtual reality technology to aid patients in overcoming their fears. They started by addressing acrophobia (the fear of heights), and then expanded their work to include aerophobia (the fear of flying) and other disorders.

FIGURE 5-30

Patients wearing a head-mounted display are able to look off of a balcony in a virtual world to help them overcome a fear of heights. The virtual world is modeled as realistically as possible within the constraints of the rendering system.

The goal of these applications was to investigate whether VR could be effective in treating people with phobias, and to create a system suitable for use in a therapist's office. The first issue to investigate was whether or not fears would transfer into the VR environment, and whether the effects of the treatment would transfer back to the real world.

Phobia treatment is typically done by what is known as *exposure therapy*. This treatment involves exposing the patient to the anxiety invoking stimulus, and allowing the anxiety to subside. Virtual reality exposure therapy exposes the patient to a virtual environment that contains the fear-inducing stimulus rather than exposing them to the stimulus in the real world or having the patient imagine the stimulus.

A hypothesis of the Georgia Tech team predicted that if the virtual reality exposure therapy was effective, then it could be used to provide a lower-cost treatment. The major factor in reducing cost comes from allowing treatment to occur right in the therapist's office. This method also provides the therapist with greater control over the degree of stimulus exposure. If required, the VR treatment could be followed up with traditional exposure therapy by traveling to a real world location that provides the anxiety producing stimulus.

Prior to the *Virtual Reality Exposure Therapy* program, phobias were treated in two primary ways. One method is to have the patient imagine the anxiety-invoking event. The other method is "in vivo" therapy in which the patient is exposed to the actual stimulus. In both cases a technique of habituation is used where the patient is gradually moved from less threatening to more threatening situations.

Rothbaum and colleages point out several of the drawbacks to in vivo exposure therapy [Rothbaum, Hodges, et al.]. It can be very expensive. Because standard in vivo exposure therapy involves both the patient and the therapist being in the fear-invoking situation, it requires time away from the therapist's office, and the time required for traveling to the site. These therapies can be very difficult to arrange logistically, which can also add considerably to the cost. With the fear of flying example, it would require

that the therapist and the patient travel to an airport, and that an airplane be available for their exclusive use and that they have a pilot available to fly the craft. Even if these details could all be arranged, they would be costly, and still not every scenario could be created at the therapist's command. For example, it may not be possible to spontaneously allow the patient to experience flying in a thunderstorm. Virtual reality exposure therapy addresses these limitations.

Another risk of in vivo therapy is that the patient may feel embarrassed about the treatment, and it may not be possible to maintain their confidentiality. Additionally, the phobia may be so great that the patient is unwilling to even try the treatment because they would have to face the fear directly, even though under controlled conditions. The researchers found that many people who were afraid to try in vivo therapy were willing to try VR exposure therapy. A possible explanation is that they realize that they are not actually facing the stimulus that causes their anxiety.

Application Description

The Georgia Tech research team created multiple distinct applications. The first was for the fear of heights, followed by applications for the fear of flying and other phobias. In all cases the patient wears a head-mounted display with headphones to expose them to the sights and sounds of the environment that cause them anxiety. The therapist can see and hear the world on a monitor while the patient is experiencing it. They can also see the reaction of the patient. The therapist is able to alter what is happening in the virtual world at any given moment to provide the optimal environment for aiding the patient in overcoming their fear.

The application that deals with fear of flying was more difficult to design than the fear of heights application, but the potential payoff was also greater in that it more fully exploits the concept of allowing exposure therapy that might otherwise be impractical. That is, it is usually more difficult to arrange an airplane for exposure therapy than to take someone to a high place.

Representation of the Virtual World

The items in the virtual worlds of both these applications were represented as realistically as possible. One of

FIGURE 5-31

The fear of flying *application allows a user who is afraid of flying to wear a head-mounted display and to virtually sit in and look around a virtual airplane. The user experiences the airplane as it sits on the runway, taxis, flies in both normal conditions and storms, and lands. The virtual world is modeled at life-size.*

the requirements for success with this type of therapy is that the participant be mentally immersed in the environment. That is, they need to believe the situation in order to feel the anxiety as they would in the real world. The developers felt that greater realism would enhance mental immersion.

The virtual world in the *fear of heights* application consists of a glass elevator, a series of bridges, and a series of balconies. The elevator has virtual buttons that can be pressed to go up and down.

The virtual world of the *fear of flying* application consists of a model of the passenger cabin of a commercial aircraft and a view of the outside as seen through the window of the plane. The passenger is seated in a window seat in the cabin, and can see appropriate views out the window both on the ground and in the air. Thus, the various airport buildings, and the runways and taxiways were modeled. While flying, the passenger can see the ground, and/or clouds.

The worlds are represented internally as polygonal objects. Specifically, they were stored as Wavefront™ object files.

Both the *fear of heights* and *fear of flying* environments were created to look as realistic as possible and to emulate the kinds of details one would find in the environment. Additionally, both environments were created to life-like scale as observed from the first-person point of view. In the *fear of heights* application, the elevator was a glass elevator that overlooked the virtual interior lobby of a virtual hotel (inspired by the inside glass elevator in the Marriott Marquis in downtown Atlanta). The participant's hand and arm are represented in the scene as an avatar of the user.

In the *fear of flying* project, the airplane seats were texture mapped to look like the actual color and fabric of actual airplane seats. The cabin was built to appropriate scale such that the seats were the right size, the aisle width was appropriate, etc. Other details such as seatbelt signs mimicked the real-life equivalent in look, size, and placement. The windows were the correct size and in the correct location.

FIGURE 5-32

A glass elevator in a hotel lobby is modeled after the Marriott Marquis in downtown Atlanta, GA. The patient can press virtual buttons to cause the elevator to ascend and descend.

The participant could also see a representation of a generic body where they sat (i.e., their avatar). They see a pair of blue jeans–covered legs and a torso if they look down. The body is static, however, and is the same for everyone.

The researchers expressed a belief that sound in the virtual environment is very important, and is a big part of the virtual therapy experience.

The early work done on the *fear of heights* application, however, had no audio representation. The *fear of flying* application made use of a variety of sound effects. The sound effects can be categorized into two basic types. One type of sound is continuously looped. Sounds like the engine fall into this category. The other type is triggered as a one-shot sound effect. Examples of this are the prelanding and tire sound effects. The sounds were coordinated with the visual display to enhance the sense of realism.

The sounds were played on a machine other than the visual rendering machine, to prevent the computational load of visual and sound rendering from competing for the same resources. The sound computational system could play multiple sounds simultaneously, allowing for a richer sound experience. More recently, PCs are now capable of handling the rendering of both sight and sound from a single (relatively inexpensive) computer.

In the two cases discussed so far, the only type of haptic feedback provided was via static physical objects. The fear of heights experience had a waist-high rail that a participant could hold or lean against, providing haptic feedback as well as ensuring the participant stayed within range of the tracking system. This aided greatly in the application, as it allowed a participant to lean over it and look down. Additionally, the platform on which the user stood was raised a few inches above the floor. Thus if users stuck their feet over the ledge, they could feel edge, enhancing the realism. In the prototype version of the *fear of flying* application, the participant sat in a normal chair with no seatbelt. However, in a later version that was commercialized, a ThunderChair™ seat with an added seatbelt was used.

For some experimental phobia treatment applications, the researchers experimented with the use of a subwoofer to provide vibration sensation to the participant. This was originally done by mounting the speaker to the bottom of the seat on which the participant sat. Later, a commercially available product, the ThunderChair™, was incorporated. The ThunderChair also uses the technique of using subwoofers to produce vibrations throughout the seat and back of the chair.

There was no vestibular feedback in either of these applications. The decision to not use vestibular feedback was made to help keep the system practical for deployment in therapists' offices, both from a cost and size point of view. The research team does not feel the lack of vestibular feedback is significant, and that the effects they are after can be achieved through the visual display.

Neither application integrated odors in the environment. The developers of these applications believed that, like sound, smell is potentially an important component in VR systems for treating phobias. Thus, in a separate project they studied the effects of other sensory stimuli such as smell, wind, heat lamps, etc. In their study, Dinh and colleagues put 322 subjects through a virtual environment consisting of a small office suite [Dinh et al.]. Subjects were exposed to different sensory conditions—the inclusion of smell or not, the addition of sound cues or not, the addition of tactile cues or not, and high versus low visual resolution. The results indicate that the addition of more senses increases the reported feeling of presence and ability to recall aspects of the virtual world. This benefit is particularly strong for the auditory and tactile cues.

Interaction with the Virtual World

These applications fall into the medical (psychiatric) therapy genre. The form is typically to mimic real-world interactions as much as possible, allowing the patient to interact and react as intuitively as in the real world.

The narrative in these applications is that the patient experiences a real life situation, in which some events are controlled by a therapist. In the *fear of heights* application, patients get on an open elevator and ride it up and look around. They then progress to other experiences such as standing on a balcony. Of course, the therapist eases the

FIGURE 5-33

A patient experiencing the fear of heights virtual reality application presses an elevator button. Note the tracking sensor on the participant's hand, and the railing he leans against, emulating the railing in the virtual world.

patients into the various steps in the procedure, which may take many sessions.

In the *fear of flying* application, the full sequence of events consists of the patient sitting in the airplane parked at the gate, taxiing to wait at a holding position on the runway, taking off, steady flight, flight with various special occurrences such as darkness or storms, and finally landing. In both applications, time passes at the same rate as it does in the real world.

Travel through the virtual worlds is based on the specific phobia being treated. In the *fear of heights* application, the interface is physical locomotion. The participant can also press the buttons on the elevator to select how high they go. In the *fear of flying* application, the ride-along method of travel is used, mimicking how most of us travel by air. The airplane follows a prescribed spline path with the patient remaining seated the entire time.

In both cases, the therapist is in control of moving the scenario from one stage to the next. In early aerophobia (fear of flying) sessions, the patient may spend the whole session sitting in the stationary plane or taxiing around the runway. In the acrophobia (fear of heights) treatment, the therapist transitions the patient from scene to scene (e.g., the elevator to the balcony) as appropriate.

The therapist has a user interface that allows them to control the simulation in a very simple way. Because the therapist's first priority is to pay attention to the patient, a complicated (e.g., menu-driven) user interface would be detrimental. Thus, the interface consists only of a three-key interface on the keyboard. The actions of those keys are context sensitive, based on the current state of the system. A state machine dictates which situations are possible from any given point in the simulation.

When the patient is ready, the therapist can quickly induce a change in the state of the system (e.g., transition from taxiing to taking off). Each state is maintained long enough to be convincing, but not so long as to disrupt the normal flow of the therapy. A state will remain in effect until the therapist takes action to change it. For example, the airplane in smooth flight will remain in smooth flight until the therapist chooses to have something new happen. The therapist may end the simulation at any time.

There are no objects to manipulate in either simulation except for the elevator buttons in the fear of heights system. In that case, the hand is tracked by a tracking sensor to sense contact between the user and the virtual buttons.

There is no agent interaction in either simulation. The virtual worlds are not populated with other people. There is a sound effect of a virtual pilot making announcements such as when it is time to land, but there is no interaction with the pilot.

All motions in these simulations were preprogrammed, choreographed motions. The therapist changes scenarios by invoking a different state in the system. For example, in the *fear of flying* simulation, the aircraft proceeds from taxiing to takeoff only when the therapist signals this to occur. In flight, the therapist can activate or deactivate turbulence while monitoring the subject's level of discomfort. In yet another application, a virtual Vietnam War experience, presentation of gunfire or radio chatter occurs only when the therapist activates the appropriate buttons.

Venue

The venue for which these applications are designed is the therapist's office. With this in mind, when doing a case study analysis of the project, a space similar to a therapy office was used at GVU. The facility has a specially constructed room with a one-way glass through which researchers could watch subjects. The site was equipped with video cameras so they could capture the sessions for future study. The therapy room was accessible via its own entrance so subjects would not need to walk through the main part of the laboratory.

Throughput of the *Virtual Reality Exposure Therapy* system mimics that of a therapist—one patient has access at any given time, with sessions lasting approximately 1 hour.

VR System

The prototype system was centered around a Silicon Graphics Reality Engine™ workstation as the main computer. This system provided the visual rendering used by the applications. The project has used several different head-mounted displays over the course of time. The *fear of heights* application used a Virtual Research Flight Helmet™. The original *fear of flying* application used the Virtual Research VR-4™.

The software was ported to a PC-based system for lower cost under a grant from the state of Georgia. This version used the Virtuality Visette™, which offers one-quarter NTSC resolution. The developers also tested some participants in a monocular Liquid Image MRG-4™ HMD. Later, the developers began to use and recommend the VR-6™ HMD from Virtual Research, Inc.

The images are displayed monoscopically. The decision to not use stereo image display was based primarily on the desire to expend their computational resources making a single higher-quality image than to create two lesser-quality images. The developers calculated the possible enhancement of the stereoscopic depth cue based on the resolution of the HMD and determined that it would not add much information for either the *fear of heights* or *fear of flying* experiences. Therefore they chose to create a more complex world instead.

Both applications use 6-DOF head tracking. In an effort to keep costs as low as possible, they opted to track only the head for most phobia-treatment applications. One exception is the *fear of heights* application, which uses an extra tracking sensor so the system could tell when the hand pushed the elevator buttons. Position tracking can be done with either the Polhemus or Ascension electromagnetic systems.

In some cases, monitors of the patient's heart rate and other body functions are used to allow the therapist to have an objective measurement of the patient's physiological responses.

Application Implementation

The *Virtual Reality Exposure Therapy* project was conceived late in 1992. The first code for the *fear of heights* application was written in the spring of 1993. By October 1993 they ran their first patient in VR therapy. For the *fear of flying* application they began taking measurements of the aircraft cabin in the summer of 1994. The cabin and outdoor model was built through the rest of 1994. The simulation program was written from January to summer of 1995. In the summer of 1995 they ran a complete case study with an aerophobic patient.

The system was developed in-house by a team that included psychiatrists and computer scientists. The study was conducted in facilities provided by the GVU lab at Georgia Tech. The project was led by computer science professor Larry Hodges at the Georgia Tech GVU, and psychologist Barbara Rothbaum of the Emory University School of Medicine. Other investigators who contributed to the design of the study were Dr. Major James Williford (U.S. Army psychiatrist who was stationed in Augusta, Georgia, at the time), Dan Opdyke (Georgia State University), and Max North (Clark Atlanta University). Rob Kooper programmed the initial application, with other programming contributions later made by Kevin Hamilton, Ben Watson, Jarrell Pair, Brian Wills, David Gotz, and Phillip Hebert.

The initial software was written using the Georgia Tech *Simple Virtual Environment* (SVE) Toolkit which is based on *OpenGL*. Because of the lack of availability at the time for good *OpenGL*-based graphics accelerator cards for PCs, the initial port of the *fear of flying* application used the *DirectX/3D* library. Later PC versions used *OpenGL* on a *Windows NT* platform. By using *OpenGL*, the developers

could more easily transfer applications from the faster Silicon Graphics workstations to the cheaper personal computer platforms.

To create the model of the cabin, a team of two undergraduate students and a high school teacher working as a summer intern at the GVU lab were allowed access to a Boeing 747 to take photographs and measurements. This process took several hours to complete. These measurements were then used to create the model using Wavefront Inc. modeling software.

The sounds used in the *fear of flying* application were obtained from commercial sound effect CDs and converted to computer sound files. To be useful in this application, these sounds had to be edited for length and content.

Related Applications and Follow-on Work

Other research groups have also been investigating the use of VR for exposure therapy. About the same time the Georgia Tech project was being prototyped, Dr. Ralph Lamson at the Kaiser Permanente health clinic in San Rafael, California, also had the idea to apply VR for helping sufferers of acrophobia. He found that virtual reality was effective in relieving the fear of heights in an experimental group of subjects [Lamson].

At the University of Washington in Seattle's Human Interface Technology Lab (HIT Lab), Hunter Hoffman has done some interesting work on arachnophobia (fear of spiders). In his work, Hoffman used tracked, physically manifested objects to transfer object permanence from these selectively enhanced objects to the rest of the objects in the virtual world, making that world more mentally immersive. In this case, Hoffman attached a prop composed of a fuzzy ball with multiple pipe-cleaners to mimic the body of a large spider. The prop is tracked, and thus is located in the same place in both the real and virtual worlds. The user can therefore feel the spider simply by reaching out to where it appears to be in the virtual world. [Hoffman, VRAIS '98]

Hoffman reported great success when his application was tested on the first patient. This patient, a Seattle-area woman, had a long-term fear of spiders that had grown so extreme that she vacuumed out her car every day before using it and placed a towel in her bedroom door jamb every night to avoid spiders. After the therapy, the woman's fear

FIGURE 5-35

Virtual Iraq *is a timely application of virtual reality. Dr. Albert "Skip" Rizzo modified a video game to create a virtual reality application that is used for treating victims of post-traumatic stress disorder. A group of collaborating researchers, including Virtually Better Inc., developed it and are involved in evaluating its effectiveness.*

FIGURE 5-34

Researchers at the Human Interface Technologies Laboratory at the University of Washington created a virtual reality application to treat arachnophobia (fear of spiders). In this application, they provided a physical model of a spider consisting of a fuzzy body with pipe cleaner legs that is colocated (via a tracking sensor) with the virtual representation of the spider. Thus, a patient wearing a head-mounted display can reach out and touch the virtual spider and feel the fuzzy physical object.
Top: Courtesy of Hunter Hoffman. Bottom: Courtesy of the BBC

had been reduced to the point where she was able to go camping.

Conclusion

The subject for the *fear of flying* case study experiment was a 42-year-old female who had a debilitating fear of flying [Rothbaum, Hodges, et al.]. Her fear had increased over

about 5 years before the therapy took place, culminating in her avoiding flying completely for the previous 2 years. This fear resulted in her missing out on things in her life such as vacations and business opportunities that required travel. Since she was embarking in a new business venture requiring travel, she sought the VR therapy hoping that it would help her get over her fear of flying—mainly the fear of crashing.

The subject completed a battery of pretherapy questionnaires, followed by seven sessions (as a paying patient) of outpatient therapy in which she was taught anxiety management techniques. Because it appeared that it would be beneficial to all parties involved for her to undergo exposure therapy, she was invited to participate (at no cost) in the *VR Exposure Therapy* program.

Once again, the patient was given the same set of questionnaires. The patient was then allowed to progress at her own pace in a series of sessions which lasted about

35–45 minutes each. Through the course of the six sessions, the patient encountered various scenarios such as taxiing on the runway, smooth flight, turbulent flight, etc. The therapist was able to observe the patient and see the view she saw. Thus, the therapist was able to aid her in overcoming her fear through appropriate encouragement and other techniques. During the testing the patient gave subjective ratings of anxiety, ranging from 0 (calm) to 100 (panic).

In addition to using standard testing questionnaires, the research team developed two forms of their own. One was a "flight self-monitoring sheet" on which the subject provided ratings for different parts of the flight experience. The other was a form that the therapist used to record what VR situations were presented to the patient. The patient filled out the self monitoring sheet several times during the testing, after the therapy, during an actual flight she took after the therapy, and again a month after the therapy had been completed. At that point she also took the original battery of questionnaires again.

Two days after the therapy, the patient successfully completed a cross-country flight with her family that she was scheduled to make. She reported that it was comforting at points to remember and picture the VR experience. Although the therapy was considered successful, the exact amount of benefit from the VR cannot be precisely determined because she had also been treated with anxiety management therapy.

In addition to the above case study, virtual reality exposure therapy has proven effective enough to move from the research lab to the marketplace. Because the *fear of flying* application generated considerable success stories and press interest, the research group received more queries about using their system than they could address. In response to this, Hodges and Rothbaum have formed a company known as Virtually Better, Inc. (VBI) to distribute the software to interested parties. However, instead of selling the hardware directly, they provide a shopping list of the necessary hardware components.

VBI reported six other sites using their exposure therapy software in addition to their own clinic at the time of this writing. This did not include the other centers that independently developed their own software for therapy using VR. This large number of actual users of virtual reality exposure therapy is perhaps the best statement of how effective VR is in this domain. Brenda Widerhold, the director of Centrer for Advanced Multimedia Psychotherapy at the California School of Professional Psychology (CSPP) is one user of the VBI system. She reported to treating 30 aerophobic patients in her first year of using the system, and 28 of these patients were able to fly after about eight training sessions using the VR experience. Widerhold used heart rate, respiration rate, and sweat sensors in conjunction with the VBI system to allow her to better monitor the level of her patient's anxiety.

Mental immersion is of prime importance for the use of virtual reality exposure therapy. People treated for various phobias using VR must be sufficiently immersed in the experience to exhibit the same symptoms in the VR experience as in the real world experience. Perhaps surprisingly, many people do indeed experience the same symptoms in VR that they do in the real world.

For example, the subject of the case study described above did behave as though she was on a real flight while she was in the VR system. She experienced the shortness of breath, butterflies in the stomach, etc. that are classic symptoms of anxiety. These indicators provide evidence that the patient was mentally immersed.

Perhaps the most significant discovery in this application was that phobias do transfer into the virtual environment. Participants exhibit anxiety symptoms when exposed to their fear-inducing stimulus in the virtual environment. Additionally, the benefits of exposure in the VR environment benefit the participant in the real world situation. Interestingly, some people are willing to undergo therapy in the virtual environment who are not willing to try in vivo exposure therapy.

In addition to the two phobia treatments described here, Hodges/Rothbaum and other groups have also developed many other virtual reality environments for phobia treatment. VBI offerings included software for treating the fear of flying, heights, malls, storms, and driving. In addition to this, they have developed software to help veterans overcome post-traumatic stress disorder (PTSD). This "virtual Vietnam" application has been developed for deployment at VA Hospitals, where it can be used by therapists to allow sufferers to relive and recall events to hopefully help them overcome the disorder.

FIGURE 5-36
Virtual reality is used by therapists to allow Vietnam War veterans to experience, in a controlled environment, many of the sights and sounds they experienced in the Vietnam War. Virtual Vietnam *includes a chair equipped with a subwoofer to provide the sensation of the vibrations of riding in a helicopter.*

Virtual Vietnam places the veteran in a few scenarios common to Vietnam veterans. These include being transported via helicopter between their base and the battle. Additionally, they are also able to experience standing in a field as the helicopters take off and land. To give the subject a greater sense of immersion, they are seated in a ThunderChair device that helps them feel what it was like to be in a vibrating helicopter and feel the roar of the gunfire outgoing from the nearby gunner and incoming from unseen enemies.

A heart rate monitor is attached to the subjects as they experience the representation of the Vietnam War.

When used as part of an overall therapy, the virtual Vietnam experience has been a useful tool in helping veterans recall past circumstances and overcome their associated problems [Hodges, Rothbaum, et al.].

Virtual reality is proving to be a beneficial tool for psychologists treating phobia disorders, but there is still room for improvement. As Barbara Rothbaum points out:

VR exposure therapy has many advantages for several anxiety disorders, primarily centered around the therapist control over stimuli, the ease and efficiency of therapy in the office, and the decreased expense of time and money. The major drawbacks at this point are the expense of the hardware and the expertise required to program the software, but these are both destined to change for the better in the near future.

CHAPTER 6

Education Applications

Take a look inside almost any classroom in an elementary school, high school, university, or a corporate training room and what will you find? Most likely, the communication of visual phenomenon is attempted using some combination of two-dimensional display devices such as textbooks, chalkboards, overhead projectors, bulletin boards, and computer screens.

Although many scholastic subjects involve learning about three-dimensional entities, the pupil's primary mode of receiving information is two dimensional. With the exception of certain cases where physical artifacts (for example arrowheads, or ball-and-stick models of molecules) are integrated into the instructional program, the student must extend the ideas that are being portrayed on their textbook pages or computer screens into three dimensions entirely within their own minds. However, research performed by Chris Dede and R. Bowen Loftin indicates that this is not an effective way to learn truly three-dimensional concepts. Often students walk away from the classroom only able to discuss the phenomena as though it were only two-dimensional in nature, unable to expand concepts into 3D.

In addition to the constraints of presentations limited to two-dimensions, common classroom displays are also not interactive. Some (such as movies) incorporate motion, and some (computers) can incorporate interaction. Virtual reality, however, provides a true three-dimensional, interactive environment in which students can manipulate, explore, and modify their environment.

Additionally, virtual reality offers the ability for students to collaborate with others who may be located elsewhere, and VR can provide anonymity for the students when that is desirable. Finally, virtual reality offers the ability to record student performance and actions, allowing either the computer or teacher to respond appropriately.

The related area of augmented reality provides many capabilities that are useful in educational settings. Augmented reality is the medium in which synthetic imagery and information are overlaid on top of the real world. An example application would be to allow a student to take a virtual nature walk through a grove of trees. In this difficult-to-implement example, as they walk and look around, students would be able to see annotations describing the tree they are seeing, as well as offered interactive quizzes, animations, and other practical educational opportunities.

One reason that virtual reality has not been widely adopted in schools is that there are relatively few appropriate applications available; another is the cost of the required equipment. These two issues are clearly related. Why develop applications if schools cannot afford to implement them in their curriculum?

Fortunately, these two problems—hardware cost and software availability—are becoming less of a barrier. Low-cost, commodity VR hardware has brought system cost down an order of magnitude over systems such as those prominent in this book. Open-source hardware platforms such as the *GeoWall* allow users to construct their own systems.

Companies such as Visbox, Inc., VisTek, Inc., and CAE-net (John-E-Box) provide relatively inexpensive commercial turnkey systems. Certainly as large-screen high-definition displays and computer vision–based camera inputs become increasingly pervasive, such systems will involve only modest costs above that of a typical classroom computer—indeed, such technology is already becoming standard in home gaming systems. Software for education is being addressed in a number of open-source efforts.

FIGURE 6-1

Third-grade Cub Scouts enjoy a tour of the VisBox-X2 system at Valparaiso University.

Visualization software for chemistry includes *Ribbons* (University of Alabama, Birmingham) and *VMD* (University of Illinois). A host of software applications covering education in engineering and mathematics is available from the Scientific Visualization Laboratory (SVL) at Valparaiso University. One of the SVL's applications (called *MaxwellVU*) was directly inspired by the *ScienceSpace* application detailed below. This application is open source, available on a number of low-cost hardware platforms, and allows students to experience and interact with electromagnetic fields in a virtual environment. The goal is to communicate the inherent meaning of Maxwell's equations relating electric and magnetic fields.

6.1 AREAS OF APPLICATION

Virtual reality is currently being used or tested in a variety of formal and informal educational settings. Formal settings include elementary school, secondary school, universities, etc. Informal settings include museums, zoos, libraries, and other similar venues. We have categorized these applications into four areas, and describe at length at least one example for each:

- **Sciences** In this chapter we cover the application *ScienceSpace*, which allows students to explore difficult three-dimensional science problems ranging from electromagnetics, to kinematics, to chemistry.

- **Constructivist** Virtual reality is particularly conducive to manifesting constructivist theories of education in that it allows students to learn as they build their own environments. This chapter describes several constructivist applications that cover a variety of student age groups.

- **Informal Education** Around the world, students are using virtual reality to learn about topics ranging from gorilla social behavior to ancient civilizations. This chapter describes several informal education settings.

- **Special Education** At a very practical level, virtual reality has been used to train critical life skills to students with special needs. Virtual reality offers a safe place to practice new skills and behaviors, and simultaneously allows instructors to gather data to help assess the progress of their students and provide new training in response. This chapter includes descriptions of virtual reality applications to help develop training skills such as manipulating a powered wheelchair, using a city bus system, and basic life-skill and social-skill training for students with autism.

6.2 OTHER AND FUTURE USES

A trend that is already emerging in the area of education is the use of augmented reality.

We envision more adoption of AR technologies in areas ranging from providing a more personalized experience for museum visitors to providing students guided exercises in prairie and other natural environments. AR offers the potential to provide extra information and annotations directly about the phenomena the student is experiencing at that moment in time, and tailored to their own interests and learning level.

VR and AR technologies are beginning to blur the line of where one "goes" to go to school. VR, AR, and telepresence allow students to experience many environments, and collaborate with geographically disperse students, scientists, doctors, and other experts while at their school, or potentially even while at home.

The possibilities of simulations carried out in virtual environments allow for compelling historical re-creations (allowing students to participate in historical events), science expeditions, and any learning experience that can make use of simulations and vignettes. Such applications can teach students emergency preparedness, social skills, and practical skills such as learning to use a new scientific or musical instrument.

CASE STUDY 6.1: PROJECT SCIENCESPACE

Executive Summary

Traditionally, scientific phenomena are presented to students as two-dimensional visualizations through a few different mechanisms: photos and diagrams in books, drawings on blackboards and overhead projectors, and more recently, interactive simulations on computer screens. All these displays have something in common. They are all two dimensional. Two-dimensional imagery has been shown to be a reasonable teaching tool, even for three-dimensional concepts, but further studies have shown that, while students may be able to answer test questions correctly, they often don't understand how those concepts extend into three dimensions as they do in nature.

Researchers at George Mason University, in collaboration with the University of Houston, developed an experimental test bed in which they studied the use of three-dimensional virtual reality for teaching three-dimensional concepts. As an experimental platform they developed three worlds for teaching concepts of physics and chemistry. *NewtonWorld* helps students explore concepts of Newtonian mechanics. *MaxwellWorld* provides an interactive space for studying concepts of electromagnetic fields, and *PaulingWorld* is focused on interactions between molecules. Collectively, the research is called *Project ScienceSpace*.

Although other applications of virtual reality in education have been explored, *ScienceSpace* specifically focused on studying the effectiveness of using virtual reality for teaching science concepts. The target audience is grade school, high school, and undergraduate students. Because most schools don't have large, projection virtual reality facilities, the researchers have developed a system that uses portable head mounted displays. Besides looking at the effectiveness of VR in general for teaching science, the researchers also explored the possible benefits of displaying to multiple senses (sight, sound, and touch).

Results of the studies indicate that immersive environments are more effective for teaching three-dimensional science concepts, and that displaying to multiple senses is more effective than displaying to a single sense.

Introduction

Trends in technology suggest that VR will soon be in the hands of a growing population of computer users. Heretofore, access to virtual reality facilities has generally been limited to large research centers and individual efforts funded to test the usefulness of the technology on certain populations. To examine and prepare for a time when VR will be widely available in grade school, high school,[1] and college classrooms, collaborators at George Mason University and the University of Houston produced a series of virtual reality experiences designed to test VR as a potential educational resource.

The focus of their work is on science education. Science was chosen because of an established teaching methodology and a well-known lack of overall student comprehension. *Project ScienceSpace* consists of three separate experiences designed to teach through scientific inquiry: *NewtonWorld, MaxwellWorld,* and *PaulingWorld*.

The goal of the *ScienceSpace* effort was to lead to better educational tools that will help students learn by allowing them to experience concepts directly, rather than merely memorize formulas and abstract behaviors. By directly interacting with the laws of physics, it is hoped that they will accept them as a valid explanation of natural phenomena, rather than as some arcane formulation presented by their teachers. It has been observed that students who ably solve physics problems on a test behave in day-to-day activities as though these concepts are not true.

The specific objectives of these studies were threefold:

- To determine whether physically immersive, constructivist learning can remedy typical misconceptions of reality held by many students

- To enhance mastery of abstract scientific concepts (e.g., relativity, quantum mechanics, molecular-orbital bonding) in an experiential, physically immersive, multisensory, collaborative environment

- To investigate the degree to which the effectiveness of using virtual reality for education is undermined as a result of physical or psychological effects caused by VR (e.g., disorientation)

---

[1] For non-U.S. readers: Elementary school children generally range from 5 to 14, and high school students from 14 to 18 years old.

The traditional method of teaching science through lectures, books (with twodimensional diagrams), and laboratory experiments (where the participation level of many of the students is limited) works only to a degree. Yet, even students who score well often don't fully comprehend the concepts they've "learned." Furthermore, this quantitative method of teaching requires that higher mathematical skills be learned before the student can pursue the scientific concepts. The result of this circumstance is that advanced science is not being taught until after many students have already lost interest in the topic.

Initial studies targeted high school and college students with a demonstrated mastery of the concepts. Their analysis of these experiments indicates that students do learn some concepts better in VR, and can spontaneously describe concepts not yet formally introduced to them.

Application Description

The *ScienceSpace* researchers did not aim to merely develop one or two pedagogically useful applications, but rather to "map the territory" of how VR can be an effective medium for education. Their hypothesis was that VR will be useful for science education because it addresses four vital components of the nature of learning:

- The novelty of VR draws the students' attention.
- The computer worlds can be used to generate meaningful representations.
- Information can simultaneously be presented in a variety of forms.
- Students can learn by doing, using "reflective inquiry."[2]

The three experimental worlds all have their own unique characteristics designed to highlight particular scientific concepts. However, they also have features in common. For example, a two-handed menu-in-hand interface is used to make selecting options more natural. The first two worlds of *ScienceSpace* (*NewtonWorld* and *MaxwellWorld*) were used in the formal analysis.

NewtonWorld is designed to teach Newtonian mechanics to beginning physics students. In *NewtonWorld*, Newton's laws of kinematics and dynamics are presented along one dimension, allowing the user to move freely outside this

dimension to view the concepts while they themselves are unhindered by Newton's laws. The concepts are presented via one or two balls that move down a colonnaded corridor with walls at each end.

Balls can be launched, caught, and "ridden" by students, who can control parameters of the world such as the mass of the ball and the magnitude of forces applied to the ball. *NewtonWorld* balls exhibit conservation of linear momentum, and demonstrate concepts of kinetic energy, as well as Newton's Laws of Motion.

By providing multisensory cues of important components of the world, students have a better opportunity to focus on the relationships between them. Examples of multisensory representations include potential energy (represented both haptically and visually) and velocity (represented aurally and visually).

MaxwellWorld is designed to allow students to explore the nature of electrostatic forces and fields, and to understand the concept of electric flux. The content of *MaxwellWorld* is a collection of point electrical charges represented as spheres, with the resulting field lines and equipotential surfaces represented as lines and surfaces.

Holding a tracked wand, students create and place electric charges in space, producing representations of the electric forces, fields and flux. Exploration of the electromagnetic properties can be done by visual inspection, in conjunction with other techniques such as probing calculated numeric values within the fields, etc., and even riding a test charge as it moves through the field.

PaulingWorld was created for the exploration of molecular structure and dynamics. Students can control their view of the molecular structure to examine it from any vantage point. They can also control how the molecule is represented, using the menu system to switch between various standard chemistry representational techniques. When multiple molecules are displayed, the student can witness the dynamics between them.

Representation of the Virtual World

The virtual worlds of *ScienceSpace* provide both common representations of introductory science concepts. By basing the representations on traditional two-dimensional representations, students can more easily relate their VR experience to the traditional representations they encounter.

------
[2]Dede et al.

FIGURE 6-2
In PaulingWorld, a similar interface is used to explore molecular interactions.

FIGURE 6-3
NewtonWorld allows students to observe and participate in elastic collisions with virtual balls.

Each of the *ScienceSpace* worlds occupies a small region of space where the concepts are presented and the participant can maneuver. While the worlds are small enough that the participant can choose a vantage point that allows them to see the entire space from an exocentric point of view, they can also move into the world and view it egocentrically.

Abstract representations are used for of all the concepts shown in the *ScienceSpace* worlds. This is necessary since the majority of the concepts cannot be directly witnessed in day-to-day life. While we can witness the indirect results of molecular docking or electric charge between two points, we cannot witness the docking itself, or the distribution of forces and energy in the charged field space. The exceptions to this are collisions in the real world, but to allow participants to better focus on the concepts, these collisions have been abstracted to occur in a one-dimensional space with no friction, and adjustable parameters.

In addition to the representations of the science concepts, menus and avatars of the user's hands are rendered as part of the user-interface, allowing the user to more easily interact with the worlds.

In *NewtonWorld*, participants view elastic collisions between two balls and between those balls and the end walls of the corridor they occupy. The corridor provides visual and aural cues of position and velocity. Columns along the corridor flash and emit a sound as a ball passes it, allowing the student to detect visual and aural patterns

related to the ball's trajectory. Shadows of the balls are rendered directly below them to help the viewer gauge their movement as they pass between lines that connect the columns on either side of the corridor. A sign on each wall indicates the presence (or lack thereof) of gravity and friction.

In the initial version of *NewtonWorld*, the size of the shadows represented the amount of kinetic energy of the ball, while potential energy (of a ball being held by the user) is represented visually by a coiled spring, and haptically as vibrations in the chest of the participant. The color of the balls represented their mass, but the researchers found that this representation didn't work well, so color was removed.

After the initial experiments using *NewtonWorld*, it was redesigned with more intuitive representations of mass, and a visual cue for elasticity of each ball was added.

In *MaxwellWorld*, a 1-meter-per-side cube with Cartesian axes provides the boundary within which Maxwell's principles are represented. Source and test charges are represented as spheres with color indicating the polarity, while pulse rate of the sphere indicates the magnitude of the charge. The force on a positive test charge is represented either by an arrow emanating from the charge or by the charge's movement through the field. In "probe-mode," the user's avatar's fingertip represents the current "potential" as

FIGURE 6-4

In this image of the updated NewtonWorld, the amount of kinetic energy contained in a ball the participant is holding is visually represented by the amount of compression of a spring attached to the ball.

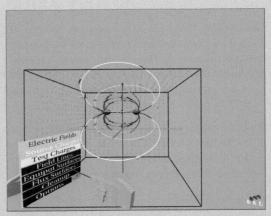

FIGURE 6-5

In MaxwellWorld, the participant can affect the virtual world through interactions with a menu and by placing objects and probing within the simulation space.

a colored plus or minus sign. The color indicates the magnitude of the potential. Similarly, a small, positive test charge is attached to the user's virtual hand with an arrow emanating from the charge indicating the direction and magnitude (again by color) of the "force [acting on] the test charge (and, hence, the electric field)." Magnitude of force was represented by the shades of color from white (neutral) to red (high), with yellow and orange in between. Potential energy was represented using the colors ranging from white to blue to green to purple.

Electric fields are represented as lines that trace a path between positive and negative source charges. To investigate Gauss' Law, the user can create spherical "Gaussian surfaces" and directly measure the flux by counting the flux lines through the sphere. Electric potentials can be represented by an equipotential surface. Field lines and equipotential surfaces are colored based on the magnitude of the force along the line or surface using the same white–red scale.

In *PaulingWorld*, molecules (represented in a variety of forms) float before the user. These forms include the familiar ball-and-stick model, a protein-backbone representation, van der Waals spheres, amino acid icons, and a wire-frame representation. Representations can also be combined, such

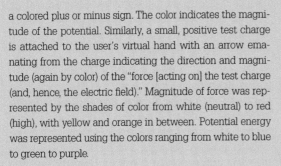

FIGURE 6-6

Several traditional molecular representations are available in PaulingWorld; they can be changed via a menu interface.

as using a backbone ribbon of the primary protein chain, and adding ball-and-stick representations of atoms that emanate from the backbone. The user can interactively adjust the representation, allowing them to expand a particular molecule into its ball and stick representation, for instance.

In addition to the *NewtonWorld* aural cues that co-represent the movement of the balls, sound is used in *NewtonWorld* to display the time of collisions between the balls, and the balls and the walls. In *MaxwellWorld*, sounds were used to represent the intensity of force or energy at a particular point. Sounds were also spatialized, so the user could localize in 3D the locale where the generating entity resides.

In all three worlds aural cues are used to provide feedback to the interaction interface. A sound is made whenever an item in the menu is selected, or when an object in the world is selected (e.g., to move a source charge).

The *ScienceSpace* development team also investigated the use of a variety of haptic feedback devices for use with one or more of the worlds. Some experiments with haptic devices included the use of a finger vibrator attached to a glove input device, an air-bladder glove to produce pressures on the surfaces of the hands, an exoskeleton glove to constrain hand motions when contacting a virtual object, and a glove that produces temperature changes to the fingertips. They chose not to use a mechanically linked force feedback device (such as the PHANToM) because of the restrictions it places on the usable working volume where interactions can take place.

In *NewtonWorld* tests were conducted to compare the possible benefits of multimodal representation of phenomenon. The comparison was between concepts represented visually; visually and aurally; and visually, aurally, and haptically. In this case the haptic representation consisted of a vest worn by the subjects that displays a "thump" on their chest or back when the ball ridden by the subject collided with the other ball or a wall. The results of the test indicated that with more forms of sensory feedback provided, the subject's performance improved. However, they did not compare the effect of each individual sensory stimulation against the others.

Use of other senses such as vestibular and olfaction (smell) were not considered for inclusion with *Project ScienceSpace* because of the added complexity and expense involved.

Interaction with the Virtual World

The *ScienceSpace* project clearly falls within the genre of *science education*. Specifically, education acquired through experiential concept learning. The form of interaction is primarily done via selecting options from a menu-in-hand interface with several methods-of-travel used, as well as by indicating desires by using a tracked single-button wand, and direct interaction using a tracked Polhemus one-button stylus.

The intended way in which the *ScienceSpace* applications would be used was to present the student with a lesson plan that included a series of exercises on the concepts, and then give them access to the immersive virtual world as the means of exploring each given problem.

Because the user's head was fully tracked, one means of traveling through the world that was always available was by simple body movement (physical locomotion). However, each world also provided other means of travel control that were more commonly used to navigate through the worlds. All worlds provided a menu option that allowed the user to fly in the direction they pointed a handheld prop (a Polhemus stylus) while pressing its button. In this point-to-fly mode, travel speed was constant and not controllable by the user. Because point-to-fly travel was a frequent activity, all layers of the menu interface included the travel option. The travel selection was indicated by selecting a plane icon placed in the lower-right corner of each menu.

In *NewtonWorld*, if a student points at a camera icon, they are instantly teleported to that location. In other words, these icons serve as predefined interesting observation points. In *MaxwellWorld* and *PaulingWorld*, the grab-the-world method of travel was also available by selecting that option from the menu. In this mode, users can reorient or relocate the world with respect to themselves. *MaxwellWorld* also allows users to change their scale to allow them to view the world either egocentrically or exocentrically. Additionally, both *NewtonWorld* and *MaxwellWorld* offer the ability to ride-along through the world on a ball or test charge so the student can experience the forces acting on the world first hand. So, in *NewtonWorld*, you can "be the ball."

Most of the interactions with the *ScienceSpace* worlds come from manipulating various objects in the world or general characteristics of the worlds. A menu system was the primary method of making modifications. In *NewtonWorld* (the first world built), a menu was placed as a head-up display, and users could interact with the menu by pointing at it and pressing a button to "pull-down" a list

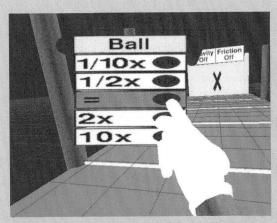

FIGURE 6-7

Two-handed menus were implemented in NewtonWorld after discovering that pull-down menus occluded important objects in the world.

of options. Having the menu constantly occupy part of the user's view was found to be intrusive and interfered with immersion, so for later worlds, the designers chose to use a bimanual (two-handed) interface for the menu.

DESIGN CHOICE

Interaction

The fixed-position menu used in *NewtonWorld* was abandoned for a bimanual menu interface for later worlds because the *NewtonWorld* users found the menu to be distracting and intrusive. By attaching the menu to the off hand, users could then eliminate the menu from view simply by putting their hand by their side, yet they could quickly and easily access the menu by raising their hand into their field of view. Because users are able to proprioceptically sense where their hand is, they always know where the menu is, without the need for keeping it in sight.

The menu system was controlled by using physical inputs from handheld props. The user uses one prop to hold the menu in their off hand, while the second prop allows

pointing, and activation via a button press. During development of the system, the creators also experimented with other forms of input such as gesture and voice control. While they found that users liked voice control, they felt that it would add too much complexity to the already large amount of new technology they would be introducing to the classroom, so they chose not to pursue it further for this project. Also, gesture recognition was found to be unreliable, and distracting to the users, so the physical prop inputs were kept as the means of control.

In *MaxwellWorld*, users can place positive and negative charges in the world. Once these charges are placed, the virtual electric field is generated, allowing students to further interact with the resultant field. The menu system is used to choose between "probe mode," "trace mode," etc.

A probe showing the potential at any location can be attached to the user's virtual hand. Also, tracers can be released into the electric field causing the released tracer object to flow along as governed by the existing electric field. Electric field lines can also be individually created and manipulated. Signaling the creation of a new field line causes a line to be generated from the current probe location. Grabbing an existing line causes it to change reflecting the potential passing through the new point. When the participant activates the generation of a Gaussian surface, the surface is generated from the current probe point. Likewise, in *PaulingWorld* representations of the molecules (and atomic surfaces) are added and adjusted using the menu interface.

The *ScienceSpace* worlds described here are not populated by agents that communicate with the participant. However, the developers later investigated the possibility of integrating some of their previous work on intelligent tutoring systems to allow students to participate in the experience without requiring a human guide. Future editions could use such agents as a form of "intelligent coaches" for the learners.

The developers have also implemented a collaborative version of *MaxwellWorld* and tested it in sessions between the University of Houston and the University of California at San Diego. However, this version was not evaluated for pedagogical benefits.

The physics of these worlds were obviously created to mimic certain subsets of formulae that describe a particular scientific theory (e.g., Newtonian physics in *NewtonWorld*). However, these physics did not necessarily apply to the user, or the form of travel they used, unless they were riding some object that was the physics model. So, features such as gravity and collision detection were only applied to specific objects to help demonstrate a particular branch of physics (e.g., Newtonian).

Venue

Thus far, the execution of the *ScienceSpace* worlds has been limited to university research labs. However, this severely limits the researchers' ability to readily engage the participation of the target subject groups (elementary school and high school students). Fortunately, as the cost of computing and VR hardware declines, constraints such as this for future educational programs will surely fall away, except in the case of *CAVE* displays, which will likely continue to be cost prohibitive for primary and secondary educational institutions. Five systems were prepared for classroom deployment to allow the researchers to get beyond the limitations of laboratory settings.

In fact, among the collaborators in this project, the University of Houston had both HMD and *CAVE* displays within its facility, and could run the worlds in either. However, at George Mason University, where many of the experiments were held, only head-mounted displays were available.

Participants of the system typically would be given some time to independently learn the science being presented, followed by time in the VR experience to either freely explore the world, or perform some specified task. Time spent in the virtual world was typically about 30–45 minutes followed by a 15-minute break, then another 30- to 45-minute session.

VR System

Since the primary venue for *ScienceSpace* is the classroom, the selected VR system must accommodate a classroom situation. However, it must be portable enough to be moved from school to school (at least until more schools have their own virtual reality facilities). Thus, an HMD-based system was constructed. In the prototyping stage of the application Virtual Research VR-3™ model HMDs were used, but these were replaced with the VR-4 model for the evaluation experiments.

The system was designed to be used while sitting down. Users can move physically by rolling in the chair, but the applications were designed such that this isn't necessary. The travel controls are typically used to navigate through the virtual worlds.

Although the HMDs match the portability and cost constraints of the project, there are some negative factors associated with them. First, the isolation factor of HMDs makes lesson administration more difficult. Students can't see written instructions or write down notes. They can converse with an instructor, but they can't communicate visually. Also, HMDs are not generally very comfortable, and less costly models (as those used in this project) are still low-resolution devices making for a less than auspicious experience.

At the University of Houston, where a *CAVE*-like projection display was installed, this application was also ported to the *CAVE*. Anecdotal experience indicates that experiencing *MaxwellWorld* in the *CAVE* is better for seeing the world from the exocentric perspective, while egocentric viewing is easier in the HMD.

During the initial development and evaluation, the computation and graphics system was a Silicon Graphics Onyx with Reality Engine2 graphics hardware. A Silicon Graphics Indy™ desktop workstation provided the audio output. This system (the Onyx in particular) was not very amenable to transporting from location to location. By using higher-performance machines during the experimental analysis stage of the project, the developers did not have to concern themselves with tweaking the software to squeeze every ounce of performance out of the hardware. They had the luxury of knowing that by the time such a system would be deployed in schools, the hardware would have improved sufficiently that they would be safe with reasonably well-written programs, and thus could spend their time developing the interface and representations aspects of the software. The systems assembled for classrooms used a single Silicon Graphics O2 system for computation, graphics, and audio rendering. The O2 system is quite small, and readily portable. Today, even a basic laptop has sufficient computational and graphical power to handle these experiences. Position tracking was done with a Polhemus electromagnetic tracking system (the *CAVE*-like projection display used an Ascension Flock of Birds electromagnetic system). Three physical items were tracked: the user's head, a 3-Ball or stylus tracked input device (with a button switch), and a third device the developers refer to as a "fixture." The "fixture" device is basically used to provide a means for allowing the user to position the menu in the virtual world.

Although not part of the "main" system, several other display devices were experimented with to render various forms of haptic sensations. Haptic displays for presenting vibrations or thumps to the chest, vibrations to the hand, or temperature changes to the hand were all forms with which they experimented.

Vibrations, or "thumps," could be delivered to the chest by vests equipped with special hardware. Two types of vests were used: a commercial off-the-shelf (COTS) device designed for use with TV video games was interfaced to the system, and a "homemade" model was created using a hunting vest and woofer speakers.

Other specialized hand-displays were used for haptic display. These glove-displays included a vibrator glove from Virtual Technologies, the Teletact bladder glove, a Rutgers Dextrose Hand-Master, and a Displaced Temperature Sensing System (DTSS) display glove from CM Research. A PHANToM mechanical-arm–based force display was also considered, but concerns about the small working volume of the PHANToM led to the developers choosing not to explore it for this application.

For experimenting with the use of voice for interaction control, the developers used the "Wizard of Oz" approach to input, where someone sat at a keyboard and entered commands based on what the user said.

Application Implementation

A collaboration between the University of Houston (UH) and George Mason University (GMU), *Project ScienceSpace* began in February 1994. Initial experiments were run in *NewtonWorld* in that summer, with experiments using *MaxwellWorld* beginning in 1995. The development of *PaulingWorld* extended later.

Development was shared between UH and GMU, with the technical development conducted at the Virtual Environment Technology Laboratory (VETL) at the University of Houston, and the pedagogical and human factors design concepts developed at GMU in Fairfax, Virginia.

Development of the project at two sites significantly distant from one another was initially done using teleconferenced conversations and faxed diagrams. Once the prototype system was running in Houston, a duplicate system was developed in Fairfax, allowing either site to run the application. The ability of both development sites to run the experience simultaneously allowed collaborative design/debugging meetings to be conducted via normal telephone communications.

The software was developed using the VR-tool software system previously developed at the VETL in Houston. The VR-tool system was built upon Silicon Graphic's *Inventor* toolkit, and used Silicon Graphics workstations. Writing the applications with *Open Inventor* enabled them to be easily portable to other platforms.

The primary design concerns addressed the use of *ScienceSpace* worlds as learning experiences. The primary focal points of design then were on user interface issues, such that the applications would be as useful as possible.

The design process involved several iterative cycles of design and evaluation. Evaluation was done by preliminary tests of small groups of students as well as by allowing a large group of physics educators to experience and comment on the project during an educational forum (the 1994 Summer Meeting of the American Association of Physics Teachers). After the initial worlds were designed and experiments conducted, the developers chose to address a younger audience, and used focus groups to evaluate and brainstorm new ideas for the experiences. They also used "talk-aloud protocols" to evaluate how the user experienced the worlds by listening to their thought process as they performed various actions.

Design of later worlds (*MaxwellWorld* and *PaulingWorld*) improved upon the design of *NewtonWorld*. For example, the menu system that had been fixed in the HMD was now dynamically positioned with the user's off-hand. Also, *NewtonWorld* was later revamped to make use of lessons learned by the experiments with both *NewtonWorld* and *MaxwellWorld*. In addition to improving the menu system, many representational idioms were modified from the initial *NewtonWorld* system to better present the concepts. For example, instead of representing mass as varying (arbitrary) colors, the level of transparency is varied from high transparency (lower mass) to near opacity (high mass). Elasticity was indicated by the surface texture changes from shiny (representing hard, elastic balls) to a "soft and squishy" (bubblegum) look.

VR DISCOVERY

One of the important lessons learned by the development team was the value of involving a group of individuals with a wide range of expertise and backgrounds as part of the project.

A major goal of *Project ScienceSpace* was to evaluate the medium of virtual reality for educational purposes. To properly do this required a considerable effort on the part of the developers in the proper analysis of their worlds. This included not only analysis during the design phase of each world as described above (e.g., the physics educators and focus groups), but also post-design experiments to compare the educational impact versus non-VR software.

While a majority of 107 physics educators felt that worlds such as *NewtonWorld* would be a beneficial means of presenting science to students, a direct comparison with existing educational software would be the real test. One area that offered a good place to perform this comparison was between *MaxwellWorld* and *EM Field*™, a "highly regarded and widely used" software product that also was designed to teach the concepts of electrostatic fields. In *EM Field*™ *(EMF)* the user interacted with a two-dimensional representation of electrostatic fields. For the sake of comparison, the three-dimensional *MaxwellWorld* had features removed that were not part of the *EMF* software, leaving the dimensionality, physical immersiveness, and type (the quantitative *EMF* vs. the qualitative *MaxwellWorld*) of interface as the primary differences between the two.

By presenting the same physics lessons for groups using *EMF* or *MaxwellWorld*, the relative gains in understanding could be attributed to the choice of software. Both groups showed an increase in understanding, with *MaxwellWorld* users were better able to define concepts, and to demonstrate concepts in 3D, and yet still were able to sketch concepts in

2D at the same level as the users of *EMF*. Also, while users of the virtual reality interface were more likely to have difficulty with the interface, and/or experience simulator sickness, they still performed better than the *EMF*-using students. The developers believe that increased motivation in using the "new" VR system might be one factor that allowed students to overcome the experienced problems of VR.[3]

MaxwellWorld was used in an experiment to compare the effectiveness of egocentric and exocentric points of view on the virtual worlds. The designers expected that egocentric versus exocentric views would each be more amenable to learning particular concepts. They found this hypothesis to be true to a degree, but more importantly, they found that the mental task of integrating the global and local perspectives provided by the egocentric and exocentric points of view was a greater cause of learning because the user had to create a mental model that accommodated both.

The application developers made many other observations over the course of their work on this project, including:

- Each additional sense presented to the participant increased the participant engagement in the experience, and in general, increased learning. This assumes that the extra sensory inputs are designed to augment the primary sense, rather than pull attention away from the focal concepts.

- A single, long (e.g., 3-hour) VR session is generally not enough to improve the student's mental model of the concepts. This insufficiency results both from fatigue and sickness from the extended periods in the VR interface, and from the need to initially learn how to operate in VR.

- Three-dimensional concepts presented, learned, and tested entirely using 2D representations are not largely understood as three-dimensional phenomena even by students performing A-level work. "A" students in a high school physics class were good at

---

[3]The authors note that while the motivation factor may decrease as VR becomes more commonplace, this could be offset by less problems with the unfamiliar style of interface, and sickness induced by the limitations of the hardware.

giving correct descriptive answers in the 2D case, but they didn't have a good qualitative understanding of the concept, and were generally not able to answer questions related to the three-dimensional case.

Virtual reality allows younger students the opportunity to learn concepts that otherwise are taught much later in their educational experience because it can present them qualitatively, without relying on knowledge of higher mathematics. In particular, students in middle school could successfully learn the basics of Newtonian mechanics. This is particularly beneficial because this is approximately the age in which their childish mental models begin to give way to Aristotelian mental models. That is, the minds of these students are ready to create a formulaic mental model, so it would be better to provide them with a more appropriate representation that would help establish a good qualitative feel for the phenomena, and lead to a better, "intuitive" understanding of the higher mathematical descriptions. One of the potential pitfalls of using videogame-like technology to present scientific concepts is that kids have become accustomed to working in the nonrealistic worlds of many video games. Since this population is comfortable working within a nonrealistic world, they need to be convinced that the physics represented by the *ScienceSpace* worlds are indeed reasonably accurate representations of the real world.

The goal of *Project ScienceSpace* was to determine the potential of virtual reality for allowing students to gain better insights into scientific principles through a learning-by-doing approach. The multiple experiments performed using the various worlds of *ScienceSpace* have demonstrated that VR can be a useful tool toward this end. The developers saw that in the current method, in which students gather most of their information from lectures and reading, students who are able to perform well on tests may not in fact have a good understanding of how the concepts work in 3D. At the same time, the VR system allows the qualitative aspects of concepts to be taught at a much earlier age, before the point in the educational process when many students have already rejected the mathematics and hard science academic path.

Both during the design process and through surveys taken as part of the experiments, the *ScienceSpace* developers found that participants were much more likely to feel a sense of presence, and in fact be more engaged in the educational activities, when additional sensory cues were provided. Whether this sense of immersion increases the ability to learn depends on how well the added senses augment the concepts being taught.

When students experienced difficulty with simulator sickness, or found it difficult to adapt to the virtual reality interface style of the experiences, their ability to learn and their sense of immersion were both diminished. Fortunately, only a few students experienced even moderate dizziness or slight nausea within the first 30 to 45 minutes, so by keeping VR sessions short, these problems can be managed. Most users were eventually able to get the hang of working in VR.

Overall, the *ScienceSpace* researchers believe immersion to be an important factor for allowing experiential learning to take place. As Chris Dede states:

> *Our research suggests that multisensory immersion for learning depends on actional, symbolic, and sensory factors. Inducing actional immersion involves empowering the participant in a virtual environment to initiate actions that have novel, intriguing consequences. For example, when a baby is learning to walk, the degree of concentration this activity creates in the child is extraordinary. Discovering new capabilities to shape one's environment is highly motivating and sharply focuses attention.*

Related Applications and Follow-on Work

How important are foundational applications when planning new applications? *ScienceSpace* has inspired a new educational effort, to which we devote the entire following section.

Conclusion

Over the course of developing the *ScienceSpace* worlds, and testing their educational value, the project developers learned many interesting lessons.

Some lessons apply specifically to using virtual reality for elementary and high school education. They found that spreading lessons over multiple, shorter sessions gave students better success at assimilating and retaining concepts. They also discovered that virtual reality provided a mechanism whereby concepts that normally require abstract mathematical description could be taught in an intuitive qualitative manner. By using three-dimensional representations, young children could learn the concepts even before acquiring the mathematical tools needed by traditional methods of instruction. However, the major problem with working with children younger than about 12 years old was that head-mounted displays are designed for adult-sized heads and are often too large for younger children, as was also seen with Strickland's work with autistic children (Chapter 5).

Some general observations about VR made by the project developers included experimental results demonstrating how adding feedback to more senses is important to the immersive experience. Higher degrees of immersion from multiple senses can improve knowledge acquisition as long as the added senses do not distract from the salient information. Another observation was that displaying the worlds in a projection-based display versus a head-mounted display results in a different method of interfacing with the worlds, although both were equally compelling.

Continuing work includes experiments designed to use *PaulingWorld* to study the value of VR for enabling students

"master counterintuitive chemistry concepts such as quantum-level phenomena." *NewtonWorld* was adapted for a younger audience, and features were added that allow collaborative habitation of the world to investigate whether the nature of social constructivist learning enhances the educational value. Finally, *MaxwellWorld* was used to explore the "contribution of immersive frames of reference to understand complex science concepts."

Project ScienceSpace has illustrated that virtual reality can provide benefits to science education. These benefits extend beyond the benefits already demonstrated by interactive computer applications such as EM Field, as revealed by the studies of the research team wherein the students were found to understand the world of electrostatics as a whole, better than the students using EM Field. [Dede et al.]

In the final analysis of course, it is not the fact that virtual reality was used in education that is important, but that education can be enhanced by virtual reality. Or, as the researchers stated: "The medium (virtual reality) should not detract from the message of learning scientific principles" [Dede et al.].

CASE STUDY 6.2: MAXWELLVU

Executive Summary

MaxwellVU is an educational application meant to augment the teaching of electromagnetics to electrical engineering undergraduate students and physics students. It concentrates on communicating the physical meaning of the fundamental Maxwell's equations to students in a virtual environment. Typically, education in electromagnetics is done through mathematical expressions and two-dimensional figures in textbooks, though time-varying media such as videos are sometimes also utilized. The revolutionary nature of the *MaxwellVU* suite of applications is to allow the student to step into electrical and magnetic fields, performing physical actions which change the fields based on their inputs. *MaxwellVU* is a suite consisting of a unique application for each of five equations,

allowing an educator to focus on the underlying meaning of each separate equation by allowing students to interact with simulations of electrical and magnetic fields. Students actively manipulate these virtual fields through hand and body motions.

The application is presently being used in teaching electromagnetics at Valparaiso University. It is available for download in two open-source formats. It has been ported and demonstrated in *CAVE* systems as well as a stripped-down desktop application for the PC.

Application Description

MaxwellVU is primarily concerned with giving students physical insights into the fundamental equations governing electromagnetics, the so-called Maxwell equations.

$$\oint_S D \cdot dA = Q_{f,S} \qquad \text{Gauss's Law (Electric Field)} \qquad (1)$$

$$\oint_S B \cdot dA = 0 \qquad \text{Gauss's Law (Magnetic Field)} \qquad (2)$$

$$\oint_{\partial S} E \cdot dl = -\frac{\partial \Phi_{B,S}}{\partial t} \qquad \text{Faraday's Law} \qquad (3)$$

$$\oint_{\partial S} H \cdot dl = I_{f,S} - \frac{\partial \Phi_{D,S}}{\partial t} \qquad \text{Ampere's Law} \qquad (4)$$

as well as the related

$$F = \frac{Q_1 Q_2}{4\pi \varepsilon_0 r^2} \qquad \text{Coulomb's Law} \qquad (5)$$

These equations are sure to appear to most readers intimidating at the least on first sight. Yet these equations comprise the mathematical expression of the laws governing electromagnetic field theory. Most physics undergraduates and nearly all electrical engineering undergraduates take a course in this subject.

Presently, undergraduate education in this subject is largely mathematical in nature. The physical meaning of the laws is touched on in lectures, and textbook material is augmented with diagrams (both 2D and rendered 3D). Additional media such as video exists on this subject, but is rarely integrated into an undergraduate course.

It is this present shortcoming in the pedagogy that motivates the use of VR to improve teaching methods. A further motivation is that electromagnetic fields are by nature invisible. VR offers the ability to render them visible, using different representations to show various aspects of their characteristics. Finally, these equations have real-world analogs, so that emulating the physical world in VR can lead to better understanding when the student finally has to tackle the math.

The *MaxwellVU* suite consists of five separate applications, one each to support understanding of each of equations (1)–(5) above.

VR DISCOVERY

Who's afraid of the big, bad math? Whereas integral signs and Greek letters may terrify the average person, seeing loops of current and patterned arrows most likely does not. VR can be used to bridge the comprehension gap from mathematic expressions to inherent understanding. Immersing ourselves in the virtual world, we can have our hands become static electrical charges and watch magnetic fields change all around us as we wave our hands around.

The VR System

The system used in the five applications is a commercially available, turnkey system made by Visbox, Inc., Savoy, Illinois. The model is the Visbox-X2 system consisting of a 4m × 3m rear-projected front screen and a 3m × 2.3m top-projected floor. Button and joystick input is carried out on a handheld Wingman joystick device, consisting of eight buttons, two joysticks, a slider, and a D-pad. Head tracking is achieved through two front-mounted CCD cameras tracking two reflective spheres on the user's glasses. The system uses passive stereo through linearly polarized filters and glasses.

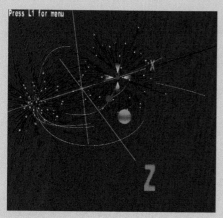

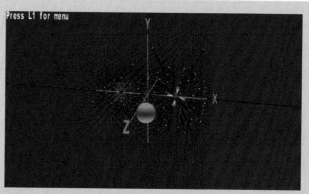

FIGURE 6-10

The ColumbVU application shows the electric field resulting from a negative and positive point charge. The green sphere is the cursor, while the yellow highlight on the red sphere indicated a selected charge. Students can place positive and negative charges within the 3D space, and view the resulting electric field.

FIGURE 6-8

VectorVU allows the user to set up a constellation of point electrical charges and then shows the resulting electric field. Users may then move a cursor around with the wand and launch test charges that leave trails as they are attracted to negative charges. This enables students to understand both the characteristic fields generated from point electrical charges, as well as perceive the effect of the field on a charged free particle.

FIGURE 6-11

The FaradayVU application, shows the electric field around a closed loop. Users can manipulate the electric field by moving static charges, yet the net sum of the electric field around the loop remains zero. Students see that in the absence of a changing magnetic field, the vector sum of the tangential components of the electric field must be zero.

FIGURE 6-9

GaussVU allows users to move their hand as a "closed Gaussian surface," reaching into and out of point electrical charges. The flux vectors are shown on the surface. The key comprehension imparted by this application is that the integration of the field vectors on the surface are proportional to the charge contained inside the volume.

The choice of linear polarization for the passive stereo puts a limitation on the orientation of the user's head. For the linear polarization to be effective, the vertical orientation of the user's head must be upright. If the user rolls their head

FIGURE 6-12

The AmpereVU application, showing the magnetic field along a closed loop. Shown is a circular loop, but other loops such as squares can be chosen. This application imparts to student the difference in the magnetic field around a closed loop when a current does and does not pierce the surface.

to the right or to the left, the polarization is lost. The use of circular polarization can eliminate this shortcoming, but suffers from higher cost and poorer filtering.

VR DISCOVERY

For a front-screen-only stereo display, linear polarization can be effective. Users tend to look straight-on to the screen and do not tilt their heads to the right or the left. This is typically not true in a 4 + -wall *CAVE* environment. When using just the front wall, SVL researchers find linear polarization effective. But the addition of a stereo floor caused users to have head motions and orientations that misaligned the polarization axes of their glasses. This resulted in loss of depth perception when users looked at the floor.

Interactions with the system are handled at two levels. When an instructor is using the system in a lecture demonstration format, students stand back from the screen such that their field of view is not covered entirely by the screen, much like watching television. The screen is projected in

FIGURE 6-13

Visbox-X2 system at Valparaiso University's Scientific Visualization Laboratory.
Photo by Aran Kessler

stereo and students wear polarized glasses. There is an area for the class to stand of approximately 5 m × 4 m, which can reasonably accommodate 20–25 students as well as the instructor. In this mode, the students are passive while the instructor holds the wand and controls the application while lecturing.

When students are using the system in hands-on mode for discovery learning, usually a pair of students utilizes the 3 m × 2.3 m projected floor surface for interaction, in addition to the front wall. Standing on the projected floor allows the bringing of objects in front of the screen and provides for a more immersive experience.

The difference between the two modes of usage illustrates a valuable lesson when it comes to using VR for education. When students are passively watching a demonstration, the system is used much like a 3D viewing screen as opposed to an immersive experience. Even if the entire group is able to fit onto the floor surface, the crowded group essentially blocks the top-projection onto the floor. Thus the instructor tends to use the front screen only. Further, though, the objects represented in the virtual world are placed "behind" the screen since they cannot be brought forward without clipping the objects by the front screen's extents.

This changes greatly when students participate in experiential learning using the application singly or with one other partner. Having the projected floor is essential for students bringing objects up close so that they interact with the surfaces, fields, and charges in close proximity to their own selves. The lesson learned: single front screens are great for presentations, but for student experiential learning, you need a floor.

Related Applications and Follow-on Work

ScienceSpace's *Maxwell's World* is the obvious forerunner of this educational effort. In fact, the chief developer of *MaxwellVU* was directly inspired by this foundational work. However, where *ScienceSpace* was limited to head-mount displays and was written for custom hardware, *MaxwellVU* uses open-source libraries and is able to be run on a variety of platforms.

This application is currently being used at Valparaiso University in their electromagnetic field theory class. A version of the software for the PC is available for free download, though the benefits of immersive VR are absent. The full-VR version is also available in open-source format

from the laboratory's website. (Links are available on the companion website to this book.)

Instructor Dale Kempf, who utilizes the software in his class, says, "Electromagnetic field theory is a challenging subject for out students, partly because it is three spacial dimensions. Virtual Reality demonstration of Maxwell's equations in three dimensions really help the students in my field theory classes understand the principles that are so difficult to visualize with two-dimensional media."

The application is actively being used today, and undergoing further development. One planned improvement is the addition of time-varying magnetic fluxes that the users can arbitrarily manipulate with hand or body movements. This would give student greater insight into the time-varying aspects of electromagnetic fields. However, calculating resulting electric fields on the fly is complicated by the high computational requirements of solving a system of simultaneous partial differential equations. Presently, the bound is computational and limited by graphics capability. As CPU power increases, it is expected that this will soon be a surmountable problem.

Conclusion

Two aspects stand out from *MaxwellVU*. First, foundational applications such as *ScienceSpace* can motivate and inspire present application development, as is seen in this instance. Present VR development tools and libraries allowed the production of *MaxwellVU* in 6 months by a team of three, whereas *ScienceSpace* was in its time a near-Herculean effort. Other applications can build on such foundations.

Second, "tough stuff" like Maxwell's equations can provide a perfect opportunity for the use of VR in education. Easing students into intimidating math by first exposing them to a virtual environment can both provide better class performance and lead to a better comprehension of the math itself.

CASE STUDY 6.3: VIRTUAL POMPEII

Virtual Pompeii premiered in the fall of 1995 (September 16 through January 7, 1996) at the M. H. de Young Memorial Museum of Art in San Francisco. *Virtual Pompeii* is a walkthrough recreation of Pompeii as it existed before Mount

Vesuvius erupted in AD 79. Covered completely by volcanic ash, Pompeii, only a few miles from Naples, wasn't rediscovered until the 16th century. The 5- to 8-meter thick layer of ash and volcanic debris plus other factors contributed to

FIGURE 6-14
The floor of the theater looking north. The stage is to the left, the beginning of the seating to the right.

this site being one of the best preserved of all archeological sites. This preservation aided in the ability to make a compelling recreation of the site.

According to Technical Director Jeffrey Jacobson, one advantage of doing a virtual recreation of the site is that it would be prohibitively expensive to create a real model. Plus, digital models have the added benefit that they can be easily replicated and distributed, even via the Internet.

By making the reconstruction available to a wider audience, it becomes more than a tool for archaeologists to envision the past. It becomes an avenue through which the general populace with an interest in human culture and history can experience the past in a way that is engaging and intuitive for non-archaeologists. The archaeologist is like an architect who can see in their mind how their plans will look when physically constructed, but whose clients are less experienced in cognitively converting the 2D plan diagram into a 3D mental image.

One of the goals of the *Virtual Pompeii* experience was to bring to life a more complete experience of what life was

like in Pompeii just before the eruption of Mt. Vesuvius. Rather than merely viewing photographs of an archeological dig side by side with a few artifacts from the dig and a drawing of how the structures were laid out, with *Virtual Pompeii* viewers can journey through the city and witness the society and culture "first hand." When *Virtual Pompeii* opened at the de Young Museum, the application developers had not reached all of their goals, but did create a world that gives a flavor of what Pompeii was like in the days prior to its destruction.

Application Description

The focus of the virtual site is the Pompeian theater complex. The complex consists of the Large Theater, ruins of the Temple of Hercules,[4] the Triangular Forum, and the Temple of Isis. These structures and other nearby streets and buildings are included in the *Virtual Pompeii* experience. Throughout the environment, animated figures (agents) add to the illusion of the resurrected Pompeii.

The *Virtual Pompeii* experience was designed to touch on the art, religion, and private life of the people of Pompeii. Participants can explore the walkways, sculptures, murals, courtyards, and structures as they existed long ago. The fact that Pompeii was nearly instantly buried served to produce a snapshot of the culture of the time. Often in other archaeological sites decay happens gradually, and new structures are built on top of the old, making it difficult to determine what things were like in any specific era.

Because the experience creators consider the work an educational application of VR, they paid considerable attention to the accuracy and detail of the recreation. The results were verified by scholars from the Archaeological Institute of America to be very authentic.

The temples provide a means by which the participant can wonder about the rites and rituals practiced in this mixed Greco/Roman/Mediterranean culture. For example, one might encounter the Temple of Isis. In the first century AD,

---

[4]The Temple of Hercules had been destroyed by an earthquake 80 years prior to the destruction of Pompeii. The structure had not been rebuilt by the people of Pompeii, so the VR experience left the temple grounds as a "picturesque ruin," as it would have been in AD 79.

FIGURE 6-15

A chanting priest stands on the front platform of the temple.

FIGURE 6-16

The small building holding the sacred water, to the left of the main temple. A fire burns on an altar before it. Sacrifices of cloths, fruits, and other foodstuffs are shown burning on it.

Isis, the Egyptian goddess of nature, had a large cult following throughout the Greco-Roman world.

The Pompeian Temple of Isis is a small, ornate structure combining Egyptian, Greek, and Roman architectural features. The Temple grounds include the gardens and surrounding colonnaded walkway. Inside were separate structures for specific purposes. The focal structure was the sanctuary on a podium, adorned with sculptures. Inside the walls was a statue of Isis, which could be viewed through the front opening. At the front was a large porch where ceremonies could be carried out with the followers below.

A separate structure to the right of the entrance of the main building was a small roofless building containing a tank filled with water from the Nile River, mixed with rainwater. Behind the main building was a small garden area with a fountain and a statue of Bacchus (the Greek god of wine, also called Dionysus). The garden might have contained medicinal herbs as well as plants from the Nile, including at least one palm tree. The priests of Isis were famed for their medical knowledge. At the back of the surrounding colonnaded walkway were rooms believed to have been used for "ritual meals" and for "the mystery cult's dramatic initiation ceremonies." The dining room contains a large marble table.

To help bring about a sense of how life was lived in the ancient city, the experience developers attempted to populate the virtual world with people, animals, and objects engaged in everyday life. Among the characters are a flautist, a chanter, and a group of singing birds.

Audio is used to enhance the sense of mental immersion. As the participant travels through the city, sounds such as singing birds, the melody of the flautist, and the voice of the chanter can be heard as the participant gets close to them. Many of the characters within the virtual world were implemented only as sound-producing agents. As the participant walked throughout the theater complex, there were several locations they could pass that would activate sounds such as a cat or a nest of birds.

Two agents that were fully implemented were a priest playing the Aulos (a double-barreled flute) from which music can be heard when the participant is nearby, and a priest singing an adoration of Isis. The singing priest stood on the portico of the Temple of Isis waving his hands out

FIGURE 6-17

This image depicts the view from the ceremonial dining chamber at the back of the temple complex. The back of the temple is barely visible to the right and can be seen just to the right of the right-most column.

FIGURE 6-19

The Grand Theater (as modeled by Veronica Polo).

FIGURE 6-18

Another view of the ceremonial chamber, showing the murals.

and up in the manner of Roman prayer. The flautist was also within the grounds of the Temple of Isis.

There were several places in the complex that would transform words from classical Latin to English as one approached the subject. For instance, from a distance the chanting priest could be heard in Latin, but up close, the words switched to English so the listener could better understand the words.

Both versions of the chant were sung by the same person with the same tempo and inflections, so the transition was remarkably smooth. A similar effect was done with the text on plaques, which can be found throughout the complex. As with the voices, from a distance, the words appear in Latin, but as the participant approaches they transform into English.

Constructed between 89 and 75 BC, the Pompeian amphitheater is the oldest known amphitheater. It could hold 20,000 spectators, nearly the entire population of the city. One of the more interesting aspects of the virtual reconstruction is a virtual re-creation of a theatrical performance in the Large Theater located in the center of the large open-air amphitheater. The play automatically begins as the user enters the amphitheater. The Carnegie Mellon University Drama Department and the University of Pittsburgh History of Art and Architecture Department helped to provide the content of the play. While in the auditorium, the participant hears the actors and the accompanying music.

The play itself was written at Carnegie Mellon and produced by Professor Don Damaellio. At the time of the eruption, Roman theater was very slapstick, with vulgar humor presented in a vaudeville-like style. Since the content of

 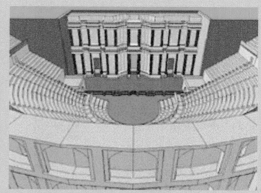

FIGURE 6-20

The Pompeian amphitheater is the oldest known amphitheater. Shown here are both a picture of the actual excavated temple and its corresponding virtual model.

actual plays from the period would be offensive to the modern museum-going audiences, it was decided to create a new play in a similar vein, but tuned to modern audiences. Roman historian and archaeologist Jane Vadnal contributed many suggestions and other input to the development of the play. The result was a political satire very much in the vein of the then popular fare, but involving modern-era issues.

The content of the play was a combination slapstick and political satire about the Emperor Toitas's older Egyptian mistress. Given the opportunity to incorporate a new play into the experience, Vadnal felt that it would be better to use a portion of a play by Plautus. By AD 79, Plautus's works were old and no longer fashionable, but were still performed in provincial places like Pompeii. More importantly, according to Vadnal, they were slapstick masterpieces.

In addition to changing the content of the play to more closely match the expectations of the modern viewer, the developers also changed the coloring of many of the buildings for a similar reason. Because the Romans liked very bright, garish colors, sticking to the authentic colors would have been distracting to the modern eye. So in effect, these changes were made to allow participants to see the world closer to the way a Pompeian would have seen the world than if the world were duplicated more exactly. A Pompeian would not have thought twice about the color of the buildings or the content of the play, whereas a modern viewer would be more distracted by these particular elements of the world.

This technique could be classified as "perceptual cue tuning," where changes are made to how the world is presented to make the world appear more natural, even though it has to be somewhat distorted to make that happen. For example, the original colors of the buildings were toned down to accommodate modern sensibilities.[5]

The play was created basically as a 3D animation that can be viewed from any angle. The movements of individual performers were recorded using typical motion capture methods. These performances were then combined and choreographed together with the help of the Jack™ system from the University of Pennsylvania. This was a very painstaking process, and in the end the look was not as good as the developers had hoped, so the visual portion of the play was left out of the final experience, presenting only the audio to the participant. The only method of interface with the world is via the travel controls. A trackball (2DOF input device) is used to move the user through the world forward, backward, or laterally. For most venues, a physically immersive HMD display is worn by one participant. This person is also given control of the trackball to move through the city. For larger, theater-like venues the *Virtual Pompeii* experience could more easily be presented on projection screens by following a preprogrammed ride-along path.

---

[5]See the "Officer of the Deck" application of Section 1, Chapter 7 for more discussion on perceptual cue tuning.

VR System

The *Virtual Pompeii* was designed to operate at regional culture centers. The first venue for a planned 2-year tour beginning in 1995 was the M. H. de Young Memorial Museum of Art in San Francisco. Unfortunately, the planned tour didn't happen, and a possible presentation at the Smithsonian Institute for the summer of 1998 also fell through. After the experience closed at the de Young Museum, *Virtual Pompeii* was presented once at the Carnegie Science Center's ElectricHorizon™ interactive theater and in many private showings at CMU.

At the de Young Memorial Museum, the exhibit was arranged such that an attendee's experience begins in the hallway leading up to a room that had been set up as a mini-theater where the *Virtual Pompeii* was housed. The mini-theater could hold about 40 people. Entry to the *Virtual Pompeii* exhibit was included in the regular admission price for the museum.

Along the entryway were real photographs of the Italian ruins used to reconstruct the ancient world, replete with explanatory text. Upon entry to the theater, one person was chosen to wear the HMD. This person was generally chosen on a first-come basis. A member of the museum staff assisted this person with the equipment and provided an informative narration. Others watched the experience vicariously on overhead screens. Both the HMD and overhead screens could be displayed stereoscopically or monoscopically. When a stereoscopic image was displayed on the large screens, polarized glasses were given to the viewers to allow them to properly see the image.

In prior experience with presenting re-created ancient Egyptian structures in a public museum venue, the application developers found that the audience could be possessive about how much time they should be allowed to remain immersed in the world. Based on this experience the developers decided to implement a clear and dramatic ending to *Virtual Pompeii*. Fortunately, for this particular scenario, there was an obvious action available that would end the experience within the context of the experience—the eruption of Mt. Vesuvius.

As the visitor's time expired, they would first hear a recording of the rumble of an actual volcano. A few seconds later, the world would begin to shake, represented visually by perturbing the viewpoint. At first, 3D particles spewing from the volcano began to occupy more and more of the participant's visual perception. After a few more seconds, the entire scene begins fading to a snowy grey image. Finally, as the rumbling sounds continue in the background, the visitor's view becomes entirely filled with ashen grey.

Just as abruptly as the lives and culture of Pompeii ceased nearly 2000 years ago, the participant's experience in the virtual world ends as they get buried in ash. Although the eruption of Mt. Vesuvius was not as instantaneous as many laypeople believe, this belief could be used as an excellent narrative device for ending the experience quickly. The entire sequence from first hearing the audio rumbling to the completely grey scene occurs in 20 seconds.

The application had controls to provide a 3-, 5-, or 10-minute experience prior to the eruption of Vesuvius. Once all vision turned ashen grey, the participant removed the HMD, and the next person entered Pompeii. The different settings for the length of the experience allowed the operators of the venue to adjust the throughput based on the size of the audience that came for the experience.

This project utilized two Silicon Graphics Indigos™ and one Onyx™ for development. A second Onyx, which included four processors (R4400, 200MHz), and a single RealityEngine2™ graphics engine were used for the traveling display. The Onyx was capable of supplying up to 30 fps at 640 × 480 resolution. Head-mounted displays from Liquid Image and N-Vision were used to display the visual images to the head-tracked participants. The head tracking was done with an Ascension Technologies electromagnetic tracking system. Large screen projection was done using Electrohome Marque projectors.

The higher-resolution n-Vision HMD (640 × 480 pixels) was deemed to be too expensive and fragile for the public show, so its usage was reserved for private demonstrations at the CMU lab. The developers felt that the Liquid Image HMD, although lower in resolution (256 × 256 pixels) was a better solution for the museum display as it was "physically able to withstand the beating it got from being in a museum show."

Similarly, a third-party trackball was used as the input device because it was sturdier than other options. The trackball also seemed to be an interface that would be more intuitive for controlling walkthrough travel, where the user can move along the surface in two dimensions.

Silicon Graphics *Performer*™ software was used for the image generation. In addition to rendering the images, *Performer* provides capabilities for handled the collision detection, database management, and stereo image synchronization. Modeling was done with the SIMLAB's preferred packages, *form-Z*™ from Auto·des·sys, Inc. The choreography was done with JACK™ from the University of Pennsylvania Center for Human Modeling and Animation.[6]

Other products used during development of the application include tools from VSI Visual Synthesis, Inc. to render the audio; Adaptive Optics Associates for motion capture; and Corphaeus Inc. and Lightscape Technologies for additional graphics support. As with the HMDs, some of the advanced features provided by some software tools were not at the de Young showing.

The creation of the virtual world model was very difficult. Roman scholars from the Archeological Institute of America (AIA) were assigned to work with Jane Vadnal, the project's Research Director. She took the information they gave her, along with data from other sources, and specified the reconstruction of the architectural details, murals, and other artwork. All of this was derived from sources such as early German watercolor paintings and black-and-white photographs. Text descriptions from historians such as Pliny who lived during the time of the eruption were also used to add details to the world. Computer modeling was done using the *Form-Z* package, and later, *Designer's Workbench*. The actual (digital) reconstruction was performed by the art team.

Virtual Pompeii was a joint project between The Archaeological Institute of America, Silicon Graphics Inc. and the STUDIO for Creative Inquiry at CMU. The team was led by Carl Loeffler, who was the research director of SIMLAB, the STUDIO's virtual reality research team. SIMLAB member Jeffrey Jacobson served as technical director on the project. It was created by programmers, artists, sound engineers, and musicians from CMU using the STUDIO for

---

[6]And later released as a product from Transom Technologies, Inc., a subsidiary of Engineering Animation Inc. (EAI).

Creative Inquiry facilities. The Archaeological Institute of America provided consultants to ensure accuracy in the areas of architecture, gardens, painting, and sculpture. The Drama Department at CMU provided content specialists for Roman Theater, and the Department of Art History provided content expertise in Roman Art.

Related Applications and Follow-on Work

In a related application that allows people to walk through Pompeii, scientists at Max Plank institute have created a "CyberCarpet" to enable visitors to a virtual creation of Pompeii to *physically* walk through the world. The CyberCarpet is an omnidirectional treadmill that allows a participant to walk endlessly in any direction. The participants wear a head-mounted display with markers on it for optical tracking. The virtual Pompeii was implemented with CityEngine, which allows creation of large-scale virtual environments. CityEngine was created by the Swiss Federal Institute of Technology (ETHZ).

Conclusion

The elements that were implemented demonstrate the possibilities for using VR as a tool for advanced and casual study of lost cultures. For the casual observer, it affords them the opportunity to imagine Pompeian life without reading a detailed book on the subject. For the serious student of archaeology or anthropology, it provides a tool to create a mental model of the world much more quickly than possible by pouring over photos, sketches, and field reports.

One of the benefits of putting site reconstruction through the rigors of creating a 3D virtual world is that the 3D reconstruction is less able to support contradictions and gaps in the data interpretation than other media. In particular, a written description or a mental model based on incomplete and unclear references are both able to accommodate gaps and contradictions without being noticed. Thus VR forces archaeologists working on a site reconstruction to confront opposing and missing data.

The *Virtual Pompeii* experience proved itself as a worthwhile effort at addressing an archaeological site reconstruction, and medium for public presentation to casual observers. During the exhibit at the de Young Memorial Museum, there was a marked increase in attendance due to the VR presentation. With a background in both art and computers, Renée Dreyfus, curator of the museum,

FIGURE 6-21

A virtual reality walkthrough of Pompeii was created using CityEngine software from the Swiss Federal Institute of Technology. The image on the right shows a participant walking on an omnidirectional treadmill to experience Pompeii.

showed great excitement about this new type of interactive exhibit. She stated: "I'm interested in seeing how far a museum can use technology for presenting contexts for works of art, and helping the public to understand the art on display. What better way than to bring them back to a world that no longer exists, but can exist in a computer?" Jacobson discusses how VR can be used to create an experience that allows a participant to experience another (no longer extant) culture:

These reconstructions open the door, not just to the buildings, but to the life that the people lived back then. We can have a sense of people going about their business. In a well-researched project, viewers will experience the weather as well as the natural flora and fauna of the time. The viewer of an historical reconstruction has a rich visual synthesis that would take years and years of study to otherwise build from books and artifacts.

CASE STUDY 6.4: VIRTUAL REALITY GORILLA EXHIBIT

Few virtual reality applications have focused on teaching about the social behaviors of the animal kingdom. The application described here is remarkable in that it realistically portrays the behavior and social interactions of a community of gorillas. The application allows a participant to *become* a member of the community. As an adolescent gorilla, the user can interact with other (virtual) gorillas to learn first-hand about the pecking order, and rituals of a gorilla society.

The *Virtual Reality Gorilla Exhibit* was a joint project between Georgia Institute of Technology's Graphics, Visualization, and Usability Lab (GVU) and Zoo Atlanta. The project had an overall goal of educating middle school children about gorilla interaction, vocalizations, and social structures. Because gorillas are an endangered species, gorilla conservation education is becoming increasingly important. The project designers felt that by allowing students to

FIGURE 6-22

Students visiting Zoo Atlanta are given the opportunity to enter a gorilla community to study gorilla social structures. In the image on the left, a student dons a head-mounted display and holds a wand. A ring platform provides a boundary for the student. Note the actual gorilla visible through the window near the VR exhibit. The image on the right shows a virtual recreation of the Zoo Atlanta gorilla exhibit that the student sees.
Photo by J. Sebo/Zoo Atlanta-copyright 1996

"become a gorilla" they might increase understanding and concern about the issues facing gorillas.

The developers (GVU researchers in conjunction with zoo personnel) established two separate educational goals. The original goal was for middle school children to learn about dominance in a hierarchy of gorilla social interactions. Later, a new goal of teaching zoo habitat design philosophy was implemented using the same underlying software. It was hoped that by enabling students to explore within the context of the gorilla society they would gain a better perspective of that society. The habitat design application provides a means for studying the psychology and philosophy of environmental design at the college level. For both projects, the novelty of VR was thought to be helpful in that it might increase the students' desire to explore the virtual world. The application of VR to middle school zoological education is what is focused on in this section. The dissimilarities between the applications supporting the two goals will be briefly discussed toward the end.

Prior to the *Virtual Reality Gorilla Exhibit* project, students could only learn about many aspects of gorilla behavior via reading second- and third-hand accounts. Direct observation of the gorillas in the zoo does allow some opportunity for study, but it is inadequate in many ways. For example, gorillas are active early in the morning and late in the afternoon, but are asleep during the early afternoon when the students would typically have the opportunity to observe. Additionally, because many parts of the zoo are inaccessible to the general public, the VR exhibit enables students to investigate many otherwise unseen aspects of gorilla habitats. The introduction of new gorillas to the community is not observable, because it is done outside the view of the general public; thus, students are unable to observe the acclimation process of a new gorilla. In general there is no way a student can join with the gorillas and interact with them as a peer. The *Virtual Reality Gorilla Exhibit* addresses these issues, and allows a student to have a firsthand learning experience related to the life of a gorilla and its habitat.

FIGURE 6-23

A variety of gorilla postures were modeled for the Virtual Reality Gorilla Exhibit. The image on the left shows a male silverback striking a pose, and the image on the right shows its virtual counterpart.
Image courtesy Don Allison

Application Description

The application designers endeavored to create as realistic a world as feasible, while retaining a relatively high visual frame rate. The application includes a model of the gorilla habitat (modeled geometrically) and gorilla agents (modeled geometrically, behaviorally, and sonically). Real-world images and sounds were incorporated into the experience as texture maps and sound samples to enhance the realism of how the world is presented.

The gorilla behavior model was created based on text and video accounts of the gorillas. Local zoo experts helped refine the model. Five gorilla models were constructed: an adult male silverback, an adult male blackback, an adult female, a juvenile, and an infant. The gorillas were created as three-dimensional entities modeled to look and act like actual gorillas. The gorilla motions were created by modeling a series of key poses. Intermediate positions are generated by interpolating between poses. When video of a pose or motion was not available for modelers to study, zoo experts would act out the role.

Each gorilla motion has an associated vocalization. The vocalization rendering is timed to correlate with the motion. More than 80 gorilla sound samples were collected for the experience. From these samples, a few general classes of sounds were created: an ambient sound of running water (from a waterfall in the habitat), mixes of male/female contentment sounds, coughing/annoyance sounds, a generic roar/charge/chestbeat sequence, and a separate chestbeat sound.

In addition to accurate portrayal of the gorilla family, a model was created of the gorilla habitat at Zoo Atlanta, including such details as the foliage, trees, and rocks. Topographical data was used to create the terrain. The creators also modeled the two associated buildings, the Cameroon Interpretive Center and the exterior of the night holding structure (they have not had the opportunity to model the interior). The Cameroon Interpretive Center is a building at Zoo Atlanta with large glass windows through which zoo visitors can observe a portion of the habitat housing a silverback gorilla (Willie B) and his family (several female and juvenile gorillas). This exhibit (called the "Gorillas of Cameroon") is also a focal point for educational activities.

As an educational application, there must be more to the experience than wandering around the habitat and watching the gorillas. The subtleties of gorilla movement

FIGURE 6-24

The Virtual Reality Gorilla Exhibit modeled the actual Cameroon Interpretive Center. These images show the actual center (the building in which the VR display is housed) and the VR model of the facility. In the gorilla experience, the students begin in the virtual center, and step through the window into the gorilla pen.
Image courtesy Don Allison

and postures can be better learned when an explanation of what is being witnessed is presented along with the view of the world. In this case, such a presentation would require both that the gorillas act in a natural fashion and that a narrator agent or other presentation mechanism be programmed to give context-sensitive information. The initial *Virtual Reality Gorilla Exhibit* included two agent gorillas with which the participant could interact with an adult male silverback and an adult female. For the initial public presentation, these tasks were performed by zoo experts, and not the application itself.

VR System

An untracked, handheld prop equipped with two buttons provides the user input interface. Travel about the environment is via a gaze-directed walkthrough method. Direction of travel is based on the direction the participant is looking. There is no means of independently rotating the world, so a full horizontal field-of-regard (FOR) display is necessary to guarantee the user will be able to always see where they are going. Thus, this interface technique works best with HMDs and projection systems that completely surround the viewer. The buttons on the hand controller activate movement in the longitudinal (gaze) direction at a constant rate of travel either forward or backward depending on which button is pressed. In the habitat design application (described later), a 6-DOF tracked stylus with

a single button is used instead as the handheld input device. The tracked stylus allows for a point-to-fly method of travel plus other forms of interaction needed for doing design work.

To enable this experience to run on lower-cost computers, some rendering tricks were necessary to maintain a reasonable frame rate. Because movement in the virtual world was constrained to areas in which the gorillas were free to roam, there were certain facets of the space that could not be seen. The developers used this constraint to enhance performance by removing unviewable polygons. Polygon count of the terrain was also reduced wherever possible. To maintain the basic shape of the terrain, some criteria were set for polygon removal. Polygon removal should not change the terrain slope by more than 5 degrees per 2-foot interval within areas the user could explore. In areas that the user could see, but not enter, the criterion was 10 degrees per 2-foot interval. The rendering system needed also to be capable of hardware texture mapping to allow all the polygons to make use of textures to enhance the scene realism.

Students experience the virtual world via a head-mounted display that provides a monoscopic image displayed to both eyes (the monoscopic-binocular display method). A student stands inside a ring platform with a railing that helps keep them within range of the cables and tracking system. The ring also provides a source of stability to aid the students in feeling assured that they will not fall down or walk into anything.

The initial application was developed on an SGI Onyx computer with an RE2 graphics accelerator. They ran the gorilla applications on either a Silicon Graphics Indigo 2 with Maximum-Impact graphics, or a "medium- to high-end PC" with a Pentium II™ Intel processor in conjunction with a hardware OpenGL accelerator card. The Silicon Graphics systems provided a better frame rate than the PC-based system (about 15 fps vs. roughly 10 fps), but at a higher cost.

Full 6-DOF position tracking (both location and orientation) was done of the participant's head. No other body part was spatially tracked. The sound is monophonic and does not vary according to head position (it is presented with a head-referenced sound stage). Sound display was done via headphones in the HMD and through a subwoofer positioned beneath the ring platform. The headphones were later replaced with loudspeakers both to allow others to hear the sounds of the experience and to allow the participant to converse with the others watching nearby. The software environment used to create the world was Georgia Tech's Simple Virtual Environment Toolkit (SVE) [GVU Tech report 93–13].

A vicarious viewing display system was also provided for the press, public, and other students to view and hear the action. Two large monitors presented the participant's view, and speakers in the pavilion presented the sounds.

Trial Run

Once a prototype of the *Virtual Reality Gorilla Exhibit* was ready, an informal study of the VR experience was held. Participants were children aged 7 to 15, most of who were already involved in the zoo's Young Scientists program.[7]

---

[7] A program of the zoo that already existed in which school children come to the zoo on a weekly basis for 6 weeks to observe gorilla behaviors and take ethological data.

Known as "the Gorilla Squad," this program gave children the opportunity to observe gorilla behavior, so most of them were already versed in watching the gorillas though from outside the habitat. The VR system was installed in the Gorillas of Cameroon center and a day was spent (amidst press coverage) allowing the students to try the VR experience. Each session began with the student participant exploring the virtual "Gorillas of Cameroon" exhibit. About 30 people had the opportunity to experience the world first hand.

The VR platform was located next to the window overlooking the gorilla habitat in the Zoo. At the start of their experience each student was placed within the (virtual) center, viewing the (virtual) gorillas through those same (virtual) windows. After getting familiar with the HMD and navigating the world by exploring the center, students were instructed to walk through the windows and into the gorilla habitat. As they passed through the window into the habitat, they were told that they were now juvenile gorillas.

Students were free to explore the environment, by "walking" around, and perhaps making attempts to initiate contact with the virtual gorillas, which would react appropriately to their actions. The gorillas in the virtual world were implemented as agents programmed with many gorilla behaviors. However, for the prototype version of the application, only lower-level behaviors were preprogrammed. High-level gorilla behavior was implemented using the "Wizard of Oz" technique. A zoo expert controlled the high-level behavior of the gorillas using a keyboard interface. This technique enabled the gorilla family to react appropriately to the student actions. The keyboard interface has keys for selecting which gorilla was under "wizard" control, and other keys to give commands to the current gorilla, such as standing, walking, or making a bluff charge. The gorillas not under "wizard" control continue performing the last request given to them. There are also key commands for administrative operations such as resetting the positions of the user and all the gorillas.

By incorporating lower level behaviors into the model, the "wizard" can instruct the gorilla to perform actions such as "move to point A" without having to specify every muscle or joint movement. As the virtual gorilla performed this instruction it used programmed "reflexes" to avoid obstacles such as holes or trees. The "wizard" could select from many common poses, which were presented with the appropriate gorilla vocalization.

In the real world, gorilla communication is by vocalization, posture, and facial expressions. Some expressions of displeasure may be perceived by human observers as physical threats. However, in the virtual world participants know that their physical well-being is not actually being threatened. This can lead to participants' actively seeking out and performing actions that annoy the adult gorillas, to provoke a threatening response. Because this goes against the educational goal of learning how to behave as a proper adolescent gorilla, an alternate form of discouragement is incorporated in the VR experience. This discouragement comes in the form of reducing the interaction with the VR experience. They are put in "time out," where they are unable to see the gorilla environment, only a message reminding them that they are being punished.

First Impressions

Overall response to the experience was positive. Students felt the experience was "fun," and that they did learn about gorilla behavior. Zoo observers saw that participants acted naively at first, but later recognized and responded appropriately to gorilla cues and signals. Most of the users interacted as they would in the real environment. For example, they did not jump into a 12-foot ditch that was there even though they were not prevented from doing so. The developers felt that the students achieved a high degree of immersion, and that there was transference of knowledge gained in the virtual world back to the real world.

Some observations made at the experience trial are similar to observations of other VR experiences at other public venues. Younger students spent more time exploring the environment, whereas older ones spent more time observing and interacting with other gorillas. Most students did not make many physical movements. Typically, they would stand stationary in the platform ring, occasionally rotating their body to look and move in another direction. However, they did travel extensively throughout the virtual habitat. Students expressed that they wanted to interact with other "student gorillas" and to see their own gorilla body. The students were disappointed they couldn't touch and feel the other gorillas, or feel the fur of their own body. Because the experience designers believe current haptic feedback

devices are not yet capable of providing acceptable representations of this nature, they plan to design future efforts to minimize the need for such devices.

One confusing aspect of the initial virtual world was that the audio display of gorilla sounds was of constant amplitude regardless of how far the student was from the source of the sound. Thus, if a distant gorilla made a sound, the student perceived it to be very close and would look for it, expecting it to be nearby. They did feel the sound was an important component, nonetheless. The problem with the audio cues was changed in later versions by adjusting the amplitude of each sound based on the distance from the viewer. It was still done monaurally, so only distance audio cues were provided, without directional cues.

Further Development

From the prototype experience, the developers found that the experience was much better when participants were "accompanied" by a knowledgeable guide who could point things out and otherwise provide assistance. However, it is not practical for the experience to require a crew of experts to act as assistants and Wizard of Oz agents. Therefore, the developers pursued an enhanced behavioral model for the gorillas capable of performing realistic high-level interactions. They also investigated integrating some form of "automatic" guide.

A significant enhancement was to further automate gorilla behavior using the same low-level poses and actions available to the zoologist running the Wizard of Oz interface, plus a built-in annotation mode that would elucidate that behavior. These behaviors were programmed with input from Zoo Atlanta zoologists. An additional significant benefit enabled by automating behaviors is that the behaviors of each gorilla can be computed in parallel. Thus, multiple gorillas can react to the participant, or even to each other.

When the Wizard of Oz approach was used, the "wizard" could only specify the reaction of one gorilla at a time. Therefore, they would always concentrate on the interaction between the participant and the gorilla nearest the participant. However, with gorillas now able to interact with one another automatically, the participant might set off a chain reaction by causing one gorilla to move, and thus change its relationship with the other gorillas, causing them to react accordingly. For example, if the participant invades the space

FIGURE 6-25
Colored shapes indicate the mood of individual gorillas.

of the silverback, inciting it to charge, the silverback may end up nearer to one of the adult females who had been sitting peacefully. The silverback may then indicate to the female that she is too close, in turn resulting in the female becoming submissive and moving away from the silverback.

Personal experience is a powerful way to learn, and is one reason why people are exploring virtual reality as a teaching tool. Bowman and Hodges pointed out, however, that "students may learn by experience, but they may also be confused or draw incorrect conclusions" [Bowman and Hodges, IJVR]. To help make the gorilla society understandable to the participant, someone, some thing, or some autonomous agent must provide an interpretation of the gorillas' postures, sounds and reactions. An initial thought was to develop an automatic guide agent that would act very much like the zoologist making comments over the shoulder of the participant. However, they later decided to use an annotation system as the primary means of presenting this information.

There were three types of annotation presented. First, a symbolic mood indicator could be shown above the head of each gorilla. Gorillas could be in one of four moods:

- Content and docile—represented as a green cube
- Mildly annoyed—represented as a yellow upsidedown triangle

- Very annoyed—represented as a red octagon
- Submissive—represented as a white pennant

The symbols chosen to represent these moods are obviously based on symbols ingrained in the target users as members of modern Western culture such as a yield sign, stop sign, or white surrender flag.

As a junior member of the society, the participant cannot cause any of the gorillas to become submissive to them, and could only witness this mood when two other gorillas interacted.

The second form of annotation is presented aurally, in much the same fashion as would be presented by a live expert companion. These annotations are presented when a gorilla's mood changes and the student doesn't know how to interpret the expressions of the gorilla. For example, mildly annoyed gorillas might make a coughing noise and look away from the offending gorilla. As a novice to gorilla society, the student will need to be told what this means. In this case, an audio annotation will state: "Coughing and gaze aversion are signs that this gorilla is becoming annoyed because you are too close to him. You should quickly look away and move away."

The last type of annotation provides instructions on how to interact with the virtual reality system. For instance, users will be told how to travel; once they have attained a basic ability, they are instructed to fly through the window, into the habitat, and are told that they are junior members of the gorilla society. These annotations are also provided vocally.

Each type of annotation could be disabled. Thus, the system could be used to test students after they had the opportunity to explore it with full annotations. Typically, the student would explore the space with full annotations until they became comfortable with it, then all the annotations could be disabled. The audio and iconic annotations can be enabled and disabled separately. Thus, students could continue to use one information source after discarding the other. Most audio annotations were programmed to be heard only the first time the participant encountered the corresponding object or event, such as the first time they climb on a dead tree. In this case, they will hear audio explaining why the trees are there, but they won't hear that message again even when they climb on a different dead tree.

A Related Effort—Habitat Design

As mentioned earlier, a separate educational experience was created using the same virtual world as the societal experience. This new version of the application was for a different audience. Rather than focusing on introductory science exploration for middle school students, the new application focused on the study of design philosophy for college architecture students.

As opposed to many other VR examples of design applications that provide the user with a blank canvas, the developers determined that it was difficult to develop a world from scratch using VR. Thus they decided to provide an existing space, and allow students to modify the design. The beginning layout was the same as the main gorilla habitat at Zoo Atlanta. This was the same world used in the society application.

Students were presented with a variety of ways to alter the space. These included moving objects such as trees, rocks, and foliage barriers. The moat surrounding the terrain could not be modified, but the terrain itself could be drastically altered. However, these drastic alterations were all predetermined based on standard zoo habitat design philosophies. For example, some zoo designers prefer to use a "bowl" design to allow visitors to more easily gaze into the area, and see the animals no matter where they are located. Another design philosophy is to use steep hills, allowing the animals to hide from view if they choose.

The application designers strove to use good design practice in creating the interface and information representation. Changes were made from the original application regarding the method of travel control, the ability to select and manipulate objects, and the amount and type of information annotations.

In the societal application, there was no opportunity for selecting or manipulating objects in the world. Thus, a new interface was necessary to allow design alterations. One way to move objects is to select them by making contact between the prop avatar and the object, and then pressing a button to move the selected object along with the prop. To allow objects to be manipulated at a distance, the representation of the prop moved using a "go-go" arm technique. This technique provides a mechanism by which movement close to the body maps directly to movement in the virtual world, but as the arm is extended, the distance covered in the virtual world increases exponentially, allowing the user to reach very far. This is essentially a drone-contact method of selection/movement, and because the prop avatar isn't always co-located with the physical prop may be confusing in a nonocclusive display (this works best in an occlusive HMD).

An alternate method for moving objects is to use a stylus and tablet interface. In this method, the user holds a prop tablet in their off-hand, and a pen or stylus in their dominant hand. By raising the tablet into view, they can see a map and menu representation on the virtual tablet. The stylus is then used to point to locations on the map, or menu options. Thus, by pointing to an object's iconic representation on the map (e.g., a triangle representing a tree), the user can press a button and slide the tree to another location in the virtual world. As the tree is moved on the map, it can also be seen moving in the 3D world.

There is also a choice of how to travel through the world. Rather than using the gaze-directed travel interface, the handheld prop can now be used to indicate the direction of travel. This allows the user to move laterally, while

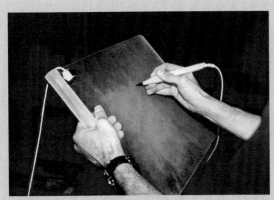

FIGURE 6-26
*A handheld, tracked tablet is used as a user interface in the
habitat design application.*

enabling them to maintain visual contact with a particular part of the world as they move. Pointing up allows the user to fly. As a gorilla in the society application, the user is constrained to walk on the ground, but as a designer, there is often a need to move back for a global view. However, the user is still constrained to remain above ground and within the horizontal confines of the habitat.

A second form of travel is available using the 2D map on the tablet. In addition to representing the location of objects in the habitat on the map, the user's location is also indicated (with a red dot). Just as moving the object icons results in movement of the corresponding objects, moving the user icon moves the user to the specified location in the habitat. The one difference is that the user movement doesn't take place until after the icon is no longer being manipulated. This delay in movement allows the user to maintain a better sense of navigational awareness.

To allow design students the ability to learn about and access the habitat, several annotations are located throughout the space. Annotations can be associated with objects (e.g., a tree) or with locations (e.g., the visitor center). Annotations can be vocal, text billboards, or pictorial billboards. Vocal annotations also have a visual representation indicating the topic of the annotation, and they can be programmed to be played only the first time they are

encountered, or every time. The user has some control over the types of annotations that are visible in the space.

The application developers conducted two disparate studies using this application. Both studies addressed the usability of VR for education, one as a general test of the usefulness of VR [Bowman, Wineman and Hodges], the other as a specific usability analysis of the effectiveness of this application's interface [Bowman, Wineman, Hodges and Allison].

In the first experiment, some members of a class on design psychology were told they were participating in tests of new technology that might be used for the course in the future. In fact, the class was split into three groups: a control group that did not have the chance to use the system, a walkthrough group that could only wander around the static environment, and a group that could walk around, and also access the informational annotations. A few days later, the class took a test with questions that could be answered based on class lectures only, the VR experience only, or both. The sample size was small, so the results were not statistically significant, but the trend was that the students who had the opportunity to use the VR system (especially those with access to the annotated environment) performed better than the control group, supporting the researcher hypothesis that VR could indeed be used as a supplemental tool to enhance learning [Bowman, Wineman, and Hodges].

Later, in the usability study, members of the class (in eight teams of three) were allowed to design their own habitat. Each team began with the actual layout of the habitat. After a brief acclimation period, one team member was selected to be the "design implementer" and work in the virtual environment. The others would give suggestions as they watched the computer monitor. Designs took about 30 to 60 minutes to complete, and still screen images were saved of the new layout so the students could present their design to the class. The VR developers recorded the errors and comments relating to the system made by the users, as well as surveyed the users before and after the experiment. The overall result was that in a short amount of time, students (the users) were able to alter an architectural space, putting their own aesthetic mark on the environment [Bowman, Wineman, Hodges, and Allison].

Conclusion

Overall, the developers feel good about the future of educational uses of VR. The exhibit can be used by students in preparation for a field trip to the actual zoo, or in cases where it is difficult for children to visit the zoo, in replacement of a field trip. The system was not designed to be travel worthy. Durability would be a key concern for creating a road show–style display that could travel to schools, libraries, and other zoos. With proper design and practice, a touring exhibit could be setup in less than an hour.

Another possible enhancement would be to include imitating the behavior of other types of animals. The developers were approached by the Grizzly Discovery Center located near Yellowstone National Park for a bear exhibit, as well as the Ontario Science Center and a German center interested in exhibiting VR experiences.

Project concept and organization was done by Larry Hodges and Jean Wineman. Don Allison designed and implemented the overall system, and created the gorilla models. Habitat and building models were by Brian Wills, and the annotation system was done by Doug Bowman. From the zoo were Kyle Burks, Kristen Lukas, and Lori Perkins, who all provided the gorilla information, and zoo director and Georgia Tech professors Terry Maple and Craig Piper, who provided access to the zoo facilities, the building used for the trial run, and some funding. Additional funding was provided by EduTech, and the Atlanta SGI field office provided the Onyx RE2 and Indy workstation. The overall effort took about 9 months from the initial work until the first public demonstration. The *Virtual Habitat* application was developed by Doug Bowman also with input and advice from Hodges and Wineman. Wineman and Maple's class on the "Psychology of Environmental Design" was used as the test case, providing subjects and evaluations of the system.

Both applications described here are designed for educational uses, outside the study of computer science or virtual reality. Thus for both to be integrated into curricula, or as part of an informal science exhibit (e.g.., at a zoo or science museum/center), they need to be made robust and inexpensive enough to be practical. This is particularly true for the "society" application, which faces the onslaught of young children. To deploy the system at a venue, the developers had to make the system more robust, autonomous, and easy to use. One specific change made to make this particular experience more feasible for a public venue was to remove the necessity of having a domain expert on hand to teach each user.

In April of 1998, a nonprototype version of the gorilla society application was deployed at the new Action Resource Center (ARC) at Zoo Atlanta for use by their guests. However, one of the greater concerns facing the Zoo was the logistics of how to demonstrate the application. The zoo has over 800,000 visitors a year, which is far too many to allow each one (or even a relatively small percentage) to experience the VR application first hand. The Young Scientists program was one group that is allowed to experience the application, as are zoo members and VIP visitors.

The installed system utilized a Dell XPS system with a 333MHz Pentium II with 256 megabytes of RAM, and an AGP Diamond FireGL 1000 Pro graphics acceleration card. A Polhemus InsideTrak electromagnetic tracker system with a single receiver was used for tracking the head.

A feature of the setup that called for improvement from the perspective of being usable by zoo visitors was to allow more group participation. This could be addressed both by having more systems and by allowing users of all the systems to interact within the virtual world, but also by allowing the people not wearing the HMD to participate in the activity. If 30 students visit the VR facility, each getting 5 minutes to wear the HMD, they end up waiting around for 2½ hours just for this short VR experience.

The developers believe that the virtual reality gorilla experience helped the zoo expand its message. Zoologist Lori Perkins explains it this way:

> By combining Georgia Tech's advanced technology with Zoo Atlanta's advanced understanding of gorilla behavior, we're able to make the educational experience more powerful and dynamic. We want students to learn from both the live gorillas in the naturalistic zoo habitat and from the virtual experience, in order to give students a way to get a richer understanding of gorilla behavior than they would get from either experience alone.

CASE STUDY 6.5: TRAIN TO TRAVEL

The Dayton Bus Ride

For cognitively handicapped individuals, tasks such as using a city bus to get to a desired destination can be difficult. Many are capable of performing this task once they have received specific training for a route they need to take. The 1990 Americans with Disabilities Act (ADA) requires that public transportation authorities address the issue of how to make their system available to all. There are some training programs available to help handicapped individuals, but learning to ride can be time consuming for many individuals, making these programs (when they do exist) inefficient. Often the transit authorities resort to using door-to-door service, which is costly, and less than efficient.

In Dayton Ohio, the Dayton Public School system had a job training program for the cognitively handicapped, and part of the skills taught included bus travel training. However, the time necessary to train each individual meant that they could not meet the needs of everyone. To reduce the need for the door-to-door service, the Miami Valley Rapid Transit Authority sought a better solution for training cognitively disabled riders.

To help reach this goal, the transit authority funded a research group at the University of Dayton Research Institute to develop a multimedia and VR system to train handicapped individuals to use the bus system. Researchers Lyn Mowafy and Jay Pollack led the research project titled *Train to Travel*. While this project focused on travel training, the developers were also interested in using VR for job training in general for the cognitively handicapped.

Application Description

Train to Travel was comprised of two separate stages. The first stage used a desktop multimedia presentation to verify that each student had the skills necessary for the basic tasks required for riding the bus. Once the basic concepts had been mastered, the student would graduate to riding the virtual bus, and later a real bus.

The two stages were designed to work together using similar audio and visual scenes. Cognitively handicapped individuals learn better when repetition and familiarity are used as tools for training. Lyn Mowafy worked with Michael Stang (a school teacher with the Dayton Public

FIGURE 6-27

In Dayton, Ohio, a virtual reality simulation for bus travel was used to train students with disabilities in using public transportation.

School system) to ensure that there was a smooth and familiar transition from one learning stage to the next.

The target audience for this research project consisted of juniors and seniors studying in the Dunbar High School job-training program. Many of them had attained jobs at the University of Dayton. The trip between the high school and the university required a transfer between buses in downtown Dayton. In teaching these students to make this trip, the designers had three goals for the *Train to Travel* project. First they desired to incorporate training methods that were already proven in the public schools. Secondly, the application needed to be able to be modified for individuals of different capabilities and needs. Finally, the implementation needed to be implemented on readily available computers to provide classroom-based alternative travel that was effective, safer, and more efficient than individual mentoring of students in the real world. [Mowafy and Pollack] The first (pre-travel training) stage taught and tested for six basic skills necessary to ride the bus using a multimedia system:

- how to properly dress for riding the bus,
- how to identify and count money, and produce the appropriate fare,

- how to tell time so they would know when to catch the bus,
- how to select a seat on the bus,
- how to identify their destination, and
- how to find the departure points.

There were also two special modules for learning how to handle emergency situations, and preparation for riding the virtual bus. Each of the module's lessons was taught by a digitized tutor. The tutor was an actor hired to present the material. The tutor appeared with the tutorial information as a talking head in a window on the screen.

Once all the multimedia lessons were mastered, the student was ready to take the virtual bus ride. One of the concerns of the student's teachers was that the HMD might induce epileptic seizures. However, after testing the system with students who were subject to such seizures, there was no indication that the system was triggering seizures even when the students used the full system for the full virtual bus ride. In fact, the students were quite excited to be using such high-tech equipment and found the experience to be enjoyable.

The actual ride from the high school to the university took approximately 45 minutes. However, the virtual bus ride distills this to an 11-minute journey, covering only the crucial portions. In a full-length ride there were long stretches of time in which not much happened, and was considered not relevant to the training. To allow the student to faithfully experience the complete ride would have required considerable effort to create the virtual world, and it was felt that this effort would "greatly exceed the training benefit." The "long boring stretches would also not engage the student in meaningful interactive learning."

The portion of the ride that was included was from the point of seeing the important landmarks that indicate the bus is about to their transfer point, and on the second leg, the landmarks they should see just before their final destination.

To ride the virtual bus, the student dons the HMD, and is given a computer mouse. In riding the virtual bus, the familiar tutor from the multimedia experience would guide the student through the steps of boarding, paying, and finding a seat on the bus. During the course of the ride, the tutor

FIGURE 6-28

During their virtual bus ride, students passed familiar landmarks. Training students to identify these landmarks was a key goal of the program.

reminds the student to look for specific landmarks. On the way to the transfer point, they watch for the Spaghetti Warehouse after seeing the Sinclair Community College. They exit the bus at the Spaghetti Warehouse, and transfer to another bus and complete their journey to the University of Dayton's Miriam Hall after seeing the Frisch's Big Boy restaurant on the corner.

A mouse was used by the student to control when they would get on and off of the bus. When the student chose to enter the bus they would be "automatically transported into the bus and set in a seat." There was no need to ring the bell on the bus to request a stop since the waypoints were at designated stops on the route, so all the rider needed to indicate was when to get off. The developers planned to allow the student to control their travel from one bus, down the street, across the intersection, to the next stop, and also to allow them to choose and move to their own seat. However, this method was not implemented, and instead a ride-along whisked the student from the bus to the next stop.

The virtual world was created by obtaining maps of the Dayton bus system, and using digitized photographs to create realistic-looking landmarks along the course of the bus in the parts of the trip encountered during the 11-minute

FIGURE 6-29
Students used an HMD and handheld controller to interact with the application.

edited version of the trip. The only sound in the virtual world was that of the tutor's voice.

Mike Stang, the job-training coordinator for Dayton's public school system, worked with Jay Pollack to come up with the basic ideas that evolved into the *Train to Travel* program. The overall design of the training system was done by Lyn Mowafy and Jay Pollack. Mowafy was the technical lead for the project and provided the principle design of the system. The overall project involved a team effort, including the help of programmers from Division Inc. VR programming was done by Andy Hamilton, Steve Hammond and Tom Congdon. The multimedia tutorials were implemented by Andy Spence, Mike Bibbey and Trish Russo.

VR System

A Macintosh computer served as the host for the multimedia training sessions. The model of the virtual world was created on a Silicon Graphics Onyx™ using Designer's Workbench™ and EZT™ by Coryphaeus. Upon completion of the model the project was transferred to a Division Inc. ProVision 100™ for the virtual bus ride. DVise™ by Division was used to animate the bus ride, orchestrate the audio components of the companion/tutor, and allow student interaction using a 3D mouse input device. The ProVision 100 VPX™ head-mounted display that was packaged with the system was capable of 320 × 240 color pixel resolution with stereoscopic display. Audio was rendered by storing

sound samples in an AKAI™ MIDI unit connected to the Division system. MIDI commands from the program would trigger the playback of specific samples.

The interactive multimedia tutorials were created on a Macintosh Quadra 950™ equipped with a SuperMac DigitalFilm™ board for full-screen video production. A standard NEC 4FGe™ color monitor, keyboard and mouse complete the system. Software packages used in the production of the tutorials included, MacroMedia Director™, Adobe Premier™, Adobe Photoshop™, Specular Infini-D™, MacroMedia SoundEdit™ Deneba Canvas™ and MicroSoft Word™.

Conclusion

A major benefit of the *Train to Travel* system was to demonstrate the real possibility in how the time and resources necessary to teach a cognitively handicapped person to be more self-sufficient by riding the bus to and from work could be significantly reduced. However, only anecdotal evidence is available to support this belief. Tests of the prototype system indicated that the number of real trips necessary to learn the route was reduced. Despite not having the opportunity to do a full study on the system, using a large population of potential beneficiaries, presentations of the system to travel trainers, teachers and transit officials met with resounding optimism that the *Train to Travel* system could revolutionize how this "very costly and intractable problem" is addressed in the future.

FIGURE 6-30
Users were provided with a first-person perspective inside the virtual bus.

Another benefit of using VR as the student's first encounter with riding the bus is that the student seems to be more independent from the outset. According to Mowafy and Pollack the presence of the instructor can be detrimental in real-world training situations because it "either modifies the experience or prevents it from occurring at all" [Mowafy and Pollack]. The virtual reality method also provides a means for the parents or guardians of the students to witness their performance in the virtual bus ride, prior to attempts in the real world. Seeing this helps to alleviate some of their fears.

According to Carla Lakatos of the RTA, reducing the number of people who must rely on the door-to-door services

allows them to better serve the people who do need these services. According to Stang giving cognitively challenged people the skills to independently travel also helps to raise their feeling of accomplishment and self-worth.

There were several features that were planned to help enhance the realism of the virtual bus ride. One such feature was to add interactive passengers to the bus. However, due to lack of funding, the project ended before these features could be added, and before a scientific study could be done to measure the effectiveness of the system.

Both of the lead developers feel that this system demonstrates the ability for using computers in general and VR in particular for training individuals with cognitive handicaps. Pollack points out the benefit of computer training over human training:

"We found that the students worked very hard when trained in this way. First the computer had infinite patience, never losing its temper after the tenth or 100th try. And very important was that the training gave each student a sense of pride since they 'got to use computers too, so cool.'"

Mowafy declares how the improvement of technology since the time they first attempted this project has made it a far more feasible use of technology:

"It was a great idea ahead of its time. Today, we could do this so much better. The major problem with projects like these is funding. Our society needs to value all of its human resources and provide them with the opportunities to be productive, responsible citizens."

CASE STUDY 6.6: FORTRESS OF BUHEN

Executive Summary
Virtual travel offers many new possibilities and advantages over physical travel. Advantages include elimination of transit time, plus cost savings once the virtual reality technology matures. However, the primary advantage of virtual travel is the ability to visit places that are otherwise inaccessible.

There are several reasons why a particular location might be inaccessible, including high degree of danger, high expense to the traveler, or restricted access for legal, religious, or other reasons. The most extreme reason is that a destination is inaccessible because it no longer exists or has become buried. Many of these reasons apply to sites of archaeological interest, making archaeological recreations

FIGURE 6-31
The Fortress of Buhen makes an ideal destination for virtual travel. The site no longer exists in the real world. However, a digital recreation of the fortress is accessible via virtual reality.

FIGURE 6-32
The Fortress of Buhen was located on the Nile River and near the border between Nubia and Egypt.

of ancient cities, temples, fortresses, etc., good candidates for utilizing the medium of VR for virtual travel.

The *Learning Sites Fortress of Buhen* project is one example of enabling travel to a place that is no longer accessible. Buhen is located on the Nile River near the ancient Nubian-Egyptian border. The Fortress was part of the Egyptian border control during the reign of Pharaoh Sesostris III. The ancient site is now submerged under Lake Nasser, created when the Aswan dam was built in 1964. A combination of factors makes the Fortress of Buhen an ideal candidate for a VR archaeological experience:

- The remains of the fortress are "extensive and well documented."
- It is "no longer available for on-site investigations or first-hand visits."
- "The site has a fascinating multicultural history dependent on economic and social cooperation."

Introduction

The Fortress of Buhen was built on the west bank of the Nile and extended over 150 meters. It had a variety of interesting features, including "moats carved three meters deep into bedrock, revetments, drawbridges, bastions, buttresses, ramparts, battlements, embrasures, loopholes, and catapult stations." It was one among a chain of fortresses along the Nile, each built near enough to be within eye-shot of the next.

Some archaeologists believe that because it was located near the border between Nubia and Egypt, Buhen probably served as both a heart of commerce as well as defense. The fortress had many sections to serve different economic and social roles. There were separate buildings that probably served for administration, storage, and occupancy. An inner city within inner walls of fortification would have housed Egyptian settlements or those of the current occupying peoples. The area between the inner city and the outside fortification would have contained mercenary forces.

There is a paradox with respect to realistic portrayal of historical archaeological recreations. VR models can sometimes be criticized for being too "cartoon-like." That is, being overly colorful and bright, and lacking the details of the actual physical structures. On the other hand, the use of texture maps can make a scene look somewhat photorealistic, and therefore can be criticized for being *too* realistic. A high degree of photorealism can be misleading to the virtual visitors, leading them to believe what they are experiencing is an exact replica of what once existed, whereas the model is more likely to be an interpretation synthesized from various bits and pieces of evidence, as well as some conjecture on the part of the experience developer.

When treated with proper consideration, a virtual reality representation of the site can actually be used to allay the misconception of which details are fact and which are speculative. A variety of data and representational styles can be merged into a system that allows the visitor to view the site from a variety of perspectives and interpretations. For example, a quick surface rendering of a reconstruction might have distinct visual qualities for data procured from different sources. Perhaps data gathered from photographic evidence might have more subdued colors, whereas the conjectured parts of the structure might be represented with bright "cartoony" colors. If multiple theories exist for how a site may have looked during its time of use, there could be an interface to shift between these views and a photographically based view of the actual remains.

Annotations can be used to provide the user with direct access to the source material, field notes, or reasoning behind particular interpretations. These annotations might contain images, sound, video, and text to help describe objects and provide background material on a particular aspect of the site.

A VR experience that provides such a multiple perspective view of the site, giving the visitor the opportunity to view the site from the eye of multiple archaeologists might lead the participant to a better understanding of the archaeological process.

The *Virtual Fortress of Buhen* re-creation used images texture mapped onto a simplified polygonal model to represent the structures of the site. Texture map images were used to mimic the visual surface textures of the mud brick coursing and stone brick walls, plus decorations on some of the interior walls. These images were constructed from drawings and photographs as well as descriptions from the reports of the excavation and discussions with the curators at the Museum of Fine Arts in Boston.

Rendered as a life-size model, participants are able to gain a sense of the enormity of the various spaces, as well as "the details of the decorations and building techniques" exhibited in the site.

Application Description

A visit to the *Virtual Fortress of Buhen* uses a tour guide metaphor to give visitors a foundation on which they can

FIGURE 6-33

A computer-generated agent acts as a tour guide aboard a pharaoh's ship of state.

begin their exploration. A computer-generated agent modeled as an ancient Egyptian scribe acts as a tour guide to show the participant around the virtual world. The tour guide follows a preset path, but the guest can look in all directions at any time, and can choose to follow the guide or venture on their own down other paths. No other interaction was possible with the tour guide.

The tour begins onboard a ship docked near the entrance to the fortress. The ship is an Egyptian pharaoh's ship of state of the period. Visitors can move about the Pharaoh's ship and accompanying cargo ships to experience them as they may have looked during the active days of Buhen. After exploring the ships, they are led onto a dock. At this point, travel control is taken from them and they are then "flown" around the outer wall, giving an overview of the site. After the ride-along flight, they are then led through the main gate of the fortress to tour the inner rooms of the city.

Representation of the Virtual World

In addition to providing the ability to seemingly experience an ancient site first hand, there are other benefits that arise from the creation of a virtual, digital copy of an archaeological site. One benefit is the ability to hold different interpretations of the site within a common context. Information about materials collected by, and owned by, different entities can be merged together into a single form. Storage in digital form also allows for the inclusion of annotations tied directly to the data, so whenever the data is accessed, a list of notes can be summoned automatically.

Digital information is also generally more transportable, and some formats allow it to be moved easily from one type of machine to another. Digital information does not gradually decay as the original source material does. The digital information can also be archived with the expectation of reasonable (though not infallible) durability.

Two other benefits arise from the ability to virtually travel. Sites or artifacts that cannot be visited or touched due to religious or other restricted access reasons can often be made accessible to the public in digital form. Also, the ability to telecommute becomes a possibility for some archaeologists. A lead archaeologist or expert on some particular topic can be consulted on various issues by archaeologists physically at a dig site.

There are some pitfalls with the digital world as well. First, there is a concern of whether the current data will be accessible on future computing platforms. Computers become obsolete fairly quickly, so data that is limited to specific platforms face the possibility of becoming unusable. The use of standard formats helps to alleviate this problem, but sometimes standards don't provide for storing sufficient detail. Also, information is often scanned and stored at a level of detail based on the technology of the day. Digital representations should be created at the highest resolution possible, with reduced resolution versions for rendering or interrogation by current computers, with the expectation that future computers will be able to handle more information. However, the limits of the scanning devices may require artifacts and the like to be rescanned at some point in the future anyway.

The other major pitfall is the legal issue of ownership. In the simpler case, archaeologists will probably not want to share any new data they uncover until after they've published a report based on it. After this, they will often be willing to allow their data to be incorporated into a global database about a particular site. On the trickier end of things, when there is a possibility of money being made from the data, people may be less inclined to share their information. This snag is becoming less of a problem as the "virtual archaeological" companies such as Learning Sites establish working relationships with the new generation of archaeologists.

FIGURE 6-34
A virtual tour guide points out an information kiosk in the virtual world of Buhen. The panel on the left shows a map of the site, the center panel displays a photograph of the actual site, and the right panel provides a text description of interesting features that are nearby.

To provide context on the *Fortress of Buhen* data, virtual kiosks are available in various locations in the virtual world. For participants interested in learning more about the site, the kiosks provide access to additional information from the digital databases. The concept is to provide the capability for visitors to explore the site as it was at any time throughout history (including points in time during its excavation) and allow them to access information on this and other sites from databases located around the Internet. Visitors could use the kiosks to make inquiries about the site at varying levels of detail, depending on how casual or engaged they are about the subject.

Interaction with the Virtual World

The kiosks in the *Fortress of Buhen* world had three panels of information. The left panel provided a map of the virtual world, with a "You are here" wayfinding aid. This panel was also intended to provide a view into a GIS database of the full site and surrounding region including geographic and topological information. The center panel shows a photograph of the actual excavation site from that spot. The right panel provides a text description of topics related to the nearby interesting features. The plan was to make it a full hypertext database of information related to this site, as well as other relevant sites, that the participant could jump to via a portal in the kiosk. The application authors had also intended for the kiosk to make available a visual database of the artifacts and archaeological remains relevant to that area.

VR DISCOVERY

The application developers found it worthwhile to provide "information kiosks" in the virtual world from which participants could access further information about what they were experiencing from the World Wide Web.

Further Educational Uses

In addition to the specific archaeological uses of this technology, the developers of the *Fortress of Buhen* (specifically Learning Sites and ERG Engineering) see other educational uses of these applications of the technology.

The ability to appreciate other cultures is enhanced when students can see how the ancestors of various modern cultures lived. In the words of archeologist and architect Donald Sanders: "Archaeology reinforces the concept of a shared human heritage and provides modern people with perspectives on their own place and time in history."

Additionally, an archaeological VR application provides students with insight into how a scientist uses fragments of information to build up a theory. Students can see how archaeology (and other sciences) is in fact an exploration into the unknown, with the scientist working to unravel the mysteries. Also, learning can branch off into concepts such as languages and mathematics by examining the languages of the ancient cultures, the mathematics used to construct buildings, or the astronomical information these cultures used to lay out structures in ways to take advantage of the movements of the solar system.

Another combined effort between Learning Sites and ERG was to make an archaeological application specifically designed as an educational device. The result was the *Vari House*, a Web-based experience on an ancient Greek farmhouse. The goal for the *Vari House* project was to enable a broader audience to experience the site in three dimensions. Since their constituent audience doesn't generally have access to high-end computers and VR hardware, a VRML solution was implemented. Although VRML models can be viewed via immersive displays, this application was designed for nonimmersive, desktop use. Using the desktop browser, the application developers combined textual information alongside the 3D visual models, allowing students to read about the world as they explore it. In addition to traversing the model of the grounds, the user can click on objects in the scene to see a detailed model of a particular artifact and/or access a textual database.

Venue

The *Fortress of Buhen* project was begun in 1993 by Bill Riseman. His overriding archaeological goals included painstaking attention to scholarly standards and a high level of detail. He was also interested in enhancing the experience by utilizing 3D models, audio, text, still images, and video, as well as enabling multiple participants to interact and share within the world. He formed a company and assembled a team consisting of archaeologists, 3D modelers, and virtual reality experts to bring about his vision. In particular, he worked with archaeologist and architect Donald Sanders and virtual reality application designer Eben Gay.

Virtual reconstructions of the *Fortress of Buhen* were based "on primary evidence and documentation (excavation notebooks, field photographs and drawings, and early travelers' views)" [Sanders]. Standard computer-aided design and drafting packages were used to create the 3D forms used in the computer renderings. Following this, details were added by texture mapping images onto the polygonal shape of the structures. At each stage of reconstruction, the models were validated by seeking out the opinion of expert archaeologists. Once the models were created, the interaction and narrative features of the experience were added. These features include the information kiosks and the guided tour elements of the experience.

Much of the documentation used to create the models and informational databases used to construct the *Fortress of Buhen* was provided by the Egyptian department of the Boston Museum of Fine Arts. This information included:

- Handwritten field diaries
- Progress photos of the excavations
- Excavation reports (including stratigraphic data and building plans)

- Topographic survey plans
- Hieroglyphic translations

In addition to the museum-supplied documentation, Riseman developed a new procedure for rendering a more accurate representation. The procedure, called by Riseman *epigraphic rendering,* used a computer program to automatically trace objects in a photograph, making the look of the resultant image more correct and easier to use for translation. As the experience toured various venues in 1994, Riseman and his colleagues found resistance to accepting his new method. Having been trained and grown accustomed to more traditional methods, archaeologists were reluctant to utilize different methods than they were used to. Tragically, however, before the project was completed, Riseman was accidentally killed in Brazil, and some of the original ideas were not completed in the *Fortress of Buhen* experience. Development on the *Fortress of Buhen* project abruptly ended with Riseman's death due to legal concerns with intellectual property ownership.

In late 1995 Donald Sanders created a new company (Learning Sites Inc.) and constructed a team to continue the work he started with Riseman. Collaborators in the new team included Tim Kendall, an archaeologist from the Museum of Fine Arts; Veronica Panttelidis, a teacher and head of the VR lab at East Carolina University; VR consultant Eben Gay from ERG Engineering Inc.; and 3D modeler Rick Morse. ERG Engineering had considerable experience in developing virtual reality and desktop virtual world products designed for education and for museum venues.

VR System
The application was originally developed on a Kubota-Denali computer. At a later time, the system was moved to an Evans and Sutherland Freedom 3000™ image accelerator with a Sun Sparcstation acting as the host. The visual display was provided by a Leep Cyberface 3™, which is a head-based display similar to a *BOOM*™. Software was written using the *Sense8 WorldToolKit*™ to develop the interactive virtual world.

The *Fortress of Buhen* was demonstrated at many venues throughout 1994, including the SIGGRAPH computer graphics conference held in Orlando, Florida. However, the original files were lost, and it is no longer possible to experience it first hand. The developers (Learning Sites and ERG) have recreated VR representations of other sites, each with their own special capabilities and characteristics, but bearing similarity to the Buhen experience. Among the other sites built are a tomb at Nemrud Dagi, Turkey, and Temples B300 and B700 at Gebel Barkal.

The tomb at Nemrud Dagi is enhanced through the medium of VR because the setting of the tomb is a breathtaking view that can best be felt by experiencing it firsthand, from the first-person point of view. The temple at Gebel Barkal is interesting because it is a currently active archaeological dig that is being used in an experiment to combine the Internet and VR to enhance the archaeological research.

Application Implementation
A JAVA-based search engine allows researchers to find information within all the documents. Active hyperlinks provide the means to jump to the excavation context in which a particular artifact was found or to which a written note refers. A 3D virtual world can be created specifically for the needs of the user. A user can select artifacts and references of interest, and a model of the world is constructed specifically for examining those specific interests.

This project could be used both as a research tool for archaeologists and for educators. Archaeologists can study the site as if they were there, jumping between excavation notes and the representation of the site. The tool can also provide the means for teaching a college-level course on archaeology. Students could freely explore the site and the accompanying information, and later be queried for possible hypotheses on how the site may have looked or how particular artifacts may have been used by the residents of the site.

Other worlds were created for educational purposes using VRML models available via the World Wide Web as onscreen walkthroughs. The Vari house is one example of the use of the Internet to provide an educational web site based on archaeology. A curriculum was developed by which students could individually explore the VRML model of the excavation, with an accompanying text description of the model followed by questions that require exploration of the site to find the correct answers. Artifacts in the site can be triggered to produce a separate rendering, with additional textual information about the particular item.

FIGURE 6-35
These four images show different aspects of a subsequent project that depicted different temples at Gebel Barkal.

ERG Engineering also demonstrated other virtual reality applications with interface features that could be applied to museum and other educational venues. In 1995, they demonstrated an augmented reality (AR)[8] application at a trade show that allowed viewers to see additional information about the trade show exposition as they explored the premises. As they looked toward different vendors, the name of the vendor was displayed above each booth, plus a short description of what each vendor sold. In this instance, the AR technology was demonstrated primarily as a navigational tool to help people locate their destination. Such technology could also be applied to applications where someone could look at an exhibit, site, or object on display and individually request specific information on what they purview depending on their level of knowledge or interest in the particular topic.

Conclusion

The *Fortress of Buhen* archaeological experience demonstrated how many features of virtual reality can be beneficial

---

[8]Augmented reality (AR) is the paradigm of display in which the user can see the actual real world in registration with additional overlaid computer supplied information.

to the science of archaeology, as well as be an educational tool using archaeology as the content around which the students learn. It also demonstrates quite clearly how VR can provide a means of travel to a locale that is no longer possible to visit.

Learning Sites Inc. later developed tools to explore the possibilities of using this technology to do "teledigging," that is, allowing researchers on site at a dig to enter information, providing access to experts in the field located elsewhere. Thus, the experts can give comments and recommendations to the onsite researchers.

Another possibility that became practical thanks to VR and new visualization techniques was the ability to use new sensor technology that could gather information about artifacts or the earth itself using non-destructive sensing. Some of this data required techniques such as volume rendering to represent the contents.

CASE STUDY 6.7: VIRTUAL MOBILITY TRAINER

Dr. Dean Inman, senior scientist at the Oregon Research Institute (ORI), is driven by a desire to help children with disabilities. Though he was intrigued by the notion of virtual reality, he initially doubted whether VR could really be of practical benefit to his disabled patients. Then, fortuitously, in 1993 his wife, Dr. Lynne Anderson-Inman, the director of the Center for Electronic Studying at the University of Oregon, heard Brenda Laurel (see Understanding Virtual Reality) speak at a conference on interactive technology. She saw that VR had potential, and also learned that suitable technology was becoming available at reasonable price points. She felt inspired and conveyed these ideas to her husband.

FIGURE 6-36

A child learns how to control her wheelchair with the aid of a virtual reality system.

Image courtesy the Applied Computer Simulation Labs

Inman had been studying the problems of teaching children to operate motorized wheelchairs for several years. There were several difficulties associated with this effort. One major problem was that it was difficult for many students to get access to motorized chairs. The chairs are very expensive, and insurance companies won't purchase them unless they are assured that the child is likely to have success with the chair, as indicated by their ability to manipulate them. Thus it is a paradoxical situation that the students need a chair to learn but can't get a chair until they have demonstrated that they can skillfully operate one. Failure of a child to learn to explore the world around them is known to be detrimental to their ability to analyze spatial problems, among other skills.

Inman began a program to teach children with cerebral palsy to operate motorized wheelchairs in 1982. Initially, this "driver's ed for wheelchairs" was done completely by putting the child in a wheelchair and closely attending to and giving the child instructions on what to do. The program later attempted to use computers (Apple IIe and later an early Macintosh) to display a simulated forward view as a means of raising interest and motivation in the children. However, this did not turn out to be a viable solution.

A significant problem is that many of the children are not motivated to learn. Without their own mobility they are attended to and waited on. Thus children may not perceive that an increase in ability for independent travel is beneficial to them. The lack of motivation on the part of the potential beneficiaries of a program that offers the chance for increasing one's ability to independently move through the world can at first be puzzling. This can at least partially be attributed to the fact that they become accustomed to receiving aid for many daily tasks. Inman refers to this as "learned helplessness."

After becoming excited by the potential of VR, Inman wrote and won a $600,000 3-year grant from the U.S. Department of Education to build a system to train disabled children to drive motorized wheelchairs in a virtual world that emulated driving motorized wheelchairs in the real world. The grant began in July 1993, at which time Inman began to build the *Virtual Mobility Trainer (VMT)* to help train and motivate children in the use of wheelchairs. He subsequently received other grants to continue this research and expand in new directions.

Application Description

The efforts funded by this grant resulted in a virtual reality system for use as a training simulator. In the *Virtual Mobility Trainer* system, children wear a head-mounted display to view the virtual world, and sit in a conventional wheelchair mounted on rollers with motion sensors. The child operates the wheelchair with its normal controls and the platform calculates movement through the virtual world by measuring the movement of the wheels.

In his previous efforts to incorporate a computer into the training, a particular wheelchair was selected and physically integrated into the system. The choice to use a platform capable of working with any wheelchair was made for the *VMT* because it allows students who already have their own wheelchair to use it as the interface to the VR system. Another benefit of placing a fully functioning wheelchair on a platform with rollers is that it allows the actual motors on the wheelchair to run. When the actual motor and wheels run in response to the input from the user, the user is provided with the vibratory and aural sensations consistent with what they would normally experience when operating the wheelchair in the real world. This effect is heightened by using rollers with bearings that are slightly off center which give the sensation of riding over moderately rough terrain such as a sidewalk or carpet [Inman et al.].

VR DISCOVERY

Inman's team found a solution to simulating inertia realistically. They simply added ballast to the rollers in the platform. By raising the weight of the rollers from just a couple of pounds to 25 pounds, the wheelchairs placed on the platforms would have to overcome the inertia of the rollers to get moving at higher speeds. This more closely simulates the real world.

Three initial virtual worlds were constructed in which students could practice specific tasks:

- An empty VR training world
- A large abstract space with interesting objects
- A model of a real-world crosswalk

The first virtual world is a simple, wide-open space with an infinite checkered floor. There are no obstacles in the environment. The main goals for this world are to learn the basic "go," "no go," "keep going," and "stop" operations. The students can also practice turns, stops, and reversing. The system can emulate the visual effects of traveling very fast, which is exhilarating for many of the children. This world is intended to allow the student to learn to manipulate the chair, and experience the sense of freedom brought about from driving a chair by oneself.

The second world is a model of a space a quarter of a mile long and a quarter of a mile wide containing ice, mud, and obstacles to avoid. The primary learning goal for this world was obstacle avoidance. Throughout the grassy world there are 3D objects and patches of mud and ice that cause the driver to get stuck or spin out of control. The 3D objects are represented as polygonal geometric shapes. If the child hits an object, a crash sound is activated, and the child cannot move the chair until they back up and turn away from the object.

In order to keep the exercise entertaining and engaging, a scenario including interactive animation, 3D sound, and simulated "hazardous" surfaces such as ice and mud was created. Some of the objects in the world are targets to drive over, with success rewarded by the display of a

FIGURE 6-37
A simple checkerboard virtual world.
Image courtesy the Applied Computer Simulation Labs

FIGURE 6-39
Learning to cross a street in VR is safer and much less stressful than in the real world.
Image courtesy the Applied Computer Simulation Labs

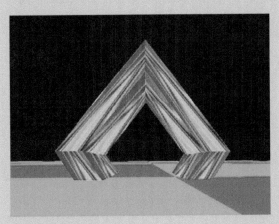

FIGURE 6-38
Fun objects in the virtual world provide interesting things to do.
Image courtesy the Applied Computer Simulation Labs

The final world was a model of an actual intersection in Eugene, Oregon. The world contained cars, crosswalks, and lights. The goal was to teach the child the real-world task of crossing the street safely. Training this task in VR is much less stressful than doing it when the child first encounters a real intersection. Part of the research study was to measure the effects of the VR training in a real-world activity.

In this realistic world, it is very important that the children not be taught to enjoy hazardous situations. The application developers expended a great deal of energy into making sure that if the child were struck by a virtual vehicle, the result was *not* fun.

Sound was integrated in the virtual world as musical themes and abstract tones. The sounds were associated with visual objects, and could be heard only when in proximity to the objects. The children enjoyed the wide variety of sounds.

It is important to note that none of the sounds were directly correlated with actions in the virtual world, other than that they were associated with locations. That is, there were different sounds emanating from different objects, and they were only heard when the student was near that object. However, the sound was not necessarily directly related to the object it was associated with.

waterfall, birdcalls, a performance by a popular entertainer, or some other fun event. If the child travels far enough, they arrive at the edge of the world and can fly by going beyond the edge. The goal of this world was to demonstrate that exploring a new space could be enjoyable. The kids found it particularly enjoyable to go through the mud and ice.

The first year of the grant was spent developing the system. The second and third years were focused on evaluating the kids that use it. The results of their study indicate that the VR wheelchair training system is effective in allowing children to gain and increase their skill in operating motorized wheelchairs. The more time children spent exploring in the virtual world, the more their skills improved.

For the first half of the grant period, subjects were required to visit the ACSL lab in Eugene, Oregon. However, a year and a half into the project the developers made a satellite facility available in a public school in Portland to make the study available to a greater number of children in the target population. Though some children were only able to participate a couple of times, others used the system dozens of times. The length of each experience varied from 15 minutes to 45 minutes per session, with an average usage of 30 minutes.

The main difficulty in training these children is maintaining their motivation, particularly in light of the fact that it can take considerable time and effort to get them to the facility. This effort caused many people not to participate, and others to drop out early, having not found the virtual worlds to be interesting enough to make the trip. The diverse group of participants demonstrates that the *Virtual Mobility Trainer* system can be beneficial to a wide population. This study has also pointed out the limitations of VR for this task.

Although the system was designed for and is capable of displaying stereoscopic imagery in an HMD, the developers found that many children prefer to view the experience monoscopically on a large monitor.

The VR System

In 1993, the system Inman's team built consisted of an Intel-486 based personal computer with two SPEA Fireboard™ graphics accelerators. The dual graphics accelerators allow images to be rendered for each eye to produce a stereoscopic view. An Eyegen3 HMD from Virtual Research was used to display the 3D world, with the head tracked by a Logitech ultrasonic tracking system. Three-dimensional audio was provided via a Beachtron 3D sound system. The headphones in the HMD do not occlude real-world sounds, so the student can converse with the instructor, and can

hear the sounds of the motors. The primary software was the *Sense8 World Tool Kit* (*WTK*). In all, the system cost was about $30,000.

The wheelchairs were mounted on a modified wheelchair athletic training platform. Modifications include ballast in the rollers and the addition of optical encoders to measure the movements of each roller. In the pre-VR setup, the students sat in a Fortress™ wheelchair coupled to the computers via an interface built specifically for this application. In the *VMT* setup, any wheelchair could be placed on the platform, but it was not directly connected to the computer. Therefore, the motors and brakes could only be controlled by the user and did not respond to the virtual world.

In the *Virtual Mobility Trainer* system, the frame rate of the simple worlds was about 25 frames per second. The more complex worlds, made up of about 750 polygons, were rendered at a rate of about 10–12 frames per second. A system today would be capable of rendering a scene with many more polygons and with more detail, at a far lower price.

In the street crossing training, a physical button was present for the children to press to activate the crosswalk indicator. The button provided an actual haptic response and resistance to being pressed.

One of the difficulties of the project was integrating the various devices from different vendors. The developers had to learn to put things together themselves because there was not a ready-to-run wheelchair training product on the market. Thus they became designers and system integrators to build the hardware and software system, and also to create the virtual worlds themselves. One thing they discovered as they implemented the project was that many different skills are required for building a VR system. These skills include knowledge about interactive 3D computer graphics, and writing interface software for specialized hardware input and output devices.

Even with their early success there were some areas they knew needed to be improved. In particular, lag and frame rate were suboptimal, and the joystick was not as responsive as desired. High lag in the tracking system resulted in delays between the time the child turns their head and when the appropriate view is displayed. Also, the HMD was cumbersome, weighed more than they desired, and had

FIGURE 6-40

Advancement in computer hardware allowed worlds to be rendered more richly.

Image courtesy the Applied Computer Simulation Labs

less resolution than they felt was necessary. In fact, some children chose to explore the world without the physically immersive, but also encumbering, head-mounted display. They chose to view the world on a nearby monitor instead.

Part of the subsequently funded follow-up project was to upgrade to a system that would take advantage of the trend of improved computer hardware to make a system that would be more cost effective, and be able to display more interesting worlds. The later system used a 400 Mhz Intel Pentium CPU system with no graphics acceleration hardware. Later, they used software developed in-house based on the Microsoft *DirectX™* rendering system.

The principle investigator on the *Virtual Mobility Trainer* project was Dean Inman. Ken Loge designed the graphics and sounds for the initial system and designed the simulation environments. He served as the manager and chief designer for the project. John Leavens and Aaron Cram programmed the systems, and Cyrus Kanga worked on the 3D and 2D graphic design.

Conclusion

Inman originally considered VR, as many do, a solution looking for a problem. He now feels that he has discovered at least one problem for which it is well suited. VR enables the team to provide a feeling of freedom and to improve the sense of space and direction to physically disabled children, as well as to teach them to use a motorized wheelchair. This helps those children feel more independent and gain more self-esteem.

Although Inman considers VR a useful tool, he does not consider VR to be an end-all panacea for solving the problems of the disabled community. He sees potential and is interested in exploring further how it can be a useful tool for the disabled population. However, merely being VR is not enough to make an experience interesting. It is noteworthy that while the novelty of VR was a motivating factor for getting children to participate in the "drivers' ed" program, VR alone is not enough to sustain the interest. The content of the VR experience must be designed to hold the interest of the participant.

On the other hand, the mass media was overwhelmingly interested in the project to the extent that interaction with the media consumed a great deal of Inman's time. Inman views the fact that his work has received considerable press as an indication that the public is interested in the idea that technology can be used for "a good, positive, uplifting purpose" [Buckert-Donelson].

CHAPTER 7

Public Safety and Military Applications

Recent world events have heightened awareness of military and public safety functions in society. A great amount of resources have been applied toward ensuring the safety and security of our nation, its citizenry, natural resources, and treasured landmarks. Virtual reality is being applied in a variety of ways to contribute to the well-being of our nation. One of the highest uses of any technology is to save lives. Virtual reality is used to help save lives indirectly by training firefighters, police, and military personnel, as well as in educating the general public, in how to respond in various dangerous situations ranging from natural disasters such as tornados and earthquakes to acts of terrorism.

Virtual reality and related technologies such as telepresence contribute to saving lives directly by insulating safety personnel from danger. One example is using telepresence to allow military personnel to carry out dangerous missions from the safety of a remote location.

It is interesting to note that many applications related to public safety and the military have been manifested as entertainment applications. For example, many virtual reality games are of the "find the villain and shoot them" genre, and ideas from them can readily be adopted for more serious purposes. Likewise, VR hardware developed specifically for gaming can be adapted for use in public safety applications. One example is the *Total Recoil* system that was developed for the Virtuality *Trap Master* application (described in Chapter 9). The *Total Recoil* system includes a life-like shotgun that provides haptic feedback via a somewhat realistic "kick back" when the gun is fired.

Many applications appropriate for public safety and military have a requirement of being very closely coupled to the physical world. As such, haptic feedback and locomotion feedback devices can be very important. Thus, many public safety and military applications are coupled to real-world input and output devices such as treadmills, bicycles, and other devices to provide a realistic sense of physical exertion.

Due to the importance of learning to do tasks correctly, it is important for VR developers to deliberately avoid any problems with the VR system that could lead to ineffective training. This means carefully studying and implementing any simulations that are included in the application, eliminating harmful lags, and other artifacts of interacting in a virtual world rather than the real world.

7.1 AREAS OF APPLICATION

7.1.1 Equipment operation training

This area of application is similar to equipment training in other fields such as the Motorola Assembly Line Trainer. Much like commercial pilots learning to fly a Boeing 747 in a flight simulator, military pilots can learn how to fly an F-117A, and they must learn not only the flight control operations but also combat maneuvers under military conditions. An added element is the ability to practice specific missions such as a particular bombing mission. There is an element of training to learn to use a specific piece of equipment and another element in which the participant learns to do certain procedures with that equipment.

Situational training In many fields, split-second timing is crucial, so one doesn't have time to make plans and rehearse for the action (e.g., firefighting); in other situations, while the action might require split-second choices, there is time to prepare for the particular situation. So, for firefighting, it is beneficial to learn about how to handle many, unrehearsed situations, whereas for military or hostage rescue actions, one can spend time to prepare for a specific operation. Of course, in many cases, the same application could be used for both general training and for a specific operation (e.g., the *VRaptor* hostage rescue).

Mission planning A specific type of VR training that can be applied to any kind of route planning or maneuver planning can be referred to as *mission planning*. This can range from presurgery planning to the practice of a rescue maneuver. It could also include the repair of an expensive piece of equipment, such as the mission- planning VR application discussed in this chapter in which astronauts planned for and practiced repairing the Hubble Space Telescope.

Why should a soldier endanger their life by being in a tank on the battlefield when through the use of telepresence they can perform the same operation from the safety of a remote location? Technology has been put to use in the military and in the local police department. The picture below shows a robot equipped with a camera, shotgun, microphone, speaker, and other facilities to assist in seeking out villains in hostage situations while the officer remains safely out of harm's way.

FIGURE 7-1

Police use remotely controlled robots in dangerous environments.

Human-guided bombs, with the operator located at a safe distance, are an example of a first-person point of view telepresence application. The operator is situated as though they were riding the bomb and guiding it down to the target.

Augmented reality has become more prevalent in military and public safety applications. As firefighters enter a burning building, they may have additional information displays that indicate where they are in the building floor plan, where volatile materials are stored, or where the home base indicates that victims are stranded in the building. The military has used heads-up displays for pilots and foot soldiers to provide additional information about their situation for quite some time. Night-vision goggles have been used to provide a view of the environment around the soldier that has been "augmented" by processing the image to allow them to see the area as though there is much more light present.

FIGURE 7-2

Primitive methods of bomb guidance often required the operators to be in harm's way. Virtual reality allows the military remote control from safe environments.

As technology progresses and applications are developed, virtual reality, telepresence, and augmented reality will continue to provide a vital role in helping to maintain the safety and security of the world. Whether indirectly via providing training or practice, or directly by keeping people out of harm's way, virtual reality can play a role in making the world a better place.

CASE STUDY 7.1: OFFICER OF THE DECK

Executive Summary

The *Officer of the Deck* (*OOD*) application is a specific instance of a larger research effort exploring the use of virtual reality in training. The *OOD* application provides a simulation in which a naval officer can rehearse navigating a submarine safely into port. The task is interesting in several ways. One is that the task can seldom be rehearsed outside of the virtual environment. Additionally, the ramifications of a failure in the task can be disastrous in terms of safety and expense.

The *OOD* application mimics the way the task is carried out in actual practice. Primarily, the officer controls the submarine via commands spoken to a simulated helmsman. The *OOD* application utilizes voice input to control the virtual submarine. The officer wears a head-mounted display and can see the harbor and navigational markers. The officer can also call for a variety of tools that emulate the real-life tools he would use.

An informal survey indicated that the *OOD* application shows that VR can be a useful tool for tasks of this nature. An interesting potential use would be to carry a portable version of the training system onboard an actual submarine and use it to rehearse harbor navigation while at sea. In fact, Advanced Marine Enterprises was recently

FIGURE 7-3

Bringing a submarine into harbor is a demanding task that requires nerves of steel and adequate training. A virtual reality simulator allows officers to practice the maneuver without risking billions of dollars.

awarded a grant to create a prototype *OOD* simulator based on the design work described here.

Introduction

The Virtual Environment Technology for Training Project (VETT) of the Sensory Communication Group at the Massachusetts Institute of Technology (MIT), and Bolt, Beranek and Newman Inc. (BBN) has investigated application areas for which VR training might be useful. Applications that have been developed include navigating a submarine to port, electronics troubleshooting, and others. Of these, we will look at one that has shown great potential for actual use in the military.

The *Officer of the Deck* VR application allows junior submarine officers to be trained in the experience of bringing a submarine into port. This is an especially useful task to train, because opportunities for learning this skill occur so infrequently. Submarines are brought to port only a few times per year, and each time, only one person has the chance to navigate the craft down the channel. In fact, only a few people can even be stationed outside the sub, on the conning tower.

The overall goal of VETT is to research methods of training using VR technology that will provide cost savings and/ or improved learning. Anticipating that computer and VR

technology will continue to become more cost effective, and portable, the researchers on this project hope to find training tasks that demonstrate good ways of providing cost effective training via this technology. Some research areas of interest include investigating human adaptability to distortions, delays, and noise of typical VR systems; the relationship of VR technologies to motion sickness; and the use of haptic display as a human interface. In general, they have focused on training techniques, cues, interventions, and evaluation methods.

The specific goal of the *OOD* experience is to provide the opportunity for training a novice to perform a task. Considering that these novices are responsible for bringing a multibillion-dollar craft into port, eliminating human error is of the utmost importance. The rest of this section will focus on this pilot task of the VETT project.

Performing the role of officer of the deck (OOD), which includes the task of guiding a submarine to port, is a requirement for promotion of junior submarine officers. They must accomplish this task at least once, yet the opportunities to perform, or even witness, this operation are fairly rare. It is only done during scheduled stops to port. At the same time, errors can be extremely costly, causing hundreds of millions of dollars in damage, and jeopardizing the careers of all the boat's officers.

The actual task involves calling out piloting commands. The OOD is responsible for monitoring the submarine's progress along the marked channel, as well as observing other traffic and conditions. Currently, the training for this task is minimal.

Application Description

A specific scenario was implemented by the VETT project to test the use of VR as a training tool for this task. The task involved only the "in-harbor" portion of navigating a surfaced submarine into King's Bay port in Georgia, but did not include the actual docking operations. This real-world location is simulated in the computer-generated environment, as is a below-deck "piloting team."

This task was selected for a variety of reasons. It can be readily implemented in a fairly portable VR system. It can tolerate the constraints imposed by affordable VR systems such as lag and somewhat simple virtual worlds. It was a task for which most subjects would not have practiced, yet for which there were enough experts available to help validate the VR experience. Also, the task was of high interest to agencies providing funding.

Viewing the virtual world in a head-mounted display, the trainee monitors the navigation aids and progress of the boat, gives spoken commands to the (virtual) helmsman, and receives back verbal confirmations. Using this method, the trainee must successfully navigate the submarine through the harbor channel to port. In-harbor submarine movement is slow, and there is a natural lag in the real-life task between giving vocal commands and the visual response. This response can be matched by the simulated response, maintaining accuracy in the task interface.

Matching the lag is important, because task realism in support of the training is a key goal. Not only does the participant interact with the simulation in the same way they would in the actual task, but the space that the officer has to move freely in the real task is constrained, which gives justification to similar constraints imposed by the VR system. In an HMD VR system, it can be dangerous to give the user freedom to walk about a large area. In this task, a mock conning tower, constructed of metal pipe, acts to protect the immersed user, to keep them located under the

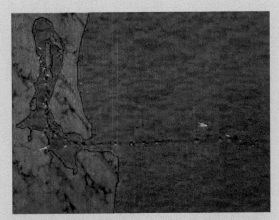

FIGURE 7-4

The King's Bay, Georgia, harbor provides the setting for the Officer of the Deck *simulation.*

tracker transmitter, and to provide a prop that replicates part of the virtual world.

Representation of the Virtual World

The harbor of King's Bay, Georgia, was modeled for the initial experiments of the training system. The surrounding terrain is fairly flat, resulting in a model with relatively few polygons. The shoreline itself put the highest demand on polygon usage. Some of the shoreline contour features were reduced to keep the frame rate at the desired 15 frames per second, resulting in a database of about 5,000 triangles.

Important features of the bay were gathered from the Defense Mapping Agency (DMA) database and nautical charts. These features include the terrain, buoys, range markers, and turning beacons. No other maritime traffic moves through the simulated channel during the task. The experimental designers decided that movement of other traffic along with modeling the associated radio traffic was unnecessary to simulating the task, and would only complicate the experimental analysis.

Navigation through a current was one of the primary skills being trained. A current is modeled, causing the submarine to drift across the channel. This is visually represented by the wake of the buoys. Other than these currents, weather

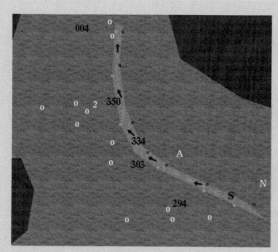

FIGURE 7-5

A "God's-eye view" allows trainees to see the course they took through the channel during a postsession debriefing.

FIGURE 7-6

Pairs of range markers are used to determine where the submarine is with respect to the centerline. In the VR display, the range markers are "perceptually tuned" so the trainee will be able to see them from the same distance as in the real world.

details did not need to be modeled. Submarines are only brought to port under good weather conditions when it is clear and with low wind. Again, the constraints of the real-life task make modeling the virtual world easier.

Tools that the trainee can use to help navigate through the channel are also made available as visual displays in the HMD. A compass display provides directional information in a virtual heads-up display (HUD). Also, the user is provided with a set of virtual binoculars that cause the user's view to zoom in on distant objects (of course, just as with real binoculars, this magnifies head rotational movement, forcing the user to concentrate more on maintaining head stability). In one experimental condition, the current was also visualized (nonrealistically) as vector arrows on the surface of the water. (The preliminary experimental results did not show any significant benefits from using this display.)

In the real-world task, the OOD brings a laminated "course-card" to the conning tower containing a list of the channel segments. For each segment, the course-card gives the pertinent navigational information regarding which landmarks indicate travel down the center of the segment (range finders), and which landmarks indicate when to begin turns (beacons). In the virtual environment task,

the spoken command "course card" invokes the display of a virtual course card in the HMD, replacing the display of the bay.

The primary goal of this experience is to design and understand the effectiveness of training in a VR environment. Realism is always subservient to this requirement. Details where realism was deemed important were rendered realistically; those that were not (such as trees) were not. In general, uses of photorealistic and audio-realistic representations of the world were used when possible as long as they didn't conflict with the training effectiveness.

The visual scene that the trainee OOD sees is a low-resolution, cartoon-like polygonal representation of what truly can be seen from the conning tower of a submarine in the harbor of King's Bay. The visual model includes the top of the submarine, the bay itself, important landmarks, navigational markers, and some optional visualization information such as flow vectors on the water and heads-up display information. Buoys are marked with identification numbers useful for verifying position. Range markers come in pairs of tall towers that indicate whether the submarine is in the center of the channel (or on which side) based on how they line up.

FIGURE 7-7

Buoys are used as a navigational aid. The number on the buoy can be cross-referenced to a chart that provides information on that buoy. Sounds are emitted by the buoys to help the officer determine their location.

The visual scene is displayed using the monoscopic-binocular method (two displays showing the same image). This requires less computational resources and does not detract much from the realism, since most of the objects in the scene (and all the important ones) are a great distance away, so the depth cue from stereopsis would not be very significant. Full 6 DOF position tracking of the head was implemented, so there are depth cues available from motion parallax.

Concern for creating a verifiable training application imposed the requirement for a method of overcoming the limitations of the display hardware.[1]

Some objects in the scene might not "appear" realistic when they are a great distance away. *Perceptual cue tuning* is the general process of matching important virtual cues to natural perceptual cues. For example, training developers must make cues such as depth cues work the same way in the display as the participant experiences them in the real world, or compensate for the differences.

In this application, perceptual cue tuning is used to make distant objects become visible in the virtual world at approximately the same distance as they do in the real world. This is particularly important for landmarks and

man made navigational aids such as the buoys and range markers [Zeltzer and Pioch]. In the HMD display used in this application, these visual aids could not be "adequately identified" without making distant ones larger. This effect was dampened as the markers drew nearer, and not used once objects could be seen at "normal size" in the HMD. The application authors tested this method experimentally and found that it did indeed achieve the desired results.

DESIGN CHOICE

Visual Representation

The application authors chose to use the technique of "perceptual cue tuning" to achieve a more realistic experience.

Audio cues were also provided to make the training session as realistic as could be feasibly implemented. The most important cue for navigation is the sound made by the buoys that mark the safe-passage channel. The two nearest buoys are selected, and 3D spatialized sounds are presented to the trainee indicating their relative location. Also important is the orders acknowledgement provided by the virtual helmsman who echoes the commands given by the OOD. Wind sound is added to the experience, providing an ambient cue that helps increase the sense of realism.

A "haptic display" is provided by the metal cage that represents the cage atop the conning tower. Though simple, this prop is effective at grounding the user in the virtual world and gives important nonvisual cues such as the direction of the bow of the boat (indicated by a knob placed in the center).

Vestibular and other sensory cues are not provided by this experience. Additions of these might increase the degree of immersion slightly, but not while maintaining the cost efficiency and portability of the current implementation. For example, one might consider the added benefits of a vestibular display of the rocking of the submarine, or of an ambient olfactory display of harbor air. However, submarines don't rock very much when going to port, and the smell won't vary much from the sea air the officers are used to experiencing.

---

[1]Such as poor resolution.

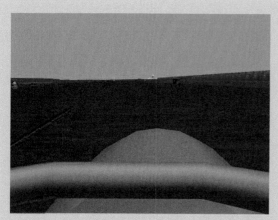

FIGURE 7-8
The handheld rail in the VR simulator is registered with a pipe surrounding the participant providing both haptic feedback as well as a constraint to the spatial boundaries of the platform.

Interaction with the Virtual World

The *Officer of the Deck* experience is primarily a training application. Part of the requirements of this *genre* of applications is that it teaches a fixed set of skills such that the trainee is able to perform to a certain standard. The *form* in which this activity takes place is a pilot-through controlled via voice commands.

The *narrative* is generally typical of a training application. The trainee is given some pre-experience instruction, including a videotape. They then don the HMD, and begin the experience. To help the trainees achieve a sense of personal context in the virtual world, they are taken on a short predetermined (ride-along) path from outside the submarine to the top of the conning tower.

DESIGN CHOICE

In response to feedback from test subjects, the application authors chose to prepend a short, predetermined ride-along flight to the training experience to give more visual context to the trainees. Beginning the experience while the participant was standing on the conning tower was often confusing.

Debriefing of the subjects is the post-trial portion of the overall experience. During the debriefing, the subjects can be shown the path of their submarine during the last trial. This God's-eye view of their efforts in the virtual world constitutes another level of narrative. After "unsuiting," they are shown a 2D map of the bay on a video monitor. A red line indicates the path traveled during the exercise. This process allows trainees to evaluate their own efforts and get a better feeling for how to modify their commands to improve their performance.

Speech was used to provide a simple navigation interface in the application. A single handheld push-to-talk button is used to indicate when commands are being directed to the virtual helmsman. There are no other handheld controllers, only a single button to push when they wish to issue commands. This control mimics the real world, where the OOD must press a similar button to speak to the helmsman. The constraint of the cage even limits physical movement to small movements and turning the head. The rudder was visually represented, and the subjects could turn their heads to visually verify the rudder's orientation, though head motion was not measured in the task analysis.

Realism of the travel interface is important for training this task. In this case, that interface is through the verbal communication with the helmsman. Thus the virtual helmsman will respond only to properly phrased commands, and with the appropriate response. An example exchange might go something like: for the command "Left standard rudder," the system would respond with, "Left standard rudder, Bridge, Helm, Aye." Though the experiment designers assume the candidates have already been trained in basic ship handling, the appropriate lag for turn and throttle is simulated and can be witnessed visually.

There are no object interactions per se in the *Officer of the Deck* experience, but there are some visual tools that can be summoned. Like the travel interface, requests for a tool are also made vocally. Tools that can be summoned include the compass, binoculars, and course-card displays.

There are no complicated visual agents populating this virtual world. The only entity that could be considered an agent is the virtual helmsman, who can only be heard and who responds with explicitly defined responses based on naval procedures.

There are no collaborative interactions in the truest VR sense. This is a single-user training system. The only thing that might fall into this category is the actual experimenter, who controls the parameters of each trial, and might be able to control some aspects of the world during a trial. Were the helmsman responses generated by a real person, such an interaction might be considered multiple-user collaboration, but in this case, it would be an example of a surrogate agent.

The simulated physics of the virtual world were designed to be as realistic as needed for effective training, and due to the fact that the world is somewhat simple, good realism was achieved. A simple submarine propulsion model was implemented. The actual propulsion system is classified, so the model was estimated. Naval officers who had served on submarines confirmed that the implemented model was near enough to be acceptable for training.

The other world physics that might have required modeling are the weather and water conditions. Since submarines only go to port in good weather, no special modeling of weather and water conditions was required. Also, water current is not rapid, and is fairly constant in the middle of the harbor where the submarine stays unless the trainee is failing the task. The submarine remains at the surface of the water during the entire procedure, so underwater currents and physics do not need to be simulated.

Venue
The venue for the experimental analysis of the application was a laboratory facility of the Sensory Communications Group of the MIT Research Laboratory of Electronics. Actual training, however, can take place either at a Naval training facility or onboard the submarine itself. Each trial training session lasted about 20 minutes.

VR System
Two prime requirements of the *OOD* training system were that it be cost-effective and portable, perhaps portable enough to be placed aboard a submarine. Most of the system choices reflect these constraints.

SYSTEM CHOICE

Display Paradigm
An HMD was chosen as the visual display paradigm (the virtual research model VR4). The full field-of-regard of an HMD gives the user the ability to look from the submarine in any direction, and is a much more portable visual system than projection VR or even *BOOM*™ displays. A full field-of-regard was a necessity because the OOD is constantly looking in all directions around the submarine as it navigates the channel. The requirements for portability and simulating the task to include the same viewing capabilities as available in the real world dictated that an HMD display be used.

The specific HMD model used was a moderately low-resolution model. Because of the low resolution of the display, the use of the perceptual cue tuning was required in order to see objects that take very little of the screen space. A Polhemus FasTrak magnetic system provides 6 DOF position tracking information of the head.

The world is rendered as monoscopic images at a frame rate of 15 Hz on a 2-processor Silicon Graphics graphics Onyx™ workstation with the RE2 graphics hardware.

SYSTEM CHOICE

Visual Rendering
Because most of the virtual world is in the distance (everything but the submarine itself), stereoscopic images do not provide a considerable amount of depth information. Thus, it was not considered essential to render stereo images. Rather, monoscopic images were rendered instead.

SYSTEM CHOICE

Visual Rendering

The pace of the task is not very rapid. Therefore, extremely high frame rates are not required. The main constraint on frame rate is the lag between head motion and the appropriate view. A rate of 15 frames per second is high enough to make the tracking system the primary cause of lag. This allows more detail to be rendered than if a higher frame rate was required.

Audio input and output is handled via a small boom microphone attached to the front, and headphones installed inside the HMD. A handheld push-to-talk switch allows the participant to indicate when they are giving commands to the virtual piloting team, mimicking the real interface in which the officer also uses a push-to-talk switch to give instructions to the helmsman. The BBN *HARK*™ speech-recognition package provides speaker independent vocal input to the application. The 3D spatialization effect is produced by the CRE *Beachtron*™ system. A midi switching device is used to select which sounds are spatialized and which sounds are presented as ambient sounds in the environment. All the audio input and output generation for the speech communication are done on a Silicon Graphics Indy™. Other sounds were stored and played from an Apple Macintosh™.

SYSTEM CHOICE

Audio Rendering

It is important to present some of the sounds in the virtual world spatialized in three dimensions. In particular, it was important to spatialize the sounds that come from the navigational buoys that help trainees to locate themselves in the world.

Application Implementation

This application was developed as a specific product for use by the United States Navy. As such, a complete version

was finalized (version 1.0). One specific feature that was not included in version 1.0 but which the developers felt was important was to add a collection of artificial instructional cues. That is, information provided by an agent in the world who can aid the trainee when they require it.

Development on version 1.0 ran for about 1 year. It began in February 1994, when the VETT project was first asked to create the application. By August of that year, a prototype version of the experience was running, and evaluated by Naval officers with submarine experience. Version 1.0 was completed in February 1995.

Many people were involved in the creation of the *Officer of the Deck* virtual environment, including principal investigators David Zeltzer and Nathaniel I. Durlach. Important programming contributions were made by post-doc Jeng-Feng Lee; graduate students Walter Aviles, Nicholas Pioch, Rakesh Gupta, and Jonathan Pfautz; undergrad students Erik Nygren and Brett Reid, and staff programmer Dorrie Hall. The *OOD* simulation was developed with the close collaboration of the BBN Training Team that included Bill Levison, Yvette Tenney, Dave Getty, and Dick Pew. Work on the *OOD* was sponsored in part by the Naval Air Warfare Center Training Systems Division and the Office of Naval Research.

The VR experiment for the *OOD* training application was put together by a team of researchers from MIT and BBN under the direction of principal investigator David Zeltzer. The VR system and *OOD* application were developed at MIT. BBN helped with the design of the experimental task and provided the speech-recognition tool.

There are many software subcomponents for a VR training application like the *Officer of the Deck*. In addition to the graphics and audio rendering, and the simulation dynamics, there were components to handle speech recognition that provided the world modeling interface, and the experimenter/instructor interface. The experimenter interface was the mechanism for controlling the experimental and training parameters, as well as recording the trial data.

The graphics software components were written in C using the *Performer* graphics library from Silicon Graphics. The submarine and world dynamics simulations were written in C++.

Related Applications and Follow-on Work

Officer of the Deck training continues to be an important part of naval training. One of the most interesting related VR-based training systems is the *Virtual Environment for Submarine OOD Ship Handling (VESUB)* project originally deployed at Submarine Training Facility in Norfolk, VA, and the Naval Submarine School in Groton, CT. Now developed by RDR, Inc. of Centreville, VA, the *VESUB* trainers are deployed at six major submarine training facilities throughout the world.

The *VESUB* trainer utilizes a HMD and provides voice-synthesized feedback in addition to speech recognition. The system has been through thorough assessment, and through this feedback it has been continually improved (see Vincenzi 2003, Hays 2000). Hays and Vencenzi found that over 90% of observers and participants felt that the system provided an increase in ship-handling skills.

Conclusion

The *Officer of the Deck* application was tested using experiments designed by the BBN training team. Subjects for the pilot experiment were MIT students who generally have a similar aptitude as Navy officers, though the MIT student subjects had little or no previous boating experience. For the final experiment, naval submarine officers were used, though these were not officers whose position would call for them to be an OOD.

In the experiment, each subject was given limited background instruction and system familiarization, after which they performed 10 trials on the training system. Measured performance improved significantly over the 10 trials. Two measures that indicated the improvement were the time spent outside the specified channel (average of 3.5 seconds in trial 1 to zero in trial 10), and the root-mean-square (RMS) distance from the channel centerline (from 28.5 yards to 6.9 yards). These results appear to validate the VR experience as a training tool.

Unfortunately, it is difficult (nearly impossible) to compare the results with a control group. This difficulty is because submarines are hard to come by and there is a general reluctance by naval officers to be measured in task performance.[2]

---

[2]Because of the possibility of its use in determining promotions.

FIGURE 7-9

The VESUB application continues to train submariners at several military sites.

Fortunately however, the *VETT* project team had a close working relationship with some U.S. Navy officers who were familiar with the task. Some of these officers participated in controlled evaluation sessions, and all felt that this system had great potential as a training and mission rehearsal tool. These kudos by domain experts further validated the *OOD* experience for training, including the use of perceptual cue tuning to accommodate for the poor resolution of the HMD.

Since mishaps involving submarines coming into port are rare, it is hard to derive specific numbers of how much can be accomplished with this application. However, if it helps to prevent even one accident, then the number of lives (and careers) saved as well as the amount of money (hundreds of millions of dollars) could be significant.

As an experiment to demonstrate the potential for use as a training tool, the project was successful. This tool provides an opportunity for OOD candidates to experience pre-training on a task that otherwise provides little opportunity for apprenticeship. Task-learning of the (simulated) task was accomplished by experimental subjects. In addition, naval officers associated with the project feel that such a system aboard a submarine would be good for performing mission rehearsal prior to coming into a new port.

This experience is unlike many typical adrenaline-rush games. It involves a much slower-paced task and is not meant to be particularly fun, so it might follow that it wouldn't be very mentally immersive either. During the times when it was "smooth sailing" for the subjects, they probably were more aware of the surrounding (non-VR) environment. However, the experiment instructor (Dorrie Hall) felt that "when the situations demanded focus, they were *there*." The purpose of the training application is to involve the subject enough so that they actually learn something.

Some interesting observations made by the application design team include noting features of good training as well as features of the VR system that may not be necessary. Regarding training, it was observed that features that make good performance-analysis tools do not necessarily make good training cues. In fact, they can become a crutch that ends up causing a negative correlation to task learning. Part of the VR system that might not be necessary for this and similar tasks (where all the action happens off in the distance) are comprehensive depth cues. The implementation for the experimental procedure did not include a stereoscopic display, but it did provide motion parallax. Not all depth cues are important for all tasks, but some cues are very important. Finding out what cues are important is vital for any training experience. The use of perceptual cue tuning was a significant part of this process. One (monocular) depth cue that they did find to be important was the perspective foreshortening of objects on the shoreline receding into the distance. The *Officer of the Deck* VR training experience demonstrated a good use of the medium to produce a cost-effective tool for a task that has traditionally had limited opportunity for training. The *OOD* development team put significant effort toward the validation and verification of the experimental task, following the advice of Fred Brooks: "Build the right product, and build the product right."

Perhaps a key validation of the overall experience is that all the officers of the U.S. Navy who they had worked with during the project "expressed enthusiasm about the simulator's potential usefulness for training and mission rehearsal." [Zeltzer et al.]

CASE STUDY 7.2: SHADWELL VR EXPERIENCE

Firefighting Trainer

Executive Summary

Not surprisingly, the Navy is interested in utilizing optimal firefighting procedures for shipboard firefighting. The Naval Research Laboratory (NRL) maintains a decommissioned ship for use as a research vessel for exploring improved firefighting techniques and training, the ex-*USS Shadwell*. One of the NRL's research projects has been to explore the potential effectiveness of VR as a tool for training shipboard firefighting techniques, mission planning, and rehearsal. The Advanced Information Technology and Navy Technology Center for Safety and Survivability branches of the NRL teamed up to create an experiment to study this issue.

Many different experiments on firefighting techniques are conducted aboard the *Shadwell*. The instructors on the

Shadwell have the ability to create controlled fires that simulate ones that firefighters are most likely to encounter. The use of VR for mission rehearsal would allow firefighters to familiarize themselves with a new ship while attempting various firefighting techniques without endangering people or ships.

Because the *Shadwell* was already being utilized for the study and testing of firefighting techniques it was also the site chosen to conduct feasibility tests of using VR as a supplement to the mission rehearsal process. A battery of such tests was held aboard the *USS Shadwell* September 18–22, 1995.

Application Description

To create the virtual training environment, portions of the *Shadwell* have been modeled at full scale in the VR environment. The application developers created a realistic model of the ship utilizing photographic texture maps to provide surface gradients for the bulkheads and decks. Objects that could be used in the firefighting procedure were modeled as 3D virtual objects. Other objects, with which the trainees would not be required to interact (such as the oxygen-breathing apparatus racks), are each represented as a simple textured polygon. A handheld input device used for interacting with the virtual world is represented as an avatar of the user's hand. No aural representation of the world was created for the initial experiment.

Two significant challenges in the fighting of fires are lack of visibility due to smoke and lack of familiarity with the area where the fire is located. Thus, a reasonable representation of smoke and fire are required to enable the participants to practice under these conditions. The *Shadwell* VR experience thus contains a simulated fire, complete with smoke plume and ambient smoke. The simulation controls the growth of the fire, as well as the smoke plume emanating from it. The fire-and-plume display was implemented as a loop of texture maps on a viewer-facing polygon. The textures were created using video of an actual fire. Ambient smoke was created using the atmospheric effects of the Silicon Graphics *Reality Engine 2*.

Collision detection was employed so users would be forced to move through the ship in a manner similar to real life. Thus, the firefighters would need to follow the same

FIGURE 7-10

Computer-generated smoke gives firefighters realistic clues regarding the location of a fire, as well as obstructs their view.

path in the virtual world as required by the real world constraints, including pausing to open doors, etc.

To open a door, a procedure was implemented that substitutes for the real-world task of manipulating the latches, wheels, levers, etc., normally required for opening ship doors. In the *Shadwell* VR experience the participant points their hand avatar at the door and presses the appropriate button on the device to open or close the door. The door stops moving when the button is released; thus the participant can control how far the door is opened or closed.

The primary travel metaphor is a *walkthrough* using a pointer-directed *walkthrough* interface. Use of this metaphor allows participants to look around while traversing the ship. This is an important feature, because they can make note of important objects and landmarks while moving through the *Shadwell*. The pointer-directed interface replaced a previous model that used a gaze-directed *walkthrough* interface. In the gaze-directed interface, the inability to look around while walking longitudinally proved to be ineffective. The *walkthrough* interface is important since the goal is for the participants to learn to travel a specific path through the ship that they will later have to traverse on foot. A terrain following algorithm moves participants vertically as they traverse stairs and ladders.

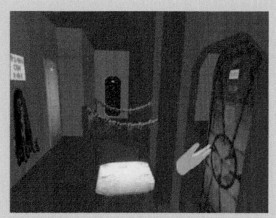

FIGURE 7-11

As in the real world, firefighters must pause to open doors aboard the virtual USS Shadwell.

FIGURE 7-12

Terrain following allows firefighters to traverse stairs and ladders in the virtual world.

The model of the world used in the experimental trials replicated portions of the *Shadwell*. A similar world was also created as a test model resembling the ship, but not representing any actual layout. This allows participants to become familiar with the virtual reality user interface (before performing the actual experimental trials) without allowing them to become familiar with the ship in the test environment.

To evaluate VR as a tool for preparing firefighters and performing mission rehearsal, a feasibility test was implemented with two experimental groups. Subjects for the test were chosen from the expected group of users, trained Navy firefighters. None of the firefighters had any previous experience with the *Shadwell*. Twelve subjects were selected and divided into two groups, with equal gender representation between groups (four men, two women). The control and experimental groups were both prepared in the traditional method, including the study of ship layout diagrams. The experimental group was given additional preparation in the VR environment.

Each VR experience was presented to the VE training group in three stages. The first stage was to tour the ship in a ride-along travel method. This was to allow the participant to locate landmarks and useful objects on the course without needing to worry about navigating. As they traveled, a narrator (the instructor) drew attention to the important features along the path. Next, the participant used the point-to-move style *walkthrough* travel interface, and manually navigated to the specified location. In the third stage, they again had to navigate their way through the course, but now with ambient smoke limiting their visibility.

Both groups were tested in two different tasks. The first task (phase I) was a navigation-only task involving no firefighting skills. The second task (phase II) involved a complete attack on controlled fire, including locating the equipment, preparing the attack team, and extinguishing the fire. After standard mission planning, and VR rehearsal for the experimental group, both groups were tested on the actual *Shadwell*. For each test, they were measured on their ability to accomplish the navigation task (in phase I) or firefighting task (in phase II) on the actual *Shadwell*. The primary measurement was the time required to accomplish the task. A count of wrong turns was also recorded.

The results showed measurable improvements in the group with VR rehearsal versus the non-VR group. Though not statistically significant due to the small number of subjects, the preliminary results indicated that the VR prepared group was able to complete each task in substantially less time, and with fewer wrong turns than the control group. Details of the study were described by Tate, Sibert, and King in "Virtual Environments for Shipboard Firefighting Training" [Tate et al.].

After the testing, the VR participants commented that the VR component of the training was very helpful and that the fire was quite realistic. Those who did not receive the VR component felt unprepared when they entered the unfamiliar ship.

Overall, this experiment indicates that VR has potential as a tool for shipboard firefighting preparation and could be used to provide a number of training scenarios. However, studies involving more subjects are needed to give statistical significance.

Areas the experimenters feel need further research and improvement include interaction techniques for manipulating objects (as well as studies for validation of those techniques) and the integration of other I/O such as 3D sound, tactile (in the form of heat display), speech input, integrated multimedia and hypermedia instruction, and multiuser interaction.

VR System

This feasibility test was carried out directly on the *Shadwell*. The application was originally designed for the subjects to be standing during the experience. However, to accommodate the tracking system in a room with a low metal ceiling, the transmitter had to be lowered by 2 feet. So, subjects were seated on a stool. The stool could swivel, allowing participants to face any direction.

This project was led by David Tate of the NRL, who also did the user interface design and model construction. Tony King provided the software design and implementation,

and Linda Sibert performed the experimental design and analysis. The NRL virtual reality lab is directed by Larry Rosenblum.

Development for this specific application took approximately five months, though it was based on work brought to the project by Tony King and Perry McDowell. Graphics programming was done using both the Silicon Graphics Performer 1.2 and IrisGL libraries.

The world is presented to the participants using a Virtual Research VR2 head-mounted display. Tracking of the HMD and handheld unit is done with the Polhemus FasTrak system. The Naval Research Lab also has a Responsive Workbench, and has installed a *CAVE*-like projection VR display. However, an HMD was used for this application because it works well with this application both because of the restrictions imposed by the venue, and the desire for a full field-of-regard display.

Conclusion

The *Shadwell* VR training experience developers have begun work with the Naval Surface Warfare Center in Philadelphia on the development of a simulated shipboard firefighting system. Some enhancements for future versions of the experience include the use of props as input devices that provide a better corollary to the real-world controls, and the addition of 3D sound. The input control will be a virtual hose nozzle with adjustable spray pattern and water control modeled to mimic the real world, allowing users to realistically control the virtual water, with an enhanced simulation of water in the virtual world. Other enhancements in this version will be the addition of 3D spatialized sounds of the fire, water, doors and footsteps. Their expectation is that this system "could be used not only as a training device in classrooms, but also for shipboard refresher training or rehearsal."

The application developers "foresee using VR as a standalone training tool where firefighting procedures can be taught through simulation of fire growth and extinguishment."

CASE STUDY 7.3: SANDIA'S *VRAPTOR*

Hostage Rescue

The Virtual Reality/Intelligent Simulation (VR/IS) team at Sandia National Laboratories created a system for *VR Assault Planning Training or Rehearsal (VRaptor)*. *VRaptor* is a system that provides the capability for end user instructors to create scenarios for situational training, including options to manipulate the environment as the training is taking place.

The VR/IS team was primarily interested in studying the scripting and control of virtual actors. The *VRaptor* system is interesting in that it demonstrates that groups such as security and emergency response forces will be able to practice situations for which they might not have a chance to rehearse in any other way.

Application Description

For testing the usefulness of the *VRaptor* system, a hostage-rescue mission was created as a demonstration scenario. Specific training scenarios, such as a "room clearing operation," typically consist of a set of defined steps such as breach the room, throw in a stun grenade, enter the room, command the room occupants to "get down," and shoot the armed adversaries. One of the crucial decisions

FIGURE 7-13

The VRaptor *system provides a relatively realistic environment for hostage rescue training.*
(Image courtesy of Sandia National Laboratories)

for the trainee to make is whether to shoot or not and at whom. The trainees must avoid shooting the hostages and getting shot themselves. The instructor can subject the trainee to a similar scenario several times with the virtual actors in different roles. Another use of the system is to rehearse an actual task to find an optimal strategy before completing the action in a live situation. The real-world method of preparing for these tasks (either as general training, or for a specific operation) is through the use of a "shoot house." A "shoot house" is a room modeled to represent the location of interest. The shoot house room is populated with "cartoon drawings or mannequins" representing the individuals involved in the scenario. Because the drawings and mannequins can only move in very simple ways, the opportunity for creating interesting situations is limited.

In the VR training paradigm, the instructor first creates the environment, places the virtual actors in their starting positions, and assigns scripts to the virtual actors to control their behavior. The trainee follows the assigned procedure while the virtual actors play their roles and realistic sound effects are triggered. When the scenario takes place, the action is sometimes very fast.

The virtual world of the hostage scenario consists of a room with furnishings, the avatar of the trainee, and virtual actors represented as human forms. The instructor can script the reactive behavior of the virtual actors. They can also trigger high-level behaviors for the actors while the scenario unfolds.

Sound effects help increase the realism of the event and augment the mental immersion felt by the participant. In the demonstration application described here, the sounds of the stun grenade and gunshots are the only ones heard.

VR System

The application interface consists of an HMD display for the trainee, and a view window and control panels for the instructor. The participant holds a replica of a 9mm Beretta, which is tracked for 6-DOF position as well as trigger pulls and when the participant inserts or removes the clip. The gun is realistic in feel and weight, but does

FIGURE 7-14
A trainee must make quick decisions as to whether or not to shoot.
Image courtesy of Sandia National Laboratories

FIGURE 7-15
The trainee holds the weapon in front of herself. The monitor reflects the image that is being viewed by the trainee in the HMD.
Image courtesy of Sandia National Laboratories

not recoil when fired. A position tracker is mounted on the gun replica and another unit is affixed to the HMD for head tracking. The participant's other hand is also tracked, as well as their lower back. These additional sensors allow both hands to be represented in the participant's view and a more complete representation of the posture of the participant in the external 3D view on the trainer console. Multiple third-person views and trainees are also possible, but were not incorporated into the demonstration system.

The instructor interface is on a multiwindow graphics workstation. One window is a three-dimensional third-person view of the virtual world including the avatar of the trainee. In another window, a set of menus allows the instructor to do activities such as assign the roles of the virtual actors (agents) to be hostages or terrorists in the next scenario. The instructor places the actors in the scene and selects from a list of scripts that describe the behavior an actor will take in different situations. One selection is what a virtual actor will do when shot at. The instructor can perform "Wizard of Oz" agent control by initiating high-level behaviors via menu interaction as the action plays out. The menus are context sensitive, providing only choices that make sense according to how the actors are positioned.

VRaptor is a system in which environments can be modeled and populated with virtual actors who respond according to the actions of the trainees. Although the developers do not see the *VRaptor* system as replacing the physical shoot house entirely, they do believe this VR version of a shoot house offers an option that can augment this live training, providing additional features, such as virtual characters that behave according to programmed actions. It also offers a lower-cost option to using a physical shoot house.

The specific work for the *VRaptor* demonstration application took approximately 4 months. However, it was built on the VR software platform under development at Sandia National Laboratories. The Sandia VR software was originally written in *IrisGL* and later ported to Silicon Graphics' *Performer* library.

The VR/IS team also integrated elements developed at other computer graphics labs. These were the geometry from the *Jack*™ system, the *KPL* language from Ken Perlin's research on behaviors for virtual actors, and *Simlet Designer*™ from Inflorescence Inc. A client/server audio system developed at Sandia was used to combine sounds into a single output.

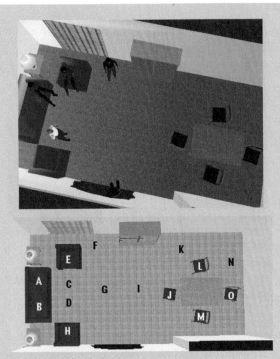

FIGURE 7-16

The instructor interface allows actors to be positioned at any of 15 different locations. Whether an actor is a hostage taker or hostage cannot be determined by physical appearance. Their actions typically reveal their status.
Image courtesy of Sandia National Laboratories

The *VRaptor* project was conducted by Sharon Stansfield and Dan Shawver of Sandia National Laboratories. Jim McGee and Wade Ishimoto provided subject matter expertise in the hostage rescue operation. Denise Carlson, James Singer, Ron Hightower, and Monica Prasaad contributed to the development of various components of the technology.

An Optics One PT01 HMD with 640 × 480 resolution and a 40-degree FOV was used to display the world to the participant. A Polhemus electromagnetic-style position tracker with four sensors tracked the participants' movements. The graphics were rendered on a Silicon Graphics

workstation. Early versions ran on the Crimson™ model deskside workstations. Later versions have been run on an Onyx™ with Reality Engine 2™ graphics hardware and on a Silicon Graphics Octane™. The VR/IS team is in the process of porting the graphics software to a Microsoft *Windows*™ platform. Audio is generated on a Silicon Graphics Indigo2™ workstation.

Conclusion

In the future, the *VRaptor* developers would like to do an evaluation on the effectiveness of this system for training, but no formal analysis has yet been done. However the Sandia team does believe their system will be suitable for many operations. To achieve a system that would meet the needs of law enforcement officers, they worked closely with a trainer for the FBI's hostage rescue team from the onset of the project. They have subsequently demonstrated the system to personnel from many other law enforcement agencies, including the Los Angeles Sheriff's Department, Department of Energy security, and the military. The developers found that most of them stated that the system had the potential to be a valuable tool.

Participants who have tried the simulator have reported favorable results. One of the features the developers would like to improve is to raise the resolution of the control of the actors' behaviors. They also would like to monitor and log the trainee's behavior to allow the performance to be reviewed.

One of the significant findings of this work by the developers is that photorealistic graphics are not necessarily the most important aspect of creating a believable virtual world. Rather, a world that behaves and responds appropriately can provide a strong sense of immersion and suspension of disbelief.

In regards to how Stansfield feels VR will be useful as a training tool for law enforcement procedures, she states:

> *While virtual reality supporting such highly behavioral, interactive simulations is still in its infancy, we believe that its application to training in high-consequence environments such as this will prove to be one of the most important and useful.*

CASE STUDY 7.4: INTEGRATED EVA/RMS VIRTUAL REALITY SIMULATION

Space Walk Trainer

The Hubble Space Telescope (HST) was launched in April 1990 to enable astronomers to gain a view of the heavens from a location clear of the distortions caused by the earth's atmosphere. Unfortunately, shortly after the deployment of the HST, the optical system was found to have disabling flaws. Repair of the telescope would require a manned space mission with multiple extravehicular activities (EVAs), that is, space walks. From 1990 to 1993 the National Aeronautic and Space Administration (NASA) put considerable effort toward the planning and crew training for a Space Shuttle mission to repair the HST.

The Simulation and Graphic Development Branch at NASA's Johnson Space Center (JSC) had been exploring VR applications in 1990 and was interested in using VR as a mission rehearsal tool. The VR training system they developed was a very ambitious project, and resulted in the first VR system used for preparing for an actual task in space.

One of the reasons they embarked on this project was to demonstrate the potential of VR as a mission-preparation tool. The goal was to help the astronauts understand the situations that might be encountered while repairing the Hubble Space Telescope and to help develop the procedures to be used in the mission. Since this mission would involve more EVA operations than previous shuttle flights (five nearly 8-hour activities), it was important that the astronauts be prepared for all the different circumstances that might arise during the operations, and be able to avoid, or quickly avert difficult situations. It also provided an opportunity to develop a communications protocol between the two EVA astronauts and the Intravehicular Activity (IVA) astronaut who controlled the Remote Manipulator System (RMS).

In December 1993 (3 years after the launch of the HST), the telescope was successfully repaired on shuttle mission STS-61. The VR lab at JSC has continued to be used as part of the shuttle mission training program. Since this first mission, all subsequent EVA procedures have been simulated using the VR system, and the JSC "Integrated EVA/RMS Virtual Reality Simulation Facility" was born, becoming a permanent facility at the space center. A large number of shuttle missions with EVAs are being planned in preparation for the space station NASA is building in conjunction with many other space agencies.

Application Description

NASA has relied on simulators and specialized training facilities since the days of the Apollo program. This has worked well, but these unique facilities with large support staff are very expensive (generally exceeding $30,000 per hour) and offer limited training scenarios, with limited availability. In addition to this, they cannot replicate the physics of microgravity well enough for all tasks. For instance, moving large objects in a water-tank is much different than in space, as a lighter touch is required in space due to the lack of resistance.

The only true way to simulate microgravity without leaving the earth's atmosphere is in the KC-135 aircraft (also known as the "Vomit Comet"). Even this is limiting because microgravity can only be experienced in 25-second durations, whereas in virtual reality an astronaut can be immersed in a simulated microgravity world for hours.

FIGURE 7-17
Astronauts Jeffrey Hoffman and Story Musgrave on a space walk to fix the Hubble Space Telescope during shuttle mission STS-61.

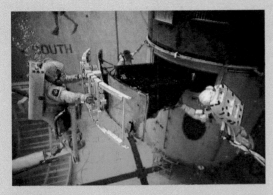

FIGURE 7-18

In the photo on top, Astronauts Story Musgrave and Jeffrey Hoffman practice removing the Wide-Field Planetary Camera (WF/PC) unit in the Weightless Environment Training Facility (WETF) water tank facility at JSC. In the bottom photo, Astronaut Thomas Akers rehearses for the HST repair mission. Note that in both photos other divers help to make the movement in the viscous fluid more closely resemble the vacuum of space.

Some of the goals of the *Integrated EVA/RMS Virtual Reality Simulation Trainer* included:

- "Evaluate the capabilities and limitations of VR technology to support integrated EVA training in a useful way.

- Provide overall situational awareness of on-orbit EVA operations as they related to water tank training configurations.

- Develop a command protocol for communications between the EVA astronaut and the RMS operator." [Homan]

Each EVA offered a different scenario in which astronauts would interact. The first HST repair mission (STS-61) involved two EVA astronauts working together with an IVA astronaut. For this mission, eight 2-hour sessions were conducted in the VR simulator. During these eight sessions, a command protocol between the EVA and RMS operator was developed and the tasks of removing the High Speed Photometer (HSP), moving it to a temporary holding device, removing the COSTAR (Corrective Optics Space Telescope Axial Replacement) from a replaceable unit carrier and placing it in the HST, and then storing the HSP into the replaceable unit carrier were practiced.

The objects modeled for the HST training application included all the objects with which the astronauts would interact. The design team constructed a computer model of the HST, the payload bay and fixtures used for transporting replacement systems into orbit, and the components that would be replaced or serviced during the repair and maintenance mission. The rest of the Space Shuttle components (that would not be seen during this task) were not modeled. Objects were created using the engineering drawings of the real-life counterparts, for more accurate representation.

Viewing the world was also implemented in a way to mimic real-world viewing conditions. For tasks such as the wide-field planetary camera replacement task, the extravehicular astronaut would be physically immersed in the VR system, while the astronaut performing the intravehicular activity would sit in front of a computer monitor that provided the portal view to the external shuttle bay. The external astronaut would interact with the environment with their hands, while the internal astronaut would manipulate the shuttle's robot arm (called the Remote Manipulator System or RMS) using joystick controls similar to the controls on the shuttle. The IVA astronaut could view the world either via a window looking into the payload bay, or on a pair of monitors that show the world through the view of cameras mounted throughout the shuttle. Four cameras are located in the payload bay (one in each corner), two are mounted on the robot arm, and others are placed in various locations in the shuttle (or are simply handheld).

FIGURE 7-19
This computer rendering resembles the graphics presented by the virtual reality system. It depicts the Hubble Space Telescope attached to the Space Shuttle as two astronauts perform repairs.

FIGURE 7-20
Tricia Mack (EVA trainer) and Jeff Hoblit (VR simulator programmer) demonstrate the VR training system as used for STS-88.

The physics of the virtual world were programmed to closely match the low-gravity environment that is experienced by the astronauts. Virtual objects were constrained to move within the limitations of the real objects. For example, when extracting long objects from the telescope, the astronaut would have to continue to guide and pull the object until completely removed.

EVA astronauts maneuver in one of two primary ways. One way was to be attached to the end of the robot arm and be moved about by an astronaut controlling the arm from within the cabin, much like a worker operating atop a "cherry picker." The other method was to be a "free floater," crawling along the structure using handrails. Handrails are placed frequently on the external structures of objects about which an astronaut may need to maneuver.

Movement in the virtual world is carried out in just the same way. Astronauts attached to the RMS move as it is maneuvered by an IVA astronaut, while free floaters pull themselves through the world by "grabbing" handles and pulling. The grabbing is done by making fist gestures that are sensed by the data gloves worn by the astronauts. Objects are maneuvered by manipulating tracked physical objects. A tracked prop is used for low-mass objects, and

the Kinesthetic Application of Mechanical Force Reflection (KAMFR) system (described below) is used for large objects.

Extravehicular activities are always done with at least two astronauts participating. Frequently (and as was the case for the first HST repair mission), one extravehicular astronaut is attached to the RMS, while the other floats freely. The RMS astronaut typically moves large objects into place, while the free floater performs tasks such as getting equipment out of storage. In STS-61, astronauts Jeff Hoffman, Thomas Ackers, Kathryn Thorton, and Story Musgrave were teamed in pairs, with two performing the EVA each day. Mission specialist Claude Nicollier was the primary operator of the RMS during the mission.

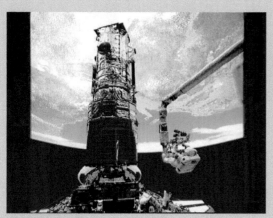

FIGURE 7-21
One of the EVA astronauts rides at the end of the RMS while the other moves by grasping handles on the shuttle and devices.

FIGURE 7-22
Inside the shuttle, mission specialist Claude Nicollier operates the RMS controls while viewing the action through four portals and two CCTV monitors.

To prepare for STS-61, EVA astronauts took turns in the HMD to experience segments of the HST repair. At the same time, Nicollier would operate the virtual RMS, and the other astronauts could watch and comment on the activities taking place in the virtual world. Movement of the virtual robot arm had the same constraints as the real thing. By putting realistic constraints on the virtual world, the trainees get a chance to not only see what the operation will be like, but also to get a chance to experience a realistic response to their actions.

Realistic avatars represent each astronaut's position in the virtual world. Working together requires that each participant knows where the other participants are and what they are doing. Astronauts also need to see their own body, so they can interact with the virtual objects. However, each astronaut's body is rendered differently from the user's perspective versus that of their crewmates. Astronauts see their own arms, hands, fingers and the inside of their EVA suit helmet. Others see the entire body of the astronaut, but the hands and fingers are not individually articulated. To reduce polygons, the entire hand was modeled as a single "mitten."

Audio in the virtual world was primarily voice communication between astronauts. Because all the sounds that an astronaut performing an EVA will hear will be those coming over their communications link, there is no need to add any sounds other than normal voice communication to the experience.

VR System

The *EVA/RMS VR simulator* provides the hardware interface to a virtual world that mimics the physical behaviors of objects and machinery in space. This world includes "a functionally correct dynamic simulation of the Shuttle Remote Manipulator System with translational and rotational hand controllers, graphical representation of the A8 control panel, and computer graphic renderings of the objects important to the scenario. The simulation also provides access to all closed circuit television (CCTV) views available from all payload bay and RMS cameras and out-the-window views" [Homan and Gott].

An HMD visual display was used for the physically immersed participants. A single Virtual Research VR-2 Flight Helmet was used in the early research. More recently, the JSC VR lab upgraded to using a pair of n-Vision high-resolution (1280 × 1024), CRT-based, head-mounted displays. These HMDs provide wide (120-degree) horizontal field of view with 50% stereo overlap. The vertical FOV is 80 degrees. After the success of the first mission, a second HMD was added to the system so both of the EVA astronauts can be immersed together in the virtual space.

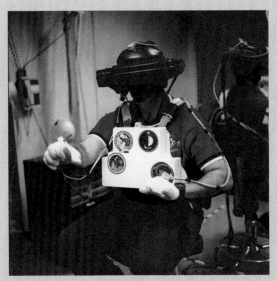

FIGURE 7-23

Astronaut Jim Newman prepares for his EVA to begin constructing the Unity *Space Station on STS-88. He wears a high-resolution HMD to view the world, and two data gloves to manipulate the world. Newman interacts with astronaut Jerry Ross (seated behind him) in the same virtual world.*

Along with the HMD, physically immersed astronauts wear two data gloves for interacting with the world, while sitting in a chair. The IVA astronaut uses a standard computer screen for monitoring the external actions, and physical and virtual controllers to manipulate the robot arm.

Position tracking is done with an Ascension Flock-of-Birds™ electromagnetic tracking system. Ten sensors were available for tracking the head, both hands, torso, and a handheld prop for each of two immersed participants. The handheld prop was used as an interface to represent lightweight objects being manipulated by the astronauts.

A large, Silicon Graphics Reality Monster™ graphics supercomputer provided the rendering power needed for the more complex rendering tasks required by the simulations. The Reality Monster provided several visual outputs. Typically, four outputs were used to drive the two head-mounted displays (two for each HMD). Another visual output shows an out the window view from within the shuttle (looking into the payload bay). Two other monitors mimic the camera monitors on the shuttle.

The prototype work done for STS-61 used an older (and therefore less powerful) Silicon Graphics workstation, with only a single HMD (used by the EVA astronaut) and Polhemus position sensors.

For communication between astronauts, much simpler technology was used. For activities taking place within the VR facility, an amplification system with headsets was used. Each astronaut in the crew, plus trainers, wore their own headset. The number of participants in the conversation is only limited by the number of headsets. For collaborations with participants in different locations, a telephone conferencing system was used. It offered the best performance for the cost and effort.

For the purpose of debriefing evaluations of trial runs in the VR simulator, the system records all the motion and other input data, as well as the voice communications between astronauts. Playback of past VR experiences can be controlled interactively to view a particular segment of time, or change a camera view.

A very important element in learning how to maneuver oneself and objects in microgravity is learning the effects of inertia from an experiential point of view. One can learn the formulae for how objects behave in space, but developing an instinct for how to work in such an environment is best done through experience. Of course, much of this experience comes from haptic interactions.

About a year after the Hubble Space Telescope repair flight (STS-61), a *mass handling simulation* system was developed at the JSC. This system consisted of a box hung on cables that are computer controlled to apply forces to the box. This system, named Kinesthetic Application of Mechanical Force Reflection (KAMFR), was built using preexisting "Charlotte" robots at JSC. The Charlotte robots were designed for use to control operations in a space vehicle or space station during crew sleep periods. The JSC VR team adapted it for use as a haptic I/O device. The "tendon-driven" KAMFR system was used to emulate the physics of objects with large mass (greater than 180 kg). As the astronaut pushes on an object haptically mimicked by the *mass handling* system, the motion dynamics of the object are calculated,

FIGURE 7-24

The dual KAMFR haptic display systems can be seen in the foreground, and far background, as astronauts Jim Newman and Jerry Ross train for STS-88.

and the robots pull on the appropriate cables to mimic the resultant forces.

Because EVA astronauta are wearing an HMD, they don't see the box on cables. What they see is whatever object the box is currently mimicking.

One way in which the KAMFR system is used is to train how to manually capture objects not stable enough for the RMS to grasp. For example, in STS-87 (November 1997), two EVA astronauts captured the *Spartan* satellite by hand after it had been set tumbling when the *RMS* bumped it. Prior to the mission, these astronauts had trained for this contingency with the KAMFR system. The system allowed them to practice handling the 3000lb payload as part of their training.

The *mass handling simulation* was first used for preparation of STS-63. It was later used for the second HST repair mission (STS-82 in February 1996), and was also used for many other shuttle flights involving EVA operations. The evaluation of the EVA crew of STS-63 was that the KAMFR

system "successfully replicated the zero-g mass characteristics of the 2700lb *Spartan* payload manually handled during the EVA Development Flight Test" [Homan and Gott]. Later, in November of 1996 (STS-80), two KAMFR systems were integrated to test the ability of the system to allow two astronauts to manipulate a single large object.

System Development

Programming for the *EVA/RMS VR simulator* was done in-house. The software core was the *OpenGL* graphics library and the C programming language. In addition to the main training applications, the JSC team developed supporting tools for creating the models, environment layout, behaviors, and feedback.

However, the simulation system is never static. When crews come to the facility to train for an upcoming mission, they use the most recently developed version of the software. The software is continually updated to include features necessary for future missions, and also to accommodate changes requested by the astronauts. Of course, this means that this is not a stand-alone system—some of the developers must always be on-hand when the system is being used to operate it.

The JSC VR simulation group is led by David Homan. Other programming and support of the VR facility are provided by contractors from LinCom Corporation. These people are Brad Bell (who has worked in the lab since its inception and works on the graphics software), Jeff Hoblit and Ken Huffman (who integrate all the dynamics simulations), and Erin Orgeron (who builds the models from engineering drawings).

While they had been experimenting with virtual reality since 1988, they began development on the *Integrated EVA/RMS Virtual Reality Simulation* about 1 year before the launch of STS-61.

User Perspective

The test of any virtual reality training application is whether it is found to be useful both through formal analysis and whether the user's themselves find the experience worthwhile. In the case of the training provided by the Integrated EVA/RMS Virtual Reality Simulation Facility, astronauts have found the facility useful for a particular subset of extravehicular training.

Astronaut Dr. James Newman found the VR facility to provide complementary training with the Neutral Buoyancy Lab (NBL). The NBL is a new, larger water tank for practicing space walks under water. But despite the increased size of the new facility, the tank is not large enough to hold complete units of the new space station, thus limiting some aspects of training.

Parts of the EVA experience that are best learned in the NBL include learning how to "work with the suit" and learning to perform precise manual tasks such as connecting cables between adjoining modules of the station.

Because the space suits are airtight, the occupant is limited in how they can maneuver the suit. For example, bending an arm might force air out of that sleeve and into another section of the suit. Thus if the astronaut wishes to constrict both arms, they may not be able to do so because there won't be any place for the displaced air to move.

Virtual reality technology has not yet advanced far enough for simulating full use of all the fingers on the hands, complete with haptic feedback. So, when trying to learn to accomplish procedures that require sufficiently learned dexterous skills with the hands, there is no substitute for wearing the actual glove in an environment where the objects one is working with might float away. On the other hand, the viscosity of the water is different than the vacuum of space, but it is still the closest one can get to simulate this task while not in space.

The virtual reality experience has been found by Newman and the other astronauts to surpass the water tank for activities such as allowing the EVA and IVA astronauts to work together, allowing the EVA astronauts to practice navigating from location to location, and practicing operation of the SAFER unit (described below).

One of the limitations in working in the water tank is that the EVA astronauts and the RMS operator cannot practice their operations together. RMS practice in the water tank involves the use of a dummy astronaut attached to the end of the RMS. The RMS operator can then practice how to maneuver the arm to put the dummy into a useful position, but the dummy cannot give feedback as to how satisfactory the position is for performing the necessary chore. In the virtual reality experience, an EVA astronaut can ride

along as the IVA astronaut moves the arm, and they can work together to find a good position and, more importantly, how best to communicate with one another during the procedure.

The EVA astronauts can also benefit from becoming familiar with how they will move from place to place while they are free floating. In space, there is no fixed horizon about which all movements can be referenced. Thus while free floating, astronauts need to be more deliberate in how they move about. By spending hours in the VR simulator, they can become familiar with the layout of the units there are working on and how best to get from one place to another.

Where VR really shines is in training for use of the SAFER (Simplified Aid For EVA Rescue) unit. SAFER is a backpack device with compressed air that allows the astronaut to maneuver in space should they become untethered and out of reach of handholds. If an accident occurs that results in an astronaut becoming detached from the shuttle or space station, they can fire the compressed air to correct their position and fly back. However, the limited amount of air in the unit may not permit the astronaut to maneuver with the unit and then return to the craft. They must know how to operate SAFER before their actual trek into space. The VR training facility makes this possible. The virtual reality experience also allows the astronauts to do sanity checks on operations that were practiced in the water tank to discover if any of the planned maneuvers are unrealistic.

Another test of how well a VR simulation works as a means of training is whether the trainees lose themselves in the experience and become immersed. Newman reports that the weight of the HMD does serve to remind him that he was not in the weightlessness of space, and he found that even with counterbalances added to the HMDs, it was good to take a break after about an hour of use: "It's hard to lose yourself in the virtual reality experience when there is this thing crushing your skull."

On the other hand, Newman did find that the SAFER training in particular provided an experience in which all his focus was on the experience:

> When you get closer to flight, and you know this
> is like the best training you're gonna get, and if
> you die in the sim, that doesn't bode well, so the

adrenaline ... really gets going. And I would say that's the closest I've come to getting lost in the simulation, with the prospect of my own demise, and what I do next makes it a real difference.

If I were to go fly again on flights this year, then I wouldn't feel the need to go into the tank near as often as we would have wanted before having done this last flight. Because there is a huge amount you learn in the tank, but once you've been outside three, or more times. Now I would be very comfortable doing some VR lab sims, a couple of NBL runs and then [I'd] be ready to go.

Related Work

At the same time the JSC VR lab was coming to fruition under the guidance of David Homan, Bowen Loftin at the University of Houston was working with the Johnson Space Center ISD Software Technology Branch, the Mission Operations Directorate (MOD) space flight training division, and the MOD flight director's office to study how virtual reality might help flight controllers understand the shuttle missions from the perspective of an astronaut. In this study, a VR system was produced independently of the JSC VR lab for use by ground-based personnel.[3]

Normally, due to the limited availability of training resources and personnel, few flight controllers have the opportunity to undergo mission training. Resources for the important hands-on training are heavily scheduled and expensive to operate. Thus, usually only the astronauts had access to the training facilities and simulations. The ground-based flight controllers and support team have much less (virtually no) opportunity for such training.

The goals of the *Flight Team VR Training System* were somewhat different from those of the Astronaut trainer [Loftin and Kenney]:

- Know the correct sequence of EVA activities
- Have an awareness of the position and orientation of the HST, fixtures, components and astronauts

- Be able to identify hardware components
- Perform specific tasks associated with the repair/maintenance of individual components such as bolts to be removed in sequence

Whereas astronauts were using VR (and traditional mission-readiness techniques) to prepare for the HST repair, Loftin's goal was to provide an opportunity for key members of the ground-based support team to interact with and learn about the operability of the various components on the HST. These flight controllers, engineers, and technicians were also trained in the related maintenance components in the payload bay.

For STS-61, several steps were involved in repairing the HST, so the VR practice task was divided into six (EVA) scenarios. The level of detail implemented for each scenario was determined by the intricacy of the procedure. The scenarios included [Loftin and Kenney]:

- Solar Array change-outs
- Rate Sensor Unit (RSU) change-out
- Corrective Optics Space Telescope Axial Replacement (COSTAR)
- Wide Field/Planetary Camera (WF/PC II) change-out
- Solar Array Drive Adapter Electronics (SADE) replacement
- Magnetic Sensing System (MSS)-Magnetometer installation over original magnetometers

The 105 flight-team members who used the system were very highly motivated. After the training was completed, the developers conducted a survey (38 were returned). The survey intended to study three facets of the program. First, they wished to study the effectiveness of this training in enhancing the flight team's performance during the HST mission. They also sought to evaluate the training potential of VR technology, as well as to assess some of the human factors issues and user-to-environment interface methodologies afforded by the training system.

Overall, the participants liked the training and thought it was enjoyable. The positive comments greatly outnumbered the negative. They thought the training was efficient and that they could compress the time required for simulating

---

[3]*Project ScienceSpace* (Chapter 6) describes additional work performed at the University of Houston.

a decent calibration setting could quickly be attained. When the glove was correctly calibrated, it was very easy to activate the fist operation.

The development on the *Flight Team VR Training System* to be used for the HST repair mission began in May 1993. Three of six planned scenarios were done by September 1993, at which point the training with the system began. By October 1993, the rest of the scenarios were completed. Throughout the duration of the training, developers continued making enhancements and improvements until the mission was deployed in December, 1993. In all, the development of the initial system took 6½ months and utilized the talents of six full-time developers and three university interns. Roughly a third of the time was spent doing data acquisition from drawings, and video of details of the specific procedures.

Loftin's team achieved their goal of giving the ground-based flight team a better idea of the situations the astronauts would contend with during the mission. In the process they trained over 120 people in the VR simulator. The large scope of this project provided a unique opportunity to gather data on the usefulness of VR as a training tool. The main finding was that the flight team found the VR training experiences to enhance their performance during the flight of the mission. Based on the success of this particular training application, the *CyberEdge Journal* awarded the JSC VR team the 1993 CJ award for virtual reality applications.

As mentioned, the *Integrated EVA/RMS Virtual Reality Simulation* was a useful tool in the preparation of shuttle missions.

More importantly, the success of the *EVA/RMS VR simulator* by the JSC researchers can be proclaimed by the fact that the system has been used on subsequent EVA missions since it was first used in 1993. For example, STS-88, flown in December 1998, involved three EVAs to construct the first components of the international space station. In addition to bringing the large components together in space, there were a lot of activities such as attaching connectors and connecting cables. In preparation for this mission, over 150 hours were spent in the *EVA/RMS VR simulator.*

FIGURE 7-25
Flight controller Paige Lucas uses VR system to have an opportunity to experience an abbreviated HST repair EVA.

a multi-hour EVA to less than an hour. Some of the negative comments referred to the slow response from hand movements and the resulting visual affect. Users disliked the weight of the HMD, and reported several problems with the data glove used for interfacing with the virtual world [Kenney and Saito].

Many of the problems with the data glove resulted from hand calibration. Calibrating a glove for a particular individual's hand is difficult and requires some setup time prior to users being able to enter the experience. If the system is not properly calibrated to each user's hand, the system can have difficulty recognizing when participants are attempting to trigger an event with a preprogrammed posture. For example, when required to make a fist, many people were unsuccessful or found that they had to squeeze their hand closed as tightly as possible to activate the posture recognition. This led to hand fatigue. A quick solution that Loftin's group discovered was to have a premade suite of calibrations for various hand sizes. By choosing a hand-size that matched the user's hand,

FIGURE 7-26

During STS-88, astronauts James H. Newman (left) and Jerry L. Ross work to connect the Russian Zarya *and United States'* Unity *modules together.*

Once the space station is operational, it too will have an RMS arm, and will be used to conduct EVA operations using the space station as the base. The VR simulation program will then be useful to simulate these missions as well.

Conclusion

It is worth reiterating that there are activities that virtual reality astronaut training provides a better method of experiencing and therefore better mission preparation than the traditional methods of experiential training. For example, VR provides the best means of learning to fly the SAFER "backpack" units that allow astronauts to fly themselves back to the shuttle if their tether ever becomes severed.

Also, the VR simulator is the only way that the entire crew can go through entire scenarios together. The water tank and other low-gravity simulators generally only allow either the EVA astronauts or the IVA astronaut to practice their tasks individually, not as a team.

When asked whether he sees VR playing an increased role in astronaut training, Newman stated:

> *I see an increasing role, and I do believe in truth, that particularly when you have experienced people—I don't need to go into the NBL near as much now, in my opinion, as I would have wanted to prior to this flight. I can do a lot of it in the VR-lab, and it's a lot cheaper to do it that way.*

CASE STUDY 7.5: INFANTRY TRAINING (NPS/ARL)

Computers are increasingly being used to mediate warfare practice exercises. To create simulations of large-scale operations requires the use of a large number of computers at a training center. The potential benefits of computer mediated warfare training are the ability to bring together

units physically located in disparate regions of the globe, and to do exercises using a far less dangerous, and environmentally disruptive methodology. However, such training is not only worthless, but potentially detrimental if it is not designed to eliminate negative training brought on

FIGURE 7-27

A soldier moves through a virtual world by walking on the Sarcos Treadport I/O device at the AUSA 1995 conference. (Photo by Michael Zyda)

by interfaces that allow the trainee easier interactions, or more information than available in the real world scenario.

At the Naval Postgraduate School (NPS) in Monterey, California, a large virtual environment simulation system was developed using the, then current, DIS protocol for collaborative communications, *NPSNET* [Zyda et al. 1993]. By freely distributing *NPSNET* on the Internet, NPS was able to test the system with users at numerous locations, operating on different systems with a variety of input and output devices. Over the course of development, many large-scale exercises were demonstrated.

A limitation of the early system was that it was heavily geared toward operations involving ground and air vehicles, but not dismounted infantry (DI). Two reasons for this are that it is much easier to create interfaces that allow participants to control vehicles in ways similar to the real world, and that the creation of Semi-Automated Forces (SAFs) used to populate the world with a greater number of opposing forces were easier to implement for vehicle-based operations. In short, a DI is harder to emulate.

Specifically, it is difficult to achieve a computer-mediated interface that effectively simulates the conditions a soldier would face in the real world. For instance, vehicles can be operated with a set of controls and viewing parameters similar to the actual vehicle. Also, constraints such as fuel consumption and maximum speeds up and down hills can be realistically imposed by the computer simulation. On the other hand, it is more difficult for a computer to know the level of exhaustion a dismounted soldier would experience and how fast they would be able to move at any given time. Interface devices that provide natural interaction for traveling through a virtual world as a dismounted infantryman (such as physical locomotion with feedback based on the terrain) have been few and far between, and those have been mostly unsatisfactory.

The NPSNET Research Group has investigated several types of input/output devices using their *NPSNET* software connected to hardware provided by collaborators such as Sarcos Research Corporation. A "Soldier Station" described by Shirley Pratt and colleagues, provides a joystick and button interface that is useful for people in the virtual world with enemy forces [Pratt et al.], but because it can't truly simulate a soldier's exhaustion, it doesn't succeed as a method of simulating how the differing amount of physical exertion required between two options will affect choices made by the soldier. For example, a soldier may be able to choose two paths to get from one point to another. The path with less chance of encountering an enemy might require a physically tiring climb and descent of a hill, while an alternate route may be physically easier but have a slightly higher chance of enemy encounter. If the only effort required to ascend and descend the hill is to move a joystick in a particular direction, the soldier will obviously choose the more cautious route. However, if a soldier tired from a long march is faced with this decision, knowing considerable effort will be needed to climb the hill, the (more dangerous) level route may be chosen.

The Army Research Laboratory (ARL) is interested in finding a more realistic interface for DI interactions with simulated warfare environments. The ARL sought to replace the traditional ICSAF (Individual Combatant Semi-Automated Force)[4] with hardware systems designed to fatigue a participant as they traverse terrain "on foot." These systems were referred to as Individual Portals, or I-Ports. As part of their research, the ARL funded the NPS to demonstrate some scenarios that make use of new I-Port systems. Three demonstrations were presented to Army personnel at the

---

[4] *Basically "Wizard of Oz"-style agents.*

FIGURE 7-28

At Fort Benning, a soldier (left) moves through a virtual world using the Sarcos UniPort for the February 1994 demonstration of NPSNET-IV at the AUSA conference and (right) a soldier moving through an NPSNET-IV virtual world on the Sarcos TreadPort.
Left image courtesy of Michael Zyda and the right image courtesy of Sarcos

annual Association of the United States Army (AUSA) Conferences in Washington, D.C. from 1994 to 1996.

Application Description

In the AUSA 1995 demonstration scenario, a squad was called upon to eliminate a sniper firing from a building. The plan was for the team to get into the building, up the stairs, and shoot the sniper. Five participants were involved in this scenario: the enemy sniper, the squad leader, and a three-member M60 machine gun team. The soldiers controlled the simulation using a variety of interface methods. Two of the

machine gun soldiers were traditional ICSAFs (controlled by someone behind the scenes), and the other three participants were stationed on different I-Port input devices: the UniPort, the TreadPort, and the StickPort [Pratt et al. 1995]. The sniper operated a UniPort, a unicycle like device that can provide a variety of resistances to the pedaling operation. The squad leader used a TreadPort, a unidirectional treadmill device, and the third member of the "fire team" used a StickPort, a joystick and button input interface.

After receiving fire from the sniper, the three members of the team provided protection by firing M60 machine guns as cover fire. The squad leader would then stand up and use a hand signal to communicate to the others that they should "Follow me." The two semi-automated (ICSAF) participants would then run to the building, followed by the StickPort participant, and finally the squad leader using the TreadPort. Once at the building, the fire team would follow the leader up the stairs. After navigating through rooms, and around furniture acting as obstacles, the team could then shoot the sniper. After this task was accomplished, one of the soldiers would wave the "All Clear" signal from the window where the sniper had been.

In NPSNET, if a dismounted soldier were virtually killed, they would see a red screen, and then view the world from a prone (lying down) position. Soldiers would return from the dead after 30 seconds.

In many dismounted military maneuvers, communication is done using silent hand gestures. The generation of these signals can be done with two different techniques: button presses that cause the avatar to move through a preset movement pattern that depicts the gesture, or by letting participants gesture naturally, with their own body. The latter method requires that enough of the participant's body be tracked to articulate their avatar in the appropriate way.

The conference audience for this particular demonstration was high-level military officials who needed to see some real benefit from using the new technology over current (proven) methods. In addition to the conference venue, the AUSA 1995 demonstration also included a network connection to Ft. Benning in Georgia, which is a location where such operations would be more likely to take place. In the demonstration described here, the participant acting as the sniper was located in Ft. Benning, and used the UniPort input device.

The scenario used for this presentation was a rather short operation based on the time constraints of quickly demonstrating the possibilities of the technology. Each of the I-Port devices supports only a single individual in the environment, so several devices would be necessary for larger operations. Plus, in actual warfare exercises, the participating soldiers would need to be "suited up" during the entire (generally more lengthy) mission.

VR System

The Naval Postgraduate School received funding to demonstrate the fourth major version of their software suite, *NPSNET-IV*, integrated with new input/output technologies and designed as a training tool for military operations. The hardware and the software involved were both key parts of what was being demonstrated. In the 1994 AUSA demo of *NPSNET-IV*, a SensorSuit was used to track the participant using mechanical means, and an HMD was used to display the visuals. For the 1995 demonstration, the UniPort device was integrated into the demonstration. In addition to this new device, other hardware changes from the 1994 demonstration included replacing the SensorSuit with a Polhemus FaskTrak™ electromagnetic tracking system, and using projectors rather than HMDs to display the visuals. New features of the *NPSNET* software were also highlighted in 1995.

VR DISCOVERY

The switch from HMD to a projection-based display was made because when soldiers used the HMD system they would routinely bump the HMD with their rifles.

The SensorSuit, which had previously been used for testing computer-mediated DI operations, was found to interfere with some of the postures necessary in conducting military operations. The SensorSuit used mechanical linkages to measure the joint angles of the participant. These angles were then used to reconstruct their avatar in the virtual world in the appropriate posture. A Polhemus FaskTrak™ electromagnetic tracking system with four receivers provided a reasonable alternative to the SensorSuit. Another disadvantage of the SensorSuit was that it took more than an hour to calibrate the SensorSuit for each user.

The Polhemus system did not provide as much detail over the entire body of the participant, but did provide 6-DOF position of four points on the user's body that could be used to approximate their current posture. The four receivers were used to track the wrists and head of the participant, plus their M60 rifle. When an HMD is used to display the visuals, the head sensor was mounted directly on the display. However, for the projection display, it is less important to know the orientation of the head than the location, so a point at the base of the neck was chosen for tracking the head's location as well as the torso of the participant. On the rifle, the tracking sensor was mounted on the stock. The developers would have preferred to mount the sensor along the sight line, but were prevented by the design of the rifle mock-up.

When the participant was holding the rifle, the *NPSNET* software was programmed to automatically snap the hand of the avatar to the rifle avatar. By doing this, participants in the world would not see the hand and rifle move slightly independently as a result of jitter caused to the electromagnetic tracking system by the TreadPort and UniPort devices.

The TreadPort and UniPort motion devices were both used to provide a means of participant input generated by leg motion. Leg motion input serves two purposes. It more closely resembles the method of locomotion used in the real world, and it causes the participant to physically exert themselves to travel over the terrain.

The TreadPort allows the user to walk on a treadmill that can sense the distance they were effectively traversing. The UniPort allows the user to sit on a device with a set of bicycle-like pedals. Rotating the pedals provides the mechanism for traveling through the virtual space, and can also provide feedback in the form of resistance to convey the difficulty of traversing particular terrain, thus requiring more effort to go up a hill than to walk across a flat region. Turning in the virtual world on the UniPort was (awkwardly) done by the user rotating their knees to the direction they would like to travel. On the TreadPort, the system would sense when user attempted to walk in another direction and rotate the scene in the visual display, and the attached robot arm would return them to the center of the treadmill.

A BG Systems Flybox™ input device provided the controls for manipulating the ICSAF characters in the scenario.

Communication between sites collaborating in the same scenario was done using the Military's Distributed Interactive Simulation (DIS) protocol. This protocol was developed to handle communication between a large

number of computers across wide distances for the purpose of creating a collaborative virtual world to enact military operations. Multicasting of the DIS information was done using the standard Mbone network protocols [Macedonia et al.]. The DIS protocol was a descendent of the SIMNET protocol, and has now been superseded by the HLA (High Level Architecture) specification.

A separate NPSNET-3D sound server [Storms et al.] provided audio feedback. The sound server software renders the sounds that correspond with actions in the world such as vehicle engines and gunshots or explosions. Sounds are filtered based on the distance and speed of the object generating the sound from the listener. The NPSNET-3D sound server uses MIDI devices (sound samplers and effects units) to control the sounds.

Vocal communication is handled separately from the sounds generated by the virtual world. In the 1995 sniper scenario demonstration, communication was done via hand gestures, so no extra effort was required. When communication is required (such as the 1994 AUSA demo) actual radios that duplicate the real-world equivalent are used.

The *NPSNET-IV* collaborative virtual environment software system is built on the Silicon Graphics *Performer*™ library for the primary scene generation and thus runs on (and only on) the full range of Silicon Graphics workstations. Human models for the 1994 and 1995 demonstrations were created using the *JACK-ML* motion library (a trimmed down, real-time version of the *JACK* system from the University of Pennsylvania). Later, Boston Dynamics' DI-Guy was used by *NPSNET-IV* for the human models.

Since *NPSNET* was originally designed with vehicular movement in mind, some reprogramming was required to correctly model DI movement through the world. In particular, *NPSNET* provides a terrain-following constraint for ground-based vehicles and dismounted infantry. However, because it was assumed that vehicles would not be entering buildings, the terrain-following would place objects on top of any objects with which they are copositioned. Thus, tanks and people would always jump to the top of any building they attempted to enter. To allow individuals to properly traverse buildings (including multistory buildings), the terrain-following constraint was modified to position the user on the nearest surface below their head rather than the highest surface at a given latitude and longitude. This modification also allowed participants to correctly move up and down stairs inside of a building.

The AUSA demonstrations were developed in conjunction with SARCOS Research Corporation (SRC). The overall system was a collaboration between NPS, SRC, the Army Research Lab, the Simulation, Training, and Instrumentation Command (STRICOM), Hughes Research, and the Dismounted Battle-space Battle Laboratory. The TreadPort and UniPort devices were created by SARCOS, and the Naval Postgraduate School integrated the systems to create the demonstration system. The 82nd airborne provided the participants who were engaged in the virtual battle.

At the Naval Postgraduate School, Professor Michael Zyda led the *NPSNET* Research Group. The main group of programmers responsible for the development of the *NPSNET* software system includes Shirley Pratt, Paul Barham, Randal Barker, Scott McMillan, and David Pratt.

Conclusion

The AUSA 1995 DI scenario provided a good demonstration of how dismounted infantry could be integrated into computer-mediated warfare exercises. However, neither the UniPort nor TreadPort devices have been widely deployed as part of the military's training program. This may be due to the cost and difficulty of outfitting each individual DI with their own system.

Although no formal studies have been performed comparing the physical exertion devices (the TreadPort and UniPort) with simpler joystick devices, there has been some comparison of traditional route training methods with virtual reality. In particular, Witmer and colleagues used traversing a particular route though a building to compare traditional visual route training methods with VR and experience in the actual space [Witmer et al.]. The results indicate that practice in the actual location results in the best route learning, while VR outperformed the use of photographic and other presentations of the route (See the discussion on the *Shadwell* firefighter training also in this chapter).

Besides the sniper simulation described here, systems with DI input devices connected to a collaborative virtual

FIGURE 7-29

An omnidirectional treadmill allows participants to walk in any arbitrary direction, and allows maneuvers such as sidestepping.

environment could be used (and have been demonstrated) for a variety of other applications such as hostage rescues, battle scenarios, police and fire training, etc.

The 1996 *NPSNET-IV* demonstration at the AUSA conference was used to introduce yet another ground-breaking I/O device—the Omni-Directional Treadmill (ODT), developed by Virtual Space Devices Inc. The ODT was created to accomplish the same result as the UniPort and TreadPort devices—to duplicate the physical exertion of traversing an environment on foot. However the ODT was designed to overcome some of the problems associated with those devices. In particular their inability to allow maneuvers such as sidestepping.

NPS and Virtual Space Devices collaborated to investigate how well an ODT could emulate real-world motions by the participant [Darken et al.]. They found that after practice many users could operate with the device, but with many restrictions. Because the device always moves to keep the user in the center of the platform, there are many circumstances that can cause the participant to stumble. Adaptation to the device generally results in users learning what circumstances are likely to cause them to lose their balance, and thus they learn to avoid these cases. Unfortunately, some of these circumstances are maneuvers that they would normally use in the real world—such as moving laterally. Also, activities such as crawling or squatting are not possible because a tether on the user will sense this and interpret it as the user falling over, and thus will kill the motors to the ODT.

As is frequently the case, a lack of sustained funding is sometimes the biggest problem encountered during the development of large VR systems. As Zyda describes the fate of *NPSNET*:

> The major limitation of the 1994–1996 AUSA demonstrations was that the work never lead to anything fundamentally reusable. Instead of providing continuous funding of the work during the 3-year demo cycle, money was provided only to slap together short-lived demonstrations. That money would be provided maybe 60 days out from the demo. The short life for the funding did not allow the full development of articulated humans in the NPSNET-IV platform and did not allow for their full testing and support. The final AUSA 1996 demo was the end of development on NPSNET-IV due to this lack of funding constancy and due to demonstration-fatigue of the NPSNET-IV team.

CHAPTER 8

Art

Artists have traditionally sought to express themselves using a variety of media. Classes of artistic expression such as the symphony orchestra, visual arts, dance, and motion pictures each have their own subforms of materials used to forge the artworks. Within the visual arts, for example, charcoal, oil and canvas, clay, steel, and even ice have been utilized as conduits for ideas. Each of these mediums has its own possibilities, quirks, and limitations.

Artists approach different media for different reasons and from different perspectives. Some artists seek to find the medium best suited to their message, while others seek to explore and extend media in different and untried ways. As a medium, virtual reality has been ripe with the possibilities for exploration and discovery.

Through exploration, artists have helped discover new uses for technology, and lead others to see possibilities beyond those originally intended and imagined. Artists are generally free of the preconceptions that constrain the creative application of new technology and are able to let their imagination soar, to show the world a glimpse of what *could* be, rather than focusing on the limitations of the medium. As a result, even for someone not interested in the application of VR as art, there is still much to learn by examining the work in this area.

In general, *art* (as it concerns exploration by artists) helps to drive public perception of a new medium. The pursuit of artistic expression uncovers interesting and sometimes broadly useful ways to interface with and make use of the medium.

This chapter discusses several uses of VR designed as artistic expression. By exploring these applications, many potential applications can be imagined. Virtual reality practitioners are only beginning to realize the potential of the medium for artistic expression, and the applications discussed in this section show a very small glimpse of the power of this medium.

8.1   AREAS OF APPLICATION

As with all the chapters on applications, putting each application into a specific subcategory does not always seem appropriate. This is particularly apparent in a chapter on art, which generally defies categorization. However, it is convenient to divide applications into similar groups for easier reference. This division of groups is not necessarily a mutually exclusive categorization.

Five categories of art applications include: *design and sketching, exploration of the medium, empathetic experiences,* and *exploration of the human condition.* A fifth category, *performance VR,* is not represented by a review of any particular applications in this book.

8.1.1   Design and sketching

The use of VR for *design and sketching* allows one to create works of art while immersed in a virtual reality environment. These works of art may be manifested as purely digital virtual worlds that must be experienced while immersed in VR, or they can be created in VR and then manifested in some other medium. That is, an architectural design may be made while immersed, yet ultimately realized as a physical building or as hardcopy two-dimensional still images. Likewise, sculpture can be created and enjoyed in the digital realm, or be taken to the physical realm by using technologies such as *stereolithography,* or by a *milling machine.*

Note that there is no restriction to creating artworks that are visual in nature. Musical compositions and other sound art may be created in VR. When one considers creating art in VR, one might first think of an immersive, three-dimensional extension of standard computer drawing packages, such as typical desktop draw, paint, and modeling packages. To think this way limits the possibilities that are present in VR for dynamics in the world physics, dynamic point of view, multiperson interactivity and other forms of interactivity, and many more. One example of an art-creation program in VR that, at first blush, resembles desktop drawing tools is NCSA *ShadowLight.*

FIGURE 8-1

ShadowLight, created by Kalev Leetaru at the National Center for Supercomputing Applications, allows architecture students to freely create full-scale architectural designs while immersed in the CAVE environment. ShadowLight offers many tools for editing, texturing, and creating polygons, including those commonly found in traditional two-dimensional drawing packages.

ShadowLight allows participants to create and place arbitrary polygons, paint and texture them, group objects, and use lighting effects, and provides many other drawing tools. However, it also exploits the interactive nature and collaborative nature inherent in VR. *ShadowLight* has been used as a sketching program for a design course in the University of Illinois Architecture Department, where Professor Joy Malnar believed it was important for students to sketch their ideas, at full scale, while immersed in the object they are creating. It was also used by middle school students to create their own virtual worlds in cooperation with a project called VR Savvy.

The Body Language User Interface (BLUI), from the Arctic Region Supercomputing Center, allows participants to create very fluid sculpture while immersed in a *CAVE* or other projection VR device. *BLUI* offers a very intuitive way to create digital sculpture. The resulting sculptures can be experienced in VR, or they can be printed out using three-dimensional prototyping printers to create physical sculptures that can be experienced in the manner to which people are accustomed to interacting with sculpture in the physical realm. *CavePainting* from Brown University allows people to freely brush strokes of virtual paint in a VR environment to create very fluid, three-dimensional virtual worlds. The paintbrushes are the analog of paintbrushes in two-dimensional computer paint programs.

This application is very interesting in its use of props as its sole user interface. That is, you use an actual paintbrush, and an actual paint bucket, etc., and are able to use techniques such as brushing and throwing paint while creating your artwork.

8.1.2 Exploration of the medium

Exploration of the medium might be considered "art for art's sake." It consists of artworks that do something different in order to appraise the end result. For an established medium, it might be those efforts that challenge the more traditional fare.

Many very early VR applications took this approach to the medium. In the mid 1970s, Myron Krueger developed walk-in, computer mediated, interactive environments as part of his *Videoplace* experience. Within *Videoplace* the position and movement of participants resulted in changes of the images projected on the walls of the space [Krueger].

Mark Bolas' *Flatlands* example reflects the expanded scope of VR over the 2D plane. In his application, the viewer is positioned in a small cubical room, and can see a representation of Mondrian's painting "Composition with Line" on two of the walls. However, the two representations differ. One places all the lines of the virtual painting in the planar field. The other representation relocates some of the lines farther away from the viewer than others. The more the viewer moves from the center of the small room, the more they can see the three dimensionality of the second representation.

Example VR applications that fall mostly in the realm of media exploration are *Placeholder,* created by a team by Brenda Laurel (*Placeholder* is discussed in Appendix D of *Understanding Virtual Reality*) as well as Charlotte Davies' *Osmose*. A primary focus of each application was to use technology to give participants new (context-appropriate) ways to travel through the virtual spaces. Each application also pushed the method of how those spaces would be seen and heard.

8.1.3   Empathetic experiences

Empathetic experiences are those that use the medium to put the participant "in someone else's shoes." Empathetic experiences are commonly presented in novels and motion pictures in which the narrative focuses on a particular protagonist throughout the story. By following the progression of one character, the reader/viewer is guided to strongly identify with the character, and the experiences they are going through.

The narrative of Rita Addison's *Detour: Brain Deconstruction Ahead* is not as imposing as most novels and motion pictures, but the ability to empathize with the artist's own personal life experience is very strong. As we share in Rita's experience, so do we share in the experiences of a great number of others who have undergone similar traumatic events, some of whom we may know well, but had previously not been able to understand how their perception of the world has been altered.

8.1.4   Exploration of the human condition

Subjects such as *exploration of the human condition* include those works that focus on how we as humans relate to one another. These works can help us explore relationships with both our contemporary terrestrial cohabitants, and those that have gone before.

Two examples of such virtual reality experiences are Cirincione et al. *The Imperial Message*, and Benjamin Britton's *VR Caves of Lascaux* experience. In *The Imperial Message*[1] the participant is put in the situation of progressing from the world of the individual, to the world of the emperor. Along the way they confront many of the conflicts between the state, and the individual [Cirincionc]. In *The VR Cave of Lascaux* experience, the participant explores a 3D representation of a real space, but at the same time is made aware that the caves are a place shared by an ancient community, a recent community, the modern world, and even those whom have come to share the VR experience together.

8.1.5   Other and future usage of VR in art

Not all artworks regarding virtual reality are implemented in virtual reality. Some artists choose to express their ideas about the possibilities of VR through other media. This literary study and cultural criticism regarding the positive and negative aspects of VR might be in the form of novels (*Snow Crash, The Hacker and the Ants*), rock-operas (*Psychoderelict* and *Lifehouse*), motion pictures (*Lawnmower Man, Disclosure,* and *Minority Report*), or any number of other media. All are valid forms of expression, but due to the difference between the medium for discussion and the medium under discussion, it can be hard to accurately convey the issues. VR is an "experiential medium" and requires intimate familiarity to fully comprehend.

---

[1] Not expounded on in this book.

Other artists breech this gap by presenting virtual reality as part of a performance. VR in performance art rides the edge between personal immersion, and detached media study. The audience doesn't experience the physical immersion; the performer does, and the audiences watch their immersive experience. Here the audience gets a better idea of how the virtual environment works, but without the need to don the equipment or learn how to control the environment themselves. The restriction of keeping the audience outside the proscenium prevents them from experiencing the world first hand.

Typically, performance VR uses a large-screen projection to show the virtual world to the audience, along with a view of the immersed participant. The immersed participant themselves may be viewing the world from the same projected image, or may have their own view, such as via an HMD. Two examples of how VR has been used in a performance include Jaron Lanier's musical world VR performance performed at SIGGRAPH 92, and "Machine Child" produced/performed by Robin Bargar and Insook Choi at the Cyberfest[2] Gala event.

Lanier's world consisted of an abstract environment in which participant/performer travel and world events were controlled via a midi musical instrument interface. Thus as the performer (Lanier) played the virtual wind instrument, the world responded. Held during SIGGRAPH's annual Electronic Theater, Lanier sat before the audience, wearing a head-mounted display, and the audience could see his view on the large theatre screen. "Machine Child" was based on a projection-VR system (the *CAVE* library), allowing both the audience and participant/performer (Choi) to see the same image. The aural/visual world still only responded to Choi's movements and input controls. "Machine Child" is also interesting in that in keeping with the Cyberfest theme it was a VR experience to explore the world of another medium(s): the world of *2001: A Space Odyssey*. Input focused on different modal controls for the different segments of the narrative: hand gesture, footsteps, and handheld prop.

The advent of the digital computer has enabled artists to explore interactive experiences as an art form. Many of the same artists who showed a previous interest in interactive art who began exploring early digital (programmable) media have now embraced this new medium enabling them to immerse themselves and their audience within another experience. This gives rise to the notion of *experiential computing*. This phrase is particularly meaningful to virtual reality practitioners developing experiences for artistic goals, in addition to trainers and therapists who rely on a realistic experience to have a valid application.

As a developing medium, virtual reality holds great promise for artists looking to pursue their ideas in a medium that provides a means of narrative flexibility and yet can relate an experience into the mind of the participant. As the cost of VR displays has gone down and the ease of creating 3D virtual worlds has gone up, virtual reality has become a much more widely available medium. New venues in public spaces are providing the opportunity to put works of VR art on display.

---

[2]Birthday party for HAL at the University of Illinois Urbana Champaign campus.

The Ars Electronica museum for electronic art in Lynz, Austria, was one of the first institutions to establish a *CAVE*-projection VR display as a permanent fixture for VR presentations. The *CAVE* is one among many digitally based installations in this museum. By providing such a VR display in a public venue, Ars Electronica provides a conduit for artists working in VR to display their work to a wider public. Each year the museum has hosted a festival including a symposium for the discussion of digital art: the "Ars Electronica Festival of Art, Technology, and Society."

The future of VR art will also see further development in "new classes" of art. For instance, storytelling, which has mostly taken the form of a one-to-many relationship between storyteller and audience, has now become more of a one-to-one relationship, with greater influence of the audience (i.e., participant) on the events of the narrative. "Interactive storytelling" has been a part of the storytelling tradition since the beginning, but with digital media, it has been expanded into the realm of "personalized storytelling." The first digital example of this is the famous *Adventure* by Crowther and Woods, in which the participant makes their way through Colossal Cave, with the story seemingly created as they interact with the world (via a text interface).

Now referred to as *interactive fiction* (see Chapter 9), these "text adventures" were very popular during the early period of personal computers. The advent of faster graphics and CD-ROMs has paved the way for fancier interactive storytelling environments, but not always richer stories. The cost of producing graphics for such stories can be very expensive, often imposing limits on the story that the text-based medium does not suffer. Full real-time rendering of 3D scenes and characters will hopefully yield a return to richer, more engaging stories, now as an extension on the tradition of interactive fiction. In fact, the *"NICE"* VR experience (see Appendix A in *Understanding Virtual Reality*) attempted to integrate aspects of interactive fiction into the application, and it is likely that more attempts will be made to include much that has been learned about interactive storytelling by the authors of text-based interactive fiction.

CASE STUDY 8.1: OSMOSE

The *Osmose* virtual reality experience is the result of Char Davies and her team setting out to explore the use of VR as an artistically expressive medium. Davies, a painter who joined Softimage in 1987 as a founding director and vice president of visual research, has a long history of using computer graphics as a means of artistic expression. Consequently, her interests have included developing new mechanisms for expression beyond those provided by conventional three-dimensional computer graphics tools.

A common thread ties Davies' interest in painting, computer graphics, and virtual reality. She desires to portray "space as a luminous, enveloping medium" [Davies and Harrison]. The *Osmose* project was a logical step in her progression from static media to interactive and immersive experiences.

From the outset, *Osmose* was meant to provide participants (or "immersants," as Davies calls them) an experience of solitude. Unlike experiences that pit one participant against another, Davies strove to provide an environment that would allow participants to commune with themselves, to explore their inner self, questioning their everyday assumptions about being in the world.

FIGURE 8-2
The worlds in Osmose have a soft feel. This image depicts the clearing world.
Image courtesy Char Davies and Softimage

Application Description

Unlike many other VR experiences, the goal of *Osmose* is not to accurately document or photorealistically portray particular aspects of the natural world. Rather, it is to convey a sense of the ethereal or a sense of being sentient and embodied in a living flowing world. The overall sensibility of the *Osmose* experience was designed to support this goal. The visual aesthetic of *Osmose* is much softer than the gaudy, chunky, cartoon-like imagery of computer games. The style for *Osmose* was derived from Davies's prior work as a painter. Renderings of Davies early work (1990–1993) with 3D computer graphics to create this effect often took as much as 40 hours for a single still image. This frame rate is clearly unacceptable for an interactive real-time application. Rather than achieving acceptable frame rates by reducing image complexity, Davies and her team looked for creative solutions to achieve acceptable rendering speeds, and at the same time presenting imagery that supported the effects and sensibility they were trying to evoke.

The rendering techniques implemented by the *Osmose* team produced objects with varying degrees of realism. Most objects, even the most recognizable ones, still had an element of abstractness associated with them. To achieve this visual ambiguity, some objects were texture mapped with semi-transparent textures. Such use of transparency and "deliberate misuse of the Z-buffer" by the developers resulted in an ambiguity of spatiality and meaning not often found in computer rendered imagery [Davies and Harrison 1996]. Colors were also carefully modified to support the artist's goal of ambiguity, as well as the desired emotional sensibility of the work.

Some of the visual elements in the application were achieved with particle systems. Paths for particles were determined a priori to achieve the appearance of flows such as streams and insect swarms. For the participant, the culmination of employing all these techniques is the sensation of being embodied yet disembodied while totally enveloped by virtual three-dimensional space.

Rather than using more traditional VR travel interface techniques (such as point-to-fly), *Osmose* required a mechanism for travel that supported the underlying artistic gestalt of the work. Davies' approach to interface design has been informed by scuba diving in oceanic space. Scuba divers control their buoyancy partially through their breathing. The amount of air in the body determines whether they will sink, float, or achieve neutral buoyancy and enable them to hover, perhaps drifting with the current. *Osmose* borrows these ideas, and uses a scubalike travel interface to allow the participant to move among the virtual worlds of the work. In *Osmose*, worlds are located above and below each other, much like the worlds at varying depths in the ocean. In *Osmose*, however, there are subtle boundaries between the worlds, and as such participants may find themselves ascending the sky in one world, and emerging from the ground into the next, or hovering in very ambiguous overlapping boundary zones.

Unlike the more common goal-oriented virtual reality experiences such as mission games, *Osmose* provides a place for inner reflection and questioning. Rather than racing against the clock to beat one's opponent or to see how many objects they can collect or demolish, *Osmose* is meant as a calming transcendental space in which the participant paradoxically feels disembodied and embodied at the same time. Not wishing to objectify the body, there is no avatar representation.

One thing that is noticed when suiting up for the *Osmose* experience is the lack of some of the traditional VR paraphernalia, such as gloves, wands, and other handheld interface devices. The designers of *Osmose* opted to discard

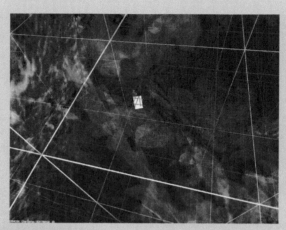

FIGURE 8-3

These images show the "subterranean forest" and the "life world." The grid is the first world that participants encounter and exists solely to allow them to learn to travel through the space by controlling their breathing.
Images courtesy of Char Davies and Softimage

these interface options because they felt that the world was something for the user to control. The interface vest, which tracks breath and balance, is all the control that is provided.

While vertical movement is controlled through breath, horizontal movement control is performed by tracking the orientation of the user's spine. This allows the user to indicate their desired direction by leaning. The participant's virtual "buoyancy" was measured by tracking the expansion and contraction of their chest. In addition to reducing the participant's feeling of "driving" the world, the technology required to implement the experience is reduced by not tracking the participant's hands or any handheld devices.

The *Osmose* experience also parallels a scuba experience in the manner in which the participant prepares to enter the foreign world. Preparations to enter the undersea world involve donning a mask and buoyancy compensator vest. To enter the *Osmose* world, a participant wears a mask (an HMD) and a vest (to measure their virtual buoyancy by tracking chest expansion and contraction). Hence, by wearing appropriate technology in either case, the participant is able enter worlds that are otherwise inaccessible.

Osmose consists of a dozen worlds based on archetypal elements of nature [Davies 1995]. Many of the worlds are reminiscent of natural elements such as trees, leaves, streams, and so on. The first world users encounter is an area in which they can practice the techniques required for traveling in *Osmose*. The practice world consists solely of a three-dimensional Cartesian grid. After practicing navigation, the user encounters worlds that include a central clearing with a tree, a forest, the interior of a leaf, subterranean earth, a pond, an oceanic abyss, clouds, and others. There is also a substratum "code world" that displays the computer code written for the *Osmose* experience. Another area, the superstratum, consists of a "text world" that displays various quotes and poetry related to technology, the body, and nature. Finally, there is a "life world" that is used to bring closure to the experience. Symbolically representing all the other *Osmose* worlds, and all of nature—indeed, life itself—the "life world" appears as a luminous sphere of flecks that fades in all around the user, until finally the world recedes and participants find themselves alone in an empty black space with only a few drifting specs of light, thus indicating that the experience has ended.

Sound is an important component of the *Osmose* experience. In order to attain an organic human nature to the presentation, base samples were taken from a male and a female voice. The samples were then processed to achieve the desired effects. Because they were built on a base of actual voices, the sounds maintained a subliminal connection with the human body presence, a key theme of the work. Some of the sounds in *Osmose* were associated with objects in the environment. Other sounds provided a more ambient quality. Some sounds were dependent on the behavior of the participant. Spatialization techniques were used to aid in the illusion that particular sounds were emanating from the appropriate location. Each world had its own sounds and a haunting melody was introduced in some. Such use of sound not only contributed greatly to the sense of immersion but also amplified the emotional tone of the work. Besides adding to the sense of immersion, the melodies also acted as a wayfinding aid by helping the participant be aware of their general location at any given time.

Thousands of participants have been individually immersed in *Osmose* since its debut. *Osmose* has been displayed in a variety of public venues such as art museums in Canada, the United States, Great Britain, and Mexico. Each participant is allowed 15 minutes in the experience, which was found to be sufficient to allow the participants to learn to navigate, gain familiarity with the worlds, and "let themselves go" until the appearance of the "life world" signals their time is up.

Approximately three people per hour were able to be immersed in the *Osmose* experience. This included the 15-minute experience as well as about 5 minutes to suit up and to remove the VR devices. With only one system available at each exhibition, reservations were taken to help organize the flow of participants. In the event that a person did not show up for their appointed time, an onlooker is selected to take their place.

Because the focus of *Osmose* is to allow people to look within themselves, devices such as projection displays were less appropriate than occlusive HMDs. The HMD effectively shut out the real world, and offered a 100% field-of-regard aiding in the impression that the participant was fully enveloped. Much like visiting the world of the sea necessitates the use of scuba gear, donning a head-mounted display was deemed to be a small inconvenience to bear to enable one to access a new and interesting space. The downside of the HMD was that only one participant at a time was fully able to experience immersion in the work.

To enable more people to get some sense of the experience, Davies added a large stereoscopic projected screen display that could be viewed by audience members wearing low-cost polarized glasses to enable them to see the three dimensionality of the world. To get a good sense of the experience, the large audience needed to see the relationship between the participant's body movement and the images shown on the big screen. The need for the privacy of the participant required that they were in a separate room where they were alone with an attendant. To balance these two needs, a silhouette view of the participant in the experience chamber was displayed to the full audience. The silhouette was projected on a translucent screen in the installation space along with the rendered world.

VR System

The computing hardware for the *Osmose* experience included a Silicon Graphics Onyx system. For full installations, the Onyx system used three graphics pipes to provide the imagery to the participant and the larger audience. One of the pipes provided the audience view, while each of the other pipes provided a single eye view in the HMD. This

FIGURE 8-4

To experience Osmose, the participant dons a head-mounted display. The view the participant sees is also displayed on a large screen for others to view. In order to allow the audience to understand the relationship between the immersed participant and the world they are viewing, yet maintain the privacy of the participant, the audience sees a silhouette of the person wearing the head-mounted display and the tracked vest.

Images courtesy of Char Davies and Softimage Inc.

division of resources generally provided the immersed participant a better frame rate than the theatre audience. The frame rate for the participant was about 20 to 30 fps, while the large audience only saw 10 to 15 frames per second.

A variety of software was used to create and run the *Osmose* application, including *Softimage|3D,* and Softimage's *SAAPHIRE* and *DKit* development libraries. Additionally, the team utilized the SGI *Performer* and *GL* graphics libraries. Once the initial framework was established, events within *Osmose* were re-evaluated and rewritten in situ. The creative process thus was the result of "planning and serendipity" similar to how, in painting, previous strokes of pigment can influence what comes next [Davies].

The head-mounted display was a Division dVisor. They selected this model because it had a wide field of view (about 105 horizontal degrees). The developers felt FOV was more important in this application than resolution (345 × 259 pixels). The participant's spine (in two places) and head were tracked with the Polhemus FasTrak™ electromagnetic tracking system. The scubalike tracking vest

was custom built, and measured the expansion and contraction of the user's chest cavity.

A variety of commercial sound products provided the sonic environment for *Osmose.* The Onyx communicated over a serial connection with a Macintosh computer to control two Kurzweil K2000 samplers via the MIDI protocol. Additionally, the experience utilized an Ensoniq DP/4+ processor to provide reverberation effects. The sounds were spatialized using a Crystal Rivers Engineering Acoustetron™.

Conclusion

People who experienced *Osmose* tended to have a very strong response to it. Many wanted to continue longer and felt a sense of loss when the experience came to a close. Some participants, typically very young males, criticized *Osmose* for being paced too slow, with too little to do. Some complained that there was nothing to kill. This is likely a phenomenon due to their expectation that VR games are meant to be high-speed, high-adrenaline, violent games. *Osmose* gives a look at a different, very creative use of VR as an artistic medium.

Follow-up interviews with participants who had the opportunity to try *Osmose* both as the immersed participant in the HMD, and as an audience member viewing the large-screen display revealed that the majority preferred the more immersive HMD display. However, the sense of presence of the large screen was quite strong, and was preferred by some participants. In fact, the sense of presence from the projected image was strong enough that the shift in perspective caused by sudden movements of the "immersant" could cause people watching the image to stumble as they stood. The application authors noticed this was more common at the New York installation, where they used a large projection system in a small space.

Osmose was produced by Softimage during 1994–1995. The initial groundwork and testing took a full year to accomplish. World building and other aspects of the immersive component took over 6 months. Since the completion of *Osmose*, Davies and her team have also constructed a follow-on VR work, called *Éphémère*, which premiered at the National Gallery of Canada in June 1998.

The aesthetic, direction and vision of *Osmose* were provided by Char Davies. Georges Mauro made the models, textures, and animations using *Softimage|3D*. John Harrison provided the custom virtual reality software for *Osmose*, and the sounds were designed, composed and situated in the virtual space by Dorota Blaszczak and Rick Bidlack.

For its beauty, gentleness, and ability to help us see the world in a new way, CyberEdge Journal awarded *Osmose* with the 1995 Art and Event CJ award.

Through *Osmose*, Davies has produced an experience that intends to "break down the barrier between mind and body leading to an osmotic interplay between sensations of embodiment (due to use of breath and balance) and disembodiment (due to being able to float)."

In discussing her quest for a medium suitable to her vision, Davies reveals in her paper "Osmose: Notes On 'BEING' In Immersive Virtual Space": "Osmose is evidence that, after more than a decade of searching, I have finally found the medium capable of expressing my artistic vision" [Davies].

CASE STUDY 8.2: DETOUR: BRAIN DECONSTRUCTION AHEAD

Executive Summary

The idea of *Detour: Brain Deconstruction Ahead* is to allow a person to experience some aspect of the world through the eyes of another. In this example, the creator had experienced a car accident in which she experienced brain damage. Although she appeared completely recovered externally, the accident had affected her vision. It was difficult for her to explain to her friends and family what it was like to see through her eyes, so she worked in tandem with a computer programmer to create a virtual reality application that permitted her to tell her story and to enable participants to see the world as she experiences it. The application was developed as a *CAVE* application and makes an especially compelling demonstration of the use of head tracking, because the participant is unable to "look away" from the visual anomalies. The use of virtual reality provided catharsis for the creator who was a professional artistic photographer.

Introduction

Detour: Brain Deconstruction Ahead (Detour: BDA) is a VR experience that attempts to communicate the impact of perceptual anomalies that result from brain trauma. In particular, the application simulates anomalies that affect the optical system. Though classified as an artistic experience, *Detour: BDA* is also useful in the medical field to help demonstrate what a victim of brain trauma might be experiencing.

The creator of the experience, Rita Addison, still recovering from and learning to live with her own brain injury, had a twofold goal for her creation. For her the goal was a means of coping with her own impaired perception and at the same time giving others the ability to "see through her eyes." Addison's hope is that a participant will undergo an "undivided moment" in which they become aware of how differently some people perceive the world. By allowing her

FIGURE 8-5

Detour: Brain Deconstruction Ahead begins with the participant in a virtual art gallery. Here, the participant experiences some of application developer Rita Addison's nature photographs.
Image courtesy of William Sherman

to give others a taste of what she suffers, and sensing that they are able to comprehend a little of what her life is like, she is more able to come to terms with her own situation.

After her automobile accident in 1992 in which she suffered a brain injury, Addison found that is was difficult to explain to her family and friends exactly what she was experiencing. The only people who understood her situation were others who had also suffered brain injuries of one type or another (accident or stroke victims). Even medical personnel had only a cursory feeling for the difficulties endured by those with these types of afflictions. Addison, and those who had suffered similar trauma as her, felt as though they had "lost their voice" to the rest of the world, since they were only able to find empathy and understanding with other head injury and stroke survivors. This experience was Addison's way of finding her "voice" again.

Application Description

Prior to her accident, Addison was an independent photographer, specializing in nature photographs. After her accident, she was no longer able to look through the camera lens, and therefore had lost her ability to make a living in that profession. Thus, she created *Detour: Brain Deconstruction Ahead*. In the first phase of *Detour: BDA*, users finds themselves in a Virtual Art Gallery, in which

some of Addison's photographs are suspended along the sides of an infinitely long corridor. The corridor itself is about 10 feet wide, with a marble floor and columns along the edge separating each image. Users are able to travel down the corridor at their own pace, stopping to look at as many photographs as they like. As they continue to move down the corridor, they will find that there are 20 images, which reappear in a never-ending sequence.

The second phase of the experience is a short (about 70 seconds) scripted path of events that represent her accident. The user begins traveling down a divided highway at night, with headlights and signs flashing past until they experience a crash. They then find themselves entering Addison's brain, watching as the neurons break apart as the voice of a doctor proclaims that "she's going to have problems."

The third and final phase of the experience returns the user to a corridor of images referred to as "The Gallery of Anomalies." It is the same corridor, with the same images, but now it runs perpendicular to the original corridor and includes representations of Addison's personal experience. The participants now finds the information presented to their own senses to be filtered by a variety of visual anomalies.

Two perceptual irregularities overlap on the visual feedback to the participant: a limitation of sight mapped to the gaze of the viewer, and a disabling mutation in shape or color mapped to each photograph. Sight is constrained by a filter over the eyes that follows the head motion like a translucent mask that changes its form. This filter changes over time, transforming from hemianopia (tunnel vision), to central scotomata (peripheral-only vision), to clouded vision, and passing through normal (clear) vision back to tunnel vision. The second anomaly is presented through the images on the wall of the corridor. Each image has a different anomaly associated with it. That anomaly is activated when the user walks toward and away from the suspended photograph. Some of the images warp space as the user moves in and out, others warp the image itself, changing color or bending lines. Ten different effects are presented this way. For example, an image might bow out toward the user from the center, indicating how one's equilibrium might be disrupted via damage to their vestibular system.

FIGURE 8-6

Left: After a press of a button on the CAVE wand, an accident sequence is triggered in which the participant experiences a late-night crash in an automobile. The consequences of the accident will be experienced later in the application.

Right: As the physicians evaluate the accident victim's condition, the participant is able to walk inside of Addison's brain and witness the snapping and exploding of the nerves that took place in the accident.

Images courtesy of William Sherman

FIGURE 8-7

After the accident, the participant is takes to the "Gallery of Anomalies" in which they experience some of the results of traumatic brain injury. In this image, the picture in the gallery of anomalies warps in shape as the participant moves about it.

Image courtesy of William Sherman

Representation of the Virtual World

The virtual world of *Detour: BDA* consists mostly of very simple objects. This simplicity does not belie the power of the experience. Rather than being constructed in a realistic manner, the world uses abstract imagery to convey the powerful message of what it feels like to live in a world with damage to one's perceptual system.

The marble floor and columns look realistic enough. However, the anomalies are abstractly represented through the warping of space, depth, image acuity, and color of the photographs suspended in the air down the infinite corridor. The automobile accident is also fairly abstract; represented by a dashed median line flashing across the floor as shapes (road signs) pass by. After a short while, one sees (and hears) a crash sending shards of glass off in every direction, reflecting Addison's loss of vision. The user is taken into a Cyberware™ model of Addison's head, going into a brain-shaped object with a simple representation of neurons (as axons and dendrites) exploding and moving toward the viewer as 3D lightning streaks.

Aurally, the user is presented with different sound cues based on what stage of the experience they are encountering. On two occasions, the voice of Rita Addison sets the mood for the galleries. At the beginning of the application she proclaims, "A sense of wonder and enchantment flow through my camera's eye." Later, as the user transitions into the "Gallery of the Anomalies," she can be heard exclaiming, "What's wrong with me? I can't see clearly." During the rest of the time in the galleries, an ambient nature sound plays.

In the accident scene the participant hears the rumble of the automobile engine, leading up to the screeching of the tires, and then the crash. The ambient sound changes as they enter the cerebral chamber, and the doctor says, "Yes, I think she's going to have problems."

No other senses (haptic, vestibular, olfactory, etc.) are displayed in this experience. Though Addison may have suffered effects to her perception of these senses too, the required extra hardware to display these effects would be too expensive to be cost-effective. In some cases, vestibular effects can be felt based on the warping of space seen in some parts of the "Gallery of the Anomalies."

Interaction with the Virtual World

Detour: Brain Deconstruction Ahead is primarily in the genre of artistic *empathetic experience* that allows participants to view the world from the particular point of view the artist has (or has had) of the world. Interaction is done via the form of a highly constrained walkthrough interface.

More than many other VR experiences, *Detour: BDA* presents itself as a story, with scenes depicting different stages of the narrative. Each scene is demarcated by the visuals and audio displayed to the participant, and signifies a different stage in the story of Rita Addison's own experience as an artist whose ability to work in her medium of choice (photography) ended abruptly with an automobile accident.

Though not explicitly stated, the VR application itself is the next chapter in the narrative. We observe, first hand, where Addison's experience has brought her. It led her to the exploration of a new medium (VR), and her use of virtual reality to communicate her perceptual anomalies.

As mentioned earlier, this experience is a highly constrained walkthrough. In fact, most of the navigation comes in the form of physical movement by the user. During the gallery scenes, the user can move only in the direction of the corridor, pointing (with a wand device) to control the speed. When pointing directly toward the wall of a corridor, the world remains stationary.

The accident sequence is begun with a button press. This is usually done by someone who is running the exhibition, allowing them to gauge when the participant (or group) has exhausted their interest in the normal gallery. After the accident sequence, the participant is automatically placed in the "Gallery of the Anomalies."

The primary objects that the participant can interact with are the photographs in the "Gallery of the Anomalies." The photographs, suspended in the gallery, deviate in form and color as the user approaches and retreats from them. The shifting in the pictures and geometry represent various neural anomalies experienced by Addison. Anomalies represent such disorders as retinal detachment, hemianopia, scotoma, subdural hematoma, and vertebral artery insufficiency that are brought about by brain injury or stroke.

Computer-mediated interaction with other users or agents is not a part of this experience. The voices of the artist and doctor might be considered a form of agent interaction because they do play a role in the narration of the experience, but there is not any interaction with them.

Detour: BDA is typically displayed on projection VR systems, which allow many people to simultaneously share the view of the experience. Interaction among all the viewers present is generally very high. Most participants in this experience are impacted by the experience, and generally immediately begin sharing their feelings with the others in the group.

The world physics of *Detour: BDA* are fairly minimal. Objects are all fixed in place. No collision detection or other interactions between the user and the objects take place, other than the photograph distortions that take place as the user walks about, as described above.

DESIGN CHOICE

Rather than subject the participants to complicated interface techniques, the designers focused on communicating an emotional message.

It could be argued that a goal of this experience is a type of *perceptually correct* representation of the world as experienced by brain trauma victims. Though perhaps it could be better explained as being *emotionally correct*, in that it attempts to demonstrate how such sufferers feel as they manage to make their way through the day.

Venue

The original venue the experience *Detour: Brain Deconstruction Ahead* was presented at was the VROOM exhibit at the SIGGRAPH '94 computer graphics conference in Orlando, Florida. This venue, which was organized by the Electronic Visualization Lab at the University of Illinois at Chicago, presented conference attendees the opportunity to see a wide variety of virtual reality applications, ranging from science to art. VROOM had a throughput for each application of five participants sharing a *CAVE* for 5 minutes. Others were allowed to watch in the background.

Ideally, a group of up to eight people can fully experience Addison's work in about 10 to 15 minutes.

Since its introduction, *Detour: BDA* has played in many other venues, including Imagina '95 in Monte Carlo, as well as research institutions investigating the use of virtual reality, such as NCSA and EVL.

Addison has also made presentations of and about *Detour: BDA* in other media. Specifically, she presented it in the form of an acceptance speech for winning "Best VR Art experience award for 1994" at the VRAIS '95 CJ awards (CyberEdge Journal) ceremony. Also, Marcus Thiebaux, the programmer of the experience, has created a videotape presentation of *Detour: BDA*, enabling more people to have at least a sample of what the VR experience is like.

The application itself has no mechanisms for enforcing the throughput of the participants. The initial gallery does not take long to explore, and the transition segment runs through a preordained sequence of events, but the length of time to explore the "Gallery of the Anomalies" is indeterminate. Users may wish to explore each of the anomalies in depth, or may rush through the different effects. There is also a significant difference between experiencing the "Gallery of the Anomalies" with full head tracking versus a secondary participant, so *CAVE* visitors will often choose to take turns giving each person an opportunity to empathize with the artist.

VR System

The VR system that *Detour: BDA* runs in is the *CAVE*, a projection visual display environment using Silicon Graphics computers. No input devices other than the standard *CAVE* wand were used to interface with the experience. On occasion, for some venues, a smaller Silicon Graphics computer was used to present a one-screen version of the experience.

Due to her condition, Rita had a difficult time using displays such as an HMD. Therefore, choosing a projection-based display such as the *CAVE* was really the only logical choice. Another choice would limit the ability of the artist herself of being able to experience her own application, which would severely limit not only its cathartic effect on her, but also her capacity of evaluating the work, and sharing it with other participants. While *Detour* has also been exhibited on single screen displays, the surround screens of the *CAVE* are an important element in fully experiencing some aspects of the experience, particularly the tunnel and peripheral-only vision.

Overall, in the opinion of the principal author of the experience, the *CAVE* is the optimal display for *Detour*. Rita considers it to provide "a sense of immersion unequaled by any single-screen display or head-mounted device."

The programming for *Detour: BDA* was done using the *IrisGL* graphics library on Silicon Graphics computers, combined with the *EVL CAVE* library. The NCSA sound server and library was also used to provide the playback of the voices and ambient sounds heard throughout the experience.

Application Implementation

Development of *Detour: BDA* took place over the 4-month period prior to its debut at the VROOM venue of SIGGRAPH '94. Programming was done almost entirely by Marcus Thiebaux, art student and programmer at the Electronic Visualization Lab at the University of Illinois-Chicago. Marcus was also working concurrently on the *Virtual Director* (Chapter 9) VR application.

The application was developed as a one-time artwork that, once complete, could continue to be experienced by many, but would not continue to be developed further. Development was led by artist Rita Addison, who worked closely with Marcus to shape the final outcome.

Funding and support was provided by Colonel Richard Satava at DARPA, who envisions many useful applications of virtual reality to the medical field, including, in this case, the ability for the experiences of brain trauma victims to be communicated to family (and doctors). Additional support was also given by the staff and students of EVL, in the way of equipment usage and some programming aid.

Given only 4 months to develop the experience, the choice of designing a simplified world was almost dictated. All of the segments are presented in a stylized manner: the infinite galleries of photographs and the automobile journey down a simple road culminating in the destruction of a work of Rita's art.

The developers chose to use a gallery of Rita's work in her former art form as the focal point about which the experience turns. At the outset, with normal perception the user moves forward down the hall as the undisturbed pictures come into view and pass. Later, everything is turned 90 degrees, forcing the participant to move sideways down the hall, perhaps representing the difficulty by which a brain injury sufferer goes through life.

Conclusion

Though no experimental analysis was done, there are many anecdotal accounts regarding the experience. Of particular interest are those from the family and friends of people who have suffered similar effects to those portrayed. The consensus is that they have been given a rare glimpse of insight inside their loved ones' trauma, and a better understanding of the person.

One of the big accomplishments of this application was its demonstration of how VR can be used to enable one person to experience the world of another. Even for those who do not personally know someone who suffers from brain trauma, *Detour: Brain Deconstruction Ahead* is often singled out as a moving VR application.

It was also singled out by the Cyberedge Journal in 1995, when it announced their annual award for best application of VR of 1994 in the Arts and Events category:

> *For creating a work of beauty, intensity, and long-lasting value, we are proud to have presented Rita Addison with the first CJ for Arts and Events! [CyberEdge Journal—Virtual Reality Products]*

The goal of allowing others to experience Rita's perception of the world has definitely been attained.

Because virtual reality deals with modifying the environmental information provided to the senses, it is an excellent medium for experiences such as Addison's to demonstrate an altered perception of the world. Many of the effects suffered can only be properly experienced in a medium that tracks the movement of the viewers head and body.

The anomalies associated with the gaze direction of the tracked participant, such as tunnel vision, peripheral vision, and others, are particularly effective for the viewer who's gaze controls where the blind spot will be. For the other viewers, who can move their heads to see around the blind spot, the effect is much less immersive. The anomalies that are affected by user movement in the space are much more easily understood by the nontracked participants (assuming the "driver" does indeed move around, triggering the effects).

FIGURE 8-8
Addison's VR application Synesthaesia *represented sense information as different forms.*

The major discoveries made by Addison were the power of VR to allow participants to free themselves from daily concerns, and in many instances, strongly impact the emotions of the participants. At the first public showing of *Detour: Brain Deconstruction Ahead*, Rita felt the emotions rise in the people around her. She knew that she had succeeded in what she had set out do accomplish.

Next up for Addison was her project *Synesthesia*, which is more in the VR art genre of *exploring the medium*, though it continues to have elements relating to how people with a disorder (Synesthesia) experience the real world. Sufferers of this disorder perceive information across senses; for example, music is seen, tastes are experienced as geometrical forms, etc.

Finally, perhaps the biggest accomplishment of the *Detour: Brain Destruction Ahead* VR experience is its role as a cathartic agent for Rita Addison. In her article in the journal *Computer Graphics and Applications*, she says:

> *Detour became a vehicle of profound catharsis for me. It helped me accept and adapt to chronic impairments and fight my way through depression.*

CASE STUDY 8.3: THE VR CAVE OF LASCAUX EXPERIENCE

Executive Summary

The VR Cave of Lascaux is an interesting combination of science and art. The application is an artistic recreation of the cave of Lascaux, but while many aspects of the experience are scientifically accurate, the goal is not scientific realism but rather a way to experience the magic of the cave. The application is typically experienced in a head-mounted display, and navigated with a six-degrees-of-freedom input device. This experience was developed as a labor of love and represents the collective efforts of the artist and many volunteers. A number of magical elements are present in the experience, such as the cave paintings that "come alive" with animation when the participant gazes intently on them.

Introduction

The cave of Lascaux is a treasured monument to a past culture. Just as importantly, however, it represents how humans relate to one another. Led by his own fear of the future, the potential damage the human animal could cause to its world, and the world of other creatures, artist Benjamin Britton looked to another time for clues to the human condition. He looked to the Ice Age, which was a time in which human culture had been decimated. His research brought him to a shrine of an ancient culture, a cave with historical as well as magical significance brought out by the paintings of a past culture. Britton decided to create an electronic version of the cave of Lascaux. The focus would be to highlight the communal aspects of the cave, and bring forth the opportunity for museum goers to participate in a modern day communal event with the cave as the basis. Out of this work came the *LASCAUX* experience.

The cave itself was lost shortly after the last ice age, and rediscovered in 1941. After the Second World War, it was opened to the public. The tremendous traffic of people who came to experience the cave caused it to deteriorate from the resulting increase in moisture and bacteria brought into the cave. To solve this problem, a replica of the cave was constructed nearby. However, even the replica had to be closed due to the ill effects of human traffic. Now, only a select group of people (mostly serious researchers with a compelling need) are allowed access to the cave.

The Ministry of Culture of France considers the cave a rare cultural treasure, and they do not wish to see the cave lose its spirit and message through commercialization. However, they were interested in Britton's work in digitally capturing the essence of the cave, because it respects the cave near Lascaux, and the Ministry has supported his work through the provision of information about the cave. With their help, Britton and his collaborators created a virtual reality experience of the Cave of Lascaux.

This experience was created as a work of art intended for a contemporary art audience. While at first blush it appears to be done as a historic travel application, the artist is quick to point out that scientific and historical accuracy was not a primary goal. Hence, this piece is an artwork, intended to communicate not just about the physical cave but, indeed, the nature of humankind. It is for audiences to

FIGURE 8-9

Texture maps are used to create the visual look of the VR Cave of Lascaux. This is a view in the center of the Fresco in the Hall of Bulls.

learn about today's world, how it relates to the past, and how it might relate to the future.

The physical cave that inspired this piece serves as a record of the populations that inhabited the area through time. Each culture has altered the cave, and the cave has altered each culture, including 20th-century man. Recent marks to the cave include the addition of electricity to some areas of the cave, as well as the deterioration of its content by the masses who wished to experience the cave first hand, and later (in the 1950's) by the vault-like door added to the exterior to control access.[3]

The design of the door itself became controversial because it was designed in a Mycenaean style of construction, and critics were concerned that future archaeologists would therefore think that the cave's door had been built during the Bronze Age.

The cave of Lascaux was chosen as the setting for Britton's VR experience because of its nature as a special place for those who have experienced it. From the outset, a goal was to maintain a sense of the cave's mystique. Thus, even the

_____

[3] In fact, before the cave was closed, the local population held occasional parties and other personal gatherings in the cave.

FIGURE 8-10
The exterior of the cave was modeled at a lower level of verisimilitude than the interior. Here one can see the entrance to the cave.

FIGURE 8-11
A view of the stylized representation of Montignac, France. From here, one can fly in "Peter Pan" mode, and explore the "Cosmos" if they desire.

VR experience is available only in certain limited venues. Britton believed that the venue and social interactions of the participants make an immense contribution to how the work is perceived. People will come because of a general interest in the history of mankind, the meaning of human existence, represented by the cave. Donning the HMD to see the cave is only a part of the participant's experience. The procedure of dressing up to visit a museum, queuing at the entryway, rubbing shoulders with neighbors, and even the effort of driving to the museum and parking contribute to a person's overall experience with the application, and the human community.

Now that the real cave is closed to most people, this is also the best way for people to have a taste of what walking through the real cave is like. At the same time, it potentially reduces the travel time and expense from that of a trip to southern France, to that of a trip to a nearby museum, although Britton states that a trip to the Dordogne region around Montignac and the real cave is well worthwhile.

Application Description

The *LASCAUX* experience replicates, in a virtual world, many of the features of an existing location on the earth. The fragility of the site means that only a few people are allowed access to that location. Yet, natural curiosity regarding the

peoples of the past created a need for an alternate way to explore this site.

The virtual world consists primarily of an interior model of the actual cave, including walls that are texture mapped with images of the actual cave walls. Outside the cave the participant can explore a small region of the surrounding French landscape (including a stylized view of the nearby village of Montignac) and the "Cosmos." The "Cosmos" refers to the world beyond the perceivable, the universe. If the viewer chooses to explore not the cave but the valley surrounding the cave, they can fly "like Peter Pan." If they fly up and into the sky, then they can fly *through* the sky and into a sort of outer space environment from where they can see the valley far below them, and the whole virtual world. This interpretation of the "Cosmos" was inspired by a 14th-century woodcut of a shepherd who climbed to the top of a mountain in order to pierce through the sphere of the heavens and witness the working of the "kosmos."

Representation of the Virtual World

Because *LASCAUX* is a work of art, a conflict of interpretation versus verisimilitude arises. How much of the work represents what the artist wants to convey, and how much is an attempt at a realistic rendering of the object of study? *LASCAUX* is a representation of an actual entity, yet the reconstruction will have impressions left by its creator. In Britton's words: "It will have a veil." His goal was to strive for the highest verisimilitude attainable, making the veil as light and transparent as he could.

With realism as a general representational goal, a survey of the shape of the cave interior along with many high-resolution photographs were used to create the virtual cave. The French government allowed Britton to make use of government data and photos for his project, thus re-enabling people to experience a likeness of the cave.

Not all aspects of the VR experience were designed to be realistic. The re-created cave also has some magical qualities. The participant might trigger an event relating the pictures on the walls. For example, a video representing more recent human history can be triggered by certain circumstances in the cave. Or perhaps, the user might notice subtle changes in the cave; finding new items in a previously visited, formerly empty, area.

Internally, the world is stored as a polygonal description of the cave surfaces plus thousands of detailed texture maps, covering nearly the entire cave. The video events are stored as full-motion video files that are loaded into the system at appropriate times.

The resultant experience is a visually engaging world, with the same shape, passages, and wall paintings as the real thing. Taking advantage of high-resolution imagery scanned from the walls of the actual cave, combined with accurate information about the physical shape of the cave, the interior of the cave is very visually realistic. The exterior of the cave is more of a stylized representation, with an icon view of Montignac nestled in the hills of the Dordogne region. During some sequences of the experience, captured video replace the center of the viewer's vision, showing related images from a more recent era.

Although the experience is decidedly visually focused, there are some audio elements as well. Most of the sounds heard by the immersed participant are long ambient soundtracks mixed together partially based on their location in the virtual world. The ambient sounds include a Chinese flute song titled "Autumn," and several sounds recorded in Kentucky's Mammoth Cave. A flute sound is heard when the listener is outside the cave, and inside, a mixture of various sounds

clips of Mammoth Cave are heard. A few other sounds such as door squeaks and bursts of wind are immediately played to correspond with appropriate events.

Because the ambient sounds were long, immediate response to movement throughout the cave was not practical. Instead, sounds were faded in and out and mixed together as the listener moved through the space. This produced an effect that Britton considers to be a *mise en scene* produced by serendipity as the program selects different sound clips.

For various reasons, including expense, no haptic or other sensory feedback is part of the *LASCAUX* experience.

Interaction with the Virtual World

We have classified the *LASCAUX* experience as part of the genre in which the *human condition can be explored* through virtual reality, although it also contains elements of other genres, such as the historical or travel walkabout.

The basic form of interaction between a participant and the experience is traveling through the space using a typical *desktop 6-DOF input device*. The *walkthrough* form of travel was chosen because of how closely it resembles the physical experience of visiting the actual cave. By putting pressure on the input device, the virtual world responds by moving the user to a new location in the world.

With exploration of the locale as the primary function of the experience, the narrative was loose. As the user travels through the cave, they can stop and ponder various paintings or other features they may come upon. Occasionally, pondering a particular image on the wall (i.e., staring at it) will cause the image to transform to a moving image. Watching the moving image might conjure up thoughts on the relationship between the world they are currently experiencing with a different time and place. As the video plays, the travel controls are disabled.

As the user travels outside the cave, they see a stylized representation of the nearby village of Montignac, France. From there, they can fly to the "Cosmos" for an over-arching view of the world.

Navigating through the world is quite simple. The participant controls travel using a standard desktop 6-DOF device such as a Spaceball™ or a Magellan™ (aka Spacemouse™). Inside the cave, the user is constrained to move only at a

FIGURE 8-12

Some imagery is associated with magical events. For example, staring at these Bison triggers the play of a video clip in the cave.

FIGURE 8-13

Although the experience in the cave is one of solitude, certain actions remind one that they are not alone in the world. This image shows a table and chairs set up in the main hall. These objects were not there when the participant first visited the hall. They appear only on subsequent visits.

fixed distance above the floor. Pressure on the device in any direction moves the user in that direction. Buttons on the device are also available to cause a jump to a predefined specific location, or to give a predefined guided tour through the cave. However, since the buttons were not visible when wearing the HMD, they would typically be used by a guide staffing the exhibit.

There are no agents per se in the application, although one might get the feeling another entity is a part of the world when they return to the main hall to find a table and chairs set up for a dinner party. Also, the "hot paintings" sense when a viewer is concentrating on them, and spring to life with a video animation have an agent sort of aspect to them.

Events such as the "sudden" appearance of a mysterious table are what Britton refers to as "dormant events." These events are only activated once the participant has visited certain locations, setting off a tripwire. The tripwire can be triggered by very specific circumstances: the time a viewer spends in a certain space, for example, or even standing in specific locations or looking in certain directions.

Because it is designed to foster a communal experience, one might think it is desirous to enable multiple users to simultaneously be able to share the experience first hand. The artist, however, considers the balance between the value of shared experience against the personalized sense of

being alone and in contact only with the cave. Each viewer wishes to feel themselves connected, and in a sense, sharing the experience can, for some viewers, dilute the experience and make it less "their own." From a more practical point of view, it is also uncommon for a museum installation to have more than one virtual reality system. Thus, for both these reasons, the added software complication was not considered worth the effort.

The physics of this world are fairly simple and deal entirely with concerns of how participants travel through the world. Since there are no objects in the world that the user can manipulate, there is no need for gravity or other worries such as collision detection between objects. *LASCAUX* uses a terrain-following method to simulate gravity, and has a "Peter Pan" mode allowing the participant to fly around the valley and off into outer space. There are also secrets in the cave that erase all "virtual physics and leave the participant immersed in virtual space without ground, and in the true zero gravity of basic VR."

Venue

The *LASCAUX* experience was specifically designed to be shown in a community museum venue. The artist views the most appropriate venue as the art museum, rather than science museums, though under the right circumstances, science museums might be appropriate. The goal was not as a scientific lesson about the cave, but rather a study of human culture, and the nature and history of humankind. The application loses much of its point and importance when one scrutinizes it for scientific and historical accuracy (although even in scientific forums, *LASCAUX* is a prime example of excellent 3D graphics and site reconstruction).

The experience is not widely available, and can be viewed only in specific carefully controlled venues. This helps to maintain the mystique associated with the actual cave of Lascaux. In Britton's words:

> I remain concerned about the tendency of the WWW[4] to present viewers with trivialized, disposable, Kleenex-culture experiences, and wish for viewers that their experience of LASCAUX can be richer than a mere mouse-clicky passthrough while logged onto their ISP[5]. For this reason, I raise the bar and make the experience require a higher level of personal investment from audience members. A viewer must really wish to see the virtual cave if they are to make that experience happen for themselves.

FIGURE 8-14
The venue allows people to see what is happening.
Photo by Lisa Britton

[4] *The World-Wide Web.*
[5] *Internet Service Provider.*

FIGURE 8-15
The museum venue allows onlookers to see the technology being used by the immersed VR participant.
Photo by Lisa Britton

Venues at which *LASCAUX* has appeared include museums in Paris and Montpellier, France, Tokyo, Italy, Austria, and Korea, the Epcot Innoventions venue in Disney World, Florida, as well as several appearances at the SIGGRAPH conferences on computer graphics.

The application was designed to allow the participant to go on a self-guided tour of the cave. In the initial exhibitions, however, Britton preferred to have it hosted by a guide. This is helpful for getting each participant situated, as well as being helpful with the flow of traffic through the exhibit. After watching many people use his application, Britton has learned that participants are able to figure out the system on their own. In a museum setting, the general length of time for being immersed in the experience is about 15 minutes.

VR System

The intended venues for the *LASCAUX* experience provided the primary constraint on the system design: low cost. Art museums frequently spend on the order of $50,000 for an exhibit. In the early 1990s it was more challenging to meet this constraint for a virtual reality–based experience. In fact, the cost of producing a VR experience is generally much higher than this, and artists working in such a technologically based medium can find it difficult to have access to the latest technology. The cost of producing *LASCAUX* was about $500,000. Individual installations of the exhibit can cost as little as $25,000.

SYSTEM CHOICE— DISPLAY PARADIGM

A head-mounted display was selected as the display paradigm, specifically the Virtual I/O unit an inexpensive model (less than $1000) that includes a system for orientation tracking.

Britton felt that by choosing an HMD display, people would be more intrigued by the application and, compelled to give it a try. The Virtual I/O system chosen also had the attributes of being light weight, inexpensive, and included its own tracking hardware (further reducing overall system cost).

Onlookers can get a view of what the participant is seeing on nearby display monitors. In fact, multiple monitors

FIGURE 8-16
A museum visitor wears a head-mounted display, and navigates through the VR Cave of Lascaux.
Photo by Lisa Britton

can be arranged to show a much wider field of view to the nonimmersed viewers than what the participant experiences in the HMD.

The tracking system on the HMD uses accelerometer technology. Thus, it only tracks orientation (not translation) and requires frequent recalibrations. The recalibrations can be handled without too much trouble by a guide staffing the exhibit. The lack of translational tracking is less noticeable because monoscopic images were chosen over stereoscopic images.

DESIGN CHOICE

The combination of a monoscopic image without translational tracking was selected for this system for better user comfort and lower system cost.

Though choosing to display monoscopically and without respect to head translation lessens the depth cues available to the participant, the designers felt the benefits outweighed this. The reason was not just because of computational and hardware costs, but also because of user comfort. Discomfort in the form of nausea is occasionally a problem in HMDs. This is generally caused by system lag and improper alignment in the stereoscopic imagery. By choosing to display a monoscopic image, alignment headaches are eliminated. While there will always be some lag in the system, the use of accelerometer based tracking reduces the amount of display lag in the tracking component.

The compute and graphics system was chosen because it met the financial goal, yet is also quite capable of handling the computational requirements of the application.

SYSTEM CHOICE

Computer System

A dual processor Intel-CPU computer running Windows NT and Intergraph graphics processors with 64 megabytes of texture memory was chosen as the computer platform to run the application.

Most of the audio was handled through the use of normal audio CD tracks. By using an audio CD, the developers could eliminate the concern of consuming large portions of memory for high quality sound samples. Mixing of different tracks, with a few shorter sound samples stored in RAM was handled by the main application.

Six degree-of-freedom input devices are typically intuitive to use for the average person, and were selected as the primary input devices.

SYSTEM CHOICE

Input System

A Spaceball™ 6-DOF input device or a standard mouse is used to allow the user to move through the virtual world.

More recently, the experience has also been publicly displayed in a projection-based ("*CAVE*-like") display system at the 1997 SIGGRAPH computer graphics conference. In this showing, viewers were not given the opportunity to control the movement through the cave, but the wide field of view provided by the surround screens was very impressive. When run in a *CAVE* environment using Silicon Graphics computers, stereoscopic imagery is presented.

Application Implementation

The original concept for this artwork began as a video wall display run by several laserdisc players. Later, a switch was made to a virtual reality interface. This switch in media led to multiple benefits. A VR interface allows the work to become much more interactive, letting participants move through the cave with total freedom. Plus, the added intrigue associated with virtual reality, would help to generate interest in the artwork. And finally, a small VR System (PC and low-cost HMD) is much easier to install into new venues than a video wall with many large monitors, each with a laserdisc player, plus a control computer.

Work began on this application on an IBM-compatible 386 PC in 1991. The creation of the full application went on for 5 years. During that time, it was exhibited on a few occasions as a work in progress. In 1996 work was completed, and with the possible exception of improving hardware, it will remain as it is. By 1998, the typical system used is an Intel Pentium running at 300 MHz and including MMX enhancement.

Although the original implementation utilized an HMD, they have also implemented a nonimmersive PC based multi-screened stationary display, providing a wide field of view. They have also demonstrated the experience running on a *CAVE*-like projection-VR display using Silicon Graphics computers.

The application was developed by a core team consisting of University of Cincinnati Professor of Art, Benjamin Britton, a technical consultant, and three graduate research assistants. Most of the funding came from the University of Cincinnati, the Ohio Arts Council, and the Chicago Center for New Television consultancy. Total cost to create the application was about $500,000. However, this does not fully reflect the amount of person-hours used to create the application. Much of the work was done for the love of the art and/or opportunity to work on an exciting VR application. Additionally, Intergraph Computer Systems donated machines for production and exhibition in support of this project.

Core tasks of designing and creating applications were handled by different individuals of the design team. One research assistant was primarily a texture map specialist and did the work, unpaid, as an independent study for college credit. Another research assistant focused on the hardware, modeling, and graphics. The remaining student was described as "rationally minded and a logical thinker." He focused on data management and other logistical details.

The technical consultant, David Britton (the artist's brother), focused mostly on the development of an authoring system, used to create the final application. There were many other tasks that were performed by about 15 volunteers during the height of production. They worked (often around the clock) to digitize the cave images, create the video clips, mix the sounds, etc.

Many tools were used to bring together this application. In addition to the custom made authoring system, Sense 8's 3D virtual world package, *World ToolKit*™, was used as the world management and rendering system. Adobe *Photoshop*™ was used to montage many of the scanned cave images together. These images were then texture mapped onto polygons. This work involved tweaking the correspondence between the polygons and the textures by hand. Microsoft *Visual C++* was used to create the custom VR authoring tool and engine for the project.

Conclusion

The artist's goal of *LASCAUX* was to bring people "into personal contact with part of our common cultural legacy as members of the family of humanity." Successfully accomplishing such a goal is very subjective. One method Britton used to determine if he was reaching the audience was to mingle with the patrons gathered at the opening of an installation and watching as they participated in the experience. In France, he found the people particularly enthusiastic about wanting to see the project, with waiting lines "around the block outside the Le Monde de l'Art galerie in Paris."

While not a life-saving type of application on the surface, it has helped to provide an opportunity for many other people to experience the otherwise restricted cave of Lascaux, allowing them to have their own encounter with the mysteries of the cave.

The experience has been successfully exhibited at several venues, providing many more people an experience of the cave of Lascaux. Also, it has generated considerable interest, with TV coverage by CNN and other networks. Britton reports that even the number of people who have had the experience is quite large. At least 12 million viewers in galleries and museums on four continents since its 1995 premiere in Kwang-Ju, Korea, have tried the experience. This includes about 10 million people who ventured into the Innoventions Pavilion at Epcot Center in Disney World,

and another 2 million at a 4-month show in Paris. Only a fraction of these had the opportunity to actually experience *LASCAUX* first hand, of course. In addition, hundreds of millions of viewers have seen television coverage on CNN, NHK, BBC, Canal+, and Korean, Italian, Spanish, Portuguese, and Dutch television stations.

Another significant accomplishment of the application is that it is a good example of successful use of technology by an artist. The artist became intimately familiar with the technology involved, and also developed new technology in support of his goals. As such, it was recognized by *Discovery* magazine as a recipient of a 1995 Discover Award in the "Sight" category.

The performance of the application was very good, giving the participant good visual cues of being in the cave environment. Even in the early systems, the only noticeable delays were during the loading of the embedded video clips. After stepping up to 300 MHz Intel Pentium CPUs with MMX enhancements, the video as well as the interactive graphics perform at real-time frame rates.

Though, it is perhaps too strong to say that it feels like you are actually exploring the real cave, that is not entirely the goal. One can easily become caught up in the exploration, and magic of the virtual world. On the other hand, when rendered in a *CAVE*-like visual VR display the feeling of being in a real place is significant.

There are two important points that are highlighted by the work done in the creation of this experience. One is that when working with technical equipment in the creation of art, artists must learn how to balance the amount of control given to the participant versus what they are *not* allowed to do. In most media, artists are accustomed to controlling the entire presentation. However, in media that allow significant user interaction, they must allow the user to make choices, to have (some) control over the overall experience.

Britton believes:

> With interactive composition, artists must anticipate viewer response and develop a meta-AI which communicates to the viewer an attitude and a sense of control. Artists do not relinquish control to viewers in interactive art, on the contrary they dangle the illusion of control in front of the viewers, inspiring and tempting them to explore and invest

their wills in the interactive art experience. Only a poor interactive composer would give up control, except as a ploy to make their audiences feel particularly empowered at some point. In interactive media, no less than in any other medium, artists control the entire presentation and provide their audience only with the semblance of control. Empowering viewers is a technique for comforting and entertaining them, not a technical necessity.

Another important point applies to work being done on computer-based historical reconstructions. As with the *LASCAUX* experience, where the goal was to minimize the veil between the physical cave and how it is presented in the HMD, anyone working on reconstructions needs to recognize that they *cannot* tell the whole truth. In other words, all media place a veil between what is represented and what is perceived, and it is important for content creators (and viewers) to realize this fact, especially when creating an experience that purports to accurately represent how the real world existed at a previous point in time.

Britton found that the context of a museum gallery was an ideal place to present art to an audience. In Britton's opinion, VR displays of this nature are well suited to display in a museum because it provides a physical space in which one can manifest a virtual environment. He believes that the use of less-encumbering immersive technology, such as Projected-VR displays, provides a more natural and inviting space, but he also believes that the flat screen—like the book, the window, and the painting—is a valuable display genre that will never disappear and will remain a vital part of virtual reality presentations.

Also, one must be aware of the clash between VR hardware that is powerful but expensive and hardware that is less expensive but can do the job. This is one battle Britton has engaged himself during the creation of the *LASCAUX* experience. He deliberately chose to use a PC system in order to make his experience affordable to museums. To accomplish this, Britton had to make use of specialized graphics hardware for the PC. In 1995, this hardware was fairly expensive compared to typical PC peripherals. Now, however, 3D graphics cards have become more commonplace, with much more reasonable prices.

FIGURE 8-17
The artist, Benjamin Britton, experiences his own work.

Next up for Britton was a project to celebrate the 30th anniversary of the first manned lunar landing. In this project, he again hoped to use humankind's past accomplishments to demonstrate hope for the species. In his project, simply titled *MOON*, Britton sought to reach a larger audience. To achieve such wide dissemination, it was distributed on mass media (e.g., CD-ROM or DVD-ROM), and was not necessarily be a physically immersive work. In *MOON*, Britton planned to integrate more storytelling elements (e.g., acts and scenes) into the narrative of the experience. In the words of the artist, *LASCAUX* is a blend of empirical human knowledge and manifest physical reality. It is not about VR. It is not about the cave. It is not about science. It features the cave for an art work of our time. It is about each individual's search to understand what it means to exist as a human being.

This experience is *about* the truth, it's not supposed to *be* he truth. It is *about* the cave, it's not supposed to *be* the cave. It is about the spirit of the cave, not the physical reality of the cave.

In closing, Britton says:

I suppose that the cave has become a spiritual phenomenon for me. In a time when we may fear the future, the cave stands as a message of hope, saying humankind will survive and prosper. Our work today builds that future world.

CHAPTER 9

Entertainment Applications

As we have seen in the previous chapters of this book, virtual reality has been put to use in a very wide array of applications. Scientists, businessmen, artists, and many others have utilized VR in ways that have helped them in their professions. The general public, however, is most likely to have been exposed to virtual reality in some area of entertainment. Whether it is via coverage of VR in the media, portrayed in some science fiction movie, or experienced first hand as a game or some other form of entertainment, the most likely avenue for the public to encounter virtual reality is in the realm of entertainment. While most people won't ever witness a physician practice a surgical procedure, they may have the opportunity to immerse themselves in a head-mounted display in an arcade and fight the evil forces.

9.1 AREAS OF APPLICATION

Virtual reality has spanned the entire continuum of the entertainment production life cycle from aiding in the creation of entertainment that is delivered in some other medium to being the end product as an entertainment product in its own right. A number of entertainment applications are illustrated in this chapter. The areas of application covered include the broad categories of *virtual reality experiences* and *entertainment production*. Each of these areas has multiple subcategories of note. Some of these subcategories include games, interactive fiction, creative expression, virtual set design and use, and virtual cameras used to choreograph computer graphics animations created for film or video delivery.

9.1.1 Games

Computer games have permeated society and become significant in the world's palette of entertainment choices. For the most part, computer games are delivered in arcade kiosks, at theme parks, on a traditional computer monitor, or on a television screen. All of these delivery mechanisms have a limited scope of interaction, and field of view/field-of-regard. In general, the participant is physically larger than other characters (whether the characters are computer generated or representations of other living people participating in the game, and there is no commonly used method to allow the participants to interact with others at life-size scale. Additionally, in traditional computer games, for the most part the participant's body is not integrated in the experience other than moving a joystick, pressing a button, or manipulating some sort of prop like a plastic weapon.

Some arcade games have integrated the participant's body to a greater degree by allowing them to stand on a surfboard or some other platform and use their body as an input device to the game. However, in all these scenarios, the participant must always physically face the screen, and the participant's head position is not integrated into the displayed point of view. Very few traditional computer games utilize stereoscopic imagery to create a three-dimensional effect.

Extending games into the medium of virtual reality offers many new opportunities for game play. VR offers the opportunity for true immersion into the game with up to a full field-of-regard, stereoscopic imagery, and natural user interfaces such as allowing the participant to physically jump rather than press a button on the controller to make their character jump. In general, traditional computer games operate from a second-person point of view (the participant is controlling their character that they see on the screen via some controller device). VR offers the opportunity for the game player to jump into the game and participate from the first-person point of view. To date, most VR applications operate from the first-person point of view with the notable exception of the *MANDALA* series of second-person point-of-view games.

9.1.2 Interactive fiction

Interactive fiction has existed for decades in media ranging from print through computer-based interactive fiction whether the experience is text on the computer or fully interactive computer graphics. The idea behind any interactive fiction experience is that there is a story line that the participant can alter based on choices they make throughout the experience. In a printed (text) interactive fiction, the person may read a page, and then go to one page if they choose to answer a dilemma one way, or a different page if they answer it another way. On the computer, the branching at decision points may be less obvious to the participant, but the idea is generally the same. With interactive fiction, there is the potential for each participant to have a different experience with the activity, and also for any given participant to have a different experience the next time they play it. One early, inspirational example of interactive fiction in the medium of virtual reality is *The Thing Growing*, created by Josephine Anstey and Dave Pape. In *The Thing Growing*, the participant interacts with computer-generated characters, generally in a *CAVE* display, though the creators have also made the application available for lower-cost displays. Throughout the story line, the participant is presented with an ethical dilemma and the outcome is based on the choices and actions that the participant makes.

Throughout the experience, there is a character that suggests things for the participant to do. The participant can choose to do them, or to ignore the character and do something else. In general in this application, if they ignore the character, the character gets more adamant and demanding of the participant. The experience culminates in a dilemma of whether to kill or not to kill with differing consequences. An interesting aspect of this application is that it was created especially for the medium of virtual reality (as opposed to translating an extant interactive fiction into VR) and exploits various aspects of the VR environment. For example, the main character instructs the participant to dance. The system utilizes the three tracking sensors (head, left hand, and right hand) to determine whether the participant did the dance correctly or not, with appropriate consequences.

9.1.3 Creative expression

Virtual reality offers the opportunity to freely create, sketch, and imagine in a three-dimensional world. In the simplest sense, one can use a three-dimensional drawing program to free oneself of the constraints of the two-dimensional world of paper or computer monitor. VR applications like *BLUI* allow one to create flowing, colored shapes in a darkened virtual world. In this book, *creative expression* applications are primarily covered in the chapter on art, but they bear a mention in this chapter because many people find the activity of using these tools find them very enjoyable. In addition to creating visual worlds, sound worlds and other senses can be represented in the virtual world as a means for creative expression.

9.1.4 Entertainment production

In addition to virtual reality applications being used by participants as entertainment in its own right, virtual reality has also been used as a tool for creating media (whether the media is virtual reality, music, film, or others) that is then experienced by the participant. For example, virtual reality applications can be used as a tool for aiding in the placement of three-dimensional sounds for playback in a standard surround-sound environment. This section focuses on applications of virtual reality related to the creation and use of virtual sets and for aiding in creating camera paths for computer graphics animation and preplanning camera moves for live-action film.

This chapter merely scratches the surface of some foundational application of VR in the entertainment arena. Many lessons can be learned from studying these applications and thus aid in the creation of new, remarkable applications both for entertainment and the creation of entertainment.

CASE STUDY 9.1: DISNEY'S *ALADDIN ADVENTURE*

When it comes to using technology to tell a story, few would argue that the Walt Disney Company does it well. Early in the development of VR technology and applications, the Disney group sought to explore how VR could be used for entertainment. One of their early efforts was to adapt the story from the box office smash *Aladdin* to an immersive theme park attraction.

In order to fully exploit the capabilities of VR, the Disney Imagineering group had to develop new hardware, software, and even a new computer language that allowed the creative team to directly build the application without requiring the intervention of technical personnel to implement every artistic choice or change.

The *Aladdin VR experience* has undergone many changes and developments over its life time, including a change from an exploratory interactive fiction world to a mission-oriented game. The Disney team had ample opportunity to observe and survey thousands of theme park guests regarding their interaction with this new form of entertainment, and fold the lessons they learned into new versions of the experience.

Introduction

Walt Disney's *Aladdin Adventure* VR attraction demonstrates several techniques of entertainment and storytelling within an interactive immersive medium. Designed as an experiment to study the storytelling possibilities of virtual reality in a public venue, the *Aladdin* attraction went through many changes as surveys were tabulated and the audience experience was analyzed. The initial experiment was conducted at Disney's Epcot theme park near Orlando, Florida, from July 1994 through 1995. After these tests, a game-style narrative was written, and the revised experience ran at the Disneyland Starcade for several months in 1996. Following this it was removed from the park. VR then re-emerged in a Disney venue at the large family-oriented DisneyQuest arcades. The new venue opened in 1998 with new VR experiences based on the *Aladdin* experiments, along with Disney's *Hercules* feature-length animation, an experience that puts the guest inside a comic book, and another allowing a raft of guests to paddle down a prehistoric river.

As a leader in using new technology, Disney wanted to explore how this new (technology-based) medium could

FIGURE 9-1

Disney's Aladdin Adventure *virtual reality experience allows guests to enter the city of Agrabah, the setting for the Disney movie* Aladdin.

be used to tell a story for a larger location-based entertainment (LBE) audience. During the preliminary period of their research the feature movie *Aladdin* was still in early design stages. This film was ultimately selected as the setting for this experimental storytelling experience.

In many respects, virtual reality is just the next step in a progression of avenues used by theme park and other large LBE venues to tell a story to a group audience. Current methods include thrill rides, shows, game arcades, large-format motion pictures (sometimes in 3D or more), etc.[1]

---

[1] In addition to stereo images, some large format venues might include "gimmicks" such as light water spray, etc., corresponding to what is occurring in the story—e.g., MuppetVision*4D.

Interactive experiences abound in LBE parks, with bumper cars, carnival games, and even with the park itself often being an immersive experience (e.g., walk-around characters and parades down "Main Street"). Previously, the only computer-generated interactive experiences were the video games in the arcade. Immersive interactive LBE venues were only on the horizon when this work began, and the Walt Disney Imagineering team has gone a long way in exploring this new medium.

Application Description

The VR experience is a computer-generated world with scenery and characters similar to those in the Disney feature film. "Guests" are given a task, or mission that fits the theme. They are then given a fixed amount of time to fly through the world of Agrabah and complete their mission. To accomplish the assigned task, the participant must interact with the characters, and navigate through several locations in the virtual world while riding on the familiar magic carpet.

In the EPCOT version (1994–1995), a character in the world, the parrot Iago, gave brief instructions, including the task of finding the thief with half of the sought after scarab. In the 1996 version at the Disneyland Starcade, a park employee informed the participant of their mission, and often gave other verbal hints during the session.

In the Starcade version, the task set forth before the guest was to explore Agrabah and collect the five pieces of the magic lamp within 5 minutes. The pieces were the base, the body, the spout, the handle, and the lid. The lid was held by Jafar in the Cave of Wonders. Once four of the pieces were collected, the guest had to fly to the Cave of Wonders, and defeat Jafar by grabbing the fifth piece of the lamp, thus releasing the Genie.

DESIGN DECISION

In fact, there were more than five lamp pieces throughout the virtual world, and the participant only had to grab any four pieces. If a redundant piece was found, it would simply be added as one of the other remaining pieces. Once four pieces were found, the extra pieces would disappear from the game, thus still requiring the final confrontation with Jafar.

Giving people a quicker way to find the required four pieces was necessary because otherwise it would have been too difficult for people to accomplish the mission in the span of 5 minutes. As a side benefit, when players found lamps in a new location, it gave the impression that the experience changed between plays.

Agrabah, the virtual world in which the guest is placed, is set and populated similarly to its counterpart in the feature film. The characters in the world portray the same look and movement. The locations had the same look and were accompanied by a thematically similar musical score. Many parts of the world were so faithful to the world of the movie, that guests could use knowledge of the location of secret passages, etc., gained from viewing the movie to their advantage in the VR attraction.

Of course, one of the considerations faced when adapting a virtual world from a linear narrative medium such as a film to an explorative medium like VR is that in the linear version, many details are not entirely fleshed out. For example, only the main entrance to the throne room is shown, but since it would be logical for side doors to also exist, they were added in the VR experience. This also benefits the VR experience creators by allowing them to branch the story based on the participants' actions. Another example would be that the complete route from the palace to the Cave of Wonders is not shown in the movie. The action simply jumps from one location to the other. However, because people bring a sense of diegesis to the movie, they have a sense that they know the complete world of Agrabah, even though they were only exposed to portions of it during the film. The fact that some specific pieces of information, such as the location of the secret entrance to Jafar's laboratory, were consistent between the animated and VR virtual worlds, the perception that the two are one and the same is enhanced.

Content is the key to any mediated experience, and is more important than the technology used to deliver it. With a background in bringing worlds to life using many different media, the Disney team was very familiar with the requirement of having an interesting world, and working with the possibilities and constraints of the chosen medium. One aspect of this project was to experiment with different styles of content and forms of interaction.

In a virtual world explored via an interactive medium such as VR, there are many ways to permit the participant to explore the world. The Disney team tried a range of "navigational narrative" styles during the implementation of the various incarnations of the *Aladdin* experiences.

On the noninteractive end of the range is the ride-along–style navigation. In this method the guest is taken along a predetermined path as though they were on a rail in a mechanical theme park ride. In another method, the guest is fooled into thinking they were interacting with the world, but is actually being led through the world. The other end of the range was to allow the participant the complete freedom to do whatever and go wherever they choose in the virtual world.

DESIGN CHOICE

In the public exhibition version of the experience, the design team chose to put the "guest" into a world with a plethora of interesting activity taking place. This gave the rider the ability to explore, making choices that lead them down different branches of the "story." However, to keep the experience moving forward, timed events such as collapsing walls or earthquakes would prod along users who hadn't made sufficient progress. As in any storytelling medium, one gets to a certain point where a crisis is needed to move the story forward.

In an environment where any activity can be done in any order, an enormous range of sequences of actions are possible (a situation referred to as "combinatorial explosion" in computer science). This freedom increases the computational requirements for the system and makes it difficult to keep the storyline tractable and intact. It also increases the time required to design, implement, and test the many possible scenarios.[2]

_____
[2]Interactive fiction and DVD/CD-ROM games face this same difficulty.

DESIGN CHOICE

To handle the problem of a world with explosive possibilities, the amount of complexity of the world at any particular moment must be limited. The creation of specific *scenes* that provide a specific setting in the world helped the designers manage this problem. As users enter a new scene, they can only interact with the objects and characters within the scene. After interacting for a while, guests will either choose, or be forced, to move to another setting or scene. By exiting a scene, all events local to it are brought to a point of closure. The use of scenes also helps control the amount of branching that can occur during the experience. Liberal use of the isolated scene technique helped keep the job of creating the experience manageable.

Representation of the Virtual World

The content of the *Aladdin* virtual world includes the city of Agrabah and the surrounding desert. It also includes the objects that can be acquired and the characters with whom the guests can interact. The general style of representation is cartoonish, as it was in the animated film.

Internally, the cartoon-like world is stored as a polygonal database. The division of the narrative into scenes helps to limit the computational requirements needed during any phase of the experience. Character motion was created and stored as an animated sequence of positions. A specialized programming language was developed (Story Animation Language—SAL) to allow the narrative to be specified by the storytellers themselves.

Visually, the virtual world of *Aladdin* is represented in a style that closely resembles the style of the feature film from which it was derived. The primary difference is that in the VR experience, the world and characters were modeled and animated in three dimensions. Buildings and characters were painted by animation artists in a computer graphics environment.

The painted texture maps incorporated the lighting effects of the scene. This technique helps achieve the desired look as well as reduce the computation requirements of rendering. There is no need to perform complex lighting operations.

FIGURE 9-2

The guest's hands are represented as an avatar that appears as white gloved hands holding a magic carpet. The guest navigates through the adventure by riding a virtual magic carpet.

A minimal avatar of the guests represents them as a pair of (white gloved) hands clutching the front edge of a flying carpet. The flying carpet is the virtual vehicle the participant rides and steers though the world. Even this limited avatar helps to ground the user into the virtual world.

Aural representation played a key role in the *Aladdin VR experience*. The *Aladdin* team felt that audio is an extremely important element of a VR application. Composer and sound designer Aarin Richard was brought to the team to work on this part of the experience and to research how 3D audio could be used to enhance the experience. He and producer Jon Snoddy discovered that different types of audio sources could be mixed without breaking the illusion, and this was used to create a more engaging sonic environment.

As with a feature film, the sound in the virtual world of *Aladdin* is a combination of many sources. General ambient sounds, as well as event- and location-driven sounds, were a major part of the world of the *Aladdin* "ride." Sounds included crowd noises in the market place, rumblings of an earthquake, and the voices of animated characters speaking to the participant. Event-driven (marker) sounds were used to indicate location or emotion in a manner similar to mood music in motion pictures. Each location had a specific introductory fanfare and ambient soundtrack.

One of the initial concerns with the design team was how difficult it would be to combine sound types. They thought it might be more complicated than with films, because not only did it need to be done in real time, but they had to combine different sound types. For example, collision sounds might be monaural, ambient music might be stereophonic, crowd noises might be user-grounded 3D recorded sounds (i.e., the sounds move when the user moves), and character voices might be presented as world-grounded spatialized 3D sounds (i.e., the sounds are stationary with respect to the virtual world).

VR DISCOVERY

In experimenting with the audio content for *Aladdin*, sound designer/composer Aarin Richard discovered that different types of sound could easily be mixed together without causing the listener to be disoriented. For example, while a spatialized crowd sound plays without relation to head movement, the voice of a specific character talking to the guest is rendered relative to the orientation of the participant's head. The combination of all these sounds resulted in a satisfactory sonic experience.

By associating audio cues with objects in the world, the team found that the level of immersion of the experience increased. This occurs because even though an object leaves the user's view, spatialized audio cues continue to indicate that the object continues to exist in its proper place in the world. When objects have no localized audio associated with them, users often move their head to follow or search for the objects, trying to keep them in view and verify their permanence.

VR DISCOVERY

User perception of object permanence is increased when objects have an aural representation that is rendered to emanate from the location of the object.

In addition to places and objects providing unique sounds, certain events also generate their own sonic representation. Collisions between the flying carpet and objects in the world were one type of event presented sonically. The exact sound heard depends on with what the guest collided. A "palette" of sounds was created for different objects and characters. Each object and character had multiple sounds associated with it. These sounds were cycled through to prevent annoying repetition of a sound that could ruin the experience of a guest who was having trouble steering away from an object in their way.

For collisions, the *Aladdin* authors experimented with different styles of sound representations. After experimenting with realistic sounds, they tried and settled with cartoon-like sounds.

DESIGN CHOICE

The experience authors chose to use the cartoon-like sounds to represent guest collisions with objects in the world. They felt that this worked better than realistic sounds, both because it matched the cartoon-like visuals of the world, but more importantly, because these sounds are more amusing. Since collisions occur when the user is having difficulty flying, hearing the light-hearted sounds is more likely to lower the amount of frustration that they are feeling.

Three types of haptic feedback were part of the complete trial experience. A breeze to indicate movement through the world was generated by a fan, a heat lamp was used to indicate when the guest flew near lava, and the physical mechanism that the participant holds onto to control the flight.

The fan and heat lamp methods of providing breeze and thermal feedback to the user were not successful. Users reported that they did not even notice the effects, despite tests with even larger fans. The reason these methods didn't work was due to the fact that the HMD's worn by the users covered the part of the body that would have been most likely to notice, the head. As HMD's shrink in size, devices such as fans and heat lamps may become more feasible.

One method of haptic feedback that was found to have a positive effect on the experience was the physical mock-carpet device used to provide travel control to the system. Although the carpet prop does not actively feed back forces or resistance to the user, physically holding the prop provides sufficient proprioceptive feedback to close the interface loop with the user. This simple, "passive haptic" feedback makes controlling the carpet easier.

Providing a prop that is consistent with what the participant sees and hears has the additional benefit of helping make the entire world seem more real. We refer to this method of providing passive physical objects that mimic the expected haptic feedback the *transference of object permanence*, that is, the physical nature of what is touched makes the rest of the world seem more tangible.

The motorcycle-style platform that the guests mount to "ride the experience" was also capable of providing vestibular feedback via a motion base that could raise and lower, and tilt side to side. Participants reported an increased sense of immersion corresponding to the magnitude of motion feedback, but reports of discomfort due to nausea also increased.

DESIGN CHOICE

Vestibular feedback was disabled from the public version of the experience due to the higher level of reported nausea. The *Aladdin* team felt that the level of involvement provided by the head-mounted display was enough that the added benefit of vestibular feedback was comparatively insignificant, and many participants did not seem to notice the lack of motion.

However, an easy method of providing motion feedback was chosen by using "tactile seats" that provide a vibration that the rider feels as a "thump."

As with most VR applications, the olfactory and taste senses were not implemented. In addition to the limited availability of hardware, the health hazards concerned with an experience designed for use in public venues make synthetic taste and smell even more impractical.

Interaction with the Virtual World

Originally, the *Aladdin* experience was designed in the genre of *interactive story*. That story was presented to the user as a world to explore, and characters and objects to interact with, where each guest was part of their own story. However, with the specific task to accomplish added to the experience, it becomes more of a *mission game* experience. This style of navigation/interaction is the platform based *vehicle pilot-through* form. In this style, all the interaction with the virtual world is done by navigating through it and flying close to characters and objects.

Since the application was created to explore the narrative possibilities of the new medium, the design team was able to make many observations about the medium. One such observation is that the author no longer has complete control over the scenic and timing elements of the experience. Control is lost as the interactivity is increased from virtually none in a rail-style ride-along experience to almost unbounded interactivity possible in a typical VR walkthrough.

A corollary observation (the flip side) is that given no direction on what to do in a world, the creators noticed that in their initial, limited world, participants remained engaged

in the experience for up to 2 minutes, and shortly after that asked for guidance in what they should be doing. The narrative needed to be more than simply go out and explore a new world. The size of the world and number of ways to interact with the world are probably a large factor in how much time people will remain engaged without direction.

VR DISCOVERY

For missions longer than the time required to adequately venture through the entire world (e.g., 2 minutes in the EPCOT version), participants expected to be given a goal.

The guests in the world of *Aladdin* are therefore given a goal to make the experience interesting. In general, people want to be directed. They want a mission to accomplish. This desire to be directed might be heightened by the fact they are in a theme park venue that customarily provides packaged entertainment to the guest.

In an LBE, the goal of the experience is often introduced during a nonimmersive, "preshow" presentation (e.g., a video segment). This can be used to give both a history of the world leading up to the guest's mission, but also to give instruction on how to travel and navigate through the virtual world. In a high throughput environment, such as a Disney theme park, the immersive experience of one group can overlap with the preshow of the next group.

VR DISCOVERY

Both the throughput and the overall experience can be improved if a pre-immersion "background story" is used to get the user "up to speed" on the events/culture/situation of an LBE virtual world [Pausch et al. 1996]. However, in arcade venues, which tend to be more "self-serve," kiosks improving throughput with this method is more difficult since the instructive preshow would likely still require the use of the VR system. On the other hand, many people learn by watching the play of previous players.

As with the natural progression of creating interesting content for any medium, the narrative went through many changes as the project was refined. Major changes in the story were made as it progressed from its original concept, to what appeared in the experimental version at EPCOT, and then to what ultimately became an arcade-style game at Disneyland.

The original idea was to present each guest with a 5-minute personalized story that takes place in Agrabah, the world of *Aladdin*. As the main character in the story, the guest would "live" the narrative based on the characters, locations, and other elements of the feature film. The story was not intended to be gamelike, but random events would move the narrative down different paths, giving a different experience to each guest.

DESIGN CONSTRAINT

Difficulties abound when creating an interesting and unique narrative within a world as complicated as that of *Aladdin*. This condition is exacerbated when creating an experience for the conventional LBE timeframe of 5 minutes. So, the narrative was designed to move the user from event to event, with fairly tight control over the path of the participant.

The experimental version of the attraction that ran at EPCOT had a few gamelike elements, but mostly consisted of the user exploring the city and interacting with (i.e., listening to) some of the characters. In fact, the goal of this version was simply to locate a specific character (a thief with the other half of a scarab) by using hints provided by characters met along the way. Once the thief is thwarted, he gives the player the missing piece of the scarab and the experience ends.

Additional game elements were added to the version that ran in the Disneyland Starcade during 1996. Expert game designer Jesse Schell created a mission for the guest to accomplish during the 5 minutes of each experience. That task was to explore Agrabah and the surrounding locations searching for four of the five pieces of the lamp. They were then to fly to the Cave of Wonders for a final battle with Jafar. Upon entering the cave, Jafar would transform himself into a giant snake with the fifth and final piece on

his tongue. To defeat Jafar, the participant had to grab the fifth piece of the lamp. Doing so would cause the Genie to be released from the lamp, Jafar to be defeated, and all to be well in Agrabah.

VR DISCOVERY

One interesting feature of making the guest search for something is the ability of the game designer to force the participant to consider the new capabilities of the VR medium. At least one piece of the lamp required them to physically look up to see it, something not possible in video games displayed on a standard monitor.

Of course, as with most arcade-style games, it is difficult if not impossible to accomplish this on the first attempt. Since there was no way to accrue time above the allotted 5 minutes, any time spent exploring side locations or listening to the world's inhabitants came out of valuable time needed to collect the pieces and defeat Jafar.

To be successful, the guest would first have to explore the world a few times, gathering the information and advice from the characters and locating the lamp pieces. Then, to win, they would re-enter the world, fly directly to the pieces, then to the Cave of Wonders and Jafar, ignoring everything else in the world. In fact, given the time constraint, some first-time players chose to ignore characters who were speaking to them (during which time they are prevented from flying away) and begin to look in other directions, focusing on the task of locating the lamp pieces.

As the guest explored the world, the mood of the experience could also be manipulated. The *Aladdin* Imagineering team implemented and tested techniques to create a mood for a scene. Specific music or lighting effects can be chosen based on the guest's current situation. A turning point in the experience (e.g., finding the palace) might cause a general shift of music and/or lighting, and therefore the mood of the guest. In more complicated narratives, the mood effects for a particular scene may be based on previous events in the guest's experience.

In experimenting with several narration techniques, the application authors felt that they had found several good ways to compose scenes designed to draw the guests' attention to specific details. Once the guest is looking toward a character, that character can point to objects or bring an object into view by walking [Pausch et al.].

Similarly, techniques to virtually move the carpet (with the guest aboard) were sometimes tried to help move the narrative along. For example, the carpet might be dragged by a character to move the guest to a specific location. The experience developers experimented with narrative techniques such as preventing flight backtracking by closing doors behind the guest, or by forcing the carpet to continue moving forward as a means to keep the story moving [Pausch et al.].

DESIGN DECISION

One method of travel that the experience creators experimented with was the "tow-rope" method, in which the carpet seems as though it were being pulled at the end of a long rope. In this method of travel, users can still move left and right, but only for a limited distance, and they remain pulled by the "rope." To allow more freedom to the participants, the creators later chose a less restraining method that used the looser concept of attractors to draw the carpet in certain directions. Guests were free to turn around and thus break the attraction.

General navigation through a three-dimensional space with 6-DOF control is very difficult. The majority of the population has little previous real-world experience with such navigational techniques. There are techniques that seem intuitive to some of the population, but might be counterintuitive for others (e.g., pilots vs. nonpilots).

DESIGN CHOICE

The *Aladdin* experience uses a piloting metaphor to transport the guest through the virtual world. As in the world of the film, flying is (seemingly) accomplished by piloting a magic carpet. Users grasp what feels like the edge of the carpet, and can tilt it from side to side, pitch it up or down, and push or pull it to control turning, climbing, and accelerating.

Since most of the interaction with the world is accomplished by flying to characters, objects, and specific locations, the importance of a good travel interface that keeps the user from floundering around or getting too lost is very high. To safeguard against these eventualities, user movements are constantly analyzed, and if they are having trouble or are far off course, the application will gently move them along in a more fruitful direction.

DESIGN DECISION

To enhance the realism of the virtual world, the creators chose to prevent guests from flying through walls. The result of this decision is that guests could become stuck should they fly into a tight corner.

The creators experimented with allowing backward flight to alleviate the frustration of becoming stuck. In the Disneyland version of the experience, backward flight was allowed, although the story strongly encouraged the guest to move forward toward some goal. For situations where reverse travel was not allowed, or the user was unable to successfully get out of a corner, the system would slowly redirect the flying carpet each time it would bounce off the wall, eventually freeing the guest from their predicament.

Gaining altitude required flying at higher speeds. This demanded some skill from the pilot in situations such as flying down the crowded streets of Agrabah. Once successful, however, the guest was treated to a breathtaking flight above the city.

Computer-controlled agents are a key ingredient in the world of the *Aladdin VR experience*. Most of the interactions with the world center around characters and the information they provide the guest.

The choreographed characters are designed to draw the attention of the participant. Once they are within close proximity, the character branches into a communication mode and relays information to the guest. The guest then chooses what course of action to follow (that is, where to fly) next.

In the virtual world of *Aladdin*, interactive characters served different roles. Some of the characters provided valuable

FIGURE 9-3
Guests are able to learn information about the world by interacting with computer-controlled agents that appear as various characters in the world.

information required to accomplish the mission. Other characters seemed to serve more to fill the world with interesting activities. In one version, Iago the parrot served as the instructor (a kind of narrator) at the beginning, and could fly along with the carpet giving hints. Jafar, of course, served the role of final antagonist that had to be defeated to *win the game*.[3]

Characters that played a crucial role in accomplishing the task were distinguished by the fact that they literally held the attention of the guest, by preventing them from flying away, until they made their statement. Characters with less important things to say would still interact with the guest within their role, such as street vendors trying to sell you something. These "filler" characters may not have advanced the story, but they did add dimensionality to the world.

VR DISCOVERY

The implementers found that using eye contact between the characters and the participant made the experience more engaging.

---

[3]Interestingly, the magic carpet itself doesn't seem to be an interactive character, as opposed to the movie. It might have been intriguing to have the carpet point to locations or be reluctant to go in certain directions during the course of the experience.

The movement and dialog of the agent-characters was scripted. Similar to standard animation practice, dialog was first recorded and then movement was formulated to match. This is typical of how animations are created.

VR DISCOVERY

In their initial experiments, body movements of the characters were created using a motion capture, performance animation system. This is also how motion is captured in many modern video games (especially sport games).

However, motion capture data is noisy and requires extensive cleaning and filtering. Because the Disney team happened to have expert animators available, they found that they could produce movements more quickly and more to their specification using keyframe animation techniques.

After some initial experimentation with multiple-guest experiences, the *Aladdin* team decided not to include this feature with the first full release in the Disneyland Starcade. They felt it would be too difficult to create a situation that enables multiple participants to collaborate on something worthwhile during the 5 minutes or so that they would be engaged in the experience.

However, 2 years later, DisneyQuest, a new customer that was more like small theme parks rather than the Starcade

arcade venue in Disneyland, requested a competitive/cooperative game. Also, by this point a single computer was fast enough to generate images for four players acting independently.

A multiple-guest experience introduces other difficulties in creating the application. For instance, if the music and lighting were adjusted for each guest, then it might be difficult to determine what effects would be experienced by the group, though something like the multiple-perspective method used by *CALVIN* (A VR application designed by the Electronics Visualization Laboratory at the University of Chicago at Illinois) could be used. In that system, each person sees the world in a unique way, even if they are in the same virtual space. Thus it would be possible for each guest to have their own theme melody that is played when other guests encounter them. This melody could be considered the audio portion of their avatar.

The physics of this virtual world are very simple. The physics consists of the flight dynamics for the guest to pilot the carpet through the world, along with other flight manipulations such as attractors to locations/characters and recovery of "stuck" guests. All other actions that occur in the world are specifically choreographed, and not the result of a simulation (cartoon-style or otherwise).

DESIGN CHOICE

After analyzing the problem of developing a world physics simulation, the designers came to the conclusion that there are too many things that work against accurately simulated physics. For example, some difficulties included only partially understood theories on how things work, and even if fully understood, the computational requirements to calculate the simulation in real time. Thus they decided they would take complete control and choreograph everything. They'd have to "cheat."

By making this choice, they can more easily create a world that is *fantastic* (i.e., in which "fantastic" things can happen, versus the mundane). Animators are also often capable of making events look "better than real." In other words, simulated falling blocks might appear fake to the participant, but an animated sequence can be made to look "right," with the added benefit that the result might better fit the narrative than a random placement of blocks.

Another strike against using simulated physics is that if it wasn't a complete simulation that included every detail, such as swaying trees, etc., then the world will look fake and cartoonish anyway. Therefore doing a partial simulation of the world doesn't do any good, and a full simulation isn't possible, because the computational requirements are prohibitive.

The participant does control their path through the world, thus a magic carpet flight simulation algorithm was necessary. A simple-but-flexible flight control system was developed that would enable most of the general population to figure out how to direct the flight of the carpet. Steering was accomplished by maneuvering the carpet control in three ways. The unit could be turned left or right to control the yaw. Pitch was controlled by tilting the unit up and down. Finally, speed was adjusted by moving the "carpet" closer to or farther from the chest. In 2D movement, this is similar to how one controls a horse. Adding flight results in a user interface that is not from any real-world vehicle, although people are able to fly reasonably well [Pausch et al.].[4]

In later versions, the altitude control was changed. It was observed that people generally aren't used to navigating in 3D space and thus got more confused and/or nauseated by the pitch controls. So the up/down tilting control was changed to simply translate the carpet and its rider up and down.

Venue

With the venue of Disney's theme parks in mind, the system was designed to be usable by as much of the guest population as possible. The experience had to be relatively easy to operate, it should cause no ill effects in most of the population, and it should fit most body and head sizes. There are also provisions for quickly removing the motorcycle-style mount to enable wheelchair access.[5]

---

[4]We were unable to locate any flying carpet or carpet pilots to compare with actual flying carpet controls.

[5]By giving the "ability" to fly to people who were not able to walk, the experience was often quite emotional for these guests and their families.

The presentation venue can also affect the practicality of the story and how it can be presented.

DESIGN CONSTRAINT

Disney's experience has shown that in ride-style LBE venues (vs. shows), experiences are economically feasible if they last 2 to 4 minutes.[6]

This is in stark contrast with a typical interactive narrative experience that people have access to on their personal computers, where a world may take weeks to fully explore (e.g., large interactive fiction, DVD/CD-ROM games, or many console video games).

Another major factor of the public venue is the concern of throughput. A general theme park ride or show needs to move about 2000 people through per hour. At EPCOT 100 people (for each 5-minute time slot) were given a demonstration that included four immersed participants selected from the audience. Smaller venues such as LBE's like DisneyQuest have lower throughput requirements, as do arcades. In an arcade, where the guests pay extra to experience the arcade machines, the constraint is merely that each game last about 5 minutes.

Some specific design choices were made for the EPCOT evaluation version of the experience. Because it was an experimental attraction, they were able to veer from conventional theme park "rides" and choose only a small subset of a group to actually experience the world *immersively*. From an audience of 100 people, 4 were picked to don an HMD and mount the four motorcycle-style platforms.

DESIGN CHOICE

For the experiment to address the needs of the entire theme park audience, a broad selection of people needed to be included, not just people with a natural affinity

for new technology. Therefore, to ensure that a broad range of people were put through the experience, the designers specifically chose to select participants from the audience who did not seem to be overly interested in the technology. This was done by giving the criteria to the park guides who ran the attraction and selected who would be given the immersive experience.

VR System

Apart from the computer hardware, almost everything in the VR system for the *Aladdin* experience was designed and developed from scratch specifically for use in a theme park/LBE venue. In particular, the HMD and the vehicle (magic carpet) platform with motion base went through considerable design analysis of what was best suited for the venue. The HMD was designed for durability, health concerns, and usability by a high percentage of the

© Disney

FIGURE 9-4

At Disney's EPCOT Center, some guests were allowed to mount a motorcycle-like platform and wear a head-mounted display while others watched.

---

[6]The overall design of the rides are created to make the experience seem to last longer, for example, the Star Tours attraction.

population. The carpet platform was designed to be comfortable for most people and to aid in the sensation that you were flying. Durability is very important because of the high throughput. One-in-a-million failures would be regular occurrences. [Pausch et al.]

The *Aladdin* team tested many display methodologies for presenting the virtual world to the participant. Based on that experience, they chose head-mounted visual displays and designed a model that fulfilled their design criteria.

SYSTEM CHOICE

Display Paradigm

In their initial assessment of the pros and cons of visual display technologies for VR, the Imagineering VR developers chose HMD over projection-style displays, such as the *CAVE*™. This was primarily based on cost and space limitations for a theme park venue. Theme park economics revolve around how many people can be moved through a certain sized area in some (short) amount of time. Putting a single person in a projection-based VR display means more space and more computer power would be needed for each guest than was feasible.

However, some other VR attractions produced by the VR studio for DisneyQuest did use a projection VR system. Specifically, the DisneyQuest experiences based on the themes of *Hercules* and later the *Pirates of the Caribbean* utilized projection displays.

DESIGN CHOICE

The HMD designed for the *Aladdin* experience was capable of providing a stereoscopic view of the world. However, the designers chose to use the two field-sequential CRT screens to provide a monoscopic image to the viewer. The HMD provided a 90-degree horizontal field of view (FOV), and 640 pixels horizontally by 480 vertically (i.e., NTSC resolution).

High-quality speakers were mounted near each ear for the aural display. To address sanitation concerns, separate helmet liners were attached to the head, to which the rest of the HMD was connected. These liners were then cleaned before re-use. The weight of the display is borne by cables that are suspended from above the participant.

This pixel count and FOV were chosen based on the design team's analysis of the minimal requirements for immersion into a virtual world. Specifically, they felt that an FOV less than 90 degrees resulted in a second-person view of the world, like peering through binoculars. Regarding resolution, they felt that using lower than 640 pixels simply made the image too fuzzy to see the world very well. At the time *Aladdin* was created, LCD displays could not meet these specifications, so CRT display technology was required. CRTs, however, add noticeable weight to the display, so a counter weighting system was devised to take some of the load off the guest.

Their HMD was designed to handle monoscopic images with bi-ocular, 3-inch CRT displays positioned to be in focus for a wide range of human heads. A single (wider) view of the world was rendered and presented (overlapping and cropped for each eye) giving the effect of a scene focused at infinity. Having noticed that many experienced VR practitioners who tested their system were often not sure whether it was a stereoscopic image, they felt that the potential problems with increased eye strain in improperly aligned displays made the benefits of stereoscopic images not worth the extra complication, and of course the additional (double) graphics computations.[7]

The primary inputs to the VR system were the carpet controls and the user's head orientation.

---

[7]There are many ways in which our perceptual system can interpret the three-dimensionality of the world. Stereoscopic images are not absolutely required to do so. Depth cues are also provided by motion, occlusion, object size, etc. While head lateral motion is not available in the Aladdin experience, motion through the world is almost continuous, and is generally more helpful for scenes with many distant objects. The effects of head motion and stereospsis depth cues are diminished for distant objects and so are not helpful for many parts of the experience.

SYSTEM CHOICE

Haptic Display Paradigm

A motorcycle-shaped platform was designed for the guest to mount in order to operate (i.e., "ride") the magic carpet. The rider was able to sit comfortably on the seat and reach forward to hold onto what felt like the front of a flying carpet.

DESIGN CHOICE

Tracking

An electromagnetic tracking system was used to track the head motion of the user. Only the orientation information was used to render the scene.

The system designers felt that the noise of the electromagnetic tracking system was more noticeable in translational movement versus rotational movement. Deciding that a noisy channel of information is worse than having no information, they chose to only use the head's orientation, which is the minimum input required to make a head-based display function suitably.

SYSTEM CHOICE

Compute System

To provide maximum frame rate, each unit was supported by a Silicon Graphics Onyx workstation, equipped with three Reality Engine 2 graphics pipelines. Each workstation included four RM5 boards providing a total of 16 megabytes of texture memory—top-of-the-line graphics in 1994.

As the initial test version was developed for display at the EPCOT Center in 1994, a requirement of 60 visual frames per second (FPS) was set in order reduce the occurrence of nausea. To achieve this rate, each of the three graphics pipes rendered the scene at 20 FPS, with the resultant images chronologically interleaved, producing the overall rate of 60 FPS [Pausch et al.]. Another beneficial effect of this is that perceptually, the higher frame rate will make the world seem more real. While the lag at the onset of each image is no different than a noninterleaved method, this method reduces the average lag of the visuals.

For the DisneyQuest version, deployed in 1998, a single Silicon Graphics Infinite Reality graphics system was capable of providing a sufficient frame rate without requiring the added complication and cost of using multiple computers. In fact, the single IR system was able to render the monoscopic views for all four of the participants at the same time, resulting in a much more economic solution.

Application Implementation

Walt Disney Imagineering developed this application for the purpose of investigating the use of virtual reality in a theme park venue. While this effort resulted in a specific mission-game VR experience, the underlying storytelling environment allowed for great flexibility. During the experiment at EPCOT, this flexibility was exercised by changing the scenario from week to week to try different ideas with a large number of guests.

Having been introduced to the immersive power of VR by simple wireframe virtual worlds seen at the NASA Ames Research Center in 1989, attraction producer Jon Snoddy and others at Disney became interested in the possibilities of applying this emerging medium to the art of storytelling. They began to seriously investigate the possibilities of VR with an experimental project in collaboration with computer graphics flight simulation company Evans & Sutherland.

For the first experimental experience, a Disney movie that featured a character that does a lot of flying was chosen as the virtual world in which to tell such a story. As the movie title suggests, The Rocketeer gave a good excuse to give participants the ability to fly. However, as the movie did not do as well as expected in box office receipts, it was dropped in favor of another movie on the Disney horizon. Aladdin was in development in the Feature Animation department, and happened to also have a tie-in to flight with a friendly magic carpet. In addition to the promise of being based on a more successful motion picture, the choice of *Aladdin* offered the opportunity to make the computer-generated world have the same hand painted cel "look and feel" as the animated film. Though this task was by no means easy, it was less difficult than making a virtual world seem like the real world, as portrayed in *The Rocketeer*.

At the same time, a switch was made from specialized flight simulator image generators to workstation-class graphics machines. Graphics workstations from Silicon Graphics Inc. were not only showing signs of being able to handle the necessary graphics requirements but also held promise for transitioning to less expensive home and set-top units.

The cost of developing the *Aladdin* attraction was significant by VR industry standards, but it was far below the resource requirements of a typical theme park venue. A Disney attraction such as the "Indiana Jones Adventure" might take hundreds of people to create. The *Aladdin* ride was developed by a team of approximately 25 people over 2 to 3 years.

Development of the attraction, including story, hardware and software, was done entirely in-house by a diverse group of Disney employees. Because it was developed as a theme park operation, the creation of *Aladdin* was led by producers whose job was in the design and construction of theme park attractions. This team was led by Jon Snoddy, then director of Imagineering's efforts to include new technologies into the Disney theme parks.

There were many personnel who provided key ideas and support of the program. In addition to producer Jon Snoddy. Executive support was given by Dave Fink (VP of R&D) and Mickey Steinburg. Innovative art direction was provided by Philip Freer, and later Gary Daines (who was mostly responsible for the hand-painted cel look of the *Aladdin* world). Composer and sound designer Aarin Richard brought the world to life with music and, perhaps more importantly, discovered the ability to combine the different types of sounds. The software technical lead for the project was Imagineer Scott Watson, who did most of the computer programming, with valuable help from the Silicon Graphics Performer™ team. Innovative hardware design came from Eric Haseltine, and Jesse Schell added the game elements to the Disneyland version.

The project was directed by George Scripner up to its presentation at EPCOT. During the EPCOT and Disneyland presentations, direction was by Bob Taylor. Taylor had considerable influence on the content that was shown to the public. This list is in no way complete. From 3D animators, to actors, to writers, many other people were involved with the creation of this application.

Many choices made by the designers creating this experience have been sprinkled throughout this section. But, because we consider content creation to be the most important element in this type of experience, the biggest design choices made were those involving the understanding and creation of intuitive ways for content designers to create the virtual world.

The visual aspects of the world were created using a combination of in-house software and *MultiGen 3D* modeling products. Character choreography was hand animated by in-house animators.

Sounds were recorded in locations similar to the virtual experience, for example, a marketplace. Musical scores were generated using traditional film-scoring techniques. Traditional sound effects techniques were also used for sounds associated with events, etc.

Narrative design was honed from being totally open ended to a mission game in order to match the time constraints of the venue. The open-ended approach was envisioned to be a world filled with interesting characters with which the guest could interact, generating a personalized story for each guests' experience. In the mission game approach, the overall plot is basically the same for each guest, although the order and timing of events may vary, and not all the guests' experiences will end with the scripted, victorious conclusion.

DESIGN CHOICE

Interactive design of the content is *very* important. The SAL (Story Animation Language) was developed specifically for this purpose. Artists (i.e., content developers) need the ability to quickly sketch out their ideas and see the results. If an artist has to wait too long between iterations, they will use a different tool or technique.

```
(spawn-task (spin-around guest clouds) `spin) (define (kill-when-stuck test-volume
max-time task) (defineguest-stuck0.0) (task-while (in-volume test-
volume guest)) (add!guest-stucktime-dt) (when(>max-timeguest-stuck) (rm-task
task-name) (kill)) )
(spawn-task (kill-when-stuck room-volume 20.0 `spin))
```

FIGURE 9-5

SAL code excerpt of a routine to help free a guest caught in a corner. (Watson)

The ability to revise scripts with rapid iterations is important to the creation of noninteractive scripts, and the design team felt this was also important in interactive narrative. Prior to the development of SAL, changes in the system required program compilation times of 4 to 5 hours, which were frequently done overnight. Thus iterations were basically slowed to one per day. If a compile failed, another half or full day was added to the cycle time.

The development of SAL allowed the team to iterate more frequently, making it easier for them to test new ideas. With SAL, a director or writer working on a project can make suggestions such as "What if you move this object over here?" "What if you change the timing on this event?" or "What if you make this object a little larger?" and see the results within a minute or two.

SAL (built on the Scheme computer language) was designed to optimize particular goals of the experience development:

- Building characters
- Creating animation of characters
- Interpreting commands provided by artists
- Synchronizing sound events with actions in the world

The SAL language was designed to be usable by animation and story artists. It allowed the artists a more direct means of expressing their ideas of the experience. Having a direct conduit helps to reduce the amount of human resources spent on entering the story, and reduce the pitfalls of misinterpretation that can occur when the writer communicates with the computer via someone else (who is more technically savvy) rather than communicating directly with the computer.

From their experience with feature films and theme park attractions, the developers knew the importance of audio in mentally immersing an audience into an experience. Using the layering technique described earlier, the main score can easily be combined with spatialized 3D sounds.

Buildings and objects in the world were impenetrable, so collision detection had to be calculated between the carpet and the walls and other objects in the world. They found this to be one of the bigger problems of the application development.[8]

In future projects, for performance and better flight, they will probably "cheat" by creating a second database specifically for determining collision events. This database would be in addition to the database for rendering the world.

With fully computed collision detection, people would sometimes get stuck in corners (e.g., between a staircase and a wall), causing them to bounce back and forth. This rapid bouncing results in the visual impression that the world is vibrating. A separate collision detection database could also be used to prevent flight into such corners and avoid the problem altogether.

Conclusion

This application was developed to explore the use of a new medium. Therefore, the developers were extremely interested in using their work to experiment with the features of the medium and analyze it. Trials were done with actual theme park attendees. Over the course of the EPCOT display,

---

[8]In fact, collision detection is a common difficulty for most projects that simulate interactive 3D worlds.

over 45,000 guests were selected to immersively experience *Aladdin* [Pausch et al.].

Each guest filled out a questionnaire containing questions regarding demographic information, what they liked and disliked the most about the experience, how it made them feel, and how much discomfort they felt. For some, this information was correlated to data gathered during the flight of the guest (their location and head orientation were stored several times a second). This logged data could then be used to analyze where guests flew and how much they moved their head, etc. [Pausch et al.]

Many results of these experiments have been published in *Disney's* Aladdin: *First Steps Toward Storytelling in Virtual Reality* [Pausch et al.]. Highlights include the relatively insignificant differences in the survey responses between male and female guests, a characteristic that also held for different age groups, which suggests that VR therefore has a broad appeal.[9]

It was hoped that analysis of the logged flight path data would show flight patterns and points of interest. They found, though, that people flew everywhere with no emergent patterns [Pausch et al.].

With such a long-running experiment, the designers were able to test many different iterations of the world, as well as many different system arrangements. Of particular interest was the correlation between the use of vestibular (motion) feedback and immersion (and nausea). The results suggest that when the motion base provided pitch movement that corresponded with the visual experience, guests gave a higher rating to the experience. However, there was also a higher report of nausea. To reduce the amount of guest nausea, they ultimately decided not to use the motion feedback.

The major accomplishment of the EPCOT *Aladdin* experience was the number and variety of people to whom it provided an immersive experience (over 45,000 from the general public). In addition to measuring some aspects of the guests' experience, it allowed the content creators to try many new ideas in this new medium. It also allowed

people to enter a world they first experienced in a linear medium: motion pictures.

The goal of this application was to experiment with and learn about virtual reality. The creators certainly met this goal, trying many different forms of navigation, display technology, and storytelling. Determining whether VR is a viable medium for a theme park, however, is a separate question that is still open. The fact that Disney chose to include VR experiences in their DisneyQuest venues suggests that VR may find a more permanent home in theme park and LBE environments.

It seems as though this application was successful at immersing the guests in the world of Agrabah. Survey respondents may have indicated this simply because it was their first use of virtual reality; however, a lot of effort was put into making the experience as immersive as possible within the constraints of the venue.

As we've indicated throughout this book, content is key, and having a good story with a familiar world certainly helps make the content more immersive. However, another important ingredient is the use of audio, especially audio that includes spatialized sound cues, sonically placing the user within a scene. Visually important was the fact that the world was an accurate representation of that provided by the Aladdin motion picture despite the fact that it was cartoon-like. In fact, choosing an animated world may have made it easier to immerse people. Pausch and colleagues distinguish between "photorealism" and "believability" [Pausch et.al., 1996]. They state that, in this case at least, the cartoon nature of the world increased the sense of "being there."

The designers made many discoveries in the course of creating this experience. Of the more significant discoveries was the ability to mix and layer different types of sounds. That is, sounds spatialized to a specific location in the world with generic 3D sounds, on top of a stereo background track. They also found that sound associated to (and spatially rendered with) an object adds to the sense of object permanence in a virtual world. Characters also seemed more believable if they made eye contact with the participant.

Many features of storytelling were uncovered in this experiment. One important feature is that people want something to do. They want a goal. Initially, people are willing

---

[9]Significantly, the questionnaires were designed in the hope of discovering differences in population segments.

to spend some amount of time exploring the world, but the smaller the world, the quicker people will lose interest without some direction. On the other hand, after the transition from the real world, participants need to have enough time to get their bearings and become familiar with the world in which they are immersed before they can set out with any sense of purpose. The length of time a participant may spend in the virtual world (as dictated by the venue) affects how open or directed the plot must be.

The major implementation discovery was that a separate database to handle collision detection between the participant and the objects (buildings, etc.) in the world would greatly simplify the task of keeping users from getting stuck in corners. At the same time, this would reduce the amount of computation needed for doing collision detection.

As mentioned, the *Aladdin* attraction was extended beyond the original test system, and installed in the Disneyland Starcade in 1996. This was also a temporary arrangement, and it is no longer available to the public. However, the DisneyQuest LBE commissioned the Imagineering VR Studio to produce a new *Aladdin* experience, as well as new VR experiences based on *Hercules* and *Pirates of the Caribbean*. Other VR experiences were installed at the LBEs, including *Ride the Comix* and a prehistoric river raft ride.

The developers are excited by the idea of giving the storyteller the ability to communicate directly with the senses. However, they feel that there are still some difficulties that currently hinder its use in the theme park venue. While the performance/price and availability are low, public VR venues often are more ride than story. Once the length of time available for participants to remain involved with the experience is extended, the ability for the storytellers to present a good interactive story in a 3D virtual world increases tremendously. As developer Gary Daines says: "If you don't have a goal, there's nothing to do—no story. This is true also for movies." After *Aladdin* was removed from the Disneyland Starcade venue, the immediate future for VR within Disney became in doubt. However, low-cost technology, and public acceptance of VR are becoming more widespread, so Disney continues to investigate potential VR projects for public entertainment.

As with any form of human communication, the message being transmitted is more important than the technology used for the exchange. Jon Snoddy drove this idea home when asked about the fidelity of the equipment used in the Aladdin experiences: "Content is the most important element (what you do), not the lens through which you perceive what you do."

CASE STUDY 9.2: VIRTUALITY GAME SYSTEMS

Many people who have experienced VR probably had their first exposure to virtual reality through VR games in an arcade, LBE, or theme park. In the future, home entertainment systems will probably be where more and more people will participate in virtual reality experiences. During the mid 1990s, this opportunity was primarily available on systems produced by Virtuality PLC. Virtuality was founded in 1987 and originally named W Industries. The company grew to become the world's largest supplier of LBE VR systems, with a 78% market share. Over 40 million people experienced VR games on one of their 1400 installed LBE systems.

The goal of Virtuality founder Dr. Jonathan Waldern and the Virtuality staff was to produce VR systems and experiences that were robust enough that they could be deployed in public spaces (and eventually homes) without requiring the venue operator or home user to be an expert in virtual reality or computer system integration. The company continued to innovate in new directions, establishing a professional VR development system—the Elysium series, developed with IBM, and a consumer prototype system developed for Atari. Unfortunately the Atari product never made it to market due to the demise of the Atari Jaguar platform for which it was designed. They also formed an

FIGURE 9-6

Many Virtuality games immerse the participant in a head-mounted display and provide a handheld controller that the participant uses to interact with the virtual world. A ring provides stability and creates a boundary for the participant's physical motion.
Photograph by William Sherman

Advanced Applications Division, which specialized in creating custom hardware and software implementations of Virtuality technology for corporate and industrial clients.

In many respects, the company was a victim of its own success. The company's exceptional growth during the first half of the 1990s led its new management[10] to invest heavily in inventory in order to speed up production of its entertainment systems. This decision proved costly during the downturn in the arcade industry in 1996 and led to a decline ending in the Virtuality Group filing for credit protection under Chapter 11 of the bankruptcy code in February 1997. However, the Virtuality name lives on. Cybermind GmbH, a Virtuality customer, cybercafe chain, and software development company headquartered in Berlin, Germany, acquired the Virtuality Entertainment business and continues to sell and support the systems worldwide. Dr. Waldern also returned to acquire the brand and certain technology assets he had been working on at Virtuality before founding his new company in California: Retinal Displays Inc.

---

[10] Dr. Waldern stepped down as CEO in 1995 and moved to the United States to pursue new display research interests.

Application Description

Two basic arcade configurations are offered on which the games are played. Both use a head-mounted display, with the graphics and simulation performed on a PC system with special graphics accelerator cards. The difference between the platforms is whether the participant stands and holds a handheld prop (model 2000SU) or sits with a steering and throttle input control mounted on the platform (model 2000SD). The VR games were designed with a specific interface platform in mind, depending on the travel interface involved.

In the stand-up system, the participant stands on a circular platform that also houses the computing equipment. A rail encircles the participant about waist high. This gives a limit to the distance the participant can physically walk, as well as something they can lean against or hold to maintain stability. The handheld prop is a 6-DOF tracked unit used for user input control (such as aiming and shooting, or activating something). Some games, such as the *Winchester Trap Master,* use specialized handheld props crafted to give a more realistic interface.

In the sit-down version, participants sit in a plastic pod with a bucket seat and a spoiler, giving it a carlike appearance. The armrests house the controllers that the participant uses to interact with the game.

The virtual world experiences appear as three-dimensional cartoon-like environments. The participant sees an avatar of the controller unit when appropriate to the game. For example, a rifle, a hand holding a pistol, or even the front of their vehicle. In multiplayer experiences, players see each other either as a human (standup platforms) or their vehicle (sit-down platforms).

As early as 1990, Virtuality realized that content was a crucial factor in how well VR arcade systems would be able to sustain market share and live beyond the initial "gee whiz, isn't VR cool" phase. Consequently, they hired someone with a background in film/TV production to help steer game development, Mike Adams. Recognizing that the content criteria for the home and traditional arcade game markets are significantly different, Adams realized how arcade games must be easy to learn and use, and provide a quick adrenaline rush worthy of the high cost per

FIGURE 9-7
Two basic platforms were configured for a wide variety of games. (Top left and bottom) Some games, such as Trap Master, *use special input devices such as the compressed air recoiling shotgun prop (top right).*
Images courtesy Virtuality PLC

game typically associated with these expensive systems. Games developed for home systems such as the Nintendo GameCube, Sony PlayStation 2, Microsoft Xbox can, or a home computer can be designed as larger worlds that can be explored in depth over a period of hours, days, or weeks.

Thus the bulk of Virtuality games were action oriented, and moved at a rapid pace for a rather brief period of play. As VR

home units become available, we can expect to see games that are more thought provoking and/or exploratory in nature. Increased opportunities for exploration and investigation give more depth to the possible content, but would take longer to play than is economically feasible in an arcade.

According to Adams, then vice president of the Virtuality Advanced Applications Division, content in the VR medium is manifested more as a location to explore than as a linear

FIGURE 9-8

Screen shot of a Dactyl Nightmare *game showing the time remaining at the top and the opponent's avatar in the middle.*
Image courtesy Virtuality PLC

story line. The story can be embedded in clues supplied in various nooks and crannies of the virtual world. Thus, the story unfolds in different ways depending on how the participants go about investigating the area.

Because the Virtuality systems were designed as platforms capable of running a variety of games, we must describe a selection of these games to give a sense of what was accomplished and motivate future design ideas. The following is a brief summary of several of the more popular Virtuality game experiences.

Dactyl Nightmare

This is the game that started it all; the first game Virtuality made available in public venues. It quickly became somewhat of a classic among VR game enthusiasts. Typically two (the minimum), but up to four, players can compete in a world consisting of five multilevel platforms. Each person appears in the world as a humanoid avatar holding a weapon. The goal is for each participant to shoot the others as rapidly as they can while avoiding being shot. This game uses the stand-up platform treating the handheld controller as the firing weapon.

The players can travel freely in the small world by pressing a button to move in the desired direction. The game designers chose to use a combination of gaze direction and the vector between their body and their weapon as the direction in which players would travel. Initially they implemented a basic gaze-directed method of travel, but during focus tests with teenage subjects, they found that the new method provided a good balance that better met their expectations.

An on-screen display shows the score of each player and the time remaining. Each player's score is simply how many times they have successfully shot another player. The person with the most points when the time runs out wins. To add interest to the game, a pterodactyl flies overhead. In addition to trying to avoid being hit by the other players, a player must also avoid the pterodactyl. Otherwise, it might swoop down, grab them in its claws, take them 200 to 300 feet above the play area, and drop them to their death, reducing their score by 1 point.

A sequel, *Dactyl Nightmare 2*, was produced a few years later that moved to a world of tunnels with the added goal of collecting pterodactyl eggs, in addition to preventing

FIGURE 9-9
Screen shot of Dactyl Nightmare 2 *showing one player adding an egg to his stack.*
Image courtesy Virtuality PLC

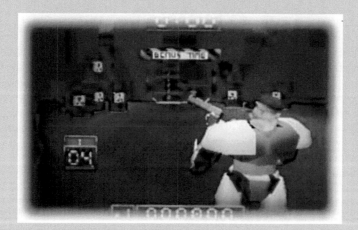

FIGURE 9-10
Screen shot of Zone Hunter, *showing a view from behind the player's avatar as would be viewed by people observing the game on a monitor.*
Image courtesy Virtuality PLC

opponents from doing the same. Opponents are hindered in their collecting by being shot or by being captured by the swooping pterodactyl. By changing the primary goal of the experience to collecting eggs, the subsequent game could now be played solo.

Zone Hunter

Zone Hunter, the second game in the Virtuality lineup is an adrenaline-based game that can be played in a single- or dual- player mode. The scenario of *Zone Hunter* is that the players are to save the earth from a mass invasion.

FIGURE 9-11
Screen shot of Buggy Ball *showing multiple cars battling for control of the ball.*
Image courtesy Virtuality PLC

Requiring a minimum of two players was found to hinder the ability to attract customers, because it would require two people interested in playing the same game. The restriction of requiring multiple players in the original *Dactyl Nightmare* was removed in Virtuality's second release for the arcade systems.

This game was also designed for the stand-up platforms. Players travel through an alien spaceship as though riding on a conveyor belt (the ride-along method of travel). The participants can look and shoot behind them, but their motion is always forward. This is a high-speed, high-adrenaline, "shoot everything in sight" game. When more than one player is participating, the players ride side by side on the virtual conveyor belt. There are several rounds to this game, and a virtual commander speaks instructions at each new level. To proceed to the next level of difficulty, players must achieve a minimum score in the preceding level.

Buggy-Ball

Buggy Ball is a sit-down game for up to four players. It was created to provide a family-oriented, nonviolent alternative to most of the other arcade content available. Thus, it is a good choice for those who prefer a game without guns and a focus on shooting things. In this game, the participants find themselves in a wok-shaped arena, driving dune buggy–like vehicles. Points are scored by forcing a large ball out of the arena. The ball is moved by driving up to it and pushing it with the vehicle. Competitors try to steal the ball from whoever has control.

Each user can choose the type of vehicle they will drive, with each providing a different set of capabilities. The four choices were a four-wheel-drive jeep, a dune buggy, a bulldozer, and a "mad" police car. Also, the overall game difficulty could be adjusted to one of four levels: easy, medium, hard, and crazy.

Pac-Man VR

Pac-Man VR is another family-oriented game for people who wish to have a less violent game. *Pac-Man VR* is an immersive, three-dimensional version of the classic two-dimensional Pac-Man made famous by NAMCO in 1980. *Pac-Man VR* is interesting in that it is a transposition of a game that was authored for a two-dimensional video game medium into a three-dimensional game in the medium of VR. Each of the Pac-Man characters is rendered in three dimensions and the game is played in a three-dimensional world. Up to four participants can play simultaneously, and each participant takes the role of a Pac-Man, seeing the world from Pac-Man's first-person point of view. The goal (as in traditional Pac-Man) is to traverse the maze, gobble

FIGURE 9-12
Screen shots of Pac-Man VR *showing the items that might be encountered in the corridors.*
Images courtesy Virtuality PLC

FIGURE 9-13
Screen shot of Trap Master.
Image courtesy Virtuality PLC

platform, but provides an added natural interface via a prop of a life-like shotgun (a close replica of a Winchester 101 shotgun). The prop uses CO_2 cartridges to provide haptic feedback via the Total Recoil™ system, which simulates the kickback felt when shooting an actual shotgun.

Participants in *Trap Master* find themselves in a simulated environment that recreates an actual setting, complete with mountains, lake, horses, and evergreens. The system employs voice activation and allows the participant to shout "Pull!" when they wish for the system to launch a clay target. If the participant does not shout "Pull!" within 5 seconds, the clay target is automatically launched. Points are earned by hitting the targets. The target shatters when hit.

There are four skill levels available, and a virtual shooting coach is available to novice shooters with tips on aim, leading, and wind judgment. A round consists of 25 targets. Twenty or more hits earn the participant a bonus of two extra targets launched in rapid succession. Since the target launcher in the trap house is constantly moving, no two games are exactly alike. This game is available in sporting club venues, such as gun clubs.

pills, and work, either in collaboration or competition with the other players, to avoid the ghosts. Another classic early arcade game translated into the medium of VR by Virtuality is Atari's *Missile Command.*

Trap Master

In 1995, Virtuality released *Trap Master.* Commissioned by Winchester™, *Trap Master* is for the sportsman who enjoys trap shooting or someone who would like to try the sport in a simulated environment. *Trap Master* uses the standup

Also using the Total Recoil hardware, the related game *QuickShot Carnival* provides a shooting gallery with fun,

FIGURE 9-14
*The Total Recoil version of the Virtuality hardware provides
a realistic interface to the sport of virtual trap shooting.*
Image courtesy Virtuality PLC

animated objects (such as leaping fish, marching soldiers, dive-bombing birds, shimmering tin cans, etc.) surrounding the participant. Participants shoot in rapid fire, and if they hit enough targets they get to advance to the next level. There are a total of eight levels, plus bonus scoring. The Total Recoil System earned Virtuality the "Best of Show" award at the arcade industry's annual IAAPA (International Association of Amusement Parks and Attractions) show in 1995.

Legend Quest
Probably the most ambitious game experience brought to the Virtuality system was *Legend Quest. Legend Quest* was a Dungeons and Dragons™–style game with multiple adventures that participants could engage in alone or with companions. *Legend Quest* was one of the few Virtuality experiences created by developers outside of the company,

and was marketed in particular (LBE) venues specifically designed only for play of this game.

In many venues, monitors are available for spectators and people waiting in line to watch. Allowing onlookers to see what is happening inside the participants' HMDs helps to attract attention, as well as helps new players know what to expect and get a basic understanding of what to do in the experience. The venue operator helps to position and suit up players, and will often supply hints to novice players such as advising them to avoid only looking forward as most inexperienced players tend to do.

The arcade games would typically last under 5 minutes and generally cost on the order of $1 per minute. There have been Virtuality installations in many major cities in shopping malls, arcades, and other amusement venues worldwide. Additionally, arrangements have been made to have systems provided for special events and parties.

VR System
The Virtuality arcade systems all use high-durability, lightweight plastic HMD units designed by Virtuality. Named the *Visette,* the initial model weighed about 8 pounds and provided true stereo display from the dual graphics cards in the Amiga based Series 1000 systems. A later model, the *Visette2,* was lighter weight and higher resolution. Although the Visett2 includes dual displays (one for each eye), the Virtuality 2000 systems render only a single, monoscopic image displayed to both eyes. The designers felt that the loss of stereopsis was an acceptable trade-off for the lower cost of a single graphics card. The other 3D cues give a sense of immersion and three-dimensionality. Stereo headphones are integrated into the HMD for the sound display.

Tracking is implemented with the Polhemus electromagnetic tracking system. Both the head and handheld props are tracked in full 6-DOF, although not all games take advantage of this.

A single computer system handles the game simulation, the graphics and the sounds of each experience. In the (earlier) Series 1000 systems, a slightly modified Amiga computer system was used. Later, the 2000 Series systems introduced in 1994 used a PC-compatible system with graphics cards

FIGURE 9-15
*A special HMD and tracker system were developed by Virtuality
for interfacing with the Atari Jaguar home gaming console.*
Images courtesy Virtuality PLC

designed specifically for the Virtuality system. At the time
there were not many commercially available real-time
graphics accelerator cards available for PC systems. A separate card handled audio computation and rendering.

In addition to the well-know arcade hardware, Virtuality
also developed several other products or prototypes for the
VR market. Some of these products include an inexpensive
tracking system using infrared light called V-TRAK for the
Atari Jaguar VR system. Unfortunately, this system never
made it to market due to the demise of the Atari Jaguar
game system. The Visette2 was sold independently from
the arcade systems, allowing VR programmers to use the
HMD on their workstations. The Elysium system (developed in partnership with IBM) was a complete integrated
VR workstation with development software. Universities
and research organizations were the primary customers for
this system. Virtuality also researched and developed prototypes of products such as tactile feedback gloves.

Virtuality developed its own software library for interfacing
with the arcade hardware and with the graphics accelerator

hardware. With this software library, programmers had
access to information about the user such as their full 6-DOF
head position, hand-controller prop position for standup
units, and driving controls for sit-down units. It was up to
the programmer of the particular games as to how they
would make use of the information. For example, not all
games use the translational movement of the head to calculate the point of view, whereas in *Virtuality Boxing,* head
location is very important and so had to be used to calculate the viewpoint. However, for applications such as *Zone
Hunter,* where the crucial movement of the participant is
through methods of travel other than physical locomotion,
this feature was often excluded.

By providing a software library to handle the VR aspects of
an experience, Virtuality hoped to attract other game design
companies to write new games for (or port old games to)
their arcade hardware platforms. Games developed by
third parties included *Sphere,* a tank simulation for SD systems, and *Shoot for Loot,* a multilevel game show spoof
by Gremlin Interactive in the UK. Unfortunately, the third-
party developer initiative suffered from the typical business model in which the arcade business operates. Profit in
the arcade game manufacturing business is made primarily
from selling the hardware units.[11]

Since Virtuality provided the arcade hardware, it was not
as advantageous for third parties to participate.

Development of games for the Virtuality arcade hardware
took about 10 months, with the equivalent of four to five
people at an overall cost of about $180,000. Each game had
a producer, who would also be responsible for other projects, a lead programmer, an entry-level programmer, and
varying amount of time from graphical artists to produce
models and texture maps. A typical Sega arcade title might
use 15 people over a year or two to produce.

Different content for different media
Aside from the differences in how software content is created for Virtuality arcade experiences, the differences in

---

[11] In the home video game business, most of the profit comes
from sales of licensed software.

what content is appropriate for this medium as opposed to other forms of entertainment is also important. VR experiences differ from motion pictures in much the same way as other interactive computer-mediated entertainment in that motion pictures are presented in a preset, linear exposition. Computer-mediated experiences are not limited to a linear path through the storyline.

This difference leads to several implications for computer experiences. Where motion pictures can hide the unimplemented details of the virtual world being presented behind facades by using careful camera placement and other techniques, worlds presented via a virtual reality interface must fill in these details. The user's ability to choose a course of action in computer experiences means the world must be prepared to handle different possible paths, which greatly affects how the experience is plotted by the authors. In fact, the nature of who is the author is brought to the fore. While the audience bears some notion of authorship in a motion picture or play, this is much stronger in media whereby the audience can affect the storyline.

Another important implication of interactivity is the loss of timing. In motion pictures, the emotions of the audience can be controlled to a certain degree by how events are timed. In interactive media, timing generally cannot be precisely controlled. There are some specific cases where timing can be controlled in an interactive experience when some action must be performed in a set amount of time. Other possibilities are to affect timing of event by bringing agents to the user or having events occur to the user that force them to react.

Although some authors of interactive fiction experiences strive to create experiences with an existing story, while still giving the participant the sense of complete control of their actions, most computer experiences resolve this dilemma in one of two other ways: by reducing the actual freedom available to the player or by limiting the action to that of a particular scenes or battles. By limiting action to events that can be scored, such as a battle, the game can let the players act freely, and their actions affect the plot by determining one of two paths. Either the battle is won, and the story can continue, or the battle is lost, and the game is over. Thus, plot exposition (if there is any) is reserved for cut scenes, or a short story of what went before to bring things

to their current state. Other experiences let players feel as though they are choosing their own course, but attempt to subtly direct their actions. Of course, if this is not done well, players will notice that their hands are tied, and their suspension of disbelief, or mimesis, will be broken.

When writing content for a new medium, such as VR, further restrictions are placed on what can reasonably be presented to the audience. For authors developing games for the Virtuality arcade systems, there was a broad set of criteria that affected the design of the games. Many of the criteria originate with the criteria of game design for any arcade game. First, one must assume they are writing for the first-time player. There must be clear and easy to follow rules. Games must give a 3-minute or so adrenaline rush and then give awards for accomplishing some goal. And, in head-based VR, when the user dons the HMD, they will be disoriented and will need time to adapt to the environment.

Probably the most constraining criterion is that the game must offer the quick adrenaline rush and chance of early accomplishment. Game designers for Virtuality arcade systems would have liked to have a game with lots of strategy and depth, but it is difficult if not impossible to create such games for this venue. Even home games such as *DOOM*™ or *Quake*™, which only offer a slight increase in control complexity over arcade games, rely on players to spend a lot of time before they begin to experience a sense of accomplishment. Richer, more complicated experiences generally require a delayed sense of satisfaction, preceded by hours of frustration. Lengthier VR arcade games cannot be developed expecting the players to pay for the hours of frustration experienced prior to accomplishment.

For Virtuality, *Zone Hunter* was the most popular title overall. This was due mostly to the fact that it was very simple and had a very low learning curve, and thus novice users could play the game without getting lost or stuck in corners. People already familiar with virtual reality preferred *Dactyl Nightmare* because it provided more controls, allowing the participants to roam freely.

Related Applications and Follow-on Work
Although Virtuality as we know it doesn't exist today, there has certainly been a progression in the creation of virtual reality and augmented reality games. One particularly

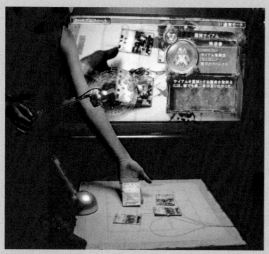

FIGURE 9-16
Sony's Eye of Judgment *game uses augmented reality technology.*

interesting augmented reality game targeted at the home video game market is Sony's *Eye of Judgment,* which runs on the PlayStation®3.

Eye of Judgment uses decks of cards with imagery as well as fiducial markers. A camera that attaches to the PlayStation is set up to point downward to where the cards are played. The system displays on the television monitor. When a player positions a card on the playing surface, the camera sees the fiducial marker and displays the appropriate (animated, three-dimensional) computer graphics on the screen. When another player places their card on the playing surface, the three-dimensional graphics related to that card are also displayed on the screen. When the cards are moved toward each other, the graphics then interact with each other.

Conclusion

Virtuality certainly set the bar for other public venue VR experiences by producing hardware that could withstand the rigors of regular public usage and providing a wide variety of game experiences. The main barrier to more widespread adoption was that the systems were expensive to purchase, operate, and play, and thus did not fit well in the established video arcade market.

At the time of introduction of such VR systems, video arcade operators typically purchased conventional game machines for about $5000 and charged $.50 per play (which might last several minutes). This is both cost-effective for the player and for the operator, who typically only needs to leave the machine sitting there and to periodically empty the money. However, the VR arcade systems generally require an attendant to help players get in and out of the equipment, plus control when the game begins and perhaps give instructions during play. For relatively short experiences, players paid about $1 per minute of play. This compared with the home option of purchasing a home game console at the initial retail price of roughly $300. If it takes the purchaser 70 hours to complete a home adventure-game experience, then their cost was $0.06 per minute, which assumes that the game and hardware have no further value.

Because arcade and other LBE environments offer a limited market for VR systems, Virtuality also made efforts to expand their market opportunities by creating an Advanced Applications Division. This division focused on the creation of custom VR applications and systems for corporate and industrial clients. Projects included marketing, training, and science museum presentations (what we might call "location-based education").

Their first marketing project was an experience brought to auto show trade floors demonstrating the Ford Galaxy.[12]

The experience consisted of boarding a virtual model of the car and being driven around by a chauffeur who explained about different features of the car. A research survey conducted at one exposition revealed that 77% of people wanted to do it again and 95% would recommend it to friends.

Another client was the Winchester gun manufacturing company. Winchester commissioned a clay target shooting experience to attract people to the sport at fairs and shows. This system proved so popular that Virtuality and Winchester agreed to market the system to LBE and arcade customers as well.

In addition to direct product marketing, two training applications developed by Virtuality including a motorcycle driving trainer and an escape route safety trainer for oil platforms. The motorcycle trainer, developed for Kawasaki, includes a special platform with a motorcycle frame for the user to sit on. The platform includes the standard motorcycle control interface. The oil-rig escape trainer used video texture maps to display prerecorded agents who lead the user through the correct escape route.

The City of Nagoya, Japan, commissioned Virtuality to develop a VR experience in which children could learn about the interactions between humans and the environment. The result was a 48-person theater. The theater was designed to allow groups of 12 to work in four teams, with one member of each group wearing an HMD (the VR rider) and the others giving instructions to that user while looking at monitors for information about the virtual world. The goal of the experience is to solve an ecosystem problem. The team lands on the virtual world from space and discovers the world to be suffering from a slight case of decay. The team finds problems using its monitor, then instructs the VR rider on what life-forms to track down and photograph. The nonimmersed

---

[12]The European name for the Windstar MPV.

FIGURE 9-17
An instructor helps the user find the way out of a burning oil platform.
Image courtesy Virtuality PLC

members of the team use the standard monitor to research the organism to learn how it relates to the ecosystem. The experience has different settings for different age groups. For the youngest ages, the system is mostly on autopilot and thus conveys the information as a story.

In 1996, Virtuality won a *CyberEdge Journal* CJ award for VR applications with its *RiverWorld* collaborative music application demonstrated at the SIGGRAPH '96 computer graphics conference. Produced by Mike Adams of Virtuality, the project itself was a collaborative project with the House of Blues, Philips, and Motorola Inc., with additional consulting by musician Thomas Dolby. Players at different sites could "play" specific instruments, and all participants could hear the combined sounds.

After Virtuality filed for Chapter 11 credit protection, the Entertainment Systems business was acquired by Cybermind, which continued to sell and support the systems worldwide. The Advanced Applications software development team went on to found a new company: Maelstrom Virtual Productions. Dr. Waldern himself founded Retinal Displays Inc., after leaving Virtuality under new management. Retinal Displays Inc. later developed new digital optical technologies of smaller, lighter, and higher-performance displays.

FIGURE 9-18

A special interface platform developed for Kawasaki allows participants to learn how to ride a motorcycle. Details such as working mirrors enhance the simulation's usefulness as a training aid.
Images courtesy Virtuality PLC

The breakup of the Virtuality team does not, however, diminish their role in the history of the medium of virtual reality. Virtuality played an important role in introducing VR to the public in a way that could be directly experienced. It produced products and games that were durable and accessible. Virtuality founder Dr. Jonathan Waldern summarizes how improving technology will continue to drive the possibilities:

The first steps toward a mass market for VR were taken by Virtuality. Today, companies are developing critical optical technologies which will allow VR and many other high performance display oriented applications to become viable for the consumer market. The computer hardware and software technologies are already there. Evolving network technologies will soon enable real time multi-participant VR experiences that cross any geographic boundary.

CASE STUDY 9.3: VIRTUAL DIRECTOR

Executive Summary

Traditionally, computer graphics animators were required to create virtual camera moves using desktop tools such as a monoscopic screen and a mouse. In order to create camera moves and perform other actions in a three-dimensional world, the animator had to manipulate the camera in three dimensions using a two-dimensional display and a two-dimensional input device. Mapping the two-dimensional interface on, say, a standard desktop system into appropriate three-dimensional camera moves was a difficult task. The virtual director application allows the animator to move the camera in a three-dimensional display with a three-dimensional input device in a virtual environment.

FIGURE 9-19
Bob Patterson, a computer graphics animator and co-developer of Virtual Director, *uses the virtual director application to collaborate on a scientific visualization project.*

In general, the output of the *VirDir* program is used to create traditional two-dimensional, linear movies. *VirDir* is particularly interesting for a variety of technological reasons. Because inputs needed to be very precise, as well as for other reasons, a speech interface was implemented. *VirDir* is also used in collaborative scenarios where animators, content experts, and other interested parties can collaborate at great distances geographically while sharing the same virtual world. The collaborators are connected via audio, as well as visually through the use of avatars.

Introduction

The *Virtual Director* application (*VirDir*) is a virtual reality tool that is a *navigation* and camera choreography tool for virtual environments as well as the desktop and acts as an aid in creating camera moves for computer graphics (CG) animations in multiple formats. The tool surrounds the user with a three-dimensional virtual world, and gives them a virtual camera with which to choreograph the camera's position in the virtual world. Voice input combined with gestures allows the director great flexibility in interactively creating camera moves. While *Virtual Director* can be used for entertainment purposes, the original application for the tool was to aid in the creation of movies of computer graphics for scientific understanding and communication. Indeed, the tool has been used as an aid creating scientific visualizations that are quite entertaining, or more specifically, "edutaining." The *Virtual Director* has been used in the production of computer animation for a variety of products, including a scientific visualization segment in the Oscar™-nominated IMAX film *Cosmic Voyage*, the PBS show *Mysteries of the Deep Space*, and animations of the ecological system of the Chesapeake Bay. It has found additional use in projects such as PBS's *Nova* HDTV special "Mapping the Universe," including simulations of cosmology.

The *Virtual Director* came about for a variety of reasons. The overriding goal was to create a tool that could be used in the motion picture production process. The primary focus of the *Virtual Director* has been to provide a variety of navigation tools to examine scene from all angles. A secondary goal was to create a tool for previsualizing camera moves for live-action shoots. Additional uses have also been envisioned, such as providing an interactive editing tool that could be used to create a rough cut of the product even before any filming takes place.

A catalyzing factor that helped to bring about the creation of the *Virtual Director* was that virtual reality equipment was available at the National Center for Supercomputing Applications (NCSA) where researchers also work on animations for scientific visualization. In particular, a *BOOM*™ head-based display was installed in 1991, followed by a *CAVE*™ projection-based VR display in 1994. Some of NCSA's computer graphics animators and scientific visualization producers were interested in how the VR equipment could be utilized as an aid in their work. After early test efforts were made using the *BOOM*, the current thrust of *VirDir* development began anew focused around a design for the *CAVE* and other projection-based VR displays.

A parallel goal for the system was to enable animators to do their work while minimizing the amount of typing required. This goal was precipitated by animator Bob Patterson, who was then working in computer graphics production at Industrial Light and Magic (ILM). Due to the severity of repetitive stress injuries (RSI) suffered from the amount of mouse motions done while creating computer animations for ILM, he returned to NCSA where he had previously worked. There he rejoined the push by Donna Cox to reestablish the efforts to create a "virtual director" driven by the need for a choreography tool for the making of *Cosmic Voyage*.

Thus, a design goal was that the *Virtual Director* would reduce the need for typing, mouse moves, and other discrete and repetitive physical inputs. Instead, voice input combined with fluid, whole-body movements are the primary method of input. Patterson looked to VR as an alternate way of working from the usual method of sitting in an office "typing, clicking, and dragging."

In the field of computer graphics, the scene is viewed through a virtual camera. This camera generally has parameters that correspond to a physical camera, such as focal distance, zoom, and a position relative to the objects in the scene. Before *Virtual Director,* camera paths for computer graphics animation were created on a desktop workstation running a tool such as *Alias/Wavefront* or *Alias/SoftImage.* Tools such as this have a very intense learning curve, and they take their input primarily from typed commands and mouse motions.

One of the more difficult aspects of using workstation tools is that they use a two-dimensional display to solve a three-dimensional problem. Hence, the user is forced to move the virtual camera in three-space via a two-dimensional interface. The moves were created by moving in one plane at a time. There had to be a better way.

For live-action shoots, camera moves are generally planned during production. While stand-ins are used instead of actors to help "block out" a shot, the crew and camera rentals eat into the budget, even if no film is shot. At $300,000.00 per day, time spent deciding how the camera should be placed and move in correspondence to the action can be very costly. Thus, it might prove prudent to use VR to previsualize the scene.

For live-action shots that will have computer-generated special effects added later, the placement of the camera is even more important. Having a preplanned camera path that is followed on the set helps the effects workers who do what is known as "match moving" to create a CG camera that follows the same path as the physical camera. On the flip side, having a virtual copy of the set and actions of the actors and props can be used on the set as CG puppets overlaid in the video playback of the shot. This allows the director to see a better approximation of what the image will look like after post-production.

Application Description

In contrast to creating experiences meant to be experienced in virtual reality, *Virtual Director* is used to exploit the three-dimensional, immersive qualities of VR to *produce* content meant for some other medium. Thus the VR experience of the CG animators is not what the final audience will see. The audience's view of the virtual world will be constrained to the scope of the virtual camera. In addition, the final rendering of the image may include many details only hinted at during the choreography work.

VirDir offers the computer animation producers a variety of tools to enable them to quickly create compelling camera moves for export to an animation system.

One thing that this allows is for directors to experiment with shots by themselves without relying on an animation technical director (TD) to be with them to support this activity. If directors care to, they can create the final camera moves themselves.

Representation of the Virtual World

The content in the virtual world of this application is dependent on the content of the virtual world of the production being created. Thus, if the *Virtual Director* is being applied to a film about star formations in the universe, the virtual world in this application contains stars. If the production is an animation for a television commercial, the virtual world is made up of characters and props related to the product. For previsualization of live-action scenes, the virtual world consists of virtual recreations of the live set, with CG representations of actors and props.

The virtual world of *VirDir* also includes elements of the user interface, the visualization of the camera path, plus avatar representations of other participants with whom the user is collaborating over the network.

Once camera moves have been choreographed, the move information is transferred to batch-animation software that renders the final results. The *Virtual Director* can be readily modified to create output suitable for many popular rendering and animation systems such as *Renderman*™, *Maya*™, and *SoftImage*™, as well as custom rendering software. For *Cosmic Voyage*, Loren Carpenter of Pixar developed a custom star particle renderer based on *Renderman*. Extra information can be stored about the camera path for renderers capable of calculating motion blur (e.g., *Renderman*).

The virtual world and interface elements are displayed in such a way as to clearly distinguish the interface controls from the scene. While the virtual world exists as a three-dimensional space that the user can travel through, most of the user interface elements are placed to appear on the surfaces of the VR display screens. This serves the multiple purposes of helping to distinguish between the virtual world and the user interface, as well as emphasizing the 2D nature of the final output and menu inputs. It also means that these elements can be more naturally viewed by the eyes because the focal distance and convergence cues will match. In fact, the stereo glasses are not even necessary to view 2D objects co-located with the screen. However, interface elements that are inherently 3D, such as the camera path representation, and avatars of collaborators are treated as part of the 3D virtual world.

The visual representational style of the animation world can be whatever the animators create. It can range from nearly photorealistic models of recognizable objects to abstract shapes, colors, and movements. The *Virtual Director* can be used to find a visual path through any form that can be represented by the computer. For example, for the IMAX movie *Cosmic Voyage*, stars and stellar gas make up the entirety of the animation world. Simple polygons and texture maps were used to represent the stars and gaseous material in the VR display.

The user interface of the virtual director has a very no-nonsense form. Menus, command inputs, and information about key frames and time values are given as text on the screen. Text is colored based on the type of information presented. For example, error messages are displayed in red to make them more prominent. The 2D "TV" view representation is simply a configurable rectangle on the screen with a rendered image inside. This TV can be formatted according to output style, such as HDTV, Imax, etc, and shows a rendering of the world rendered in 2D from the perspective of the computer graphics virtual camera.

Camera paths within the virtual world can be shown either as a series of points through the space, or these points can have axes added that show the direction that camera is looking, and a vector pointing toward the top of the view. Key frames are distinguished from the in-between positions of the camera by yellow squares. A dodecahedral wireframe highlights the current key frame. For the camera itself, the user can select different representations ranging from a simple forward/up axis pair to a "viewfinder" that shows an image of what will appear on the screen.

In the initial phases of the project, audio was not a high priority and was not implemented. Developers put forth several possibilities to improve the audio quality. One is to provide feedback to commands. The initial implementation was done via a text display. Another possibility would be to attach audio to objects in the virtual world scene. Also, sound could add the capability to do sonification in the environment, mapping sounds to various data parameters. This is important because *VirDir* is often used for producing scientific visualization.

Another potential use for audio is to enable the audio tracks from the production to be edited in the *CAVE* concurrently with the video production. This could be especially useful for editing three-dimensional audio in the scene.

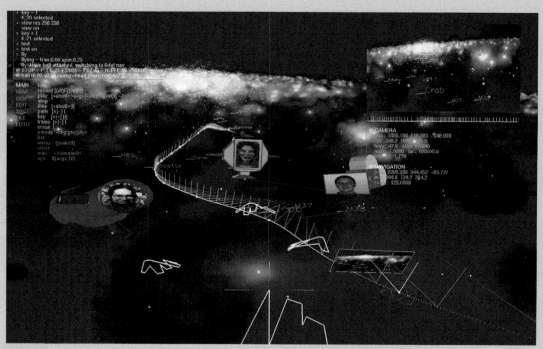

FIGURE 9-20

Many elements of the Virtual Director *user interface can be seen in this image. Collaborators are depicted by avatars that include their photograph, and an icon of their hand. The path of a computer graphics camera is shown as a line with axes that show the direction of the camera. Text information such as messages and commands can be seen in the upper left corner, while a two-dimensional image in the upper right corner shows a two-dimensional rendering of what the computer graphics camera sees.*

FIGURE 9-21

Two of the application developers collaborate in a CAVE to fine-tune camera moves for a scientific visualization animation.

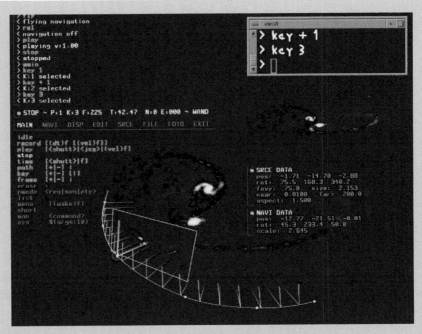

FIGURE 9-22

The Virtual Director *application allows speech input for its commands. In this image, the window in the upper right shows text translations of commands that were issued via the speech interface.*

Apart from holding the physical wand input device, there is no haptic feedback in this application. Originally the *Virtual Director* was displayed in a *BOOM,* which gave the feel of putting hands on a camera and directing it through the space. However, this was lost when the project was transferred to the *CAVE* system.

Since the *Virtual Director* is designed to create content for a medium that is limited to sights and sounds, the addition of other senses to the *VirDir* application itself must be beneficial toward this preeminent goal. The application designers and developers have not found a compelling reason to pursue the use of senses beyond mostly visual, and partially aural and haptic feedback.

Interaction with the Virtual World

The genre of this application is *iterative design*. It is often used by a single user, who begins by exploring the space and sketching out some camera moves, eventually refining the choreography to meet the narration goals of the animation.

It can also be used as a *collaborative design tool* allowing multiple people to sketch path ideas, share interesting point-of-view paths and to comment on the ideas of others. The primary form of interaction with *Virtual Director* is free-form flying through the space, augmented with voice commands to govern the movement, and to adjust various features of the interface.

The narrative of this application is free exploration of the animation virtual world. The goal is to find interesting and insightful views and camera motions through the world. Participants can create camera moves that persist from session to session, allowing them to come back later and pick up where they left off.

Over the course of developing an animation, or live-action previsualization, the director will go through a sequence of phases that are all accommodated by the *Virtual Director*. At first, the director will simply want to explore the space of the world, flying around to determine where some

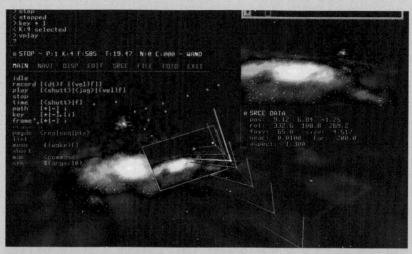

FIGURE 9-23

Virtual Director *has been used as a tool in the creation of many scientific visualization animations that have been seen by many people on television, in planetariums, and in IMAX™ movie theaters. This image shows a snapshot from the development of a scene illustrating colliding galaxies for the IMAX movie* Cosmic Voyage.

interesting and informative viewpoints are located. In the case of scientific visualizations, this will often be done in collaboration with the researcher that produced the data being visualized. The next phase is to "sketch" some preliminary camera paths and create rough animations from these paths to see how well they work. Once some good sketches have been produced, the director will probably create new paths based on the better sketches. Again these paths will be used to create test animations. If the results of the test animations are favorable, the director may go back into *VirDir* to fine tune a few key frames to create the final choreographed camera path.

In most cases, the scene for which the camera path is being created will itself have some form of narrative that evolves over time.

Because the goal of camera choreography is to help the viewer find their way through the space of the virtual world, it is vital that the "virtual director" be able to easily navigate the space themself. Thus, a variety of methods are available for the user to accomplish this task within the framework of the *Virtual Director* application. Using wand inputs in combination with voice commands, each of the different methods of travel are useful for different subtasks.

The most common method of travel is a style of *fly-through* control that allows the operator to simultaneously manipulate their location and orientation through the space. The particular method of flight control chosen is based on relative movement of the wand from the point where travel was activated. Translation is controlled by moving the wand fore and aft from the original position. Orientation is controlled by rotating the wand about its axes. Because users can begin by slowly moving the wand and gradually increase the offset from the "zero point," they can easily do moves that follow the traditional CG maneuvers of "ease-in" and "ease-out." The degree to which the particular magnitude of arm and wrist movements are translated to flight through the world is defined by the users, so they can select whether they want gross arm movements to be necessary to move at high speeds, or if only subtle physical movements will produce the same results. Voice command activates and deactivates wand-gesture input to the various functions.

As the user becomes skilled with the *Virtual Director*, they learn to perform several common physical maneuvers for different kinds of moves. An example of a move that is straightforward in *VirDir* is to choose an object and orbit about it while keeping the object in view of the camera. While this type of shot is not overly difficult to accomplish on a workstation screen using a mouse for a stationary object or point of interest, if the object itself is moving or there are other complicating factors, then the desktop method can quickly become tedious, requiring the user to move the camera a bit, then adjust the angle a bit, followed by moving the camera a bit, and again changing the angle a bit, ad nauseum. Such a camera move can be easily accomplished with *Virtual Director* by using a tool that automatically keeps the camera centered on a specific point of interest. However, while this is useful for a novice user, Patterson finds this mechanism too artistically constraining and instead chooses to maneuver the wand in three-dimensional space to achieve a satisfactory result. The *VirDir* point-of-interest tool allows camera-orbiting capability that allows orbiting around any point of interest, including camera paths while tracking some phenomenon. A second form of *fly-through* travel control is also available that is a little easier to use, though less flexible. This method of travel was added to allow novice users to explore the virtual world without requiring a lot of practice to become familiar with the controls. This can be important when a scientist collaborating with the director wants to point out an important visual element of the world, even though the scientist might not be a regular user of *VirDir*.

For some animations, the director may desire to affect the relationship between the scale of the world and the viewer. To this end, controls over changing (travelling through) scale are also provided. In life-like shots, the scale is generally set to be 1:1 with the real world. However, in many visualizations, such a scale would not serve the purpose of the animation, which is to allow the viewer to see the interesting features of the world.

The ability to adjust scale also provides for a method of travel we refer to as *scale-the-world* travel. In *Virtual Director*, scale-the-world travel is accomplished by scaling the user up relative to the size of the world about the point at which they are currently located. By them physically moving to another location in the apparently diminished world, and rescaling to the original size, the user is now located at the new location. In the case of *VirDir*, scaling is done about the location of the wand, so the user can move with a few simple movements of the wand. Scaling the user relative to the world also achieves the effect of allowing the user to make fine or gross location adjustments with the wand.

In addition to the fly-through modes of travel, the user can also *jump travel* to particular positions in the data. Voice commands allow users to select a particular (existing) key frame they would like to jump to, or they can jump to preset locations and times, or for particular types of scientific simulation data, to a region based on the resolution of the data.

Jumps to key frames move the user to the location of the frame without changing their orientation with respect to the world. Preset jumps can also be set to jump to a location while retaining the orientation, or can be set to orient the viewer to a particular view. Presets can also set the scale between the user and the data. For scientific datasets with varying degrees of resolution based on the data (referred to as Adaptive Mesh Refinement (AMR) simulations), the user jumps to the specified region at the appropriate scale for viewing the specified region.

Existing camera paths can also be used to control travel in a manner familiar to film and video editors, through *shuttle control*. Since each camera path denotes a path through space (and time), the user can select a path and then move along it in animation time[13] by twisting the wand with their wrist.

As a control mechanism through story space and time, *VirDir* must pay equal attention to moving through time as it relates to the virtual world. Just as in live-action motion pictures, slow-motion photography, time-lapse photography, and gimmicks such as a rapidly moving clock or calendar pages falling away are used to indicate that time is passing in the virtual world at a different rate than the physical world of the audience, the same is often true of animations. This is often the case with scientific visualizations. As the camera

---

[13]By "animation time" we mean that the camera moves along the frames of the path as though shuttling through the animation.

moves from frame to frame (advancing in "animation time"), the time in the virtual world might remain fixed, flow at a steady but faster or slower pace than reality, or even make discrete jumps in time.

In the case of *Cosmic Voyage*'s colliding galaxy segment, 25 million years are covered over the course of 5 seconds of the audience members' lives.

Because the worlds that the camera is moving through are often dynamic, a camera position is defined by where the camera is in space as well as exactly when in time. Thus, the application is dealing with time in three ways: data time, animation time, and real time. Part of the difficulty in maintaining acceptable results is that the various methods of keeping time must be unified in a harmonious fashion. The time-varying data does not necessarily vary at the same rate as the rate the frames in the animation are being displayed. For example, if there are 18 time steps per second in the dynamic dataset, yet the animation will be played at 30 frames per second, the application must reconcile what data time is to be displayed in each frame of the animation and, if necessary, create appropriate data by interpolation or other means.

Other than turning on and off menus and the "TV" display, the main objects within the *Virtual Director* that can be manipulated are the interface elements that exist within the virtual world: key frames, and whole camera paths. Additionally, the user can turn on/off the display of visualization elements, change isosurface values, create data slices, etc.

It is important to note that the aforementioned methods of travel through the space did not necessitate that camera paths were being created. In fact, users can fly the camera through the space without changing their own view of the world. For example the animator can move the virtual camera through the world much like a child might fly a toy airplane through the space around them without letting go of it. However, these methods of travel are a necessary part of camera path creation.

Directors can choose to create camera paths in a variety of ways. They can physically fly the handheld prop through the scene. They can discretely create keyframes and allow the application to create a spline path from key frame to key frame. The third option is to capture the path taken as they fly-through the world. The first choice listed (physically moving the wand through the scene) is the simplest, but also the least used method of creating a camera path. This is likely due to the fact that to accomplish this, the entire scene must be scaled to fit within the *CAVE*, and that situation doesn't allow for subtle control.

One common method of camera path creation is to find a few interesting views and connect them together by moving to each view, voicing the command to create a key frame at the current position, adjusting time, and then moving to the next view adjusting the key frame. The application developers and users state that this technique is very valuable, as long as the user maintains an awareness of their scale and the rate of passage of time. *Virtual Director* provides visual representations to aid that awareness.

Another common method of camera path creation is to maneuver to a good starting view and then activate a travel-recording mode such that either the position of the user's head or the center of the *CAVE* are used as input to the camera. If the user does not travel anywhere, then the camera will remain stationary (though time will pass in the simulated world). As the user flies through the world, the camera will follow along dropping key frames at regular intervals, creating a path that will be mimicked upon playback.

By creating multiple camera paths, camera path sequences can be created and edited. There are several possible sequence-editing constructs in the system, including:

- *Regular,* in which the camera stays on one path

- *Priority,* where the camera follows a master path, but can be overridden at any point in time by a higher priority move for brief parts

- *Sequential,* in which each camera path is executed in order, even if that means jumping back in time to begin the next sequence

- *Edit list management,* though not yet implemented, the future plans for *Virtual Director* include the capability of allowing any arbitrary sequence of paths and portions of paths to be strung together in a straightforward manner

The editing of camera paths is done by adjusting, adding, or deleting key frames on the path.

FIGURE 9-24

Many collaborators are visible in this image. These scientists are collaborating on their investigations of the Chesapeake Bay.

Each key frame contains information about the position in space and time of the camera within the simulated world. The actual camera path is a spline curve fitted to smoothly pass through all of the key frames. Fine-tuning a camera path is done by manipulating individual key frames.

Key frames are individually adjusted using menu input and wand movements to perform operations such as slight translations and/or rotations, gross movements, or deleting the key frame altogether. A key frame to be modified or deleted is selected by voice. Once selected, the key frame can be adjusted with the wand using either *relative* or *absolute* manipulation. Absolute manipulation causes the key frame to jump to the current position of the wand. When this is done to key frames that are a large distance from the viewer, the key frame will be moved considerably, and in the process is likely to terribly distort the camera path on which it resides. This problem is avoided by using the relative manipulation mode that only moves the key frame from its current position in the same direction and rotation as the

wand is moved. Fine control is obtained by moving the key frame a fraction of the wand movement.

For some applications of *Virtual Director* it is possible for the camera choreographer to interact with objects in the scene of the simulated world, as opposed to only with the camera and key frames, for example, enabling a view of fish concentrations in a body of water for one segment of the animation. To allow this, *VirDir* uses hooks into the simulated world to manipulate the world. A submenu is provided under the normal menu selections, giving command access to the user for manipulating the world.

No agents are added to the virtual world by the *Virtual Director* application. While some of the worlds themselves may incorporate avatars that represent characters in the animation or live-action plan, these avatars do not interact with the director, and thus do not qualify.

The *Virtual Director* application includes a set of features to allow collaborators to work together in the virtual

FIGURE 9-25

In this image, collaborators are depicted by spheres with faces rather than photographs. The participants can indicate facial expressions such as the winking eye on the avatar on the right.

space over vast distances. One such example of this was a collaboration between NCSA and Old Dominion University (ODU) in which the scientists in Virginia (Glen Wheless and Cathy Lascara), who were studying the ecosystem of the Chesapeake Bay, worked with the animation team in Illinois to jointly create an animation that shows the important scientific features of the simulated world.

Specifically, features added to support collaborative work include avatar representations of all the parties connected to a *VirDir* session, options to share choreography data (camera paths) between sites, as well as allowing users to broadcast commands to other sites for remote control.

Voice communication between sites is not supported directly within the *Virtual Director* application. Rather, voice is transmitted either by telephony communication links, Internet (e.g., M-bone) communication tools, or (when the collaborators are across the hall rather than across the country) via direct microphone-amplifier-speaker connections.

In general, the *Virtual Director* operates as a "no physical law" system, allowing the user to maneuver through the space unconstrained. The virtual world being explored in *VirDir* might operate under its own, separate world physics, however. Since the virtual director was built first and foremost for scientific visualization applications, most of the datasets displayed in the world are driven by a scientific simulation. Thus, the objects in those worlds adhere to the rules enforced by the simulation code. When it comes time to produce a visualization of the simulation however, the camera is not affected by gravity, high winds, galactic collisions, or otherwise.

However, in the case of preplanning a live-action shot, it would be desirable to have the virtual camera operate under the same physical laws in which the real camera will have to operate. Thus, for preplanning a live shoot the virtual camera should be able to be made to follow constraints imposed by cranes, tracks, and other real-world camera manipulation

FIGURE 9-26

The Virtual Director *Application has been used with many different hardware display configurations. Here, Donna Cox, a developer of* Virtual Director *uses the NCSA PowerWall as her means of entering a collaborative session.*

tools. Real-world production equipment simply can't move as freely as a virtual camera in a virtual world, and it is important to consider those constraints in the planning for a live shoot. Features to support a live-action mode are planned for a future version of the application.

Venue

The *Virtual Director* currently runs in the *CAVE* at NCSA and a few other research institutions. It also operates reasonably well on large wall and table VR displays. The developers would also like to see it in operation at movie production facilities, but this has not occurred yet.

Currently, the *Virtual Director* is designed for a single person operating the controls. However, being a *CAVE* application, it is easy to have a small group in the *CAVE* seeing the view as determined by the primary (tracked) user.

A typical session with the *Virtual Director* during the making of the *Cosmic Voyage* was 1.5 to 2 hours. Often the sessions extended to 3 hours, and sometimes became 6-hour marathon sessions immersed in the *Virtual Director*.

Any discomfort felt from using the *Virtual Director* for extended periods of time were attributed mostly to "issues of the contraptions," that is, pressure on the head from the glasses and tracker, rather than from other aspects of being immersed in a virtual environment. For relief and relaxation during the long sessions, Patterson enjoyed listening to music with the lights dimmed while he used the tool he and his collaborators had created. He felt the lighting and music contributed to creating a less tense, more creative environment.

VR System

The VR system supporting the *Virtual Director* is a typical *CAVE* environment consisting of the *CAVE* screens, head tracking with the Ascension Flock of Birds, and the typical tracked *CAVE* wand. The computing power is provided by a Silicon Graphics Onyx II system with Infinite Reality graphics hardware.

In addition to the normal *CAVE* system, voice input is provided by a small, head-set wireless microphone connected to a PC running *Dragon Dictate*™ voice recognition software. The voice software can be combined with software that allows the user to send text commands and control windowing and other system commands, enhancing the power of the voice interface.

The voice system in this particular application is speaker dependent and must be trained for the particular speaker. This makes the whole *Virtual Director* system unsuitable for random, walk-in users. Each user must train the voice system for their voice prior to using the *Virtual Director*. Each user can train the system to recognize aliases as well, so training the voice system is one way of creating macros and user-specific commands. These single commands can actually execute a string of *VirDir* commands. Another aspect of the training is that the user can allow the voice software to have many different voice commands map to the same activity. This prevents the user from getting tired of saying the same commands over and over.

Anecdotal evidence indicates that the voice system works correctly about 95% of the time as long as there are no other people present who are talking. Soft music playing in the background does not seem to interfere; however, human voices do. Thus, if there are kibitzers in the *CAVE*, their voices can confuse the voice-recognition system. As an aid in preventing this problem, one of the users (a male, Patterson) prefers a push-to-talk switch on the microphone. Another primary user of the system (a female, Cox) prefers instead to use commands such as "wake up" and "go to sleep" to activate and deactivate the voice system. Cox says she doesn't like "futzing around in the dark trying to find the switch." She notes that one possible reason for this preference is that her women's clothing does not have pockets onto which the switch can be clipped, whereas the male user, wearing jeans, does.

Application Implementation

The development of this application began in the early 1990s at the behest of Cox and Patterson. The first, experimental version utilized a FakeSpace *BOOM*™ device for display and tracking. The *BOOM* looked and handled somewhat like a camera and gave a camera-like feel to the operator.

In this version, there was no voice recognition. Instead, input from finger gestures were measured by a VPL data glove to issue four commands to the system. The four commands were data time forward, data time backward, data time stop, and record a camera move. The users found that using the glove as a gesture input device was difficult because users had to remove one of their hands from the typically two-handed task of moving the *BOOM* display. Also, it required

calibration for each usage, and still only provided a handful of commands. Another problem with this version was that the *BOOM* offered only a "through the camera" view.

The user was not able to see any of the world beyond the camera as is possible in the *CAVE*. The original version was programmed mostly by Peter Fritzen, a computer graphics programmer visiting NCSA from the Fraunhaufer Computer Graphics Institute in Darmstadt, Germany. Some additional programming was done by University of Illinois undergraduate programmer Brygg Ulmer.

A new version was built from scratch by graduate student Marcus Thiebaux when a *CAVE* was installed at NCSA in 1994. The project team for this version consisted primarily of Cox and Patterson of NCSA as the designers of the *Virtual Director*, and Marcus Thiebaux from the Electronic Visualization Lab at the University of Illinois at Chicago as the primary programmer. Development of this version was handed off to a single other (but full-time) programmer (Stuart Levy) in 1997, when Thiebaux graduated.

The *Virtual Director* library uses *OpenGL* as the graphics interface, and uses the *CAVE* libraries to handle the tracking tasks, multiple-wall display, and stereo display. As a library, *VirDir* is in fact not a single application, but a suite of applications that use the same interface. New real-time rendering code is written for each application and linked to the *VirDir* library. In some cases, the entire rendering system is written from scratch (e.g., *The Cosmic Voyage*), while in other cases, existing code is merged with the *Virtual Director* as was the case for the Chesapeake Bay visualization.

Because the *CAVE* and other system hardware and software already were available, the primary cost in developing the *Virtual Director* was the time of the designers and programmer.

The *Virtual Director* system has been tested by (in fact, spearheaded by) the intended users, who were primarily computer animation artists. A variety of different interfaces have been tried. Some of them continue to be used, others are not. It is, however, significant to note that much of the early interface design was done by the programmer (also an artist) who worked alone to bring ideas discussed with the users to fruition. Many times, this resulted in the expectations of the users not being met. Other times, the expectations were surpassed. Thus, along the way, the overall design was the result of give and take on the part of the users and the programmers based on what was considered desirable versus what was considered feasible to program.

This project was developed at NCSA as a long-term development project. Often, in production studios, only a small amount of time is available to experiment with new techniques before one must go into full production mode. At NCSA, the designers have been able to experiment and develop the *Virtual Director* as an ongoing project, and investigate new ways of doing computer graphics animation production. Thus, major shifts in the design such as moving from the *BOOM* interface to the *CAVE* were not out of the question.

One of the biggest design changes was moving from the *BOOM* VR environment to the *CAVE*. There were several reasons for making this switch. One was a very pragmatic reason. The programmer (Thiebaux) was more familiar with programming in the *CAVE* environment. This, however, was not sufficient reason alone to justify the switch. A major reason was to gain the view of the world beyond the camera that the *BOOM* was not able to offer in an intuitive way. This was chiefly possible because the field of view in the *CAVE* was much wider than that in the *BOOM*. Also, the *BOOM* that was available at NCSA was an older unit with low resolution and a monochromatic display. In the *CAVE*, the user was able to "see" the computer graphics camera, whereas with the *BOOM*, the only view was through the camera. The *CAVE* that was available was much higher resolution, and color. The final reason for the switch was that the *BOOM* was somewhat limited in the possible motions the display head of the *BOOM* could move. For example, the *BOOM* cannot be rotated directly about the Z-axis. This was a move that was sometimes desired for virtual camera paths.

In the *CAVE* available at NCSA, the primary method of input was a wand with three buttons and a pressure joystick. Because the main objective was to create a path through space, the prototype version for the *CAVE* managed to accomplish this, and a simple key-frame editing tool using only the wand buttons. However, this offered only the "physically move the wand through space" method of path creation ("performance" mode) and provided only a

fraction of the necessary functionality, and there were no more buttons available on the wand. To allow a more robust set of controls, a broader input mechanism was necessary.

For the next version, a system of menus was chosen as the best means to allow for all the options desired for controlling the animation camera. By this time, it had been decided that voice would be a crucial element for input, so the menu system was designed to operate off of text commands, that is, from the keyboard. Since the voice system operated by emulating keyboard input, commands can be entered either by voice or by actually hitting keys on the keyboard.

Using the text method of input allowed a straightforward means of integrating voice software. With this method, the voice software only needed to convert voice commands into ASCII text strings that are fed to the command line menu interface.

In addition to solving the health problems associated with constant, multiple button/key presses, voice input was found to have another important benefit. When wand buttons are pressed, the wand inevitably moves. This can interfere with the desired input. By using voice, an event can be triggered while the wand is held steady.

There is a downside to using voice as well. When it works properly, voice input has a small but nonzero amount of time required to utter the command and for the command to be recognized. This poses a problem for inputs that need to be instantaneous. The other problem with voice recognition is that, while improving, it does not provide 100% accuracy. Users of the *Virtual Director* have learned to work within these limitations.

Since interacting in the *Virtual Director* is not a means unto itself (as is true for many other virtual reality applications), a method of determining the quality of the resultant animation and, ultimately, a method of creating the final animation are required aspects of the system. To be able to judge what the animation will look like requires both a good representation of what the animation package will produce and good real-time display of the simulated world to see how the action will appear to the audience.

In order to see a decent real-time rendering while using the tool, a representative sample of the full dataset is used.

In the case of scientific data this might mean a fraction of the particles in the world are shown, or more crudely formed shapes. In recreating a real-world set, a combination of cruder forms and lower resolution texture maps help alleviate the real-time crunch. When the final rendering is done in batch mode, a high-quality renderer generates the frames outside of real time, using the full dataset.

Typically, the camera path data is transferred to an animation package that performs the rendering using the renderer of choice. Occasionally, the choreographer will want to see a better representation of the animation without waiting for a batch animation job. To provide this option, the *Virtual Director* can use the computer's graphics hardware's rendering ability to render the images, compact them into an animation file, and play the animation. The quality is not as good as typical animation packages, but this provides a result that is improved over the real-time rendering, and thus lets the director continue working without leaving the VR environment.

For real-time rendering, the frame rate in the *Virtual Director* can be improved by turning many of the display options off. A common use of this is to turn off all displays except the "TV view," which is enlarged to fill the screen. Doing this gives a reasonable play back of the camera move. The fact that turning off the 3D view of the world allows the animation to be displayed monoscopically also helps the frame rate.

Conclusion

There have been no formal studies on the ergonomic benefits or increased productivity resulting from using the *Virtual Director*. However, as they say, "the proof is in the pudding," and it has passed this one important test: It has been used, and continues to be used, in the production of professional computer animations. Two prominent jobs in which *VirDir* has been put through a significant work cycle are the creation of the *Cosmic Voyage* colliding galaxy animation sequences, and subsequently, to choreograph a segment for the PBS series *Mysteries of Deep Space.*

Thus far, the system has primarily been used by the team that developed the application. However, other researchers (such as the oceanography team at ODU) have also used *VirDir* for their own animation work, and other researchers have expressed interest.

However, the *Virtual Director* has not yet infiltrated the movie studios. *VirDir* would need to be more closely integrated with existing computer graphics technology in a cost-effective manner if studios are to embrace it as part of their production process.

The main accomplishments of *Virtual Director* have already been espoused: the creation of multiple and significant animations for scientific visualization.

Although the developers say they do not "lose themselves" in the virtual space, they do find it to be more satisfying to create camera moves when they are surrounded by the world they are animating. Patterson says: "It's like your data is suspended in front of you, and around you. You're in it and you can place the camera in absolute space as if you're holding it. The floor makes the *CAVE* different than other displays because you can see that space goes on below you. It's like flying around space in a free-form manner on an invisible platform." Cox notices that she feels "immersed until the tethers pull my hair."

Patterson points out that it has become totally natural to place the camera in a 3D space. In fact, he has "stopped doing camera moves at the desktop when [he] can go down to the *CAVE* and produce a variety of moves easily in less time."

Over the course of development, many design options have been tried and discarded, or tried, kept, and expanded on. Lessons learned by the development team range from whether VR was even usable, to comparisons between different display paradigms, to the benefits VR can provide over desktop interfaces.

The application designers were reluctant to use VR at first because of the lower-quality imagery that is produced by real-time rendering systems. They were unsure if the live rendering would produce results useful for judging an animation camera move.

The design team also discovered that the *CAVE* seemed to be the most suitable VR display paradigm for this particular problem. One of the positive aspects of using the *CAVE* as the display device for the *Virtual Director* is the fact that it provides a "view beyond the camera." Because the target output of the *Virtual Director* is a flat screen, the front wall in the *CAVE* is considered the most important, but the side walls and floor also contribute to the user's ability to see what is in the periphery, and beyond the domain of the camera. This is much like what a camera operator in the real world would experience; they are able to see the camera's view through its lens, but also the much wider real world outside the camera. Because the front view is the most important, other large-screen projection display devices such as large wall displays have also been found to be suitable, but they are less effective at showing parts of the world that are in the periphery.

Another positive feature of working in the *CAVE* is that it offers a break from sitting "stagnant in front of a radiating monitor clicking and dragging." That is, the typical mode of operation with this application in the *CAVE* is walking about and using the arms actively. This is a much more active, holistically healthy environment than working in standard animation environments.

Voice input is also a key contributor to the holistic nature of the application (this was expected). But voice was found to have other benefits as well. One of the key advantages of using the voice software is that the user does not need to take their eyes off the scene to interact with the system. This can aid in not losing one's train of thought, or having to interrupt a camera path capture in order to issue commands.

When the project began, the developers were interested in exploring VR, but they were not interested in being VR content developers. They were interested in using VR as a tool for creating high-fidelity images meant for display in other media such as film and video. To this end, they have largely been successful. But there is more that can be done, and so they continue to push *Virtual Director* in new directions.

One future development that has been mentioned is to expand the feature set of *VirDir*, increasing its suitability for preplanning live-action camera shots. They also plan to improve the editing capabilities, including the inclusion of edit list features.

The developers envision a scenario in a production facility where a computer graphics studio might have six ImmersaDesks or other relatively low-cost displays running *Virtual Director* where technical directors can schedule blocks of time to create moves, test models, and other activities. Using the collaborative capability of the system, a film director who might be working in another city could use a local VR display to view and discuss camera moves with the technical directors (TDs). In the future, the developers plan to expand the system to enable *Virtual Director* to animate more than just the camera. Any object in the world, such as lights or world entities could be animated. Additionally, through integration with other software packages such as was done with *CAVE5D*, they can manipulate the representations of the scientific data being displayed from within *Virtual Director*.

CHAPTER 10

Putting It All Together

10.1 EXECUTIVE SUMMARY

In this chapter, we review the characteristics of the applications described in this book. The characteristics of the applications are manifested in the form of a database a query interface to which is available on this book's companion website. This chapter also includes some sample figures that depict the relationships between applications and their characteristics.

10.2 INTRODUCTION

The basic premise of this book has been that in order to build compelling new virtual reality applications it is wise to study the characteristics of extant applications. By studying other applications, the VR experience developer is able to draw on ideas that are suitable for their new application, while avoiding the pitfalls of weaknesses that other VR application developers have encountered.

Throughout this book, we have pointed out the various characteristics of dozens of VR applications that are foundational to the field. Applications are categorized by their genre, their hardware, their field of application (such as medicine, business, education, etc.), and various other categorizations. Additionally, we have noted the existence and nonexistence of various traits of each application. For example, we have noted whether an application uses audio or not, and if so, whether the audio is placed in three dimensions or not, etc. Another example is whether the application included haptic feedback, and if so, whether it is a tactile response or kinesthetic feedback.

All of these characteristics can be gleaned by reading the application descriptions included in this book. However, in order to make this book especially useful as a reference resource, we have encoded the characteristics of each application into an online database that supports queries by application developers to quickly allow them to drill into the relevant information from applications that provide the characteristics that they are interested in. So, for example, if an application developer is interested in including audio in their new application, they can query the database and find which applications described in the book use audio. The database supports much more complex queries as well, such as "Show me all of the applications that use 3D audio that also use head-mounted displays, but don't include haptic feedback." Conversely, it is also possible to query the database to learn the characteristics of the applications described in this book. For example, one could query the database to learn the characteristics of the *Officer of the Deck* application.

10.3   THE DATABASE FIELDS

In order to use any database to its maximum potential, it is important to know the types of data that it includes and what is meant by each data element. A full listing of the database fields is included in Chapter 2 and a definition of each field is available on this book's companion website.

The easiest way to explain the schema of the database is via an example or two. Continuing with the "audio" example, one can query for applications that use audio. Figure 10-1 shows the list of applications in this book that use audio.

Another level down, one can query for specific audio characteristics. In this database, subcategories of audio include "3D audio," "Nonspeech audio," "Sonification," "World-referenced audio," and "Head-referenced audio."

Figure 10-2 shows the applications in the book that use three-dimensional audio.

One more example is speech recognition. One can query based on the general characteristic of "speech recognition." Beyond that, one can also query about various characteristics of speech recognition. The subcategories include "Speaker independent," "Speaker dependent," "Push-to-talk," "Name-to-talk," and "Look-to-talk." It is important to note that the subcategories are not simply a list from which you can choose only one. For example, an application could use speech recognition—that is, "Speaker dependent"—that uses the "Name-to-talk" method of invoking it. If a subcategory is invoked without specifying one of the attributes, the results will be returned as though all elements in that subcategory were specified. So, if a query is made to return all applications that use speech recognition that is invoked by the "Name-to-talk" method, the results will include all applications that include "Name-to-talk" regardless of whether the speech recognition is "Speaker independent," or "Speaker dependent."

In the applications in this book, the two applications that use speech recognition are *Officer of the Deck*, and *Virtual Director*. Refining the query to seeking applications that use speaker-independent systems limits the results to the only application that fulfills the criteria, *Officer of the Deck*.

Figure 10-3 shows the relationship between the two applications that use speech recognition. The diagram shows that both applications use speech recognition, they both use the "push-to-talk" method to invoke speech recognition, but also illustrates that *Officer of the Deck* uses speaker independent recognition whereas *Virtual Director* uses speaker dependent speech recognition.

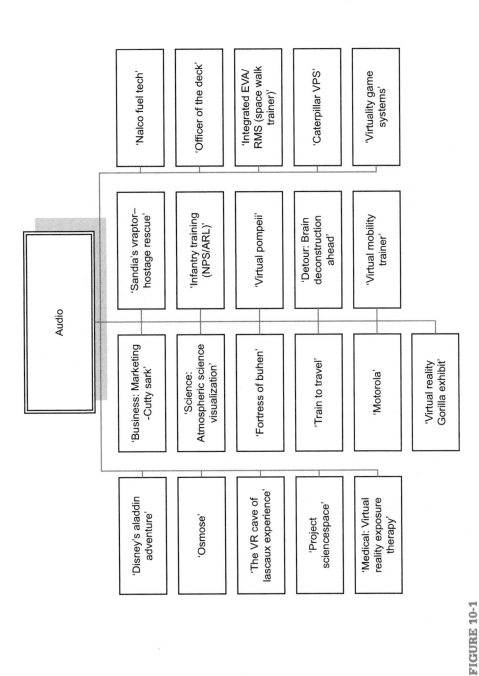

FIGURE 10-1

This diagram depicts the applications in this book that use audio.

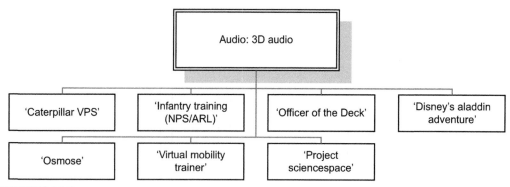

FIGURE 10-2
This diagram shows which applications in this book use three-dimensional audio.

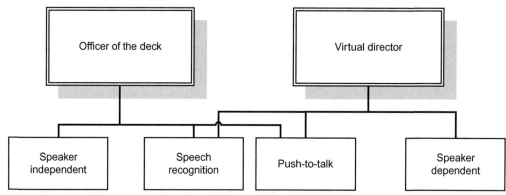

FIGURE 10-3
This diagram shows the relationship between the two applications in this book that use speech recognition.

10.4   FINDING APPLICATIONS WITH SPECIFIC CHARACTERISTICS

One of the most helpful ways to use the companion database is as an aid in identifying specific applications that possess the characteristics you are interested in. So, imagine you are considering creating an application that uses a head-mounted display, and you are planning to use it in a public venue with a large throughput of end users. By querying the database for applications with those traits, you would learn which applications fulfill those criteria. In this particular example, one of the applications that would be returned is Disney's *Aladdin Adventure*. Even though your goal was not to create an entertainment application that was for a theme park, you could benefit from the *Aladdin* application developers' experience in using head-mounted displays in a public setting. Their experience with the durability, hygiene, and "suit-up" time issues of head-mounted displays in that setting could help you avoid similar trial and error when you deploy your application.

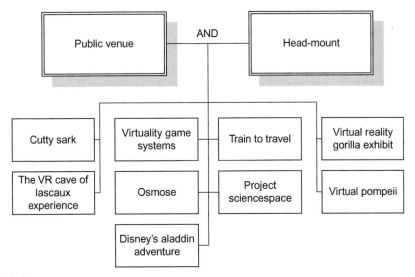

FIGURE 10-4
The diagram above illustrates which applications described in this book use head-mounted displays in public venues.

As an example of the scenario described above, the following diagram lists the applications described in this book that use head-mounted displays in venues that are public (theme parks, museums, etc.).

10.4.1 Showing all the characteristics of a specific application

It is often helpful to have a list of all the characteristics of a specific VR application. One reason such a list is beneficial is that it shows some of the characteristics that are commonly found together in successful applications. For example, by viewing a list of all the characteristics of the *Officer of the Deck* application, one can see that "push-to-talk" speech recognition is used in an application that uses a platform. By then studying the application write-up, it becomes evident that in that application end users hold the "push-to-talk" button in one hand while steadying themselves by holding the platform rail with the other.

By querying the online database for the traits of the *Officer of the Deck* application, you can see a list of the characteristics of that application. An example of the results of that query is shown below.

Another reason one might desire to create a list of all the characteristics of an application is to see what elements are commonly used in applications from a certain field. For example, one might want to see the characteristics of all the medical applications that are covered in this book. By querying the database for all "medical" applications, the following results are obtained.

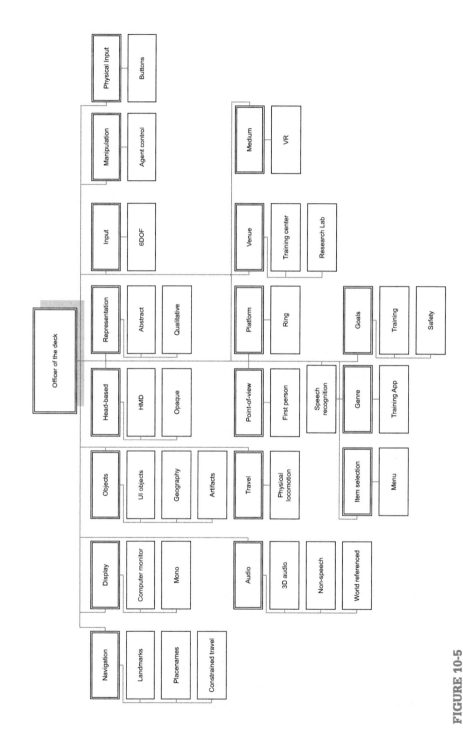

FIGURE 10-5

The diagram above shows the various characteristics and techniques that are used in the Officer of the Deck *application.*

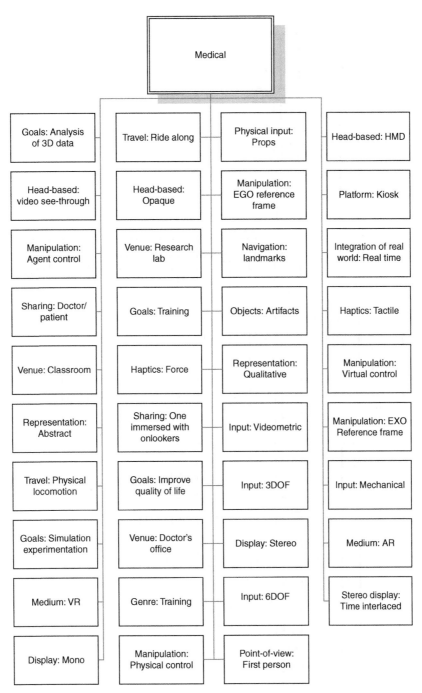

FIGURE 10-6

This image shows the results of a query to the database for a list of the characteristics of the union of all the medical applications described in this book.

10.4.2 Application taxonomies

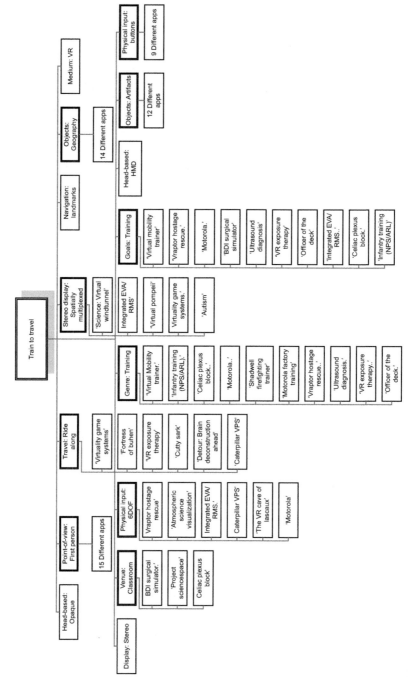

FIGURE 10-7

A second-level diagram, showing an application, its characteristics, and the related applications having each characteristic. For characteristics that have too many related apps to list, these have been omitted for space purposes.

The final example we show is a way to create taxonomies given the database access. Suppose you were especially interested in a particular application. You could list all of that application's characteristics. But then you may wish to know all the other applications that also have that attribute. In Figure 10-7, we show a diagram of "Train to Travel," and all of its characteristics. Then, under each of those characteristics, the other applications described in this book that share that characteristic are listed. In this way, the database can guide developers in shared "learned lessons" between seemingly unrelated applications.

Bibliography

Bajura, M., Fuchs, H., and Ohbuchi, R., "Merging Virtual Objects with the Real World: Seeing Ultrasound Imagery Within the Patient," *Proceedings of SIGGRAPH '92*, Chicago, IL, July 26–31, 1992, *Computer Graphics 26, #2* July 1992, pp. 203–210.

Bowman, D.A., Wineman, J., and Hodges, L.F., "Exploratory Design of Animal Habitats Within an Immersive Virtual Environment," *GVU Center Technical Report, GIT-GVU-98-06*, 1998.

Bowman, D.A., Wineman, J., Hodges, L.F., and Allison, D., "Designing Animal Habitats Within an Immersive VE," *IEEE Computer Graphics and Applications*, Vol. 18, No. 5, September/October 1998, pp. 9–13.

Bowman, D.A., Wineman, J., Hodges, L.F., and Allison, D., "The Educational Value of an Information-Rich Virtual Environment," *Presence*, Vol. 8, No. 3, June 1999.

Brooks, Jr., F.P., Ouh-Young, M., Batter, J.J., and Kilpatrick, P.J., "Project GROPE — Haptic Displays for Scientific Visualization," *SIGGRAPH 1990 Conference Proceedings, Computer Graphics*, Vol. 24, No. 4, August 1990.

Bryson, S., and Johan, S., "Time Management, Simultaneity and Time-Critical Computation in Interactive Unsteady Visualization Environments," *IEEE Visualization*, 1996, pp. 255–261.

Buckert-Donelson, A., "VR People: Dean Inman," *VR World*, January/February 1995.

Darken, R.P., Cockayne, W.R., and Carmein, D., "The Omni-Directional Treadmill: A Locomotion Device for Virtual Worlds," *UIST '97 Proceedings*, Banff, Canada, October 14–17, 1997, pp. 213–221.

David, J., Homan, C., and Gott, J., "An Integrated EVA/RMS Virtual Reality Simulation, Including Force Feedback, for Astronaut Training," *AIAA Flight Simulation Technologies Conference*, San Diego, CA, July 19–31, 1996, NASA Reference Publication: AIAA 96-3498.

Davies, C., and Harrison, J., "Osmose: Towards Broadening the Aesthetics of Virtual Reality," *ACM Computer Graphics: Virtual Reality*, Vol. 30, No. 4, November 1996.

Dede, C., Salzman, M., Loftin, B., and Ash, K., "Using Virtual Reality Technology to Convey Abstract Scientific Concepts," In *Learning the Sciences of the 21st Century: Research, Design, and Implementing Advance Technology Learning Environments*, 1997.

Dinh, H.Q., Walker, N., Song, C., Kobayashi, A., and Hodges, L.F., "Evaluating the Importance of Multi-sensory Input on Memory and the Sense of Presence in Virtual Environments," *IEEE VR 1999*, Houston, TX, March 13–15, 1999.

Du Pont, P., "VR for Thermal Visualization: Analyzing Air and Temperature Flow," *VR World*, May/June, pp. 58–59.

Foley, J.D., VanDam, A., Feiner, S., and Hughes, J., "Computer Graphics: Principles and Practice," 1990.

Fong, T.W., Pangels, H., Wettergreen, D., Nygren, E., Hine, B., Hontalas, P., and Fedor, C., "Operator Interfaces and Network-Based Participation for Dante II," *SAE 25th International Convergence on Environmental Systems*, San Diego, CA, July 1995.

Fuchs, H., Livingston, M.A., Raskar, R., Colucci, D., Keller, K., State, A., Crawford, J.R., Rademacher, P., Drake, S.H., and Meyer, A.A., "Augmented Reality Visualization for Laparoscopic Procedures," *Proceedings of Medical Image Computing and Computer-Assisted Intervention—MICCAI '98*, Cambridge, MA, Berlin, Heidelberg: Springer-Verlag, October 11–13, 1998, pp. 934–943.

Garrett, W.F., Fuchs, H., Whitton, M.C., and State, A., "Real-Time Incremental Visualization of Dynamic Ultrasound Volumes Using Parallel BSP Trees," *Proceedings of IEEE Visualization '96*, San Francisco, CA, October 1996, pp. 235–240, 490.

Holloway, R.L., "Registration Errors in Augmented Reality Systems," Ph.D. Dissertation TR95-016, Department of Computer Science, The University of North Carolina, 1995.

Homan, D.J., "Virtual Reality and the Hubble Space Telescope," *AIAA Space Programs and Technologies Conference*, Huntsville, AL, NASA Reference Publication: AIAA 94-4558.

Inman, D., Loge, K., and Leavens, J., "Virtual Reality Solutions for Children with Physical Disabilities," *Proceedings of Militar Applications of Synthetic Environments and Virtual Reality MASEVR '95*, Stockholm, Sweden, December 6–8, 1995.

Jacobs, M.C., Livingston, M.A., and State, A., "Managing Latency in Complex Augmented Reality Systems," *Proceedings of 1997 Symposium on Interactive 3D Graphics*, Providence, RI, April 27–30, 1997.

Kenney, P.J., and Saito, T., "Results of a Survey on the Use of Virtual Environment Technology in Training NASA Flight Controllers for the Hubble Space Telescope Servicing Mision," URL: http://www.vetl.uh.edu/Hubble/longpaper.html

Krueger, M.W., *Artificial Reality*, Reading, MA: Addison-Wesley, 1982.

Lamson, R.J., "Virtual Therapy of Anxiety Disorders," *CyberEdge Journal*, Vol. 20, No. v4n2, March/April 1994.

Loftin, R.B., and Kenney, P.J., "Training the Hubble Space Telescope Flight Team," *IEEE Computer Graphics and Applications*, September 1995, pp. 31–37.

Macedonia, M.R., Zyda, M.J., Pratt, D.R., Barham, P.T., and Zeswitz, S., "NPSNET: A Network Software Architecture for Large Scale Virtual Environments," *Presence*, Vol. 3, No. 4, Fall 1994, pp. 265–287.

Mine, M., "Characterization of End-to-End Delays in Head-Mounted Displays," Tech. Rep. TR93-001, Department of Computer Science, The University of North Carolina, 1993.

Mowafy, L., and Pollack, J., "Train to Travel" Ability, *Journal of the British Computer Society Disability Group*, Vol. 15, pp. 18–20. ISSN 1352–7665.

Pausch, R., "Disney's Aladdin: First Steps Toward Storytelling in Virtual Reality," *Proceedings of SIGGRAPH 96*, 1996.

Piguet, L., Fong, T., Hine, B., Hontalas, P., and Nygren, E., "VEVI: A Virtual Reality Tool for Robotic Planetary Explorations," *Virtual Reality World 95*, Stuttgart, Germany, February 1995.

Pratt, D.R., Barham, P.T., Locke, J., Zyda, M.J., Eastman, B., Moore, T., Biggers, K., Douglass, R., Jacobsen, S., Hollick, M., Granieri, J., Ko, H., and Badler, N.I., "Insertion of an Articulated Human into a Networked Virtual Environment," *Proceedings of the 1994 AI, Simulation, and Planning in High Autonomy Systems Conference*, University of Florida, Gainesville, FL, December 7–9, 1994.

Pratt, S., Ohman, D., Brown, S., Galloway, J., and Pratt, D., "Soldier Station: A Tool For Dis-mounted Infantry Analysis," *Proceedings of the 1997 Spring Simulation Interoperability Work-shop*, Orlando, FL, March 3–7, 1997.

Roberts, R.J., "Passenger Fear of Flying: Behavioural Treatment with Extensive In Vivo Exposure and Group Support," *Aviation, Space, and Environmental Medicine*, Vol. 60, 1989, pp. 342–348.

Rothbaum, B.O., Hodges, L., Watson, B.A., Kessler, G.D., and Opdyke, D., "Virtual Reality Exposure Therapy in the Treatment of Fear of Flying: A Case Report," *Behaviour Research and Therapy*, Vol. 34, 1996, pp. 477–481.

Sakas, G., and Walter, S., "Extracting Surfaces from Fuzzy 3D-Ultrasound Data," *Proceedings from SIGGRAPH*, 1995, pp. 465–474.

Sanders, D.H., *Archaeological Virtual Worlds for Public Education*, Learning Sites, Inc., 1997.

Sheridan, T.B., "Musings on Telepresence and Virtual Presence," In T. Middleton (Ed.), *Proceedings of Virtual Worlds: Real Challenges—Papers from SRI's 1991 Conference on Virtual Reality*, Westport, CT: Meckler Publishing, 1991, pp. 55–66.

Sherman, W., and Craig, A., *Understanding Virtual Reality*, Boston: Morgan-Kaufmann Publishers, 2003.

Sherman, W.R., Craig, A.B., Baker, M.P., and Busherll, C., "Chapter 35: Scientific Visualization," In Allen B. Tucker, Jr. (Ed.), *The Computer Science and Engineering Handbook*, Boca Raton, FL: CRC Press, 1997.

Spitzer, V.M., Ackerman, M.J., Scherzinger, A.L., and Whitlock, D.G., "The Visible Human Male: A Technical Report," *Journal of the American Informatics Association*, Vol. 3, 1996, pp. 118–130.

State, A., Hirota, G., Chen, D.T., Garrett, W.T., and Livingston, M.A., "Superior Augmented Reality Registration by Integrated Landmark Tracking and Magnetic Tracking," In H. Rushmeier (Ed.), *SIGGRAPH 96 Conference Proceedings*, New Orleans, LA, Annual Conference Series, ACM SIGGRAPH, Addison Wesley, August 1996, pp. 429–438.

State, A., Livingston, M.A., Garrett, W.F., Hirota, G., Whitton, M.C., Pisano, E.D., and Fuchs, H., "Technologies for Augmented Reality Systems: Realizing Ultrasound-Guided Needle Biopsies," In H. Rushmeier (Ed.), *SIGGRAPH 96 Conference Proceedings*, New Orleans, LA, Annual Conference Series, ACM SIGGRAPH, Addison Wesley, August 1996, pp. 439–446.

Storms, R.L., Roesli, J.T., Biggs, L.J., Falby, J.S., Barham, P.T., and Zyda, M.J., "The NPSNET Sound Cube," *Presence*, Vol. 7, No. 5, October 1998, pp. 503–507.

Strickland, D., "A Virtual Reality Application with Autistic Children," *Presence*, Vol. 5, No. 3, Summer 1996, pp. 319–329.

Taylor III, R.M., Chen, J., Okimoto, S., Llopis-Artime, N., Chi, V.L., Brooks, Jr., F.P., Falvo, M., Paulson, S., Thiansathaporn, P., Glick, D., Washburn, S., and Superfine, R., "Pearls Found on the Way to the Ideal Interface for Scanned-Probe Microscopes," *1997 IEEE Visualization Conference*.

Taylor, V., Stevens, R., and Canfield, T., "Performance Models of Interactive, Immersive visualization for Scientific Applications," In *Proceedings of the International Workshop on High Performance Computing for Computer Graphics and Visualization*, July 1995, pp. 238–252.

Wheless, G.H., Valle-Levinson, A., and Sherman, W., "Virtual Reality in Oceanography," *Oceanography*, Vol. 8, No. 2, 1995, pp. 52–58.

Wloka, M., "Lag in Multiprocessor Virtual Reality," *Presence: Teleoperators and Virtual Environments*, Vol. 4, No. 1, Winter 1995, pp. 5–63.

Zeltzer, D., Pioch, N., and Aviles, W., "Training the Officer of the Deck," *VR Blackboard, IEEE Computer Graphics and Applications*, November 1995.

Zeltzer, D., and Pioch, N., Validation and Verification of Virtual Environment Training Systems, In *Proceedings Virtual Reality Annual International Symposium '96*, Santa Clara, CA, March 30–April 3, 1996, p. 123.

Zyda, M.J., Pratt, D.R., Falby, J.S., Barham, P., and Kelleher, K.M., "NPSNET and the Naval Postgraduate School Graphics and Video Laboratory," *Presence*, Vol. 2, No. 3, pp. 244–258.

Index

Printed and bound by CPI Group (UK) Ltd, Croydon, CR0 4YY

03/10/2024

01040312-0004